What's Wrong with Us?

by

Ronald Duane Crawford

D1515591

3 Carrick Lane Bear, DE. 19701
ronald.c @INyaPJs.com

for
INyaPJs, LLC.

What's Wrong with Us? © 2005 by Ronald Crawford

Library of Congress Cataloging in Publication Data

Crawford, Ronald Duane, 1966-
    What is Wrong with Us?

    Includes bibliographical references.

    ISBN-13: 978-0-9826268-0-1

Disclaimer: To the best of my knowledge, all quotations included here that do not appear in the bibliography section of this work fall under the fair use or public domain guidelines of copyright law in the United States.

For

the children of the world whose innocence, love and freshness inspire and sustain us all. Try to move upward and onward toward the light, dreams do come true if we are true to them.

For

Wisdom, Bryan and Julian Speight, may I continue the quest.

And, For

the sake of Love and only Love.

My Life's Map

Acknowledgements

The Alpha, Omega, and everything-I thank you.

Mother Earth, thank you for sustaining us.

I want to send thanks and prayers to everyone in the entire world.

I would also like to thank my family for being patient with me all these years. I know I am a difficult person to understand and even more difficult to love.

I could write a long list of individuals who have helped me in my life, but that would mean mentioning everyone I have ever met. Ann, Milton, Buck, Karen, Misha, Mother, Terry, and Willard thank you so much for everything you have done and will do for me. I focus on not letting your belief in me and efforts made on my behalf go to waste. I love you all.

To the women in my life I want to say, "Thank you", "I am sorry", and "You're welcome."

To those I have considered enemies, or those who have considered me an enemy, I want to say I am sorry and thankful for the learning opportunity. Without our interactions I could not possibly be where I am now. I sincerely hope we get to meet each other again, so that we may act more like we should.

I would also like to say thank you to and acknowledge the fact that without life or the opportunity to live, I would never have had the opportunity to experience anything.

Lastly, I want to thank myself for continually enduring the trials of life.

Introduction

We are headed down the wrong path. We make our own lives hard, and, we all know it. What is wrong with us?

Why do we LIE, even to ourselves? Why do we become JEALOUS and/or ENVIOUS? Why do we JUDGE one another? Why does everyone think they are RIGHT and no one wants to be WRONG? Why do most say, "RELATIONSHIPS are supposed to be hard and you have to work at them?" Why is SEX so wonderful and horrible at the same time? Why does FEAR compel us to lunacy? Why do we hurt those we say or have said we LOVE?

Why are we so ignorant in the technological age? Why have we been ignorant throughout history? Why do sexism, bigotry and racism exist? Why are we murdering and raping? Why do we steal from one another? Why is there hunger and needless death? Why is there hate? Why are there religious wars or war at all? Why is it that the opinions of others matter? Why is life hard? Why do we need a slave population? These questions and more, made me think. After deliberation, I came to the conclusion that there is something wrong with not only me, but all of us.

These questions and more, made me think. After deliberation I have come to the conclusion that there is something wrong each and every one of with us, and we are regenerating, recreating our own existence into future generations. Why?

Before I begin, I think it is important that I address this work. The concepts within are interconnected and incomplete if not taken as a whole. I encourage you to write in the margins, answer the questions, and ask some of your own.

I have been saying for years that I would like to write a book about human nature, that is animal nature as applied to human behavior, from my point of view; and use, not only my experiences, but also the experiences of others to illustrate *the truth*. After all, we all have or will share the same experiences. The places, people involved, circumstances, or lifetime may be different, but when we hear a story told by someone else, if it has not happened already, we will have the same thing happen to us. There is nothing new under the sun and others throughout history have already said what is contained in these pages because we are all plagiarists.

Where shall I begin? I referenced my diaries and want to write about the disappointment I have had in my own behavior. By that, I mean I am writing about the trespasses (the lies and deception I portray in order to perpetrate a plan) I have committed against humanity, which is as much a part of me as my hands or eyes. I am speaking of the general disintegration in the human spirit, soul or collective consciousness as a whole. I really do not think there is a distinction, but for those who are not ready to believe that we are of the same cloth, I typically separate you from me and me from us, just for the sake of conventional distinction.

I have been able to read people since I can remember and so have you. It has gotten me into all sorts of trouble, because I am unable to control what I say in response to the lunacy I have witnessed. I have always said exactly what is on my mind, even as a child. It has been my "Excalibur" and still is; the truth always cuts to the heart of the matter. My mother said, "You have always had too much mouth." Moreover, because of this, I have been labeled and chastised. I have been told that I am "too smart for my own damn good" so many times, and in so many different situations, that it must be true. I have been told that I am not properly socialized. This was said by my high school principal to my mother. He explained that I needed to learn how to fit in. I will not and cannot. I have been called arrogant though I try to be humble, unfeeling though my heart breaks when I see injustice, manipulative when acting in self defense, a smartass when I say, "I know" and different because I refuse to follow the "norm". A friend warned me not to be so untouchable, so solo, so alone in thought and action. When I asked why, he said that people are vulnerable when they stand - alone.

I have seen and known hunger, both as a child and as an adult. I know *Lies* from both sides of the coin. And, the Truth, *Lie's* older brother, has evaded me and I him. I am acquainted with pain (both physical and mental), through the giving and receiving of beat – downs, and through the cruelty of words and actions designed specifically to hurt. I have hated so much that it hurt and I have been justifiably hated. Poverty and his twin brother, Plenty, play hopscotch in my living room and sit at my dinner table, fighting one another to see who gets to dance with my fate next. *Jealousy and Envy* have been my intimate friends and still are unwelcome guests. I have had the gavel of *Judgment* fall on me and I, in turn, have used it on others. I have stolen for no other reason than Greed and I have had things stolen from me in reprisal and for the same reason.

I have witnessed the most beautiful souls in others and they do not know how beautiful they truly are, because society has told them they do not fit the defined norm of what beauty is. It has destroyed self-esteem and executed spirits. It has shaken my belief system and challenged my morals.

I have fought many battles on the streets, in ward rooms and in conference rooms. I have cried for no other reason than memories and sorrows forced on my existence by the experiences that I have and have not yet had, or cannot recollect at the present. Innocence has been lost at my hands and surrendered by my heart. I have been so *Right* that no one could prove me *Wrong,* and I have been so wrong, that not even I could make it right. *Relationships* have taught me both permanence and impermanence. I have made bad loans and taken even worse ones. *Sex* has unbridled my morals and destroyed my trust. *Fear* has stunted my growth and propelled me to new heights. *Love,* in its many shades and different levels of development, has walked in and out of my life. In short, life has been my constant companion and yours since the beginning.

I am trying not to see with my eyes or hear with my ears. I want to see, hear, and feel with my heart and soul. The mirror of existence once scared the hell out me, but not anymore, for I shall not fear. My existence is what I make it and the last thing I should fear is myself.

Try to remember this: animals exist to procreate and serve their part in the equation of natural balance. *Human Beings* exist to transcend to a higher spiritual plane as a species, not individuals. That means, we all go or none go. Personally, I refuse to remain in my present state.

I am beginning to know myself through the thoughts and actions of others. They are my own. Realize that with experience perspective changes. I hope that by the end of this work, everyone will be able to see that by doing to others, you do to yourself. We are one and are constantly driven by unseen forces to merge. It is my quest and reason for being to become a complete Human Being and to bring as many others with me as I can.

Please hold my hand as I walk you through this labyrinth I have called life.

Chapter I

Lies

Lie: *to make an untrue statement with intent to deceive*[1].

I don't take people at their word anymore, my feelings would get hurt much too often.

We are liars and I can prove it. You just lied to yourself if you thought, "No I am not." That implies that you have never lied and what are the odds of that? It also implies that you will never lie and what are the odds of that? "I will call you right back."

We also say we want to hear the truth. That is generally true, if that truth is flattering or to our advantage. If it is critical of our person or anything relating to it, especially our children, we do not want to hear it because it hurts. "The truth hurts." This is not a new idea, but it is true.

If you are old enough to talk, you have lied before and will more than likely lie again. I am an admitted liar. I do it because I am good at it! I have an excellent memory and everyone else is doing it. Lying has allowed me to level the playing field and to avoid conflict, tasks, accountability and unwanted close personal contact. Lies seem to be momentarily the path of least resistance.

There is a developmental process by which an individual learns how to lie. The concepts of lying and of truth telling are intertwined; like right and wrong, each requires the other. It is impossible to consciously lie without a perceived knowledge of a truth.

I am tired of living a lie. I am tired of living as I am expected, and not as I was meant to or want to. I am tired of not being able to say exactly what I feel inside without being labeled as maladjusted, cynical, abrasive, flirtatious or arrogant just because we do not see eye to eye. I also want to hear exactly what others want to say, but few people are secure enough with themselves or their relations to tell the truth.

I am tired of reading and listening intently to what I know to be untrue for the sake of civility. I am tired of trying to communicate through the filters between subconscious thought and spoken language. I am tired of trying to be what others expect me to be and behaving in the manner I was taught in order to be socially acceptable. I am tired of mixed signals and programming on a global scale. I am tired of having to remove masks to see real people and be seen. I am tired of being driven by selfish desires and instinctual needs. I am tired of not being able to ask the hard questions and get an honest answer from most people. I am tired of people telling me that they do not know why they do what they do. I am tired of having to dream about a better way of life. I am tired of the lies.

As I said in my introduction, I have lied. I lied to get into college; I never graduated from high school. I lied to get in the Navy; I said I never used drugs. I lied to get into Corporate America; it is called a resume. I have lied on my taxes to increase my refund. I have lied for sex and to be loved; you should hear some of the rehearsed lines I have used to obtain women. I have

---

[1] Merriam-Webster's

lied to impress people who mean less to me than their opinions. In other words, I have lied to get what I wanted and to manipulate situations and people for my own benefit. I should have been a lawyer or a politician. However, by far, the worst lies I have told have been to myself.

I told myself that I was happy working for someone else. I told myself I would be happy if I only had someone to love me. I told myself that material concerns make the person. I told myself that if I have to be in the food chain, then I would be a lion, not a lamb. I said I can do it all by myself.

How perspectives change as we grow.

Who Lies

If you throw a stone into a crowd, only those you hit will scream.

First and foremost, it is obvious that I am not the only person who lies. The difference among people is in the frequency, target and degree of the lies. This is the main reason why we do not believe or listen to each other. I often warn people not to listen to a damn thing I say, but to watch what I do. If I had five dollars for every lie that has been told to me, I would be rich. If I had the same for every time I have lied, I would be wealthy enough to sign a check for Tiger Woods.

I was chosen to participate in the interview process for potential students. The administrators thought it would be a good idea to have a student on the interview board. Being a student who had gone through the program made me an ideal candidate. I sat and listened intently as everyone asked his or her questions, most of which seemed rehearsed and superficial. I finally, asked, "Have you ever cheated?" I was never invited to another interview.

If you take time to analyze a normal conversation with most people, you will find that they do not listen, hear or understand most of what we say. Many people cannot think and listen at the same time. And, because we all lie and know it, in the course of conversations, people often drift off into inner space to digest, compute and then decide whether what they have just heard is true or not. You see it in the facial expressions and can almost see the two hemispheres of the brain fighting as they think about something you said and miss the meat of the discussion.

Meanwhile, back at the ranch, the conversation continues and is lost on deaf ears. You did not hear what the other person has said while you were thinking. I try to avoid this by interjecting questions when I have them. It is infinitely better than trying to decipher what someone has said or allowing someone to lead me astray with fishermen's tales. What usually has caused you to start thinking was the sound of something uncertain; there is no fault or judgment in this. Many do not interrupt to ask the definition of a word, but lose some of the conversation asking themselves what the word meant. Any distraction is enough to corrupt verbal communication, the sound of a possible lie or some unbelievable fact, some associative thought or simply thinking about sex.

Face it; most people are passive listeners, unless there is gain or threat involved. Instead of questioning what we hear, we are conditioned to listen politely, to accept exceptional lies as the truth. You do not have to believe me, ask someone to repeat what you have just said to him or her in order to check for understanding.

Wade Rowatt[2] asked 112 men and women how willing they were to use 78 different lies to get a date. Results showed that 90% admitted being willing to tell a lie to a prospective date.

We all know a lie when we hear one, and feel it necessary to ascertain the reasoning for the lie instead of facing it head on. Facing a lie head on is considered by many people to be rude, intrusive, or abrasive. To openly question another's comments is like saying, "Are you lying to me?" The issue is that we are so used to hearing bullshit that we do not distinguish the truth from a lie anymore. We accept lying as a normal part of everyday communication. It is as if we have lost the art of communication because of lying; favoring our own analysis of conversations to what the other person was actually trying to say, a mask on top of a mask, on top of their truth.

I do not care why we lie; we do it and we know we do it. Just admit it, be aware of it, and try to stop telling and believing. Keep this in mind; if you told the truth all the time, you would not have to remember shit.

Most people see the relative value of honesty; many do not view it as a principle of right or wrong. We lie to protect our own interests, and it seems as though it has become a necessary evil. Many professional men and women assume that it is impossible to perform their jobs with integrity; just ask any lawyer who has suppressed evidence, any politician who has compromised, or any sales representative who has stretched the truth when it came to a product's capabilities. A friend once told me she could not possibly tell the troubled children she manages the truth. She went on to say that it is difficult to socialize in general and be honest. I agree; it is difficult, but not impossible.

A survey by Careerbuilder.com revealed that 1 in 5 people lie at work "at least" once a week. There are 52 weeks in a year. The reasons are as follows: to appease a customer-26 percent; to cover up a failed project, mistake or missed deadline-13 percent; to explain an unexcused absence or late arrival-8 percent; to protect another employee-8 percent; and to get another employee in trouble or look better in front of a supervisor-5 percent.

I discovered that my older brother and I came into being because of a lie. My mother and father met each other, became pregnant and married over the same lie. I came along after the fact. What was the lie? My father faked having money. He stole $2,000.00 from a young lady he was dating. She made the mistake of showing him where her father kept a drawer full of stacks of $20 bills. Dad removed the key and stole two stacks of twenty dollar bills. With this money he seduced my mother. He bought her so many clothes that she had to hide them over her friend's house, so that my grandfather and grandmother would not ask where they came from. His spending $2,000.00 in 1964 on a virgin was enough to convince my mother it was true love. When I asked my mother what drew her to my father, she said, "Those bowed legs and that white leather jacket walking down the hall like he was the king of the planet." She also told me that

---

[2] Wade Rowatt: Psychologists University of Baylor. Specializes in experimental social and personality psychology.

they danced well together and she thought that was love. Two and half years and one and half kids later, Mom realized she had been duped. Duped by her own expectations, the lies she told herself, and duped by the lies my father told her and himself.

All I want to say is that lying has become so much a part of our lives that we seldom distinguish it from the truth unless it is to our benefit or we catch someone in a blatant one.

Humble Beginnings

The major problem with human attitudes toward self-serving behavior is that most people practice what I term "morality of convenience". Individuals expect others to follow the moral guidelines in respect to human interaction, but are quick to justify their own selfish actions. Morality is wonderful, until it somehow restricts your own ability to gain at the expense of others. Until people realize that the universal moral codes apply equally to all members of the species and not just to people other than themselves, there will not be a lasting solution to mankind's problems. B. W. Holmes[3]

Like most of our other behavioral characteristics, we learn to lie first, at home and from those who surround us during our childhood (I touch on this concept in Chapter IV: Right and Wrong). We learn that we can avoid accountability, doing some undesirable task, and/or gain advantages and attention by exaggerating the truth or lying. For example, "Who opened the cookies?" asks a mother of her children, after leaving explicit instructions not to open them until after dinner. A typical response is, "Not me," even though there are cookie crumbs on our chins, or in our desire to join in a conversation we exaggerate a truth and/or tell a complete lie in order to be included, if just for a moment. This behavior, by the way, does not stop with childhood, but continues throughout life. The lies and exaggerations increase proportionally as the profit from telling them.

Excuses

I can show you my hand, but you cannot play it![4]

Not only do we learn the benefits of lying, but we also find imaginative ways to justify why we lie, making it almost noble. Our subconscious builds a self-protection mechanism so that we do not feel bad about the decision we made to lie. Excuses are what our desire tells our morality in order to persuade it to go along with the plan, and suppress the unpleasant feelings associated with making these decisions.

The excuses we tell ourselves allow us to function in a somewhat normal fashion, while continuing to violate natural, spiritual and civil laws. They tell us that we are not bad people for doing things we ourselves, not others, deem inappropriate. Excuses tell us that everyone else does it, so it is acceptable for us to perform the same type of behaviors. An example of this might be finding a wallet and keeping the money. I like to think I would at least mail the wallet back or call the owner. I know that some people keep irreplaceable items in their wallets. Some people

---

[3] B.W. Holmes: Philosopher. Author of www.reasoned.org
[4] Poker expression used by my grandfather, Julian.

justify cheating on or using their mates by stating, "They cheated on me first!" Why not leave the relationship? Excuses tell us it is everyone else's fault that we are not getting what we want. There is a constant battle going on inside of each and every one of us between our morality (spirit) and desires (body). Our wanting (desire for) something usually over rules our own sense of right and wrong, self interest over altruist nature and design. The justification we rationalize for doing this is called an excuse. For example, alcoholics keep drinking, drug addicts keep getting high, head doctors keep making billions and people keep working at jobs they hate. Children often explain away a bad grade with, "The teacher does not like me". It is because "I am a woman", "I was molested or abused", "I am an alcoholic", "I am African-American, Latino, or White", or "I have an over active thyroid." Regardless of the reasoning, excuses give us easy answers to even easier questions.

There is a file as thick as a set of Encyclopedia Britannica in every major law enforcement agency in the world about the "Excuses Gang", headed by "NOT ME". The members are Not Me's brothers, the triplets "Wasn't", "Whatn't" and "Beats Me", his cousins "Who Knows" and "I Don't Know", rounded out by their close childhood friends, "Let Me Think About It", "I'll Get Back to You", "I Had a Flat Tire", "It's in the Mail", "The Dog Ate It", "Honestly", "I am not Feeling Well", "I am on My Period", the infamous "I am on the Pill" and, the notorious, "I Promise not to Come in Your Mouth". They have infiltrated every crevice of society and often disguise themselves to avoid detection. I know my mother wants to hang them for the shit they did in our household, and the shit they are still doing all over the world.

Excuses are the tools of the incompetent; they build monuments of nothingness and bridges to nowhere. Those who excel in excuses, seldom excel at anything else. Unknown

Let me tell you about some of the lies I have told myself. The biggest one is that I am better than most other people. I used to get so mad at people for stealing from me. I have no idea why I thought that I could judge anyone for doing exactly what I have done to others. I remember stealing from my mentor as a child. I used to take quarters from his change dish when I went to his apartment to do work for him. The amount is not important and my age was no excuse for my behavior. I did it; and I am ashamed to have taken anything from someone who was doing everything he could to help me. And, even though I have confessed to the person I have stolen from, I am still haunted by that choice and am trying to find a way to make up for it and not do it anymore… I think maybe I already have. While living abroad, I used to let people sleep in my living room when we hung out late. I kept a change dish in the same room they slept in and they partook. I got mad as hell. I am not mad at them anymore. I understand their motives.

I have taken advantage of women. I used emotional attachment to get the money and for whatever reason not paid them back. But, if I put the money borrowed on a scale balanced against money given, it would tilt heavily on the side of monies given, but that does not excuse not repaying a loan. I truly want to track down every one and make things right. The boys on the block would call me a "P.I.M.P." for doing this and would not see anything wrong with it. I am not on the block. "I" judge what I have done as wrong and it eats at me because I want to be a better person than I am now. What is worse is that I have borrowed money from friends and have not been able to pay them back. I am determined to make good on them all. I want to be in a position where I can give aid to others in need to make restitution for my past. I want to balance the scales before they balance themselves.

A person digging a hole can only dig so deep without burying themselves.

Denial

If I could buy you for what you are worth and then sell you for what you think you are worth, I'd be wealthy.

I have always found a way to make the negative things that have happened to me someone else's fault. In reality, the things I viewed as bad were faults of my own. Am I any different from everyone else?

I awoke once to a shipmate masturbating in his bunk not four feet away from me; it was the sound of springs squeaking. I told him. "Do it in the shower like everyone else." He became angry when I told others on the ship what he had done. It was funny because we were all doing it. He confronted me in our stateroom. You should have seen him posturing and denying what we both knew to be true. It was not until I told him there was not a damn thing he could do about what I said but flap his gums that he calmed down. I understand his being embarrassed about being caught "whacking it" and upset about my telling others, but he had no right to try to convince me that what I saw was not real. In addition, just for the record, I am not so callous as to want to embarrass anyone on purpose. When I was telling the story, I did not use a name. It was not until someone asked me what I did that his name slipped from my lips. I felt bad about it, but it was the truth and I was not about to take any shit from him about it. "Oh, you think you're Billy Badass?" "Nope, but I can take you!" He shut the fuck up. He got me back by using alliances, later.

One of my acquaintances does not like her current boyfriend. I call him her boyfriend loosely (benefactor might be a better description). She has several other prospects. She said the sex with him is bad and he is not that attractive, but he buys her presents. So for the moment, she is with him exclusively. What is wrong with this picture? Nothing. Someone giving to us makes us feel wanted and valuable or loved. It is about self-worth. Just be careful that you do not lie to yourself or to your mate about what is going on. The guy doing the buying knows already; that is why he tries to compensate financially for what he thinks he lacks physically, and more importantly, spiritually. And please remember that self-worth comes from within and cannot be measured with monetary values. It is literally priceless; you cannot buy it. If you do not love yourself, you are incapable of loving others. Instead we end up looking for our worth in the praise received from others.

I have watched grown men and women who are supposedly secure with themselves arrive in countries and become someone they are not. They reinvent themselves in order to feel good. The standard and price of living in the United States and Europe is so much higher than that of many nations. Picture a minimum wage of $90.00 US a month, and that is if you have a full time job. $2 - 3 US per day is normal. Many people work when they can, and barely have enough to eat. So when foreigners go there with $1000.00 to blow on their 10-day vacation, they seem like they are rich and many of them act that way. They buy people and play at being Ballers[5]. They flagrantly lose their inhibitions and respect for other human beings; this is sexual tourism at its peak. My vices are mine to control or let control me. I went elsewhere, "Never shit where you sleep!" I have since learned that everything comes to light. What about you? Someday, somehow, that demon comes. I have faced them, ran from them, and fought them. They belong to me and are my excuse for not doing more.

I have heard the poor referred to as "monkeys", "chimpanzees", "animals", "fuck machines", "whores" and a host of other names. These comments have come from whites, Latinos, African-Americans, males and females alike. I remember listening to the conversation of two American women at a club one night. We were at the bar and they did not know I spoke English. Two local men accompanied them. The things they said about their companions amazed me. Imagine their surprise when I told them, "You two need to be careful about what you say. You never know who is listening." People like this cannot seem to get enough attention from "these animals".

The situation is the same in many other impoverished and wealthy countries alike. I have seen and participated in it. These same people could not and do not have sex with the same frequency in their native countries and it shows. They are telling a lie to themselves. The lie is I am the "Man" or "Woman" and people want to love me. The quest for love continues, so what if it is false and paid for. Wealth = love. I call it Pri$e-Tag-Roman$e.

I dated The Pro for six months. She was beautiful and an excellent partner in bed. How many people confuse good sex with love? She showed her affection openly, and believed that she received affection and love through frequent sex and financial assistance. It was a pleasant arrangement for a while, but she slowly became very possessive and began demanding more of a commitment from me without wanting to grow. She never wanted to be out of sight for long. I do not think it was so much about love as it was about protecting resources that could be diverted from her and her child to other women. Our lies started to surface. I was not a rich American and she was a not a hard working girl (actually she was a hard "working" girl).

She was a whore who did not want me to know she was one. I knew I had no future with her; she would be a burden for as long as we were together. When someone more refined, more financially independent and just as satisfying in bed came into my life (actually Dani weaseled her way in, and I let her), I slowly stopped the financial support. My friend was gorgeous and soon found other sponsors, but she still came to visit me periodically.

Please do not judge me too harshly for this attitude. She did not tell me she had a child, but I figured it out because she was lactating. I thought to myself, "She has a child that is breast feeding or has been recently weaned." I did not say anything for three days. When I finally asked, she admitted she had a child. The baby was 18-months-old and staying with her family not ten minutes away by cab. I remember thinking that she has a child and she has not left me for three days to go home. My assessment of the situation was that the monetary gains that I represented outweighed the biological necessity to be with her child. I did not judge this; I had experienced the same thing with my mother.

---

[5] Baller: African-American slang term relating to people, usually men, who have large amounts of disposable income.

I have always felt a need for unconditional love. For me, the purpose of any intimate relationship is to be in and feel loved. I have heard the stories of failed relationships and infidelity all my life and I believe I know why they failed. The relationship was based on something other than love. Because of this I have always questioned the motives of people, especially the women with whom I have been involved. I know that we interact because we want love, but most people want something that they perceive as love and do not understand that love is free and pure. It is not an exchange of property or favors; it is an exchange of spiritual energy and dream building.

I listened to Dr. Phil one day. He said, "The main reasons marriages and relationships fail is because we get involved with the wrong people at the wrong time for the wrong reasons." He went further to say, "People put so much time into planning weddings and not enough time into planning their marriages."

I have always looked for women who could satisfy my needs. They have to be stimulating mentally and physically, gainfully employed, secure and willing to show unconditional love. I even have a checklist for my perspective long term mate: no children[6], educated (self or formal) and working towards something better (drive), beautiful, sexual, lovable, independent, emotionally stable and open-minded. The purpose of the list was to prescreen women before I invested too much into them. It is hard to find anyone who fits all these requirements. Most women have children, have been married before or want to get married. Those who are not married are either too young or there is a reason why they are not married.

The women who do fit into this mold are frequently very high maintenance (princesses or bitches depending on who is giving the feedback). It is as if males are expected to pay for the quality of the product with constant attention and affection (those of you who <u>are</u> bitches, have dated one or are married to one know what I am talking about). Oh, before you get it twisted. A bitch can be any gender. I have said many things about the Princesses I have dated, but by far the most common comment about the Princess is, "She can be a bitch." Believe me I have tested this theory.

So where do I turn to find this unconditional, pure love that we all want? I have the choice of settling for less than I want and deserve, or being alone because most do not have a clue to what unconditional love is.

Because most of us have not found what we want, we are willing to put up with what we view as deficiencies in our mates because we obtain or maintain security and/or the feeling of being loved. It is like a balancing act; we calculate that if our mates possess most of the qualities we like, we can deal with or change the ones we do not. Eventually the scale tilts toward the characteristics we do not like or did not know about in the beginning. For most, it is better than being alone.

People realize how hard it is to change their own behavior, but for some reason we are not able to transpose this idea to others. At this point, complaints and requests or demands for change start. "I do not like it when you..." Did they do it before you got together? "I do not like

---

[6] Women with children will protest. Did you have "No Children" on your checklist before you had them?

the way you squeeze the toothpaste." How did they squeeze the toothpaste before? "I am not satisfied." Did they satisfy you before?

They say that women marry males expecting that they will change and they do not. And males marry women expecting that they will not change and they do. People cannot change other people; only experiences can do that and why would you want to change what you say you love?

Women constantly complain about men lying. Women lie first, faster, better and more often than men. They just do not scrutinize their imperfections as readily as they do those of others. Do not take my word for it; ask an honest woman.

I personally have not met anyone who I liked totally. At this point in my life, I am not willing to "bark like a dog" for anyone, and I do not want anyone doing it for me. In layman's terms, I do not want anyone to perform in a manner that is designed to please me in order to gain some form of affection, and I will not groom them in order to gain. We all revert to ourselves after we tire of acting/lying to please other people. We cannot become the person we think our partners or anyone else wants. We can only act like that person and that cannot last forever. Usually it begins to fade after about 6 months of living together. I said, "living together" not being in a relationship. Why? I know and have known of women and men who only clean up when they have company. One would get the impression that they are an extremely neat person when in fact they are slobs. By the time you figure it out, it's usually too late. You have invested feelings, and even though you do not like untidiness, you continue in the relationship. As time passes other inaccuracies begin to crop up and are added to the list of dislikes. This drives me nuts, but we would never know this about a person, if we were always visiting. I honestly think that there should be a six-month trial of living together before marriage. It gives both parties time for the truth to emerge and the lies to die.

The Civil War

Did you know that the primary reason for the Civil War was not slavery?[7] It was about political power in Congress, economics, tariffs and States' rights. I know, I said the same thing about cotton. Most of those who fought and died in the Civil War did not own slaves. Owning a slave was like owning a house and a nice car today. They were expensive. Typically it was the plantation owners, corporations and wealthy who owned numerous slaves. One day I am going to look at the slave records of my family and sue the corporations for back pay plus interest. That is what they do to me when I am late with a payment.

Abraham Lincoln's Emancipation Proclamation of January 1863 was a propaganda campaign. He threw the idea out to his cabinet in early 1862 and received horrible feedback. By this time, I think his conscious was kicking his ass. He had seen the carnage of the front line and wanted it over. Can you imagine seeing tens of thousands of dead and knowing that your decisions caused it? Can you remember the last time a president was on the frontline of a battlefield?

---

[7] Gordon, Cause of the Civil War.

In his Annual Message to Congress in December, 1862, Lincoln proposed that each state should have its own plan of gradual, compensated emancipation to be completed before 1900. That opportunity ended January 1, 1863, with the issuance of the Emancipation Proclamation. Lincoln's September 22, 1862 proclamation warning the South to return to the Union within 100 days or face the loss of their slaves had gone unheeded.

In truth, Lincoln and most other Republicans thought the Civil War was a "white war" to be fought by white people. "Honest Abe" may or may not have been an abolitionist, but one thing is sure; he was desperate, wanted abolitionist votes, needed African-American troops, which were originally paid less than their white counterparts, and would have tried anything to end the war because it was bankrupting the treasury (income tax was first initiated to help pay for the war). The Enrollment Act of Conscription (the draft) caused civil unrest and rioting in New York during July of 1863. The South my ass! They were hunting and killing black people in the North. They even burned the black orphanage on 5th Avenue and 43rd Street to the ground. That's Midtown Manhattan[8] today.

FYI: There was a provision in the Northern draft that allowed for a payment of $300.00 to be excused. In the South, if you owned twenty or more slaves, you could go home after your initial enlistment. Have things changed all that much? Think on who have started wars in the past, and who have fought them?

During his first campaign for President, Lincoln read the following speech in his fourth debate with Stephen Douglas in Charleston, Illinois on September 18, 1858: *"I will say then that I am not nor ever have been in favor of bringing about in anyway the social and political equality of the white and black races; that I am not nor have been in favor of making voters or jurors of Negroes nor of qualifying them to hold office, nor to intermarry with white people; and I will say in addition to this that there is a physical difference between white and black races which I believe will "forever" forbid the two races living together on terms of social and political equality. And inasmuch as they cannot so live, while they do remain together there must be the position of superior and inferior and I as much as any other man am in favor of having the superior position assigned to the white race. I say upon this occasion I do not perceive that because the white man is to have the superior position the Negro should be denied everything"* (Basler).

I always thought of and was taught in school that Lincoln was the great "Emancipator" and believer in equal rights. This tells me that at the time he was running for President, the first time, he had a more practical and rational approach to slavery. By the year 1900 all slaves should be free (with compensation), but not equal. Abe's plan called for forty more years of gradually decreasing and compensating cruelty. I compared this speech to the Gettysburg Address and wondered what affected the change of heart during his first term. I think it was the ceaseless lobbying of Frederick Douglas' and others, to attach the Civil War with the slavery issue.

Lincoln issued the Emancipation Proclamation as the nation approached its third year of bloody civil war. The proclamation declared, "That all persons held as slaves within the

---

[8]World-famous commercial buildings such as Rockefeller Center, Radio City Music Hall, and the Empire State Building surround the area today.

rebellious states are and henceforward shall be free" The Emancipation Proclamation freed only those slaves in states or territories outside of Union control. It did not mention Maryland and Delaware, which did not secede and, it did not mention Tennessee, Kentucky and Missouri, which were loyal states. West Virginia and parts of Virginia and New Orleans also got passes.

Only areas under Confederate control were affected. How many of those slave owners do you think freed their slaves? The Southern states under Union control and the loyal Border States that allowed slavery were able to keep their slaves in bondage[9]. If any of the Confederate States laid down their arms and returned to the Union, they would have been able to keep their slaves as well.

I was not taught this part of history. Lincoln used the "slave issue" after the fact to turn the Civil War into a sort of crusade for freedom. He imprisoned thousands of suspected spies and Southern sympathizers without trial for years and used the war as the reasoning behind it. He did it to save the Union during a "Civil War".[10] Sound familiar? Another president used this precedent to condone torture.

FYI: Lincoln suspended the Writ of Habeas Corpus[11] in 1862 and then jailed thousands of suspected southern sympathizers and traitors. Does that sound familiar? The Military Commissions Act does the same thing to anyone that the President deems a suspected terrorist not to mention the Patriot Act.

The legal end to slavery came with the ratification of the 13th Amendment on December 6 1865, but the right for everyone born in this nation to be a citizen did not come until three years later with the ratification of the 14th Amendment. The right for all males to vote did not occur until 1870 with the 15th Amendment. What were they waiting for and why? Every swinging "Dick" could vote. What about the women? Why did they have to wait 50 years for the 19th Amendment? Even after the passage of The Civil Rights Act in 1964 "the land of the free" needed The Voter's Rights Act of 1965 and still does[12]. Why? I do not believe the hype. Why not? I remember the "Amistad[13]" and the following story will tell you that things have not changed.

"You better move your black ass!" That is what he whispered in my ear as he followed too closely behind me. Normally I would have turned and confronted him. This time I was out numbered and felt punked in front of my girl. "Shit! Mother-fucker!" was the silent prayer of the moment. It is hard to swallow shit from another male, knowing that it would be different, if we were without spectators, allies, a badge or the advantage of a weapon.

---

[9] National Archives and Records Administration.

[10] Many are doing the same even now with the "Terrorist/Islam/Oil Issue".

[11] Writ of Habeas Corpus: a judicial mandate to a prison official ordering that an inmate be brought to the court so it can be determined whether or not that person is imprisoned lawfully and whether or not he should be released from custody.

[12] The Voter's Rights Act received 33 "NOES" in the House of Representatives when it came up for renewal in 2006, all Republicans. I wonder why and I wonder what race.

[13] Amistad: Name of a Spanish ship which a slave rebellion occurred in 1841. It went to the Supreme Court and President John Quincy-Adams argued for the slaves. President Van-Buren, under pressure from a teenage queen and southern separatist, especially John C. Calhoun, intervened after a lower court had ruled for the slaves.

There are few things worse for a male than to be belittled in front of those he is supposed to protect. Men do not understand the woman's way, and we assume that we will be looked on in a different and lesser light.

Maybe if they were civilians I would have put up at least a verbal fight, but police officers? I would go to jail. My Commanding Officer would be called. I would be finished. Just like the time I stole some Kool-Aid from the grocery store and was caught, decisions, decisions.

It started innocently enough. We were exiting a new club that had opened its doors in an upscale neighborhood. There was an opera house directly across the street from an African-American nightclub. It was interesting to see the way the opera crowd mingled with the hip-hoppers. Three weeks after the club opened, and it was a nice establishment, the police showed up and started harassing groups of black males. I dismissed it. My girlfriend pointed it out and I replied, "Look at whom they are targeting. They won't touch someone like you or me." I was referring to the guys who hang outside of clubs. They tried to look gangster and drew the police like flies to dead flesh.

It was winter and cold. "I'll go get the car." The place was so popular that I had to park three blocks away. I did not want my companion to walk that far in the cold after dancing all night. Besides, her cute coat would not protect her from a light breeze.

I admit that I drove up a bit aggressively. I could not help it. There was a policeman standing in the drop-off/pick-up area. I thought it would be funny to scare him and get him out of my way at the same time. I waited until I was 30 or so feet away from him, and then, putting the car in neutral, I hit the gas. The engine surged. He turned. The instinctual "startle" response made him jump at the sight of headlights and the sound of a high revving engine, when in fact I was braking. A few of the patrons smiled while others laughed aloud.

My fraternity brother was sitting in the front seat and moved to the rear. "Hey! You can't park there," one of them yelled as I exited the car to close the door for my date. "I am not parking. I am just stopping long enough to pick up my date. It's cold out here. Is that OK?" I thought it was reasonable.

"No, that's not OK," came from the group in a different voice. It was deeper and older, authority and trouble. "Oooh shit!" "I know!" I do not like authority and will buck it every chance I get without going to jail. My partner hurried to the front seat and I closed the door, removing any doubt that I was supposed to be in the pick-up zone.

I saw him walking briskly toward me. He had to set an example for his men. I could almost hear, "I'll show them how to handle this type of ..." I was on my way back to my side by the time the pissed off sergeant closed to within six inches of my left ear and then whispered those words, "You better move your black ass." I know had pulled a funny, but I think that was a bit harsh and meant to illicit a response. I considered his actions as leaning on the shield (authority), numbers and a gun. "Walk away son... Live to fight another day," I bit my lower lip.

A patrol car followed me to the city line. I had to obey the speed limits and signal every turn after a night of drinking and dancing until four AM with blinking yellow and red lights, with no one on the road but me and my chaperone. It was just like the driving test I took when I was 15. No sweat. I told myself that I am a pilot and that I could monitor my speed, stay in the lines, signal my turns, stop properly and not give the "MAN" another reason to mess with me.

Everyone was scared. I had to tell both my companions, "Stop looking back at them. That is what they want." It made me regret ever telling them that we were being followed. I used the cruise control when I could. That let me concentrate on the road and ignore the fear. When we reached the turnoff for the tunnel, our "shadows" did a u-turn. I felt like I was being escorted out of town by the sheriff or rather the system. "To Protect and Serve" whom? That is one of the reasons why I do not believe the hype.

FYI: Did you know the original 13th Amendment, House Resolution No. 80 - the "Ghost" or Corwin Amendment of 1861, which was not ratified by Congress, but is still on the books as a proposed Amendment, protected slavery in states where it existed? In 1963 lawmakers, Rep. Henry Stollenwerck and seven other representatives, introduced legislation to not only ratify this Amendment in Texas, but also asked the other states to ratify it. President Lincoln sent letters to states urging that they support the Amendment. The Civil War interrupted the process. Maryland, Illinois, and Ohio did ratify it.

A lie told often enough becomes the truth. Vladimir Lenin[14]

National Lies

People lie and people run governments. Therefore, it is logical to assume that the people involved with governments lie. Knowing this, it is a good idea to assume that politicians are "guilty" until proven innocent[15].

Before I begin, I would like to try to explain why I am addressing National Lies. I am a patriot not an idiot or a blind follower. The government of the United States does not have a clean past and if we are to continue on our current path, we are doomed to repeat the errors of every other super power. Those who forget the past are destined to repeat it.

When I read the Preamble of the United States Constitution I am aware of the big lie "Our", their blood runs through my veins as well, forefathers told:

---

[14] Vladimir Lenin (1870-1924): Russian revolutionary. Leader of the Bolshevik party. First Premier of the Soviet Union and the main theorist of Leninism.

[15] Reagan first said Iran-Contra did not happen. Clinton said he did not have sex with Monica. Foley said he did nothing wrong concerning teenage male pages.

"We the people of the United States, in order to form a more perfect union, establish justice, insure domestic tranquility, provide for the common defense, promote the general welfare and secure the blessings of liberty to ourselves and our posterity, do ordain and establish this Constitution for the United States of America."

How is it possible to write such an inspiring piece of literature demanding justice, liberty, tranquility and welfare for all, and own slaves or condone the institution of slavery?

By signing this document every male present was condoning slavery and avoiding the inevitable. It is a direct contradiction. I do not care what excuse you choose to believe in order to justify this act; it is neither logical nor humanistic. The Constitution was a compromise between 13 different states and a multitude of different agendas, all of which were being conducted by white men, many of them Virginia planters and most of them wealthy[16]. For whom do you think they were looking out? There were no female or minority voices heard or considered. How many of them were Catholic, Jewish or other?

In order to qualify the Constitution, individual slaves were not even considered single complete persons. Because some states had large numbers of slaves, they wanted them to be counted. It was a compromise because the states with small slave populations did not want them counted at all. Slaves ended up being counted as three-fifths of a person (for congressional representation). The two sides were fighting over the number of seats that each state would have in the House of Representatives (House of Commons in England). The Virginians with their enslaved population and other Southern states made out like rats in a cheese factory.

In reality slavery became all about cotton. And, after the invention of the cotton gin[17], the need for manual labor on cotton plantations increased significantly just as it had in Virginia, North and South Carolina with tobacco years earlier. The Industrial Age, the fabric industry and the demand for cotton worldwide spawned global debauchery. England took over the East Indian cotton fields and established what might as well be considered a serf system for the 3 million orphaned English children and the poor who were forced to work in the sweatshops. Here in the states we always blame only the South, but it was the Northern factories that processed this cotton into fabric. Only the wealthy and governments can finance these types of power plays. It was a business arrangement with both the North and South profiting from the deal. No wonder it took a hundred years after the Civil War for the Civil Rights Bill to pass. Did you notice I said a "Bill"? It is not an "Amendment". Congress can revoke it. Why end slavery? It is a lose-lose for everyone concerned, except the slaves, whatever color or nationality they are.

American slaves were considered to be a fraction of a person. How is that possible among learned men then and now? Show me differences in people and I will explain environmental adaptation. Ask about behavior or intelligence and I will say what I know about nurturing, opportunity and leading by example. Where did I gain or lose the two-fifths that separated them from me and us? What fraction of the human quality did my ancestors not possess? Did I gain this lost fraction when my ancestors became pregnant by their masters, or did I gain it when the mistress seduced that side of my forefathers? They were using the issue of slavery as leverage

---

[16] At the time, the Virginia Colony's boundaries were much larger than they are today.
[17] Eli Whitney invented the cotton gin in 1793.

and ended up with a compromise between those in favor of slavery and those who wished to abolish or limit slavery to existing states. The main cause of contention, however, was political power and wealth, not the well being of Africans. "Massa" had his brothel and free labor to boot. Misses did not have to cook or clean. She did not even have to have much sex with her husband or even nurse her own baby. I swore an oath many times over, "To protect and defend the constitution from all enemies foreign and domestic..." That is what I am trying to do now, protecting and defending the words, not the intentions behind them.[18] If shit ain't going right; I have the right to dispute it! It is written in the "Declaration of Independence."

When the colonies decided to separate from British Empire, they drafted a diplomatic document to legally state their reasons for doing so. Take a look at the first paragraph of the "Declaration of Independence":

"We hold these truths to be self-evident: That all men are created equal; that they are endowed by their Creator with certain unalienable[19] rights; that among these are life, liberty and the pursuit of happiness; that, to secure these rights, governments are instituted among men, deriving their just powers from the consent of the governed; that whenever any form of government becomes destructive of these ends, it is the right of the people to alter or to abolish it and to institute new government, laying its foundation on such principles and organizing its powers in such form, as to them shall seem most likely to affect their safety and happiness...."[20]

I think that is a wonderfully written wish. But, in order to write a document like this and still have individuals in bondage takes a strange thought process that is still in existence today. This process allows us to dehumanize others. The slaves were not considered people, so those certain unalienable rights granted by the Creator did not apply to them. The Nazis used this form of reasoning to justify the "Final Solution". America used the same process of thought to justify slavery, the violation of treaties with the indigenous peoples of this nation and most recently during times of war. Look at how we have demonized Islam. Look at some of the World War II propaganda and how the Axis powers, the Japanese in particular, were portrayed. They were little bucked-teethed, slant-eyed "Japs".

If you ever read the complaints of the founding fathers, think of the women, non-whites, non-Protestants[21], indentured servants, and slaves that they did not represent. If you read the list of grievances against King George[22], you will find that we, as Americans, have and are committing the same atrocities in our country and in the countries of others. I say this because I read the complaints. I specifically point to the following original complaints: for quartering large bodies of armed troops among us (occupation forces), for cutting off our trade with all parts of the world (sanctions), for depriving us in many cases, of the benefit of Trial by Jury (many have been held for years without trial or charge), for transporting us beyond seas to be tried for pretended offences (Guantanamo Bay and the secret prisons), for exciting domestic insurrections amongst

---

[18] FYI: George Washington and Congress banded the recruitment of African-Americans into the Continental Army using the words "wretched assistance" to describe them. "Fuck you, George!" Jefferson supposedly abhorred slavery, yet he held over 100 slaves and fathered several that he kept in slavery. "Fuck you too, Tom!"

[19] Unalienable or inalienable: incapable of being alienated, transferred or surrendered.

[20] The Continental Congress removed all reference to slavery from the Declaration of Independence.

[21] Protestant: referring to any group formed from the Protestant Reformation started by Martin Luther.

[22] George III (1738-1820): King of England. Suffered from porphyria. Declared insane in 1810.

us.... (USA sponsored Regime changes). I also remember both Tuskegee Experiments. Read the "Federalist Papers"[23] and then read "Common Sense[24]". The "Declaration of Independence" is now and was then an oxymoron, a lie told by blind men, who were mainly concerned with their own self-interest or too afraid to take a firm stand against what they knew was wrong. I sincerely believe in those words, but I have not seen many capable of putting these ideals into practice.

... in the Declaration of Independence there's a remarkable poetic track but, you know, down toward the end of it, it says, you know there are all these men signed on, committing treason I believe when they signed the Declaration... Bono[25]

FYI: 52 of the 56 delegates owned slaves or supported slavery in some way. And, the "War for Independence" was partially financed by the "slave trade". And, the signers of the Declaration of Independence removed the following from Jefferson's original draft: "he has waged cruel war against human nature itself, violating its most sacred rights of life and liberty in the persons of a distant people who never offended him, captivating and carrying them into slavery in another hemisphere, or to incur miserable death in their transportation hither. This piratical warfare, the opprobrium of infidel powers, is the warfare of the Christian king of Great Britain. Determined to keep open a market where MEN should be bought and sold, he has prostituted his negative for suppressing every legislative attempt to prohibit or to restrain this execrable commerce and that this assemblage of horrors might want no fact of distinguished die, he is now exciting those very people to rise in arms among us, and to purchase that liberty of which he had deprived them, by murdering the people upon whom he also obtruded them: thus paying off former crimes committed against the liberties of one people, with crimes which he urges them to commit against the lives of another." They did not want to be seen as hypocrites.

The constitution provides for equal protection under the law. Tell that to the thousands who have been lynched or raped, their lands taken, treaties broken, their children kidnapped and their families murdered. Let us bring back Strom Thurman and ask him about his black child. Tell it to those who have been denied the right to vote, the right to eat in public establishments, the right to buy land, the right to equal education and to benefit from a level playing field. Tell that to the people who have had laws created to stop them from becoming equal, or in many cases, from living the American dream of life, liberty and the pursuit of happiness. I am not speaking exclusively of African-Americans, but Asian, Irish, Chinese, Italian, Islamic-Americans, especially the indigenous population, and anyone who is not or was not a part of the established power base.

Laws were designed to stop the immigration of Irish in New York and Boston. San Francisco and Monterey made atrocious laws to quell the Chinese expansion before and after the railroad barons brought them here to use their labor to complete the Union Pacific Railroad[26]. Think

---

[23] The Federalist Papers are a series of 85 articles that argue for Constitutional ratification.
[24] *Common Sense* was a pamphlet first published in 1776 by Thomas Paine.
[25] Paul David Hewson (1960-): Irish main vocalist of the rock band U2. On Larry King Live October 13, 2006. http://edition.cnn.com/TRANSCRIPTS/0610/13/lkl.01.html.
[26] There was a shortage of labor due to the gold rush of 1849.

about the infamous "Jim Crow" laws and Grandfather clauses in the South after the Civil War. Try to remember that the Cherokee were forcibly removed from Georgia even after the Supreme Court ruled that they had a legal right to stay. President Andrew Jackson reportedly replied, "John Marshall[27] has made his decision; now let him enforce it." The Cherokee were relocated at gunpoint. The move, sometimes called the "Trail of Tears", resulted in the deaths of one in four of those who began the march. All of the above are perfect examples of America's National Lies.

If an African-American, white or Latin male graduated from the same college, with the same class ranking and degree, who do you think will get the highest pay and the most job offers? Who would get the most promotions and mentors?

Article I, Section 9: "The Migration or Importation of such Persons as any of the States now existing shall think proper to admit, shall not be prohibited by the Congress prior to the Year one thousand eight hundred and eight, but a tax or duty may be imposed on such Importation, not exceeding ten dollars for each Person." The newly formed US government wrote provisions into the Constitution to profit from the slave trade. They debated for hours about slavery. But they did not end it - then and there.

One of the biggest lies is, "We have a democratic government". For one, we have a Federal Republic.

For one, we have a Federal Republic[28], not a democracy. The popular vote does seem to matter when we are on the verge of a landside majority. The Electoral College controls the Presidency[29]. Who are they, and what are their affiliations with one another and how are the lobbyists involved?

Our forefathers designed it this way to protect against "the tyranny of the majority". That has not worked very well. Before you think I am bashing the United States with that statement, think about minorities and what has happened to them after and before this form of government was established. It did not work for them. When the forefathers wrote of the "tyranny of the majority" they were referring to the majority of white men (not wealthy and landless) against a minority of white males (wealthy and landowning). We still see this power struggle between the GOP (Greedy Opportunist Party) and the Democrats today (The Jack - Ass Party[30]). They did not even consider ethnic minorities.

Our government is for sale to the highest bidder. Whoever raises the most money wins elections, and Lobbyists all but control the Congress. I cannot believe that I can pay a member of the Senate or House of Representatives to promote or fight against legislation through a third party. I do not care if we call it a campaign contribution or a fact-finding mission that requires golf clubs; it is a bribe meant to peddle influence.

---

[27] John Marshall (1755-1835): 4th Chief Justice of the United States (1801-1835).
[28] A federal republic is a state which is both a federation and a republic.

[29] We found that out in 1876 and in 2000. They were both political compromises made up on the run. Both sides were vying for the best deal. Friends fucking each other over what color hat Esu was wearing.
[30] The Democratic Party received this nickname because of Andrew Jackson. A columnist pictured him as an ass and it stuck.

If the members of the Senate are all millionaires, how can they be expected to relate to the issues of the common people or be concerned with any bill that will benefit those they supposedly represent? In some shape, form or fashion we constituents end up working for them. There are more "have nots" and "have nothings" in this country than "haves" and "have mores".

When a small portion of a population controls the majority of the wealth, there is something very wrong. There is something wrong when the wealthiest nation in the world establishes $11,201 per year as a poverty threshold[31]. How would you live on or under $11,000 a year?

Congress approved their pay raise because of the "price of living", but shot down a minimum wage increase. The land of milk and honey is not so for the majority of its citizens. If it was, we would all be happy (the pursuit of happiness) and debt free. Many say that the United States is the greatest nation the Earth has ever seen. I disagree. We are a great nation, if we could take off the rose colored glasses, and we shall be the greatest when we finally learn to use our most effective resource, the American people.

George Bush got into office because of a lie told to the entire world. I am not upset at Karl[32] for working the system; everyone does it. The United States has troops in Iraq right now because of a lie. Al-Qaeda was not there in cooperation with Saddam. Colin Powell [33]has come forward to say that he had not seen any evidence that there was a connection between Saddam Hussein and Al-Qaeda. To be sure, there is a legitimate threat in Iraq now.

In June of 1954 Mr. Eisenhower and the Dulles brothers stretched the truth about the communist in Guatemala to protect the economic interests of United Fruit, importers of Chiquita banana (Eisenhower and the Brothers Dulles had stock in United Fruit). The result was a CIA[34] sponsored coup (complete with US aircraft flying overhead) and the reversal of land reforms that gave 100,000 poor people land and homes. This is the same United Fruit that had so much invested in Cuban sugar. This is our government or rather these are the people who we have put into power and allow to stay in office. We often forget or choose to forget the lies, favoring distortion; or maybe we just do not give a damn as long as we can have our SUVs. Why face reality when fantasy is so comfortable? The fact is that money talks.

I watched the Senate Armed Forces Committee question former Secretary of Defense Rumsfeld on television. I wanted to listen to some of his responses. "Rummy" was asked, "Are you comfortable with the way the… program is preceding?" He responded by saying, "I am never comfortable. Programs always seem to cost more and take longer than planned, but they have their arms around the problems and I am confident that they will solve them…" His answer was, "NO, I am not comfortable and our (DOD) projects are always over-budget and behind schedule." No one on the panel said anything further about the matter. I was shocked. First, what kind of person is never comfortable? Second, if it were a stockholders meeting, he would have

---

[31] US Census Poverty Thresholds 2008: 1 person under 65 years old
http://www.census.gov/hhes/www/poverty/threshld/thresh08.html.
[32] Karl Rove: the political brain behind Bush.
[33] Interview with Barbara Walters on ABC's 20/20 09 September 2005.
[34] You may read about the CIA's involvement in Guatemala at www.foia.cia.gov/guatemala.asp.

been flayed with other questions like, why? Those dinosaurs, the Senators, just sat there; they are either too dumb to understand what is going on, too unconcerned to care, or in on it. The whole thing looked like a staged lie to me. Frustrated, I changed the channel. "Damn Lobbyist!"

J.F.K. wanted nothing more than for the Civil Rights Movement of the 1960's to go away. If it were not for the bad publicity being sent all over the world via television, and particularly to the countries undecided on whether a democratic or communist government would serve them better, Mr. Kennedy would have continued to stall the civil rights movement, but we hail him as a proponent of equality. Kennedy was more concerned about being reelected, communism and world opinion than equal rights. He also had more girlfriends than a casting director at a major studio.

The Kennedy administration took office in 1961 as national sentiment in favor of stronger civil rights legislation, with means of enforcement, was growing. President Kennedy, however, was loath to ask the Congress for strong legislation on the issue. Although he was personally sympathetic to the plight of African-Americans, his political instincts warned against taking action. Then came one of those events that forces the hand of a cautious leader.
On May 2, 1963, a horrified country watched on television as the Public Safety Commissioner of Birmingham, Alabama T. Eugene "Bull" Connor and his policemen and firemen descended on hundreds of African-American marchers, including schoolchildren, with attack dogs, nightsticks and fire hoses (Gittinger and Fisher).

FYI: Did you know that Joseph Kennedy gained his wealth through bootlegging during Prohibition?

Did you know that in November of 1963 Ngô Đihn Diệm Jean Baptiste, the President of South Vietnam and his brother, Ngô Đihn Nhu, were assassinated during a coup d'état. The CIA knew the coup was going to occur, and that the President and his brother would be killed. Our government assured the incoming regime that we would not interfere, the proverbial blessing. We did this because Diệm stopped following orders. Our government then showed great public disapproval after the event. When Madame Nhu, the wife of Ngô Đihn Nhu, heard of the assassination she said, "Whoever has the Americans as allies does not need enemies" How true. I am not saying Diệm was a good guy, but a country whose battle cry is "freedom" and "democracy" cannot condone murder. JFK was assassinated 20 days later and Robert followed in 1968. ..."Live by the sword..."

I registered to vote for the first time in my life recently. I do not think it makes a difference, but I wanted to scare the hell out of the GOP and Democrats by registering as an Independent. I am not from Ohio, Florida, or any of the "Ignorant about my rights" states. Challenge "Me" at the polls with whatever means at your disposal! I hope and pray that I will be forgiven for tearing (whom ever does it) a new asshole with my understanding of the Constitution and its Amendments. And, I pray and hope the Creator will forgive me for saying, "Fuck you and the horse you rode in on." It is time to do what is right for a change, and not compromise on what it is. Pork barrel spending, earmarking bills, lobbyist and interest groups have to go if we are to survive as a "FREE" nation. I think we should lower the salaries of Congress to $50,000 a year,

23

so we can raise the minimum wage, and if you are a millionaire, you should serve for free. Call it "public" service as Ben Franklin tried to....

"Mother's may still want their favorite sons to grow up to be President, but they do not want them to become politicians in the process." John F. Kennedy

FYI: I think Kennedy would not have been reelected because he refused to invade Cuba.

International Lies

The National powers have been lying to each other since we first started raiding the neighboring villages, towns and countries. Throughout documented history there are stories of war and broken promises. False treaties, false marriages and land grabbing have created ripples that are still felt today. Too many times one region has promised friendship and peace to another, only to renege later. Hitler and Stalin agreed to divide Poland and signed a non-aggression pact. Hitler invaded Russia two years later. After being invited to a celebratory dinner by the Inca Emperor, Atahualpa[35], the Spanish Conquistador, Francisco Pizzaro, kidnapped him. After the ransom was paid, Pizzaro had him throttled (strangled). Makes you want to rethink that guest list. In the 1500's the French and the Spanish became allies in order to divide the Kingdom of Naples and other portions of Italy. It did not matter who was married to whom. It was about growth or death. Many a monument was built through conquest. The Spanish took all of Naples, and then promptly told the French to "fuck off".

Genghis Khan promised peace to the Chinese then took the entire empire. They promised him protection. Native Americans saved Jamestown, the first successful English settlement in North America, from starvation. I wonder if they would have done so if they could see the nation today. "We the people" should read "Us the people and them".

The Romans promised citizenship and protection to the conquered, in exchange for tribute; that sounds like extortion or is it taxation? Hitler signed a treaty with British Prime Minister Chamberlain, promising he would not invade any more countries, after he took part of Czechoslovakia. This just wet the lips of the wolf, who was now convinced that the French and the English would not fight, for blood. The Spanish, French, Danes and Portuguese decimated the native inhabitants of South and Central America in the name of spreading different forms of Christianity while obtaining wealth. The English, Spanish and French did the equivalent in North America, but were more upfront about their intensions to plunder for natural resources. The Germans, Italians, French, English, Belgians, Dutch, Spanish and Portuguese carved up Africa like a pizza and took away not only its resources, but also generations of its people.

All invaders leave their mother countries with the sole purpose of taking lands (colonization) and resources from other people, under one pretense or another. Grow or die is the main driving force. The Mongols, Greeks, Persians, Egyptians, Punts and most other strong people have and will do the same. If you are strong and want something, kick ass and take it.

---

[35]Atahualpa (1502?-1533): Inca Emperor of Peru. Illegitimate son of Huayna Capac.

In most cases, the cultures and populations of these stolen lands were all but destroyed and displaced by the "civil" culture of the conquerors. In my opinion, only people who are able to live together in peace and harmony can be classified as civilized. Yet, the so-called civilized countries have been fighting each other for eons over land, resources and religion. How is it possible for a teacher to teach what we ourselves do not know and cannot practice? Since 1798, our nation has been involved in well over 100-armed conflicts on foreign soil[36]. In my opinion a warring nation does not know peace or how to be civil.

The British were not civil in India, America, Southeast Asia, China or Africa. I admit that slavery and slaving had been going on for centuries, but nothing compared to the wholesale slaughter inflicted by the Europeans and Muslims on Africa. Entire generations were removed from the gene pool by the civilized nations and we wonder why the cradle of humanity is in such a sad state.

Those who supported Apartheid are by far some the most uncivilized people on the planet. The Spanish decimated some of the most advanced societies of the Americas for gold and riches. The British and the United States used germ warfare (smallpox-infested blankets) against the Native Americans. British companies imported large amounts of opium into China and instigated the first international drug war because the Chinese instituted laws against its importation. The Chinese ban interfered with the profit margin of the British East Indian Company. As a result, the British military warred on China. The resulting treaty gave Hong Kong and other territories to the British. The British invented the concentration camp during the Boer Wars[37]. The Germans got the idea from them and Winston Churchill was the architect. The Portuguese held on to some of their colonies until 1976, and even today countries claim territories gained from war or colonization.

In my lifetime Britain, France, Belgium and others have held countries under foot. Australia had a law established in 1901, the *Immigration Restriction Act*, also known as the White Australia Policy until 1972. The United States and every other country started its climb up the Empire ladder first by fighting like dogs among themselves. We called it a Civil War. Then we united under one banner and began to expand beyond our immediate borders. Throughout history, after unification, militarily strong countries seem to get in many fights over property.

There is a proverb that says something about a dog turning on its master, but I cannot remember it.

Our latest acquisitions, Iraq and Afghanistan, were taken to fight terrorism, to prevent the use of weapons of mass destruction and then to affect regime change. Now, it is about freedom and democracy. Yeah, right! When a country does have free elections and the results are not to the liking of the United States, we protest and pressure that country to capitulate to our desires through the use of alliances, threats, economic strangulation, and other forms of coercion. A perfect example is Hamas[38]. The Palestinians freely elected the radical anti-Israel group to 74 of

---

[36]http://www.history.navy.mil/wars/foabroad.htm.

[37]Boer Wars (1880-1881) and (1899-1902): The British forcibly took possession of the Free Orange State and Transvaal Republic for the gold and diamonds that were discovered in those regions.

[38] Hamas (Islamic Resistance Movement): Reported terrorist group of Sunni Muslims originating in Lebanon.

132 seats of the parliament in January 2006. The US government responded with economic and political pressure because of Hezbollah[39]. When these efforts did not work, a blind man could have seen what came next-the 2006 Israel-Gaza conflict (the use of force). We are hypocrites when it comes to democracy. I have heard "The World's A Safer Place without Saddam Hussein," so many times that it should be a rap song. Is it really? I must have special vision or need a new prescription for my "rose colored glasses" because it seems better for a very few, the same for some and worse for the majority of others.

FYI: Did you know the only reason the United Nations did not intervene in Rwanda was that they refused to call it "genocide". If that "one" word were used in any of the correspondence to describe what was happening, via its charter, the UN would have been obligated to get involved, so no one in the higher echelons dared to say "genocide". Of course, we all "now" know it was genocide, but when does the truth matter when pertaining to poor countries with no economic interests to the "Great 8"? Ask the Congo, Sudan, and Uganda about the UN and what genocide is.

Middle-East

For those of you who do not know it, there is no defense against someone who is willing to give their life for a cause.

The Middle East is in such bad shape today largely because of the external influence of Britain, Russia, France and recently, the United States.

Britain was concerned about Russian expansionism into Persia (Iran) during the 1800's. Remember that India was the "Jewel" of the British Empire until Gandhi came along and gave the cash cow back to the original owners in 1949; we call it independence. If you know your geography, you can see that Afghanistan, the "graveyard" of great powers, is a natural buffer zone between India and Russia. The British invaded Afghanistan in 1839-1842 with 16,000 troops and got their asses kicked. In January 1842, out of 16,500 soldiers (and 12,000 dependents) only one man and one horse survived. They tried again in 1878-1890 because the King of Afghanistan said "No" to a British Mission (embassy). This time they succeeded. The British are the ones who designated the current boundaries of many Middle Eastern countries. In 1919 the Afghans declared independence. After some fighting, the British conceded. In 1979 the Russians finally got their turn to invade. They stayed 10 years. It was during this time that the United States got involved as well. Many viewed it as an opportunity to do to the Russians what they had done to the "US" in Vietnam and Korea.

The United States financed, equipped and trained some of the anti-Communist Mujahedin rebels to fight the Russians during the 80's. As a matter of fact, at one point Osama Bin Laden thanked the United States for its support in Afghanistan. We even gave them the Stinger missile. [40] I wonder if we got the unused ones back. The Taliban and Al-Qaeda emerged from this group of fighters and are now using the very guerilla tactics "our" advisors taught them against us in Afghanistan and Iraq. What happened between then and now?

---

[39] Hezbollah (Party of God): reported terrorist group of Shi'a Muslims originating in Lebanon.
[40] The Stinger missile is a sophisticated heat seeking anti-aircraft missile.

When planning the invasion of Afghanistan the Bush administration rightly went back in history to find the last time the Afghans were conquered. They had to go back to 1219 when Genghis Khan and the Mongols ravaged the region. However, they did not emulate the Mongolian tactics - the use of overwhelming force and the decimation of the male population. Instead, they relied on tribal leaders and money, despite requests from the soldiers and CIA operatives on the ground for US troops.

Iran is no different. An oil concession deal was struck in 1901 between the Shah of Persia and William Knox D'Arcy, which gave the British Empire a 60-year hold on Iranian oil. After oil was discovered the Anglo-Persian Oil Company (APOC), now British Petroleum (BP), was founded in 1909. It was the first foreign oil company to begin to exploit the oil in the region. Winston Churchill argued that oil, not coal was the future. The British government agreed and partially nationalized the APOC in 1913 to secure fuel supplies for its immense naval fleet. The British and Russians were rivals in Iran as well. In 1941 both countries invaded Iran. They did so to secure the vital oil resources that sustain the war machine and fuel dependent economies. They forced the Shah to abdicate and put his pro-western son, Mohammad Reza Pahlavi, in power. He remained in power, except for the four days of the 1953 coup, until 1979. This Shah used oil revenue to purchase more military equipment from the United States than any other country. Much of the profits from Iran's oil resources were used to support the United States' industrial military complex. But, you cannot buy bullets, live in grandeur, provide no bread for the people, restrict freedoms, and still expect to stay in power. Ask the last Czar of Russia. Ask any governmental body that has pursued this course.

FYI: We have nothing to worry to about with Iran and nuclear weapons. If they keep building their nuclear program, the Israelis will bomb it just like they did Iraq's in 1981.

Iraq came into British possession after the partition of the Ottoman Empire following World War I. The Turks were dumb enough to enter the war on the side of the "Axis" powers. When they lost, the British moved in, taking Iraq as a mandate. They installed a Saudi, King Faisal, on the throne. Iraq gained its independence in 1932, but the British maintained the right to military bases in the country. What kind of independence is that? In 1941 a coup d'état by former Prime Minister Rashid Ali occurred which was supported by the Nazis. They did this with hopes of shaking off the English. The British response was not only predictable, but looking at the history of Imperial powers, it was all but guaranteed. They invaded and reinstalled their "Yes Boy". Six years later the British left and the country pretty much went through a series of coups until the Baath Party in 1968 and Saddam in 1979. In 1980 Saddam saw the regime change (the Shah was out. United States hostages and the Ayatollah Khomeini were in) in neighboring Iran as an opportunity to seize more oil rich territory[41]. He invaded. The war lasted 8 years and brought the United States into Iraqi politics, all for oil, power, revenge and greed.

Did you know that Iraq invaded Kuwait in the first Gulf War because the Kuwaitis loaned Saddam huge sums of money to finance the war with Iran? Saddam did not want to repay the loans, wanted to settle a border dispute that had existed since the British established the new borders in the 1920s, and wanted to reduce the production of oil to make the prices rise.

---

[41] The Ayatollah Khomeini purged the military much like Stalin had done before World War II. The result was Hitler invading Russia in 1941. Saddam must be a historian because he did the same.

Just so you know Iraq bought many of its ingredients for chemical cocktails, and biological weapons from other countries that routinely produce them. Iran also purchased technology from someone. As a matter of fact, the United States gave Iran its first nuclear reactor during the Carter administration. When Iraq and Iran fought who supplied the weapons? The Unites States supported Iraq and Russia supported Iran, more Cold War shit. As a matter of fact, Ronnie Reagan sent Donald Rumsfeld to Iraq as a special envoy in 1983 to make sure that the stalemate that had developed would swing in Iraq's favor. We supplied the Iraqis with finances, equipment, satellite images and intelligence on the Iranian Army. Why? We were pissed because the Iranians stormed the US embassy in Tehran in November of 1979. They held US citizens hostage for 444 days in reprisal for the United States not only supporting the Shah, but also allowing him to take up residence in the United States. To their credit, they did release the female and African-American captives.

FYI: The United States later sold arms to Iran as well (Iran-Contra)-playing both ends against the middle. And, the Senate Subcommittee on Terrorism, Narcotics and International Operations of the Committee on Foreign Relations 1988 report included findings indicating: "Individuals who provided support for the Contras were involved in drug trafficking, the supply network of the Contras was used by drug trafficking organizations, and elements of the Contras knowingly received financial and material assistance from drug traffickers. In each case, one or another U.S. Government agency had information regarding these matters either while they were occurring, or immediately thereafter... Payments to drug traffickers by the U.S. Department of State with funds authorized by the Congress for humanitarian assistance to the Contras, in some cases after the traffickers had been indicted by federal law enforcement agencies on drug charges, in others while the traffickers were under investigation by those agencies... The Subcommittee made only one legislative recommendation in its report that directly pertained to the Intelligence Community: 'No U.S. intelligence agency should be permitted to make any payments to any person convicted of narcotics related offenses, except as authorized in writing by the Attorney General in connection with the investigation or prosecution of criminal activity.'[42] "

We have to remember that the CIA had already sponsored a coup d'état in Iran, operation TPAJAX[43], in 1953. They intervened on behalf of the Shah in a power struggle against his Prime Minister Dr. Mohammed Mossadeq, Time Magazine's "Man of the Year" in 1951. The Anglo-Iranian Oil Company (British owned) exerted enormous pressure on the Truman administration to intervene after the Iranian Government decided to nationalize its oil wells in March of 1951, but Truman said, "No". The issue was profit sharing. Other countries in the region were receiving 50% of the profit from the Western companies that were extracting oil from their lands. The Iranians on the other hand, had long since sold their shares to the British for £40,000 and a small percentage of the profits. When Eisenhower[44] was elected in 1951 and Winston Churchill[45] in 1952, the answer changed to "Yes" It was about "oil" then too.

---

[42] https://www.cia.gov/cia/reports/cocaine/report/background.html.

[43] http://www.odci.gov/csi/studies/vol48no2/article10.html

[44] Dwight Eisenhower was concerned about Russian influence in the region (more Cold War crap).

[45] Winston Churchill was conscious of the fact that Britain had just lost India in 1949 and was concerned about the unraveling of the British Empire. Remember, Churchill is the same man who denigrated Gandhi and invented the modern day concentration camp.

The United States has been directly involved with Iraq since 1983, Iran since the 1950's and Afghanistan since the early 1980's. The Taliban would have never come to power had we done it right after the Russian withdrawal in 1989. Instead the United States and its allies lost interest and did nothing to help rebuild the country. The Taliban stepped into the power void.

Modern day Palestine is what it is because of the British and the French. In exchange for siding with the British against the Ottoman Turks, the Arabs were promised a homeland by T. E. Lawrence, better known as "Lawrence of Arabia". After the end of WW I the British and French reneged on their promises. The British took the Mandate of Palestine and the French took the Mandate of Syria. Go figure? This is probably the start of the contention between the West and Arabs.

After WW II, the British started losing control over Palestine because of the terrorist activities of the Jewish "terrorist/freedom fighter" groups like Irgun, Lehi, etc. Some holocaust victims wanted to settle in Palestine and the British prevented any immigration on the part of Jews. A friend had a good suggestion that would have settled this mess before it started. The United States, Britain, France and Russia should have given Germany to the Jews after World War II, but that would be too much like right.

Throughout history super powers have always tried to spread influence and fight when their heads butted. If you cannot see the pattern, you need an eye transplant, need to pick up a history book or use that computer for more than e-mail or solitaire, a little deprogramming would not hurt either. Do not listen to any other reason for being in the Middle East except oil. Everything else is rhetoric, politics and PhD (piled high and deep) bullshit. Try to remember that most politicians are professional liars and that a hornet can run a jackass.

We are very civilized people indeed, who will do anything to justify our gaining or protecting wealth and power.

FYI: Exxon-Mobile made $45.2 billion for 2008 in profit, the most of any US company ever in a year. They broke the record they set in 2007[46].

Two Tier Justice

If you show me a person without a vice, I will show you one you cannot trust.

The justice system in the United States is one of the biggest lies alive. It is a two-tier system. People like lobbyist Jack Abramoff, Enron, DuPont, Universal Life, Halliburton, Merck, Boeing, Marsh & McLennan, PBHG Mutual Funds, Riggs Bank, Time-Warner, AIG, Fannie Mae, Conoco Phillips, WorldCom, Citigroup and others know what I am talking about. They all broke the law and are in the process of, or have already bought their way out. A few of the culprits will go to the federal country club for a few years to "pay" their debt to society. You can send me to prison for four years too, if I can keep the $500 million I stole minus the $300 million fine. That

---

[46] 2008 was the fifth year of the Iraq occupation. Hurricane Katrina supposedly destroyed so much of the east coast's fuel supply. OPEC received $60-$70 per barrel. And, FYI: Afghanistan had a bumper crop of heroin. It was all but eliminated under the Taliban.

is a $50 million/year job. When my sentence was commuted or the President pardoned me, I would write a book, join the lecture circuit, and get a syndicated radio or television show.

G. Gordon Liddy, AKA "Mr. Watergate", had his sentence of 20 years commuted by Jimmy Carter after serving 4 ½ years. He has written several books and has had several television and radio spots. Elliott Abrams, an admitted liar in the Iran-Contra scandal, was pardoned by Bush Sr. along with five other conspirators, and used to serve as the Deputy National Security Advisor for Bush Jr. - what a "hook-up". He has also been accused of having a hand in the 2002 coup in Venezuela. Gerald Ford pardoned Tricky Dick Nixon. Nixon received a state funeral. Patty Hearst served 22 months of her 7-year sentence before Jimmy Carter commuted her sentence in 1979. Bill Clinton granted her a full pardon in 2001. George Steinbrenner, the owner of the New York Yankees, pled guilty of making illegal contributions to Nixon's re-election campaign and obstruction of justice in 1974. He was fined a total of $35,000, restricted from baseball for two years, and then Reagan pardoned him in 1989. Jimmy Hoffa, "Mr. Teamsters", was convicted of attempted bribery of a grand juror and sentenced to fifteen years in 1964. Nixon commuted his sentence in 1971 for a reported $300,000. Angelo DeCarlo of the infamous Genovese crime family was convicted of extortion and sentenced to 12 years in 1970, but Nixon pardoned him after a year and a half in 1972. Marc Rich, a billionaire, fled the US for Switzerland in 1983 to avoid tax evasion charges. Clinton pardoned him after he paid $100 million fine in 2001[47]. Scooter Libby was his lawyer. Roger Clinton Jr., the President's half-brother, was convicted of cocaine possession in 1984. Bill pardoned him in 2001. Robert McFarlane, Reagan's National Security Advisor, and Caspar Weinberger, Reagan's Secretary of Defense, were both accused of lying to Congress about Iran-Contra. McFarlane pled guilty, was fined $20,000 and sentenced to 2 years probation. Weinberger was indicted and due to stand trial before Bush Sr. pardoned both he and McFarlane after he lost his reelection bid. Bush also pardoned Edwin L. Cox Jr. who is from one of Texas' richest families. Cox had pleaded guilty to bank fraud in 1989 for falsifying collateral on $78 million in loans. He spent six months in prison and paid $250,000 in fines. Cox Sr. then donated between $100,000 and $250, 000 to the Bush Presidential Library[48]. Ted Kennedy killed Mary Jo Kopechne in Chappaquiddick and received a two month suspended sentence. Neil Bush was on the Board of Directors for the Silverado Savings and Loan when it collapsed. It cost taxpayers an estimated one billion dollars. The Federal Deposit Insurance Corporation (FDIC) brought charges against Neil and the other members of the board, but it was settled out of court for $50,000.00. I wonder if his daddy being Vice-President had anything to do with. Paris Hilton stole a video of herself 'doin' it' from street vendor and was involved in a hit and run. Both were caught on tape, but nothing happened. She also received a 45-day sentence that was reduced to 23 days for good behavior before she crossed the threshold of the jail. After 5 days she was released for medical reasons. Do you see the pattern? If one is in the "know"…. Sometimes, instances like these make me wish I had a little "white privilege" and were wealthy. Ask Roman Polanski.[49]

My cousin was convicted of armed robbery. He robbed a 7-11 for a few hundred dollars and then had a change of heart. He took the money back. He received ten years in prison with no

---

[47] http://jurist.law.pitt.edu/pardons6.htm.

[48] http://www.time.com/time/nation/article/0,8599,101652,00.html.

[49] Roman Raymond Polanski (1933-) : French film director, producer, writer and actor. Convicted of raping a 13-year-old child. Fled the US in 1977 and kept making films.

hope of parole because of the states handgun laws. Will anyone pardon him or commute his sentence? I doubt it, unless he comes up with a healthy campaign contribution. The well off and connected have such tough lives when compared to the average citizen criminal, who has issues getting a job because he or she has to check "yes" in that box that asks, "Have you ever been convicted of a felony?"

I want to talk about lobbyists. Jack Abramoff was said to keep very detailed e-mails. I wish the prosecutors would make them public. I want to know everyone who received money from him and why. It should not be that difficult to find out. As a result of the Abramoff scandal, Congress was finally forced to address lobby reform. The issue was very public for about a week. Numerous Congressmen gave the monies they received from Jack to charities - rats jumping a sinking ship. Congress eventually passed a watered down Lobbying Reform Bill, so that they can keep the corporate money flowing into their campaign funds, bank accounts, and spider holes. This whole affair was swept under the rug and a few individuals or sacrificial lambs will take the fall. Investigate Tom Delay, the former Republican whip, Bob Ney, a Republican Congressman from Ohio or Randy "Duke" Cunningham[50], a Republican Congressman from California and see who and what "fall out."

George Bush Jr. immediately said he does not know Abramoff personally; Jack or his firm has had over 400 contacts with the White House, over 80 with Karl Rove and Abe's 'used to be assistant'; she resigned. I cannot wait to see where the trail of e-mails goes. Do not get me wrong; the Democrats are just as dirty. The $90,000 found in Congressman William Jefferson's (D-Louisiana) freezer proves it. We should clean house as a nation and not let these Powercrats police themselves. If it were up to me, members of Congress would not be able to except any form of payment or contribution in exchange for influence. If someone's argument for or against proposed legislation is legitimate, they do not have to dress it up in "green" or free shit.

I have real issues with people who steal millions or billions and go to a federal prison for a few years. Andrew Fastow, the man responsible for the financial schemes that doomed Enron Corp., was sentenced to six years in prison, four years less than he had agreed to in a plea bargain, by a judge who felt he deserved leniency. I wonder what would happen if I robbed a store of $100.00 and were caught. Well, that would be very dependent on how much I could spend on a lawyer. Madoff was sentenced to 150 years in the Butner Federal Correctional Complex near Raleigh, North Carolina for stealing $65 billion. It is a country club. The Mrs., who obviously had nothing to do with stealing the money, bought a house nearby so that she could be near him. I wonder if he gets congenial visits.

I remember being asked about how I felt about the O.J. Simpson verdict. I walked into the middle of a conversation between four or five of my squadron mates. The verdict had been given the day before and I was not one of those who stayed glued to the television to watch it. The question made me a little uncomfortable because white people were holding the conversation and it felt like my peers were setting me up. If I said I was happy about the verdict, I was screwed in their eyes. If I said he should have fried, I would be a sellout because of all the African-American people who have died at the hands of whites over the centuries. When I heard the verdict on the news, I remember thinking, "He got away with murder", even though I knew little

---

[50] Being an aviator, Cunningham used to be one of my heroes. He was a fighter ace during the Vietnam War.

or nothing about the case. Surprisingly, I was not upset. I remembered the case of Emmett Till[51] and how his murderers went free and then they were paid $4,000.00 for the story four months later. They beat him and shot him in the head for showing undo attention to a white woman on a dare.

Because of this, and because people in positions of power have been getting away with murder and a virtual plethora of other crimes for years, I saw nothing different in the O.J. case except the color of his skin. O.J. was not an activist and he had been accepted into the higher echelons of our society. But I remember watching the reaction of people on the television. It was scary. Most African-Americans celebrated and most whites damn near lost their minds. This is America. I think we all know why this happened, but if you are unsure, spend some time being still and think about it. I think: "An African-American, black man, nigger killed a white woman and got away with it. What is America coming to?"

There is a two-tier justice system; my squadron mates knew it, just like I did. So, why ask me? They already had a quorum. I responded as tactfully as I could. I simply put on a blank face and said, "I think it is a damn shame when a man with money cannot get away with murder in our justice system." I still laugh at the expression on all their faces, "What?!?" utter and total confusion. I wonder if any of them got what I said right then and there, or if it was one of those delayed fuses that blew up long after I escaped. At any rate, I planted a seed in their subconscious. I gave them something to think about.

I once got a ticket in North Carolina that I did not pay. The following year I got another one. Because of the first ticket not being paid, my license was suspended in the state. I went to renew my license in California and found out that I had to pay for the two speeding tickets in NC first, which I promptly did. However, because I paid the second ticket, I was in essence pleading guilty to driving without a license and my license was suspended for another year. I had to get a lawyer and pay $900.00. It was convenient that the clerk at the Courthouse in Eastbumfuck, N.C. had several numbers handy. The lawyer had the first charge reduced from a moving violation (speeding) to improper equipment (broken tail light). Because of this, the second ticket was not driving while on a suspended license and my driving record was cleared. All it took was $1,500 and three days to clear it up; my point? Money talks in our justice system; it always has and if you get a speeding ticket; the smart person pays it! The way information is shared today; you cannot fart without someone knowing it.

Nixon lied, resigned, got amnesty and had a state funeral honoring him as a great "Man". The former Chief of Naval Operations, Admiral Jeremy Boorda, committed suicide over a lie. The fall from grace was too much for him because he stressed integrity so much and did not live up to his own standards. Reagan's boys brokered the Iran-Contra[52] deal to fight the Sandinistas[53] in

---

[51]Emmett Till (1941-1955): 14 year-old murdered in Mississippi allegedly for improper advances toward a white woman. Because of double jeopardy they were able to sell their story to a magazine and not be tried again.

[52] Iran-Contra Affair (also known as "Irangate"): 1980's political scandal in the United States. President Reagan's administration sold weapons to Iran, the enemy at the time and used the proceeds to support the Contras. The efforts of the Nicaraguan Contra organizations to unseat the Sandinista Government in Nicaragua spanned much of the 1980s but had their roots in earlier events. A 1911 treaty between the United States and Nicaragua gave the United States the right to intervene in Nicaraguan affairs, and U.S. Marines were dispatched to Nicaragua in 1912 to protect

Central America and free the hostages Hezbollah kidnappers had in Lebanon. When Congress asked him about it, he said, "I do not recall", and he got away with it. I guess he had Alzheimer's a lot earlier than diagnosed. Bullshit! He lied and Oliver North lied to protect him. Ollie now has a television show.

FYI: The first of the arms for hostages deals were brokered through Israel, which sold TOW missiles to its mortal enemy, Iran.

Clinton got a blowjob in the Oval Office and got to stay there[54]. But no one I know examined the mindset of the woman. Think about it. What kind of woman saves a blouse with sperm on it? She set his ass up and made him pay for it. The term "gold digger" comes to mind. I once told a colleague that a picture she showed me at work was "nice". I did not think it was nice. I thought she looked like a hoochie mama, but what do you say when you see someone's picture? This is complicated, so bear with me. I was the third shift manager. One day my department head insisted that I work second shift. I could not rationalize why. We had a second shift manager who rarely worked her shift anyway. I did not see the need and questioned her as to why she wanted me to work off my assigned shift. Her answers never did add up until later.

I did as she requested. I did my usual walk around. When I got to "Hoochie's" station I looked at the display monitor as usual to see how her line was doing. Stuck in the lower right-hand corner of the screen was a picture of her. It was one of those $5.00 Polaroids in front of a ghetto backdrop. She had her back to the camera and her head turned so that you could see her face. Her skirt was so short you could read her mind. The picture was accented with her hand on her extended left hip.

My first response was confusion. I thought, "What the hell is this doing here?" "Why'd she put that there?" She got mad at me six months or so later and accused me of sexual harassment because of the way I said, "Nice Picture." My manager and she set me up.

There has been a rash of female teachers having sex with their male students. If a male teacher did the same, they would go directly to jail. One woman got probation and then sent a sexually explicit video over the internet to the student. One woman's lawyer had the nerve to say, "My client is too pretty to go to prison." Before you start with the "males view sex differently", a crime is a crime and females are just as culpable as males, but our justice system does not work that way. If a female hits a male, she probably will not be arrested. If a male hits a female and she is upset enough to press the issue, the male will go directly to jail. Add to this the fact that we show preference to those we consider attractive, and you have an unbalanced system.

U.S. economic interests. The two-decade military occupation that followed helped foster the development of a guerrilla opposition, led by Augusto Cesar Sandino that sought to rid Nicaragua of U.S. influence.
[53] Sandinist National Liberation Front (FSLN): Nicaraguan political party that ruled Nicaragua from 1979-1990. Faced heavy opposition from the United States due to its predominantly Marxist ideology and resulting closeness with Socialist countries (Cuba and Soviet allies).
[54] If I were President, I would try to make it a daily requirement (not from Monica or anyone like her). The most powerful man or woman in the world should be as relaxed as possible.

I have a question. Why do we still fuck with Cuba? I know they are Communist, but so are the Chinese and we do so much business with them it "ain't" funny. We also are allies with the Russians. Did I mention we were at war with both China and Russia in Korea and Vietnam? Hell, the Russians put medium range nuclear missiles in Cuba and we forgave them and, evidently, China too (They have a trillion dollars in reserve. As sure as God made lil' green apples China is going to make a power play, maybe Taiwan because we are spread thin militarily). We tried to murder Castro, but no one wants to remember that. No one wants to hear that our government, with Allen Dulles at the helm of the CIA, solicited the aid of the Mafia to help complete the deed. [55] The mob had a vested interest in seeing Castro dead; they had invested heavily in Cuban casinos and lost money as well when Castro came to power. If someone tried to kill me, they had better not screw the pooch.

I know that Castro is not the best of leaders, nor is Cuba the best example of a democratic government, but neither is the former President of Pakistan, Pervez Musharraf, nor many of the Arab royalty, the Saudis included. Boys as young as 4-years-old have been kidnapped and smuggled into the United Arab Emirates to serve as camel jockeys. It is just a question. I am not un-American and I am not a mindless, deaf, blind automaton. That means I question inequity, as every true American should. It is our duty. No, it is our obligation to challenge those in power. Otherwise, as throughout history, those in power frequently become uncontrollable and stop leading for the people, and instead lead for the power, influence and wealth of a chosen few: "The haves and have mores."

The great masses of the people... will more easily fall victims to a great lie than to a small one.
Adolf Hitler

The Other Twin Towers

Did you know we have another set of twin towers? They are the Federal Budget Deficit and the Trade Deficit.

Let us forget the politics, and concentrate on the budget issues and our tax dollars. The projected budget deficit is estimated at over $611 billion for fiscal 2009[56]. It is only going to worsen because we are not doing anything to stop it. If we ran our households in the same manner that the federal government is being run, we would go to debtors' prison, file a chapter seven or 13, or be out on our butts because we would continually have to "rob Peter to pay Paul." I have had budgeting issues like this in my household. I tried to solve my issues in much the same manner as the government does; I borrowed money to support a lifestyle that was beyond my means (bullets and butter). In the end, something had to give. It is impossible to keep borrowing forever. Eventually the Repossession Man, Mortgage Lender and/or Utilities Company will come for theirs. You do not have to believe me; ask any of those institutions that have received funds from the Federal bailout. The same is true of our government; something is going to have to give. Medicare, the VA (even in wartime) and education would be my bet for the first budget cuts. We are dishing out more than we are bringing in. I do not see the sense in driving a Mercedes and living in a trailer park.

---

[55] http://www.odci.gov/csi/kent_csi/docs/v39i5a04p.htm
[56] http://www.whitehouse.gov/omb/budget/fy2009/pdf/hist.pdf

Once I figured out that approximately 48% of what I made is taxable in one form or another. Between Social Security, Federal and State Taxes, FICA, Medicare, and sale tax, I was left financially hurting after working long hours. I have to be honest and tell you I felt like a slave and too busy to be human. I had enough to survive, but survival is not my mission in life; freedom is. Do not get me wrong; I do see a need to pay into the society I live in for the greater good. I just do not want to make someone else rich. I want to see tangible gains from my investment in my society. Throughout my life, I have not seen these gains. I see the gap between the wealthy and the poor getting larger. When I heard the former leader of my nation say, "The haves and the have mores... You are my base" and then laugh about it, I want to kick his ass because I see more and more "have-nots" and "have-nothings." I know he meant what he said. Shall I translate for you? He said, "You rich and wealthy people here tonight are the base of my political power. Without your money I would not be here. I won't abandon you," and he did not.

It is our money that is being spent. If I do not have a say in where it goes, that is "*taxation without representation*". If I had my way, 21.7% of my taxed dollars would not go to defense contractors ($651 Billion in 2009)[57]. I can comfortably say without any research that we spend ten times more than any other country on the military. I would elect to put my cash into education, the VA, Social Security or housing, employment and medical insurance programs. A trillion dollars for Iraq so far, I read it costs a billion dollars a week... How much for Katrina[58]? Who are more... No, what is more important, Operation Iraqi Freedom and a favorable government with huge oil reserves or US citizens?

For the record, I am no socialist or communist; I am a humanist. I like prosperity and the concept of capitalism, but I do not like having to screw anyone to get what is mine. I also do not like being screwed without permission.

The United States is moving towards Conspicuous Consumption[59] just like the ancient Romans. We have stopped producing much of what we need and now import cheaper goods from foreign markets. We are consuming more than we are producing. When these markets become volatile we are forced by the desire to survive as a society to intervene for our own interests, like the British, Israelis and the French did when the Egyptians nationalized the Suez Canal[60]. A similar instance is Castro nationalizing the corporations in Cuba after their revolution. He saw what the foreign companies were doing to his country. They were taking all the wealth for themselves and paying General Fulgencio Batista y Zaldivar, the Cuban President before the revolution, not to complain. The common people, however, got little or nothing, reminds me of "Trickle Down Economics". What is even funnier is that the common Cuban still does not have much. They just changed masters.

---

[57] http://www.whitehouse.gov/omb/budget/fy2009/pdf/hist.pdf.

[58] March 2006: In an emergency spending measure, The House of Representatives approved $62 Billion for the wars and $19 Billion for recovery.

[59] Conspicuous consumption (American economist Thostein Veblen): the consumption of expensive goods, commodities and services for the sake of displaying social status and wealth.

[60] The Suez Crisis aka the Suez War or 1956 War: War fought on Egyptian territory in 1956. The conflict pitted Egypt against an alliance between France, Britain and Israel. Eisenhower did not back their play and the Russians threatened to intervene on the side of Egypt. As a result, the British Prime Minister, Anthony Eden, was forced to resign.

As a side note, I have a warning and a prediction. If Social Security is privatized, there will be corporate fraud and mismanagement. Whoever is in political power at the time will appoint a crony to head the department, and he or she will give preferential business and investment treatment to political supporters. Look at the estimated 1,100 pension funds that are in trouble. The Social Security Trust Fund is the largest trust fund held by the federal government. The Defense Trust Fund is second largest and a blind man can see what is being done to it.

Wealth and power motivate us to keep repeating mistakes. The prominent culture in the United States and that of most other Western societies is based on the Roman and Greek models. If this model did not work then, it will not work now. Expansionism and peace through force do not work. You win hearts and minds by going in like Green Peace or the Peace Corps. When we use the Marines, people get pissed. Every known civilization based on Roman and Greek principles are declining or have declined, whether through internal rot or external conquest. You do not have to take my word for it; look at history. Look at Great Britain, once the mightiest empire on the planet. They are now our lap dogs. Look at Spain and Portugal; once the wealthiest nations on the planet. Portugal is now one of the poorest in Europe. Look at Italy; the former Roman Empire. What happened to the Mongols and the Egyptian Dynasties? Where is Alexander's Empire? Where is Nubia, Timbuktu or Carthage? Look at the Zulus, the Huns, the Goths or the Visigoths. Where are the Czars and absolute monarchs of old? The list goes on and on. One of the biggest lies we are telling ourselves is that we are acting in a civilized and rational manner. We are headed for a train wreck of epic proportions. The credit crisis, mortgage defaults, and the bank bailouts are just the tip of the iceberg.

People have a right to govern their own country. No one has the right to force their values, culture or views on others. If you disagree with me, think about an unrelated stranger coming into your home and changing the way it is to suit him or her.

When asked, "What do you think of Western Civilization?" Mahatma Gandhi replied, "I think it would be a good idea." I do too.

FYI: the national debt for 2009 is $ 12.1 trillion and rising. The budget deficit for 2009 is going to top $1.71 Trillion[61]. Let the congregation say, "Cha - Ching!" Obama was handed a shit sandwich. I do not know how he going to stop it or if he can.

Ask me no questions and I will tell you no lies.

Do You Love Me

"Do you love me?" I have thought a multitude of answers to this question, yet, rarely said any of them unless I was angry or in love. I have come to interpret the meaning of the question to be, "Do you still love me?" 99% of the time the answer was, "No I don't. You are not the person you said you are. I loved her. "

---

[61] $482 Billion for the everyday bad accounting, $700 Billion for the bank bailout and $787 Billion for the stimulus package. http://www.whitehouse.gov/omb/assets/fy2010_new_era/Summary_Tables2.pdf

Does anyone know what love is or do we define it by what we have learned? Whether or not we know it, we definitely want to be loved unconditionally. We all want to return to that warm and fuzzy feeling we had when we were safe and protected. We absolutely want someone to tell us they love us and more importantly, because we know that people have learned to use this phrase to disarm, we want someone to show it.

Newborns die if they do not receive nurturing and love. No adult with eyes or ears needs to ask how another person feels about them, but we ask and have been asked the Love question many times.

One of the reasons behind not telling the truth is self-interest. We want to avoid discomfort and we do not want to lose the attention, affection, social status or financial support (security) that we gain from our association. We kill two birds with one stone. We satisfy programmed self-interest and the instinctual necessity to be loved. So why ask a question to which you already know the answer? Why would anyone ask someone whom they know does not love them or someone who does, "Do you love me?"

It is for the same reason we need confirmation of someone's lying. We want to believe that we are loved with the same type of conviction that a mother loves her child. To complete the illusion we will gladly listen to and believe a convincing lie. We go so far as to perform maneuvers that are designed to show our level of devotion and hope to precipitate a reciprocal response. When the maneuver fails to elicit the expected reaction, we doubt our partner's level of commitment. When our partner does not display the "expected" levels of attention or affection, we doubt their love for us and "Do you love me?" It is the subconscious at work.

Instead of saying directly what our concerns are we send subliminal messages via the subconscious through the filters of language and conscious thought, hoping that our partner will get the hint. The message is a signal saying that we need some form of reinforcement because we are feeling insecure. I know many people, including myself, who are in and have been in relationships that were destined for failure from the beginning, yet we continued down that road. You do not believe me? Just look at the divorce and separation rates; look at how many partners you have had in your life; and look at the infidelity rate among relationships. We have listened to many people speak about the dissatisfaction they are experiencing with their significant others. I have heard complaints about bad cooking, the lack of or unsatisfying sex, possessiveness, lack of affection and a multitude of other B & M's (bitches and moans). What amuses me is when I ask, "So, why are you with them?" The answers I have received in reply range from funny to bizarre. The answers I have given myself are scary, but there are common denominators in every one.

I think the most influential factors that make us want to hold on are security and intimate satisfaction. The answers to the questions we ask are sometimes worse than the reasoning behind the question. We are programmed to believe that lying is acceptable as long as there is no positive proof to the contrary. We tell lies to ourselves to keep someone, anyone, in our lives. If you do not believe me, examine your life and the lives of those you know. You will find that most people spend more time in relationships than out of them. Ask yourself what is the longest period of time you were purposely single, and went without wanting sex or intimate contact.

Ignorance

I think the hardest lie to destroy is ignorance because it is bliss. If we believe something completely, it cannot be wrong. It requires a shift, a change in the thought processes and it has a domino effect. When one idea dies so do those connected to it and so on. Try convincing some that homosexuality is not a bad or good thing. I do not care either way. Try telling some that America is not the land of freedom for all. Say that Mary was not a virgin or worse that Jesus was not. Use a racial slur. Draw a defamatory cartoon featuring Allah....

Me, Myself and I

If I tell you a mosquito can pull a freight train, all you have to do is hook it up.

It took me the longest time to realize what the above statement meant; your word is your bond, your fabric, what you are made of. One day I hope to hook my own mosquito to a freight train.

I am trying to ignite a rebellion: INDEPENDENT RATIONAL THOUGHT, for TRUTH and FREEDOM or DEATH! Forget what we were taught; it is time to do what is right with us.

I believe that the majority of us prefer to live life with blinders. That is, many among us do not want to see any of the unpleasantries or truth around us. We prefer to see and listen to lies in order to maintain our own matrix of personal comfort. In seeing the issues that plague our world, we are forced to feel the pain of our brethren. This is too much to bear for many because it forces us to want to do something about the plight of others or requires us to look internally at ourselves.

Internal checks for clarity scare the shit out of me. They usually force fundamental change, and change is scary. Instead we make excuses that allow us to ignore what is right in front of our faces. "Not my problem" We have excuses for almost everything we do and they do not even have to make sense. Someone once said, "There's nothing imperfect in my world" This is what I believe and how I try to live, without seeking imperfection in others or myself.

Wearing blinders puts us to sleep and offers a false sense of security. Not only do we not see the illness that plagues our species, but we also do not see other falsehoods for what they are. Most of all, we cannot see our true selves anymore; we are too busy trying to be what our surroundings demand of us. I think individuals who prefer blinders need controls to live. We need to be told what is right and wrong, and led so that we may avoid responsibility for what goes on around us. We give up choice to avoid responsibility for our own actions.

With knowledge comes responsibility and not many are willing or able to take on responsibility or leadership. Governments, religions, gangs, hate groups, support groups, corporations, television and all sorts of different organizations take on this responsibility and gain tremendously from it. They gain the power of decision-making; they gain from our power of choice surrendered. Those with power define the direction of everyone who is dependent on them. That is not for me. It does not qualify me as un-American or non-spiritual; it does qualify me as an individual capable of and willing to make my own decisions, come to my own conclusions, and face my own consequences without doing harm to anyone else or bitching about it.

I can no longer go with the flow or listen intently to the lies I have been told throughout my life in order to feel secure, have the right job or fit in. The answers provided by society, school, the government, corporate America and family are no longer enough to satisfy the questions I have about the world, the universe and myself. I have found that the truth, thinking for myself, asking the questions we naturally have and not simply accepting any answer given in response is usually enough to understand the basics of most subjects. I have learned to sit still and wait for answers. What is mine is mine, and meant for no one else.

One thing I have learned is that I have a responsibility not only for myself, but also for everyone else. That is right, everyone. I may not be able to give something material to every person (or myself for that matter) but because I believe that we are connected, I must make an effort to help, even if it is just a kind or a harsh word, or a prayer for peace and forgiveness. This is contrary to the competitive, go for the jugular mentality prominent in our society.

One of the things I am determined to do is to stop making promises. It will help me in my quest to stop lying. I look at a broken promise as a lie, and I know that for whatever reason, we cannot always do what we say we will do. I think that this is one of the most powerful ways to elevate the species and myself at the same time. I am also on a personal quest to take the blinders off. To see through the lies I have absorbed as truth and take on the responsibility that I have surrendered because I was afraid.

I have learned that the lies I have told and continue to tell myself are the most harmful to me. They also hurt those whom I love. I have learned that the world is mine, my destiny is mine, and I have a responsibility to do better than those who have come before me.

There are so many lies which started long ago and are still alive today that it is difficult, or next to impossible, to recognize that they are lies anymore. That being said, I have typed no lies. I love us too much! But, I am still left with the question, "What's wrong with us?"

Do not believe in anything simply because you have heard it. Do not believe in anything simply because it is spoken and rumored by many. Do not believe in anything simply because it is found written in your religious books. Do not believe in anything merely on the authority of your teachers and elders. Do not believe in traditions because they have been handed down for many generations. But after observation and analysis, when you find that anything agrees with reason and is conducive to the good and benefit of one and all, then accept it and live up to it. Buddha[62]

---

[62] Buddha or Siddhartha Gautama (560-480 BC): A Buddha is one who rediscovers the truth, the nature of reality, of the mind, of the affliction of the human condition and the correct path to liberation by enlightenment.

Chapter II

Jealousy and Envy

Jealousy: hostility toward a rival or one believed to enjoy an advantage.

Envy: painful or resentful awareness of an advantage enjoyed by another joined with a desire to possess the same advantage[63].

> *They envy the distinction I have won; let them therefore, envy my toils, my honesty and the methods by which I gained it. Sallust[64]*

I have a theory. Without the need for love there would be no jealousy, and without physical ranking or material wealth, or rather the emphasis we place on them, there would be no envy.

I believe our society promotes competition and our social structure is based on rewards. I also believe that all of our actions are an attempt to attain love or what we perceive as love. Using these givens, I think we are ultimately competing for love. Even if you disagree with my givens, we have all seen or participated in some form of competition for love at some point in our lives. Whether the competition was experienced as a sibling trying to get more of your parent's attention, or developed when vying for a mate or a promotion, it was there and it was real.

Whatever we perceive as love, whether it be attention, affection, praise, recognition or material possessions; we want it all to ourselves, and will compete to retain what we have and attain more. These are the origins of jealousy (the belief there is spiritual competition) and envy (the belief in material fairness).

Every relationship is either cooperative or competitive at its most basic level. Most lasting relationships are cooperative the majority of the time. I cannot think of any social behaviour that is neither cooperative nor competitive. People's motivation and behaviour, if it involves others, is generally a conscious effort to accomplish a common goal, or to take advantage of a strength or weakness to obtain something, usually at the expense of another. I put on my mental body armour when I leave the comfort zone. It is a dog eat dog world.

I think that most competitive relationships are destructive. I think this because the objective of competing is to win. Only one team, country or person can win. The other competitors are considered losers[65]. This means that a significant portion of those who compete will not receive praise, rewards, recognition or love regardless of the level of effort they put into the cause. Our self-esteem and mental well-being are affected adversely by losing, and we all know how fragile our esteem is. I know that I hate to lose, so I have removed myself from competing. I will never have to compete for what is rightfully mine and I know that there is plenty of love to go around.

The basic premise of competition thrives in most societies because it fits hand and hand with some of our primary instincts, survival being one of the strongest. The self-centered conditioning that most of us experience does not help. We seem to think that if someone gets more attention, more money or more of anything, it means that they are getting more than their share and it is not

---

[63]Both definitions are from Merriam-Webster's.

[64]Sallust (86-34 BC): Roman historian and politician, a friend of Julius Caesar. Governor of Numdia, North Africa.

[65] Strange that we live on one planet and are of one race. Who are we competing against?

41

fair. Why should they have more love? Our self-centered training and natural instincts make us think that someone else having something means that we cannot have it, and it pisses most people off.

In recent studies monkeys have displayed the same sense of fairness or justice[66]. If you give one monkey a grape or some other favored treat and the other a less favored treat to perform the same task, the monkey who perceives that the favored treat he received is of less value than the grape the first monkey received for performing the same task will often throw the treat out of the cage, refuse to eat it, or refuse to perform anymore tasks until he gets a grape or a treat of equal perceived value as well. I always thought I was smarter than a monkey.

Dr. Steven Covey[67] and Dr. John F. Nash[68] both believe that there is enough of the pie to go around, and by working for the greater good together we can all have what we want. Unfortunately, few people believe this. We are stuck in the mindset that if others have something, they are taking away from what we think is or could be ours. Hence, we are usually jealous and envious of those who have more of anything that we do not have.

Jealousy is simply and clearly the fear that you do not have value. Jealousy scans for evidence to prove the point-that others will be preferred and rewarded more than you. There is only one alternative-self-value. If you cannot love yourself, you will not believe that you are loved. You will always think it's a mistake or luck. Take your eyes off others and turn the scanner within Find the seeds of your jealousy, clear the old voices and experiences put all the energy into building your personal and emotional security. Then you will be the one others envy and you can remember the pain and reach out to them. Jennifer James[69]

Throughout the "Book of the Courtier[70]", the speakers warn about exciting the envy and jealousy of others. Specifically it says, "for indeed we are more prone to condemn mistakes than praise what is well done and it seems that out of some innate malice, many people, even when they see what is clearly good, strive with all their might to find fault or at least what looks like fault. Thus in everything a courtier must be cautious…" This was written during the 16th century in Italy. They knew then. It seems human behavior has not progressed at the same rate as our technological efforts.

I have been passing by you for 70,000 years and have seen you metamorphose like insects in the corners of grottoes. Seven minutes ago I looked at you from behind the pane of my window and found you ambling in filthy alleyways, led by the devils of apathy, the chains of servitude shackling your feet and the wings of death fluttering above your heads. You are today as you

---

[66] Brosnan, Sarah, B. M de Waal, Frans and Schiff, Hillary C. Yerkes' Division of Psychobiology.
[67] Steven R. Covey Ph D.: Author and Founder of the Covey Leadership Center.
[68] John F. Nash Ph D.: Father of Non-Cooperative Game Theory. Winner of the Nobel Prize for Economics in 1994. He was also a paranoid schizophrenic. Featured in the Film "A Beautiful Mind".
[69]Jennifer James Ph D.: Urban Cultural Anthropologist.
[70]The Book of the Courtier by Baldassere Castiglione, count of Novellata (Dec 6, 1478 – Feb 2 1529), a diplomat and prominent Renaissance author.

were yesterday and shall remain tomorrow and thereafter, just as I saw you in the beginning.
Kahlil Gibran[71]

One could open an orphanage, feed the poor or perform some other magnanimous deed; yet, someone else will try to find a fault or a crack in our effort. Many will go further. They will go out of their way to convince others of your faults. I think it is a shame that we have to be cautious in our actions and the phrases we use, because someone will not like what you to have say or have done regardless of the intent to do good - ask Tiger Woods.

Ask Bill Cosby[72] about the issues he faced because of a simple truth he stated. All of the marvelous and helpful things he has done have been nullified by people who want nothing more than to topple him because of what he has said and what he has done in the past. A senior officer once told me, "Ten *attaboys* are erased by one fuck up." Before you decide to destroy another person's reputation, open your closet and let us see your skeletons. You know the files (memories) I am referring to; they are the ones you do not want to look at because they show you in a less than favorable light. They are the ones with layers of dust on them; they are the ones we hide in our super-subconscious.

Jealous and envious people attack. We have all participated in ugly conversations belittling others who seem to possess what we do not or wish we did. We have berated people who look different, dress a certain way or hold themselves in high regard. It disappoints me when I hear people speak poorly about someone. It hurts more when I find myself consciously or unconsciously doing it.

I remember seeing a male wearing a yellow suit, yellow bowler with a feather and matching yellow shoes. I was walking up a stairwell and he was descending. The first thing that entered my vision was his yellow shoes and socks. I stopped and examined him from head to toe. It was quite rude of me to stare, but I was genuinely taken aback. The cane made the scene complete. I was looking at *Huggy Bear*.[73] This is by no means my style of dress, but what right do I have to criticize it? I described him as looking like *Tweety Bird* with a yellow *Chicken George* hat. He just wanted attention and evidently it worked. Though I was not flattering, I did talk about his outfit for weeks. I even wrote about it.

I have had people criticize my manner of dress. A girl once told me, "You look like you'd go to the grocery store in slacks." I usually dress conservatively and neatly, preferring a more reserved and comfortable look. I am not faddish, but have been known to stretch the envelope. I have noticed that no matter what we wear, someone will have something unflattering to say. I once had a weight lifting type from college tell me I had no business wearing a very nice summer vest, not because it was ugly but because he thought I did not have a broad enough chest. Another individual was upset because we went out and he asked me what I was going to wear (I know, sounds like women but think of male birds). I told him I was dressing casual. I wore a pair of jeans and red oxford. He was upset because his definition of casual was a T-shirt. I wear what

---

[71] Khalil Gibran (born Gibran Khalil Gibran bin Mikhā'īl bin Sa'ad: (1883-1931): Lebanese born American writer, poet, and prophet.
[72] Bill Cosby: Actor and Comedian. First African-American to star in own television series, *I Spy*.
[73] Huggy Bear: Fictional character of a pimp from the *Starsky and Hutch* television Series.

I want and so should you, with no regard to what others may deem appropriate or not. Who are we to judge?

Hating

I have seen and performed too many actions of jealousy and envy in my life. I can go back to my childhood and tell you about the time my brother vandalized a dictionary I received for scholastic excellence. I received praise and he did not like it. I been recognized for a high-test score and was awarded the Brown Book Award. It was a dictionary from Brown University with a dedication in the front written with my name. The inscription, though a form letter, meant a lot to me. It was the first time I had seen my name in print. The inscription had everything to do with drive, intellectual achievement and excellence. I loved it. I loved how it gave me bragging rights and recognition from anyone who came in the house. No wonder my brother scribbled over the dedication with crayons and acted like our four-year-old sister had done it.

I learned about the award in physics class. It happened to be right after several of us were discussing our scores. My score embarrassed me because I thought it was low, compared to the Ivy League standards for a scholarship, so I did not want to tell anyone what I received. I listened intently to what everyone said, and who contradicted or questioned whom. According to what I heard, my real score was lower than all of theirs. One classmate finally asked me, "What'd you get Ron?" I did not want to say. We all took the examination because we were in college prep. We also took the same classes. These were the brains of the school. Some of them were in the 12th grade and I thought I did not measure up. I was heartbroken that I was not among the smart anymore. Something told me to tell the truth; I did. The student who questioned me was a rival for Valedictorian. After I answered she smiled and said she got the highest score of the group.

When the teacher said, "Congratulations, Ronald," I was puzzled, "For what?" She then said that I had the highest score in the school. Everyone who had heard the girl say her score was higher than mine now knew she was lying and they questioned her with their eyes. She was sitting behind me when the announcement was made. I turned and looked at her with the same questioning expression. She rolled her eyes at me.

It hurt me to the core of my being that my brother hated me that much for shining. When I confronted him, he first told lies and then excuses for why he had marred the book. The simple reason was jealousy. I had done well and gloated; he did not like it. He retaliated by defacing my reward. The girl retaliated by rolling her eyes and not speaking to me anymore. Misery makes company. My classmate gloated as well.

I was at a party with my girlfriend, and an ex/secret lover showed up with her friends. It made for an unforgettable night. I was dipping some punch from a plastic trashcan only used for punch production. I had to bend at the waist to do this. When I rose, my lover stuck her tongue in my ear. The girlfriend was standing close enough to see it all. As my lover chased me around the party, I did my best to stay away from her, and keep my girlfriend close at the same time. The lover was not having it. She slapped me on the ass while girlfriend and I were dancing at least three times. I ignored the first two, but not even girlfriend could ignore the third. She danced near us the entire night and touched me whenever she could. It got so bad I had to leave the party. I ended up having to explain to my girlfriend that I did nothing to provoke this type of behavior. I had not, on this particular night, but knew full well it was my continuing to have sex with her that sparked the episode. Why will the human animal be just as satisfied by negative or positive attention? Why was my secret lover hatin'? She slept with me many times afterwards.

I learned that even family members exhibit the *crabs in a basket syndrome*[74]. It was not the first time I experienced this and it would not be the last, and guess what? It is not a phenomenon strictly limited to me. Doing well will guarantee that someone will be gunning for, trying to dethrone or denigrate you. Do yourself a favor and remain humble. This is the only way to avoid the envy and jealousy of others. Down play your results, put it off on luck, God, or good timing, anything but individual accomplishment.

Seeing White, Black

I can tell you about the envy I had because of the social advantages enjoyed by whites, "White Privilege". They seemed to have more of everything and I did not and still do not think it is fair. I was taught in school, at home, in the community and by mass media that lighter skin not only implied more intelligence, but also more beauty, more success and more wealth.

When I was younger it was rare to see anyone who looked like me on television who was not cleaning or performing some other servile, violent or secondary role. Even now, with a few exceptions, Hollywood does not aggressively promote or expect high returns from productions that star African-Americans who are not "paper bag brown," or even white women who are not a hundred pounds skinny with blond hair and blue eyes. But, I was fortunate enough to have positive Afro-centric influences that made sure that I was exposed to positive role models who looked like me. Regardless, I began to think that white people were more beautiful than I, or more to the point, they were in control of every aspect of my life and the lives of everyone I knew. Is that slavery?

My natural features were and are not considered attractive by our society. Hell, at one point in my childhood I remember wanting to be white and wishing I had been born to a white household. Recently I read a book by Benedita da Silva[75]. She went so far as to take bleach baths to try to lighten her skin; I was not alone when having those thoughts. The movie *Watermelon Man* is a satire revolving around this idea of white privilege. "You better get out of that sun; you *gonna* get black," is what my 'redbone' grandmother used to say. I cannot get black; I have tried. I get darker. Besides, color in skin is beautiful, if it were not, companies would not be investing so much R & D money on tan-in-a-can and people would not pay money to lie in human microwaves.

I wanted the same materialist wealth and the obvious social advantages that whites have, so I resolved within myself to have what they have by emulation. Do as they do and the privileges will follow was my rationale. How do you think that panned out? That explains my hate or envy of/for whites and to a large extent it explains my eagerness to fight them at any opportunity. I

---

[74] Crabs in a Basket: If a crab tries to escape from a bushel basket, other crabs will grab it by its limbs and prevent it from climbing to freedom.
[75] Benedita da Silva: Brazilian Politician. Autobiography, "An Afro-Brazilian Women's Story of Politics and Love"

wanted to prove that I was not only as good as they, but better. The fistfights I got in did not prove anything except that I had more experience defending myself with my hands. White people, like most others, like to fight. First, using verbal attacks, mental posturing and alliances to ensure they have a comfortable numerical advantage (intimidation), and there are a lot more whites everywhere in America, except jail. I now know that I am no better or worse than anyone else, but the process of losing that conditioning took years of trying to be what I am not.

We are conditioned to want to be in positions of power. Our innate motives tell us that it is better to be at the top of the food chain because we have more access to mates and a greater portion of the available resources. Unfortunately, white males hold the majority of these positions in our society. When someone who is not white or male gains one of these positions, they are put under a tremendous amount of unnecessary pressure to perform, and their mistakes are often magnified tenfold. America says, "Look! We gave them a chance and see what they've done with it." It reminds me of the big push for naval aviators that allowed me to become one. I was in class with history and philosophy majors (not that a history or philosophy major is stupid, but the studies performed on aviators in previous years had proven that technical majors, i.e., math, physics, etc. do better and are more successful). Aviators must have a fundamental and all most natural understanding of the relationship between three-dimensional space, time and gravity, physics - part of the Natural Law. Anyone who has not already flown in their heads has often has difficultly with real flying. The mechanics keep them behind the aircraft and they never get to enjoy the freedom the flight. It is the same as working at a job you hate, too much energy trying to understand the mechanics of life instead of enjoying the flight. It does not matter that those who defy the odds have to consistently work harder to gain half the recognition. Ask Margaret Thatcher[76], Stanley O'Neal[77], Richard Parsons[78] or Kenneth Chenault[79] what they had to go through. Ask Oprah about her experiences in a market dominated by males. She is not paper bag brown or skinny, nor does she have Arian features, though I suspect she did have some work done. I draw inspiration from these people and hope to emulate their tenacity, persistence, and determination toward a goal that is so obvious that we all are striving to reach it.

FYI: Did you know that the majority of Chief Executive Officers, CEOs, in the United States are white males over six feet tall? Yes.... We still judge peoples abilities and rank them high or low on the social totem pole by physical appearance. If I only I had breasts and white skin, this is not a judgment; it is a fact.

I once wanted what whites had. I was conditioned to think material wealth identifies whom you are. This is true, but I had little experience with credit and no experience with profiling. It was not until I got a chance to closely interact with people from different cultures that I realized that I too am fortunate. After going to school with them, I found out that no one is smarter or better. After fighting them with my hands and competing at sports with them, I found out they are not stronger, and they do not have more will or heart as I was led to believe; they are not John Wayne. When stationed with them in the military, they showed the same weaknesses. When working with them I realized they are as afraid and fragile as everyone else.

---

[76]Margaret Thatcher: "The Iron Lady" British stateswoman. Prime Minister 1979-1990.
[77] E. Stanley O'Neal: Once Chairman and CEO Merrill Lynch & Co., Inc.
[78] Richard Parsons: Lawyer. Former Chairman and CEO AOL Time Warner.
[79] Kenneth Irvine Chenault: Lawyer. Former CEO of American Express.

I once pondered the history I was taught before elementary school. I went to an African-American owned and operated pre-school, "The Center for Black Education". I was taught about the history of my ancestors and their version of the truth about African-Americans and the experiences since our forced exodus from the continent. I am not talking about anything like the history I was taught in public schools. That history brushes over African history and mentions nothing about Africa being the birth place of humanity. I asked myself how many people could live on a hand full of mush, while confined with shackles in an 18-inch space, with unclean water, rampant disease and cruel captors for 30 days or more on a ship crossing the Atlantic Ocean. Sometimes slaves were forcibly marched for months from inland slave camps. The answer depends on the source; estimates vary from 85% to 71%[80] of Africans endured these trials and lived. If you take into account the number of healthy slaves that were thrown overboard because of food or water shortages, the percentage increases, to what level no one knows.

Only a strong people could have survived the Middle Passage, slavery, segregation and discrimination. These same strong people are my ancestors and the ancestors of every other person on the planet. I am not only referring to physical strength. Add to this the fact that some slave owners practiced eugenics on slaves, some even interbred with slaves. They are my ancestors too. I cannot reject them even if they do not accept me.

Like many of the offspring of slaves, I have a variety of people's blood running through my veins. I know I have American Indian (Cherokee, Seminole, and Sewanee), German, Chinese, Portuguese, Scottish and the obvious African blood. That is why I have bronze or brown (depending on sun exposure) skin. So what does that make me? My driver's license says I am "BLK", but Africans, who are truly black, say that I am a white male. My birth certificate says "Negro". What is a Negro, but black in Spanish? Is it a coincidence that black is associated with evil and negativity (black cat, black magic, black Monday, black September, etc)? Electrical outages are called blackouts even if it happens in the middle of the day. Maybe it is the same reason a white male answered, "A mongrel" when I told him the different tribes that have contributed to my being and asked him, "What does that make me?"

It's sad dog that can't wag its own tail.

I Want Some

I remember being envious of one of the neighborhood kids. He lived in one of the better homes on the block, and had more expensive apparel than most of the other children. We used to say he thought he was better than the rest of us. I went so far as to pick fights with him to make myself feel better. Now I know that he was not the source of my frustration and fear; I was. I knew his family was better off economically than mine and I resented it. I only hurt myself with this attitude.

There were many times during my childhood when I was envious of the older kids who hung out on the corners (Interestingly enough, I do not typically get jealous of anyone's intelligence or looks. My envy usually is based on economics). They enjoyed an economic freedom I wished to

---

[80] Lovejoy, Paul E. (2000): Estimates 5-15% mortality rate.

have. They did not have to go to school, they did not have jobs and they seemed to have the most desirable girls. In short, they were my closest role models outside of the home. I did not want my grandfather's life style: working every day, coming home to eat dinner, and then starting all over again the next day or the next week. It seemed like a boring, endless cycle. I did not see much difference between what he was doing and slavery. On the other hand, the guys on the block had it going on. I thought they were cool and wanted to be like them so I too could have what they had: money, power and respect, at least until the real authorities popped up to show who was really in charge.

Envy is the ulcer of the soul. Socrates[81]

How viewpoints change as we grow older and experience different things. Actually they do not change, our perspective does or it should. Whenever I go home and run across one of the old crew, I see that I was in error. Most of them have become statistics. They look old for their ages. Most are dead, in jail or stuck in the same endless cycle of ignorance and poverty that they tried to avoid during adolescence. They were drug dealers, high school dropouts, and guys who had nowhere to go. They lived on the fringes of society, but I did not see anything wrong with it at the time. They preyed on the weak and profited greatly from their exploits for a while. The quick money and opportunism of the drug trade has been the pitfall of many people; young African-American men are not the only ones to fall. I am thankful that my road did not head in the same direction when it easily could have.

Do not forget how we treated some of our classmates. Remember the kid we teased as being the teacher's pet? Remember the pretty or ugly girl, the handsome or fat guy? What about the star athlete or the dunce? I do. I remember being teased for getting good grades. I remember bullying and being bullied for no other reason than being different in some way. These things are enough to make others angry.

We all know that childhood is just the training arena. By the time we are grown, we have had time to perfect our techniques of hurting and discrediting others to make ourselves look and feel better. It is not an honorable thing to witness, or worse to participate, whether as the leader or as some mindless minion who is just following the pack.

A heart at peace gives life to the body, but envy rots the bones. Proverbs 14:30

I have a favor to ask. When someone rubs you the wrong way, check yourself first! Ask yourself why you are afraid of them or why they are afraid of you. More often than not, if you do not like someone, you will find that the origin of your disgust is within yourself not within them. I am ashamed of the intentional pain and suffering I have inflicted on others and have pity for those who still intentionally inflict pain, including me, but I am trying.

---

[81]Socrates (469-399 BC): Greek Philosopher. Plato's mentor. Tried and convicted of impiety and for corrupting the youth of Athens and made to drink hemlock.

And oft, my jealousy shapes faults that are not. William Shakespeare[82]

I believe jealousy and envy are born of our own insecurity and doubt. We sometimes hate to see others achieve a level of excellence that we too could achieve with effort. My pity comes from the knowledge that envy not only hurts the person of whom we are jealous, but also destroys us from inside. And that is where we must look for solutions. We have to do internal searches for sources of inspiration and excellence. However, overcoming "me-ism" is hard as hell to do. I know older people who have not been able to do it in all their years on this Earth and have suffered terribly from it. I am trying to avoid the same fate.

Stop the Madness

Sibling rivalry is an example of selfishness when it comes to love. Most parents love all of their children equally or should. The expression of this love may manifest itself in different ways, but it is love nonetheless. Children and many adults do not see it this way. People seem to think that there is a competition for this resource. I know I used to try to have all the love that was around me as a child. I would pull all kinds of humorous stunts to get "all eyes on me". I was the fool, the court jester. If we were animals competing for the most nourishing teat to suckle in order to survive, I could understand this behavior a bit more, Jacob and Esau.

We reward one child for having good grades. We believe that this will motivate the other children to do as well to receive the same rewards in the future. It does not always work that way. Many who are not on the receiving end of the rewards become resentful, and will usually commit some random act of defiance in order to get attention (remember the monkeys in side by side cages) or rather to draw attention away from their rival and towards themselves. They throw the treat from the cage. Children love to pout. What are they trying to accomplish by showing their disapproval and who are they hurting? Adults pout too. I have seen it and done it.

I remember getting new shoes when I was in elementary school. I asked for and got what I thought were the popular brand that all the cool kids were wearing. I was trying to show my worth through possessions. My brother followed suit. The next day we wore our new shoes to school. To my surprise, I received ridicule instead of praise because the shoes were imitation leather. I did not know the difference when we bought them. My brother must have received the same treatment. Later that day while playing on a fence, I fell while performing a "tightrope" act. The sole of my left shoe caught the top of the fence and ripped as I fell. I reluctantly went inside and explained what happened. My grandparents decided to buy me another pair of shoes. Witnessing this, my brother left the house and returned later with damaged shoes. I do not judge his actions; he wanted a different pair of shoes too. He did not want to be made fun of anymore than I did.

In 1937 Margaret Mead[83] wrote *Cooperation and Competition among Primitive Peoples.* Although I disagree with her calling people who can live together without war primitive, she makes some observations about these cultures that are quite interesting. For instance, there are several societies that place a negative value on competition, and positive value cooperation. I

---

[82] William Shakespeare (1564-1616): English Poet, Playwright and Dramatist.
[83] Margaret Mead (1901-1978): American anthropologist and writer on "Primitive Societies".

think I would like these cultures better than the one in which I was raised. People who are this civilized cannot be called primitive just because they have not developed the same levels of technology that Western cultures have. We need to examine why they do not support competition or need modern technology. Cultures that are more technologically advanced are that way because technology is the best way to ensure military victory, and victory means material wealth.

I was taught in a management class that it is necessary to address people according to their individual needs in order to become a successful manager. This same concept can be used in manipulating any relationship, but I had issues with this because I did not see the need to nurture people in order for them to do their jobs, gain their trust or favor. I believe that a paycheck should be enough to motivate performance at work. After all, we go through an interview process where we may lie (padded resume) or practically beg for the job with which we are now unhappy.

Being open and honest should be enough to gain respect, affection and friends. But because Western society is based on the reward and competition system (another expression of love), the better performers or the more popular individuals are those who wear multiple masks, consistently receiving more attention and making others jealous. Of those who do not receive an equal amount of praise, some frequently cause problems in order to get what they deem is their fair share of attention. Remember that to many, attention is interpreted as love; it does not matter if the attention is good or bad. I ended up spending 95% of my people time attempting to manage these individuals. Anyone who has been in a position of perceived power (manager, teacher, coach, parent, etc.) has experienced this phenomenon.

Because even in the most team-oriented environments there is competition, there is also jealousy. I once incurred the wrath of a co-worker for working too hard. While in the US Navy a fellow officer told me that I was making the rest of them look bad. They were spending most of their time flying and ignored the paper work. All of them were getting out of the Navy and trying to head for the airlines. I had training manuals to correct and I had lost my love of naval flying. I did the paper work first and flew as a secondary role. Which was what we were supposed to be doing, but we had little or no supervision, and flying is a lot more fun than sitting behind a desk. At the end of every year we received evaluations of our performance and were ranked against each other for the next promotion cycle. In essence my co-worker was asking me to scale back so that they would not look as if they were neglecting their duties.

At the manufacturing company I worked, one of my managers told me that my peers were concerned that I was working too much. Can you imagine someone I am in direct competition with for promotion being concerned about my work ethics? My manager told me that he thought their real concern was that I was making them look bad. Truth be told, I was trying to make an impression on the higher ups by working harder and longer than my peers. It was my intention to raise the bar. If they could not or were not willing to keep pace with me, then they would be working for me soon. There is nothing like putting yourself on the fast track.

Contrary to accepted wisdom, competition is not basic to "human nature," but actually poisons our relationships, damages our self-esteem and holds us back from doing our best. Alfie Kohn[84]

If you threaten the security of others, keep an eye on them. It does not matter if the position is job related or more personal in nature. People are extremely protective of what they think is theirs. We are territorial. If you do not believe me, openly flirt with someone's mate.

When people find that direct competition is unsuccessful, many resort to denigration, grooming and/or treachery. This type of behavior often reflects badly on the persons who use it. I think that if we spent half the time we do being jealous on more productive endeavors we would all be better off. I have a suggestion. If someone brings you anything but good news, question his or her motives. Ask yourself what they have to gain by bringing you negative information.

One of the contributing factors to envy and jealousy is our consumerist/disposable society. It has embedded in all of us the fear of being replaced. Being traded-in for a newer, better model is a real concern in relationships. Not enough marriages are immune to this. We may think we have become irreplaceable in love, work or society, but when "competing" relationships emerge, we feel threatened and Mr. Jealousy takes this as an invitation to visit.

How many times have you been caught looking at another male or female? Here is the scenario. You or your partner sees an exceptionally beautiful person walking towards the two of you. It is obvious at some point you both will see the person. We see them, but we are not allowed to stare or look more than once. This could be interpreted as a competing relationship. Looking means we are aware of their presence. Staring means we think they are attractive. Sneaking a second peak means they are exceptional. We may have to hear about it later, but it was worth it. Some people purposefully divert their attention from the source of attraction to their mate in order to avoid the inevitable.

When we do stare, we do it in such a way as not to be obvious. As soon as one of you acknowledges your attraction, you can be sure that your mate will disapprove, view it as inappropriate, and make it clear that it will not be tolerated. "What are you looking at?" "The same thing you were!"

I have taken this to a completely different level. If I see something that is attractive, I mention it aloud. The object of my attraction could be a person, art, or anything/one. I know that beauty cannot be hidden and if I see it, then so does everyone else. I try to take the bullets out of the gun before there is a reason to shoot. Why is it that so many people see fault in this? Is it insecurity over our own appearance that makes it a capital offence to see beauty in others?

My mother said it is a matter of respect. My question is respect for what? Why is acknowledging the beauty of someone else disrespectful? We can look at a sunset together, say it is beautiful and agree. The same stands true for art or a handsome child. Is it disrespectful to consider anyone of the same sex as your mate attractive? The logic being that if we find someone else attractive, there is the possibility of being replaced or traded in for a better model. I remember hearing a friend of my mother saying, "Every time I see a young girl in a bikini

---

[84] Alfie Kohn: American lecturer and author in the fields of education, psychology and parenting.

without stretch marks, I want to scratch her eyes out". My mother opened the topic by commenting, "I remember when I did not have stretch marks". She happened to be looking at a teenage girl in a bikini. I saw the girl; she was beautiful and young. The simple fact that I remember it tells of its importance to me then and now. I asked myself why she was jealous. It was her choice to have children. Does she regret that choice?

My ex-girlfriend once took a picture of a guy walking down the beach. I was sitting beside her when she said, "Damn!" and hurriedly reached for the camera. I looked up to see a nice looking guy with muscles everywhere. I found myself getting jealous, momentary insanity. I snapped out of it, but her attraction made me wonder why she was with me, if she liked guys who worked out. I asked, "You like muscles?" "Yeah." "Then why aren't you with one?" "They spent too much time working on themselves." I thought that was interesting; I was a compromise, not Adonis, not the 90-pound weakling.

I found myself dancing between two of the most attractive women in a club. One was mine and the other was a hopeful. They both were hot and I was happy being the meat in their sandwich. At one point I looked at the table where my supervisor was sitting. His eyes were on us. We made eye contact and then I looked up to the heavens then mouthed, "Thank you God" and smiled. It was a joke. When I got back to the table he told me, "Ron, I am your God." People are a trip. Do I have to say what color he is?

Me, Myself and I

My mother and I got into an argument one day over something I consider trivial. I was in the car with her, my brother and sister. We were at a stoplight and I saw a homeless male standing with a sign: "Hungry Veteran." I retrieved a dollar from my center console, left there for such instances, and waved him over. "God bless you." "You too." After the exchange, my mother protested. She said that she does not give money to grown men. I responded with, "I give to the homeless whenever I can." My brother chimed in with, "You have done that for as long as I can remember." What came next has been a subject of friction between my parent and me since that day. "If you want to give money to someone, it should be me!"

There is a concept that is immune to jealousy. It works on the premise that love is infinite. If you divide infinity by the total number of people on the planet, you still would have infinity. The same is true with love. Inside of each of us is an infinite supply of love. As difficult as it may seem, allowing everyone to love everyone else does not rob us of what we think is ours solely, the love of someone we love.

Another method I use to try to avoid jealousy is to look within. No one knows us like we do. If we think about the causes of jealousy and reflect on our own self-worth, we realize that we do not have to be jealous of anyone. There are enough men and women, praise, money, attention, and most importantly, love to go around.

I have no reason to envy anyone. Neither do you. Nature made us all strong spiritual and physical beings, regardless of what we have been taught and why we have been taught it. Besides, it was our choice to be who we are. I would not trade my heritage for that of anyone else. I can put on a suit, have all of the needed qualifications, nail the interview and underneath it all I will still be me. And, I do not want "white privilege" anymore. Privilege blinds many and I am attempting to see.

I shall say it again: we have no need for jealousy or envy. Its roots lie within our own insecurities and fears. If we become comfortable with who we are, set and achieve individual goals, no matter how big or small (little accomplishments lead to big ones), we would have no reason to be jealous of anyone.

I have learned that words have the power I give them. If someone calls me a "Nigger", "Nigga", "Liberal", "Sexist", "Stupid", "Ugly", "Arrogant", "Beautiful" or "Sexy", it is not the word that empowers the user; it is my reactions that do this. Reactions dictate the course of the interaction. And, my reactions have the energy and purpose I give them. Besides, if someone is trying to push buttons, they want something from us and I believe that something is misinterpreted or misrepresented love. Can you see anything wrong with this?

Chapter III

Judgment

Judgment: mental faculty by which people ascertain the relations between ideas[85].

I remember the happiest time of my life. It was that carefree time before I understood stratified social inequity and the judgments that result from them.

I do not think judgment is about who has committed the most heinous or more numerous of crimes. We have all stolen from and lied to ourselves. We all have regrets. We all wish we could change something about our past and have dreamed of a magical time machine. I think judgment is about the choices we have made.

You are a hypocrite if you just thought, "I do not judge people." We all do. I try not to, but then I see a three hundred pounder in Speedos or a bikini, a big head, a nice pair of breasts or something else that appeals to or repulses the eye.

Judgment is based on individual perceptions of right and wrong, and observations that do not necessarily represent what is true. In the past it was acceptable, and even expected behavior, to kill and eat a member of the surviving crew when marooned at sea. A sperm whale sank the whaling ship Essex[86]. The surviving crewmembers drew lots to see who would be sacrificed for the good of the others and who would be the executioner. It was the Captain's first cousin who drew the short straw, and ironically the Captain drew the long straw. He would do the killing. When rescued, the courts did not prosecute the survivors, but dismissed the crime of murder because of the necessity of existence. What do you think about this? How do you judge this practice of human sacrifice and cannibalism?

The crew of the Peggy ran out of supplies after being battered by a number of storms and losing her sails. First, they killed and ate the only slave on board. After starvation returned, they drew lots, but decided to wait until the next morning to carry out the execution because the male who drew the short lot was very popular. They were rescued before that time arrived, but the man who was to be sacrificed went insane during the night.

Just because a majority agrees something is wrong or right does not make it so. There is a logical possibility that we can be mistaken. People used to think the Earth was flat and the center of the Universe. Some still do.

Our cultural conditioning has a huge influence on what we think is wrong or correct. I remember being caught skipping class by the vice-principal. The offense is punishable by a three-day suspension. The vice-principal told me to go to class and the matter was forgotten. "What are you doing?" He asked. "My homework," I answered. "Go to class." If I had been smoking, it would have been a different matter. It did not hurt that I was an honor roll student.

Feelings are individualized, affected by genetics, based on personal experience and influenced by our different environments. Therefore it follows that feelings are not a very reliable basis for making a judgment unless you are one of those rare individuals who has learned to nullify what they have learned and listen solely to the inner voice. Feelings are generally too

---

[85] Merriam-Webster's.
[86] The story of the Essex inspired the novel, <u>Moby Dick</u>.

subjective to be dependable. Lawyers say that the law and justice are separate issues, and have nothing to do with judgment. Keep this in mind when judging others.

True and False

The ability to distinguish between true and false is relative to the experiences and knowledge base of the individuals involved. For example, if someone says that the war in Iraq is right and believes this to be true; they are telling the truth as they know it. Remember when witches were burned at the stake or drowned? Jesus Christ was charged with sorcery and eventually crucified because he performed what some thought to be miracles and others witchcraft. Be careful before judging; you may fall off the edge of the world, be burned at the stake or crucified as well.

"Let he who has not sinned cast the first stone," Jesus said this to the crowd that wanted to stone a woman who had sinned in their eyes. According to the story, she sought refuge at Jesus' feet. No one threw a stone. Some sources believe this woman was a whore or an adulterer. If she was a whore, I bet some of her regular customers were in the crowd with stones in hand. How many of us have stones in our hands?

Expectations

My grandfather told me that at eighteen he expected every male to leave his house or at least contribute. That is what I did, but then I saw how he treated the females. They came and went like everyone else, but he gave them money, and less static. But, he demanded money from the males. He would go so far has to guess how much money we would make and ask for a percentage.

I remember when I was a flight student. I was having financial issues. I owed $750.00 for expenses I had incurred when in Aviation Officer Candidate School (AOCS). I did not pay the bill and they sent a letter to my command. I was in "beau coup" trouble. What followed was purposeful humiliation. I was given a flight failure for headwork[87]. Granted my self-generated financial crisis had nothing to do with flying, but this is the way my command chose to discipline me. That meant I did something stupid. Just before the letter arrived, I had asked an instructor to drop me off at a car dealership after our flight. I had to pick-up my car. I explained that I had an I.O.U. for an upgrade from the factory-installed radio that came with the car. I negotiated the deal when I bought the car a year before, but did not have the time to leave my car for two days while in flight school. I thanked the instructor for the ride and went about my way.

One of the many things my Commanding Officer said was, "I wanted to break my sword over your head when I heard you bought a new radio and are in debt." That hurt. I explained to my Commanding Officer about the I.O.U. as I had with the instructor. It did not make a difference; I was condemned. It was hard to stand there and listen to an old man tell me what he wanted to do to me and know he would need help if he wanted to complete that mission. What makes the matter stick and hurt so much is the fact that the instructor saw me in the hallway some time later and smiled in my face as he asked me how I was doing. "I am fine, Sir." In my

---

[87] Students get three failures (strikes) before they can be processed out of the Navy. You can receive failures (also called "downs") because of test scores or poor judge or performance in the aircraft or simulator.

mind I thought, "No thanks to your lying ass." He threw a log on the fire when it was not needed or right. "Fuck you, LT. Jones."

I was assigned to an instructor who was supposed to sit down and go through my finances with me. It was my hope that I could learn how to effectively budget. After I showed him every bill I had and where they stood, he looked at me and said, "It is a damn shame that you are worth more dead than alive," I thought to myself, "You are really enthusiastic about helping me, asshole." I ended up getting a loan from my girlfriend to pay off the debt, but the damage was done[88]. The judgment had been made and my reputation in the Navy was shot. People talk and reputations follow you. Pay your bills or wait seven years.

At the end of training it is typical for the graduating class to have a sit down with the Commanding Officer to give him feedback on the training. Every student who was leaving to go to the Fleet sat in a room together and answered his questions. I sat silent, but attentive through the entire event. By the end, I was looking at the Commanding Officer with contempt. It must have shown all over my face because he said, "What about you?" "Excuse me?" "Don't you have something to say? You have been in and out of my office more than a janitor." He paused to see my reaction; it was provocation. "Danger, Will Robinson. ... The wrong word in front of witnesses will kill your naval career." "I know." "It ain't worth it kid." "I know, but I want to remember this moment and him." I hardened my facial expression so that he could read me. I showed him what he wanted to see, my true feelings: "I hate you, you vindictive son of a bitch... I think you are a poor leader because even this stupid Nigger remembers what he was taught in Leadership Class: 'Praise in public; reprimand in private'. This is malicious." He then said, "Just kidding." I remember thinking that I had withstood their assaults, personal and professional, and still survived to become an aviator. On top of this, I had written what I thought about the command and the way it handled my situation in the feedback sheet we all had to fill out. My feedback required two additional sheets of paper. The Commanding Officer already knew what I thought. He did not have to ask in front of my peers or in that fashion. Why was he taking a Parthian[89] shot at me? I answered with even more internal contempt, "It was fair." I wanted to choke him for trying to embarrass me in front of my peers, but that taught me restraint.

The Commodore read every feedback sheet. No command or commander likes it when a student says anything that could be deemed as negative. I pointed out the lack of support I received and the way I had been treated for being in debt. I was 21 and did not know it was all about reputation; it does not matter that I owed maybe $36,000 total ($25,000 for a hot car, $10,000 in student loans, and one credit card with a $500.00 limit. That is nothing compared to the Government's debt or many of theirs.). What matters is the appearance of propriety. Today I am almost debt free. I wonder how much debt my executioners have accumulated over the years and how many bills they had to pay late or not at all. I wonder how many of them defaulted on their home loans.

---

[88] How do you get a loan from someone you supported for years?

[89] Parthian shot: the Parthians were excellent horsemen. Their Calvary used bows as their main method of attack. They perfected a technique of charging the enemy while firing arrows. They would then turn 180 degrees and retreat before they came within range of the enemy's weapons. While riding away, the rider turned backward to face the enemy and let one last arrow fly. It was called a Parthian shoot. We call it a parting shot. "Take that, Mo Fo".

My finances did not improve. I kept spending money as fast as it came in. But, in the military they take responsibility for every aspect of your life, if a problem arises. So when anyone has an issue with a service member, all they have to do is call your command to get results.

At my next command, I had an unexpected expense. My car needed $700.00 worth of work. Why does shit happen when you are dead broke? I paid with a rubber check, knowing I could muster the cash before the shop owner got too impatient. It just so happens the rent was late as well; I was courting a woman. My landlady called the command the same day the shop owner got impatient. They told me I had financial problems. I knew by payday I would not have them anymore, late fees included. It was not a big deal to me. I owed money and I intended to pay it. That is the way I was raised, but there are people who have never gone without and have never had to scrape a living. These people were among my judges. I was not in debt except for student loans, my car and, now two credit cards. It was not financial problems; it was a financial discipline issue. I liked to spend money to have nice things and female companionship. I explain this in depth in Chapter V: Relationships.

The naval aviation community is very small. The community is even smaller for African-Americans. My reputation had preceded me to my next squadron and I was not welcomed. When they got word of a bounced check, they hammered me. I felt this was legitimate. For punishment I received a letter of reprimand, and had to stand in front of the entire squadron and give a brief on financial responsibility. As embarrassing as it was, I gave the brief in as professional a manner as I could. I did not want to give anyone the satisfaction of thinking they had taught me a lesson or broken me. I did what I was told to do and bit my lip-to hell with pride.

Sometime later, I was at a red light. I heard my name called. Tom, an instructor pilot in the fleet training squadron, was in the car beside me. I exchanged "hellos" as politely as could be expected. I say that because after my financial responsibility presentation I was pretty much put in a shit pile. I did not even have a real job in the squadron. They placed me under the leadership of an older lieutenant with over twenty years in the service who watched me like a hawk. Officially I was Assistant Administration Officer. I led a total of two sailors. Both of whom had over ten years of service. They did not need me to manage them. I was jobless. I was not able to compete with my peer group on evaluations right from the start. I placed a wall between them and me. That is why I thought it was unusual for Tom to try to be on such cool terms. He was the instructor who had received the phone call from the auto repair shop about my check. He was probably feeling bad about that considering he was a bit more down to earth than the other guys in the squadron. His background was inner-city; I trusted him to be more up front and honest.

He asked me, "Did you hear about what happened to Hamilton?" I said, "No." He said, "I told them if they did not do anything and you found out; you would scream racism." I asked him what Hamilton did. He said, "Trust me, it was bad." I asked if it was worse than what I did. He said, "Way worse!" He said that they took Hamilton to Captain's Mast. [90] I never did find out what he did, and found it strange that no one told me. Even Tom only hinted at the offense. They had to know. When it was I, everyone knew and discussed it openly. Some were even happy about it. My offence was so heinous that they openly punished me to the point where a fellow officer came up to me after the Financial Brief and said, "That was the bravest thing I have ever

---

[90] Captain's Mast is an inquiry to see if there is justification to send the defendant to a Court Martial.

seen anyone do… I just wanted you to know that." I have no gripes about what they did to me. I did not uphold the standard. I do however question the severity of the true punishment and the two-tier justice. No matter what I did or how I did it from there on, I was judged.

When new aviators get to their fleet squadrons, it is customary to have a "Hail and Farewell". There I was standing in front of the entire squadron with two other new pilots. One guy had the biggest smile in the world. They named him "Joker" and everyone laughed. When it was my turn at bat, the crowd started shouting out suggestions and someone said, "Stupid". I ended up with "Sammy", after Sammy Davis Jr., I did not trip. Previously even African-Americans had said that I resemble Mr. Davis. It must ring some truth. But, the "Stupid" comment hurt. I am not stupid. I gambled and lost. I never knew who said it, but it sent me a message. "You will never belong here." The largely uniform laughter throughout the room confirmed it. I cannot tell you how raging mad I felt after that. I resigned myself not to try to fit in anymore.

I was once assigned to develop a Judge Advocate General (JAG) Report. If you have seen the television show of the same name, you have an idea of what that entails. I was assigned to investigate the shooting of one of our sailors, Seaman Joe. He was at a party when he was shot and his friend was killed. Because he was in the Navy, it was required that we investigate the circumstances surrounding his inability to perform his duties. It was not an assignment anyone would want. That is probably why I got it. I was to be judge, jury and executioner. I was supposed to investigate and then give recommendations as to a course of action.

I did the investigation and found out the 19-year-old sailor had taken a gun to a party where people were smoking dope and drinking heavily. Seaman Joe had purchased the weapon legally, but I found out he was waving it around in the party before he put it in a gym bag. His friend got into an altercation with the male who eventually ended his life and shot Seaman Joe. The male had seen Seaman Joe's gun earlier and assumed he still had it in his possession when the fight broke out. The shooter did not hesitate to pull the trigger.

Here I am judging the actions of another human being. Was it stupid? I thought so, but because I had done the same thing before (waving a gun around in a party); I was reluctant to label this guy for making a mistake. If I had really done my duty, he was going be Dishonorably Discharged and possibly scarred for life. How could I personally justify doing this? I could not and told him as much. I also told him if he told me the truth I would do everything in my power to help him. He did and I kept my end of the bargain. I was fortunate that the trial had not taken place yet. So my investigation could not include the testimony of the shooter. I wrote in my findings of fact that he had made a mistake in judgment. My recommendation was that he spends time in Extra Instruction. Extra Instruction is a lot like detention. I sent this to the base lawyer, who promptly rejected my findings, and asked that I reevaluate the recommendations after the trial had finished. I never finished the investigation. I was transferred to my next duty station just as the trial finished. FYI, the shooter was found not guilty by reason of self-defense. I have no idea what happened to Seaman Joe, but I imagine they nailed his black carcass to the cross.

What I learned from my experiences is not to listen to what people say about others. If one must judge, do it with the eyes and ears of the judged. I evaluate people not by their interactions with others, but how they act with me. I try to understand motives and behavior. In doing this I can better predict how they will react in different circumstances and choose to interact, with them or not, based upon this evaluation. For example, I know several people who are crack addicts. I would not leave my wallet in their presence unaccompanied, but it does not mean that I will not associate with or try to help them. If that were the case, we would not associate with most people.

I was in a country where one eats with chopsticks. It was the first of many lunches at a family run restaurant across the street from the factory. I know it was the first time they had seen a person with brown skin. White foreigners were common, but a beige brother was something to stare at. The waitress brought us four pillows to sit on and three sets of chopsticks and a fork. "Where are my chopsticks?" "Foreigners do not eat with chopsticks" "I want chopsticks."

It does not matter where or who we are; others will judge us. Our family, friends, associates and anyone who meets us will make an assumption about us because of what they observe. Some people get preferential treatment, but they are judged as well, just not harshly.

I love to dance and I love women. So when I asked a taxi driver to take me to a club where I could dance and meet girls, I assumed I was going to a disco or at least this country's rendition of one. When I entered, I knew I was in the wrong place by the reaction of the patrons. It was *Blazing Saddles* when they saw the sheriff. I remember thinking, "Uh, Oh." I spied an empty table and quickly sat down. I thought about turning around at the door, but I figured the patrons would not learn a damn thing if I did, and I felt my "Manhood" would have suffered in some way.

There were booths and tables of people sitting drinking, talking and smoking. No one was over twenty-five. I scanned the room and I swear I felt hate. I could not understand how my simple presence could invoke such a unanimous reaction. Several of the males started posturing by raising their heads like many people do when saying hello with an upward nod. I could not understand the purposely louder than conversational words from a few others, but it made everyone laugh. "I guess I am not welcome here." After about five minutes a waiter appeared with a menu. He looked surprised; his smile was questioning but polite. I asked him why there was no music and if the dancing would start later. "There's no dancing here." I got up and walked out. I heard the roarous ovation of patrons before the door closed behind me.

You will be or have been stoned by individuals who have committed worse or equal crimes as you have. I have done it; you have done it. Humanity listens intently and with great pleasure to the silent screams of its brethren. We are silly little creatures who in our self-righteousness forget our own trespasses and magnify those of others. We seem to be reluctant to dust off the old file cabinets in our minds and look at the incidents from our own past. We would rather forget some of the more unpleasant things we have done. We like to feel superior to those around us and say things like, "I would have…" I do not know what I would do if I was in someone else's shoes, but it would probably be the same thing they did. I do not know what I will do in the future. All I know is what I have done in the past and what dreams and hopes I have now, but they keep changing, having to adapt to metamorphing circumstances.

I have been fighting a personal battle not to judge anyone for anything, because I know that depending on the circumstances, I can be the worst of the bad and the best of the good. I am trying to walk the middle road between everyone's right and wrong. It is like walking through a minefield.

Pulling No Punches

I have fornicated with the wives of others, lied, cheated at cards, on women and on tests, and I have committed acts of violence that could classify me as a barbarian. I have also performed acts of mercy like feeding the hungry, giving time and sharing knowledge. I have given money to the needy, and protected some who could not protect themselves with my own body and have the scars to prove it. Does this classify me as a pious American or a humanitarian? That would depend on who is doing the judging. What does that make me, normal, animal or human?

I used to wonder why my grandfather drank so much. It embarrassed me to see him so drunk he could not walk, and it hurt because he was my idol. I did not like seeing him in a state that, through my young eyes, belittled him as a male. The chides of my peers did not help. I could not understand why he would do that to himself. It seemed stupid and self-destructive to drink to the point of being incoherent until I did it myself. Experience is a teacher like no other. I realized I was not so hurt that I told him to stop, not that he would have, and I was not so upset as not to accept his generosity when he was in this state.

I started drinking hard when I went to college. I looked forward to the weekend break as much then as I did when I was working in corporate America. It was free time to do with as I pleased, a break from reality and doing the things that were necessary to get ahead, but painful and somehow unnatural. Damn near every weekend was for partying. Drugs and alcohol seem to soothe the ills of the cruel world, to provide an escape. They are drugs and that is exactly what they are supposed to do. I would rather drink alcohol or smoke marijuana than be prescribed drugs by some quack that knows as much or as little about me as I allow. I considered it self-medicating. Come Sunday, I would snap out of it and start studying for the week while glancing at the football games.

After helping numerous people who have drunk too much and indulging myself, I understand the temporary relief that drinking allows, just do not over do it. I like people when they are intoxicated. They lose some of their inhibitions and become more like themselves. One thing I can say about myself is that I do not change when I am drunk or high. I am the same blunt, thoughtful and freaky person I was before I got intoxicated, though I may be a bit more talkative.

I Am Not My Father

I vowed not to become like my father. In many ways I have not and in others I have. I absolutely hated him for his lack of responsibility in helping to raise the children he created. I have come to grips with the fact that living with another person is not the easiest thing to do. My father did not have the financial resources to support himself, not to mention a family; and he was too young for marriage and parenthood. Passion led to the creation of my brother and me. Necessity led to my father's departure.

It was irresponsible, but no accident. I realize that with or without Robert in my life, I have a mission, a goal that cannot be changed. My destiny was to be born, live and die having accomplished or learned from whatever I experience in my time here on earth. I do not want children right now, so I probably do not have to worry about my children growing up without a father. It is not that I do not like children; I think they are our most precious resource. I just know that my path does not include fatherhood at this time or in the classical sense. I feel like I still have a lot to do before I am ready for the ultimate commitment, raising a child. Growing up, becoming free and becoming a "Man" are among the things I still have to do.

My parents can be included in those statistics about domestic violence and divorce. My mother told me stories of his coming home drunk late at night. He would demand that she prepare food or pick some other reason to establish his dominance as the head of the household even though they lived in my grandfather's basement. My mother is strong willed and would often resist. This led to fights. I do not know who was kicking whose ass, but I know my mother. She is not the type to be a physical victim and if she was anything like she is now, not only did Pops have his hands full, but also probably got as much as he gave. My father confirmed the stories of fighting, but could not give me an explanation as to why. I did not care who was at fault. Besides the end result was inevitable, separation and divorce.

How things change as we grow up. It is my experience that if you allow anyone to hit or mistreat you once without repercussions, they are more than likely to repeat the behavior. Some people like to hit (physically and verbally). The blows are often disguised as love taps, but they always occur after you do something that they do not like (an unflattering comment, a joke at their expense or anything else that they deem inappropriate). I immediately say, "Don't hit me!" "I did not hit you." "Yes, you did." "Oh, that was just a tap." I played the "hit game" as a child. The meaning of hitting (physical or verbal) and not being hit back has not changed with age.

I have heard some of the foulest words exit the mouths of the most pristine women when they get upset. People like to bring up, and frequently use, experiences that they know will hurt when they are upset. Sometimes these experiences are so painful that they promote a violent reprisal. It is as if people want to push you to the point where control is lost. They go out of their way to hurt you the way they were hurt. I like these exchanges; they are truthful and healthy, though painful, lessons.

Alternative Lifestyles

Allow me to tell you of some of the homosexual experiences I have had. Before you start licking your lips or throwing up, let me say I have never had sex with a male or even been remotely close to doing so, but there have been males who wanted to have sex with me.

The first time, I was young when a boy asked me, "Ronnie, can I suck your dick?" We were in the same bed at the time. My brother remembers it better than I. He reminds me that he woke up to find me beating the boy. "Why are you hittin' him?" "He asked if he could suck my dick!" I still wonder who taught a child how to do that.

One of the older guys in the neighborhood and I conveniently found a joint in my aunt's stash. We smoked it. It was not my first time smoking a joint, but I was not accustomed to the effects. He was older and had more exposure than I. He dry humped me. It is weird to write about it now because I have never told anyone about the experience before. As a matter of fact, I always denied ever having any homosexual experiences because of the stigma attached to it. I could have passed a lie detector test. I really believed I had not had any homosexual experiences until I sat down and thought about it. Denial is a bitch.

I was at a bus stop late one night and some guy said he wanted me. I did not understand him and I guess it was evident that I did not because he repeated himself. He said, "I want you. Like a male wants a woman." I was repulsed and afraid. I stepped away from him and he left me alone. When I tell that story to other males, they ask me what I did. When I say I just distanced myself, many say what they would have done. Usually it is a violent recourse, but I think I did what was right. The puzzled look on my face told my potential lover not only that I was not interested, but I was insulted as well. I could not tell you whether I was more pissed because of the male-gay thing or because of social-economic reasons (he looked unkempt).

I once suspected that one of my line brothers was gay. We had to practice a series of routines for the presentation of new pledges to the campus. One of these routines required that we line up in very close proximity with our arms locked together. My back was to his front; his back was to the front of the person behind him, etc. While we were practicing he got a "woody". I could feel his erection on my butt. I was pissed and protested aloud. It turns out he was gay, or bisexual, or whatever. I do not hold it against him and I do not care anymore.

It is interesting that my next experience with homosexuality came with this same person. I was staying at his home during a break from school. I was waiting for some money to arrive from my mother via a friend who lived in the same city so that I could go home for the break. I was only there for a day or two, but one night two of his friends (brother and sister) came over. We began drinking. I was attracted to the sister, but the brother was attracted to me. It was a trip. The drunker he got, the more aggressive he got. It came to a head when I got tired of politely dodging his advances. Somehow we ended up wrestling because I wanted out of the house. He grabbed me from behind and bit me on the shoulder. It was not an angry bite; it was an intimate one. Nothing happened and I am not upset. It was funny as hell. Picture a movie with a homosexual who is sloppy drunk chasing another man around the house. You could call it *The Unwilling Partner*. It was just another experience.

I used to work for an elderly male who I thought was gay. He constantly surrounded himself with boys and treated them well. I was all about the money. I could tell the way his employees looked and treated me that something was up. I did not care. After the summer I would never see these people again. I kept telling myself, "I am not gay." I do not remember how it happened, but one night I ended up spooning with him. Actually he was spooning with me. I was surprised when his sleep arm found its way over my shoulder. I was petrified and insulted at the same time. I did not move. I was waiting for what he would do next. I moved away. He rolled over and he fell asleep. I moved to the couch. That never happened again. I was too uncomfortable.

I have had experiences in other countries where it can be difficult to tell a person's sex. I was with a companion and we walked into a strip bar. I was busy looking at the menu when my partner in crime tugged on my arm and asked me if the women on stage were boys. I looked up and saw fifteen or so topless g-string clad people with numbers on their hips. I looked down at the menu to see that only half of it was for beverages, the other half had the specialty of the numbers on the stage. I looked back up and I had to ask the waiter if they were boys. We exited to all of their amusement and giggles when he said, "Yes."

During the same trip, I had an opportunity to talk to a transsexual. It was an enlightening conversation. She told me that she was born with the anatomy of a male, but she is a female inside. Everything about this male was feminine, everything! If I had not asked, I never would have known. My lover was surprised at how much empathy I showed this person. She said, "You were really feeling for her." I was. I have to admit I felt sorry for her. Not because I thought she was confused, but because of the stereotype and judgment she will face for the rest of her life for being her true self. For the first time I was able to feel for someone who had defied nature, and found compassion, not judgment.

There is a place the locals called "the four floors of whores." I could not believe that such an establishment existed in this particular country because of the strict laws. I had to see it for myself. I stood outside after the clubs closed at 2 AM watching the negotiations between potential clients and the service workers. I got into a conversation with a Brit about how things worked. He and his partner were bargain shopping. At this time of night, the girls had to score or get nothing for the night. I saw his partner in crime talking to a boy-girl. I asked if he knew that they were talking to boys. He said, "Yes" When his friend was within earshot he repeated what I had asked. His partner's response was, "Who cares as long as you can fuck them in the arse." I was taken aback. The transvestite trying to land the guy standing beside me overheard and started yelling, "Nigger" over and over. Then one of the foreigners said, "Good on you," to the transvestite. I was puzzled and asked him if he agreed with the transvestite. He had "the cat that ate the canary" look on his face. I wanted to knock the shit out of him. My blood pressure was rising and I could feel the adrenaline pumping through my veins. The police showed up right about the time I was hitting boiling point. All of the transvestites ran. I remember seeing the two foreigners walking towards a taxi with two boys. Both of the men were wearing wedding bands. I could not help but wonder if their wives knew they were gay. Later I realized that I should have immediately known.

My immediate supervisor and his wife happened to be in the same city I was temporarily working. I joined them for dinner accompanied by my married lover. We had dinner at a hotel restaurant. Not our hotel, but the hotel of a VP of our company. My supervisor met him at the airport and identified the hotel, as well as the VP's room. We charged the meal (it had to be $1000.00) to his room. The company could afford it. When the bill arrived I realized what my supervisor was planning. He told me not to mention it and I went along.

We ended up in a club that just happened to be the hottest spot in town on a Wednesday night. We reserved a table. A bottle of vodka and mixers appeared from my favorite waiter, a nice kid who happened to be a virgin at 25. We took him to dinner once. I picked his brain about life in that part of the world.

My supervisor's wife put my camera under her shirt and took a picture of her breasts. I was shocked. Then I heard the story of how they met. He was traveling and she was a club singer. OK, that explained it. She was a freak, meaning she liked to have sex, all kinds of sex. Kind of like the woman who was accompanying me. It was going to be an interesting evening. I thought they wanted to swap and told my date. She was not attracted to either of them, and especially not the wife. I was not attracted to the wife either, and the husband was off limits. Remember I am not gay, but will try anything sexually once that does not include another male. I did an orgy once and I could not get an erection with other people in the room. When we were walking out he groped my ass. I retaliated by swatting his. He liked it. "Oh, shit! They are swingers!" After that realization my partner and I departed.

No strange thing that they called at home one Saturday to tell me, "A five liter bottle of wine just fell out of one of Jesse's boxes." "Who's Jesse?" "Jesse's a friend who moved to Thailand three years ago for six months." "Ohhhh, so a five liter bottle of wine fell out of a box that has been in your garage for three years?" "Yep... You coming over?" I came up with an excuse.

What have I learned from these experiences? First, I am not gay. Second, I learned not to judge people by their sexual preference. I have also learned that in any situation, if I am offended by someone else's choices, I need to ask myself, "What am I afraid of?" What have you learned from yours?

Opinions

If you defend your opinion, you are blind, deaf, and dumb.

Have you noticed that people have a habit of asking for the opinions of others only to do what they want to anyway?

I thought I could live a perfect life. That was until I realized that I could not live up to the expectations placed on me by society. I cannot be the "Man" of anyone's dreams. I cannot be the perfect employee. I cannot be the perfect leader. I cannot be the perfect worshipper. I cannot be anything perfect unless I stop looking at myself through the eyes of others. I believe that the key to success is not others, but one's self. The realization of self-need and the execution of strategies to attain our objectives have been, and are, based on the principle that what we need, must be obtained from others. I am done being dependent on others for a perception of who I am. I define me; the opinions of others do not.

Recently I have been doing job interviews. I am running out of resources and need a source of income. I hate interviews. I hate the fact that I have to convince someone that I am qualified or that I can do the job; but more importantly I have to convince them that they like me, that I am not a psycho and that I will fit into their company culture. That is hard for me considering the fact that most people feel comfortable around those who look like them. I always feel like I have a strike against me before I walk in. How does one make an accurate judgment about someone in an hour or two? Truth be told, I doubt if I will ever fit into anyone's culture the way they want me to unless it is an exceptional company. I have tasted the freedom of not having to chase the dangling carrot.

One of the common questions I have been asked is "Tell me about a time when you have failed at something." Shit, where should I begin? I realize that the question is a double-edged sword. Everyone has failed at something and they know this, but what they are looking for is an answer that shows you are humble, willing to learn from mistakes and persistent. If you give the wrong answer you fall on your own sword. I will tell you what I dare not tell any prospective employer. I have failed at many things. I should have graduated with super honors. I have the ability and the intellect, but I did not concentrate on the task at hand. Why? I had too many distractions and not enough discipline. What distractions; drugs, alcohol, women and lack of money. Though the partying was a contributing factor, I kept it to the weekends. I really did not need money considering I had access to three meals a day, but to party and treat the girls nice, you need cash. The real distraction was immaturity and a healthy libido.

In the Navy I should have done much better. Again, even though I consider the Navy and the Marine Corps among the last bastions of "white male supremacy", that is no excuse for my not doing well considering the tools we all have been given. I allowed others to influence how I felt about myself. They dogged me, but that is no excuse. When I look back at those dusty files, I see that I could have silenced my critics with sustained superior performance. Instead I adopted the fuck it and fuck them attitude. This was reinforced when I was assigned another shitty job that no one else wanted.

Our Commanding Officer wanted our squadron to participate in "Clean the Bay" day. It is a day when people basically pick trash from the Chesapeake Bay and its tributaries. We were assigned several different areas. To make a long story short, we received the Virginia Beach Community Service Award that Year. I put a great deal of time and planning into the event. I solicited hardware stores for gloves and equipment. I asked local establishments if we could use their parking lots as staging areas, and so on. My Commanding Officer was interviewed on every local news network that day. We did a good thing. I got no recognition at all. This was expected, but it felt like I had a knife twisted in my gut when the squadron gave another officer a medal for organizing a Boy Scout weekend on base. There were distinguishing factors that I saw; he was white, well liked and he did not have issues.

I really should have soared at the manufacturing company and the semi-conductor company as well, but I did not. They both started well, but the same distractions hindered my progress. At the manufacturing company, it was my female boss trying to sleep with me, working third shift, long hours, low pay, insecurity and a female accusing me of sexual harassment. There were other issues as well, but those were the big ones.

My semi-conductor job was a disappointment. I was laid off because after 9/11 the bottom fell out of the market. It felt like a final blow to me. I asked myself why am I giving my time, energy and heart to companies that really do not give a damn about their staff. I decided to try it on my own. I sold all my shit and moved to another country, but that is another story in itself.

I judge myself much harder than anyone else. One day I am going to live up to my own expectations. There is no excuse why I should not. I am in good health; I am educated and talented; and, I believe in my own abilities. The rest should be easy if I dedicate myself to a cause, remain honest and do no harm to others.

Look into the depths of your own soul and learn first to know yourself, then you will understand why this illness was bound to come upon you and perhaps you will thenceforth avoid falling ill.
Sigmund Freud[91]

Instead of judging others, I try to understand the motives behind human behavior. I now know that my attraction to married women was an attempt to have both sex and freedom. My acts of violence were a quest to feel empowered. On the other side of the same coin, I cried like a baby for the victims in the Twin Towers and do the same when I see children hungry or sleeping on the streets. It felt like the world screamed when the tsunami hit Southern Asia.

Knowing the reasoning behind behavior helps in not being angry or sad with others in their pursuit of self-interest. After all, I have done what I have to get what I want. Why should I be angry when others do the same, even if they make out better than I? We are hypocrites and need to be less critical of one another because we all make mistakes and not only deserve an opportunity to try again, but also are destined to try again, and again, and again until we get it right.

Who Are We

Paul wrote in 1 Corinthians (5:9), *"I have written to you in my letter not to associate with sexually amoral people (5:10) not at all meaning the people of this world who are immoral or the greedy and swindlers or idolaters. In that case you would have to leave this world."* Even then, people were aware of the state of denial of humankind. We are far from perfect, but we do not have to be. Remember that the next time you are pissed off at someone.

You are young, my son and, as the years go by, time will change and even reverse many of your present opinions. Refrain therefore awhile from setting yourself up as a judge of the highest matters. Plato[92]

How many times have you made a wrong first assessment about a person? First impressions last and although you can read a person's spirit instantly, the physical impressions are not sufficient to gauge the real personality of another or what actions they are likely to perform. You are seeing an act meant to attract attention and impress. Pay it no mind; typically it is only a partial representation of the real person.

Usually, "What do you do?" is one of the first questions out of a person's mouth. This may be followed by more qualifying questions: "Where do you live? Where are you from? Where did you go to college? Are you married? Do you have children?" As we answer these questions, think about this: "Why are they asking you these particular questions?" How many people ask, "Who are you?" and if they did (assume they already know your name), what would you say? Would you start with your career or your family? Or would you be able to give a true answer. I have looked all over the world for myself and found him in the mirror staring at me with the eyes of a predator.

---

[91] Sigmund Freud (1856-1939): Physiologist, medical doctor, psychologist and considered to be the father of psychoanalysis.
[92] Plato (429-347): Greek philosopher. Teacher and mentor of Aristotle, who taught Alexander the Great.

We have learned to piece together a person by gathering bits of information through interrogation. Armed with this information, we place others on a social totem pole. Afterwards, we choose to associate with them depending on what we want or think we can gain from them. What if all or part of the information passed, gathered and processed is a lie? Then, the assumptions are based on inaccurate information and the judgment is based on flawed assumptions and choreographed behavior. It is a fact that most are not forthcoming with their perceived flaws and faults. This is especially true when we are trying to impress. People lie about jobs, income, names, phone numbers, age, etc.… How do you get to the real person?

How many times have you found, that depending on the surroundings and individuals involved, people seem to change or show a different side of their personality? People often go through a metamorphic transformation to fit into an environment (work, school, family, club, church). We wear masks. We are chameleons. I love to hear the change in people's voices when they try to have a professional telephone conversation. I am amused when guys with guts suck in their stomachs when women are present. I like to remind them that they can start breathing again after the women leave.

The term "well rounded" comes to mind when describing those who perform these transitions well. Character after all, is the psychosis we show the world. We all should be nominees for the Academy Awards. Just ask any politician, con man, manager, actor, lawyer or potential wife or husband, all of whom show many different faces to their audiences.

My manager propositioned me in her kitchen one night when I went to her house to get a copy of an old evaluation. It was that time of the year and I had no clue how to write an evaluation for this company. I asked my manager and others several times for one of their old evaluations to use as a template. It was now Friday and the reports were due Monday. Neither she nor the others I had asked, brought in the evaluations (competition is a trip), so I had to go to my manager's home.

I should have been suspicious when I got there and the report was not on the coffee table. I called ahead of time and totally expected a quick exit. Her daughter was home and I finally got a chance to meet her. I had seen her before, but she was shielded from view when picking her mother up from work. Trixie was nice looking. She was carrying an overnight bag and a diaper bag. Her mother was lighting candles, making drinks and turning off lights. I felt like one of those cartoon characters that ends up in a boiling kettle and does not know how they got there. "Shit! I have been had." I tried to think of a way to get out of this mess. I asked for the evaluation again. She had to go out to the garage to find the box. I assured her I had time and it was important. I got two of her old evaluations.

While she was going through boxes that took her 20 minutes to find, I finished my drink and so did she. I was offered another drink; free alcohol, free sex, free is good. I volunteered to make them. I like margaritas, but not when she made them, and I did not want her to stop looking for the evaluations.

I was cutting limes when she cornered me from behind and was trying to force me to kiss her. I felt her breasts in my back and her hands on my waist. At 190 lbs, she outweighed me and could have chosen to fight me for it. That is too much woman for me and she was my direct supervisor, and supposed mentor. I could not have sex with her. This was a definite "double don't", even then I knew that. Keep your personal and professional life separate. One is for making money and the other is for spending it. Work does not define you; it pays you.

I gave her a bird peck and said, "That is all you'll get from me." I used the professionalism excuse. I even reminded her I was married (I was not married. I told them that so that Housewife could take advantage of their relocation package and sell her condominium. They paid all the fees and the points). I also wanted every woman in the plant to think I was married. It means I am off limits or so I thought; I wanted to concentrate on learning the ropes. As far as my manager was concerned, I was married but she obviously did not think it mattered. I was so wrong about her, and she later went out of her way to make sure I knew it.

We frequently wear so many different masks that we do not even know ourselves. Unfortunately, we judge others by the masks we see and wear. We either like or do not like them. If we do not like them, we rarely get a second opportunity to see the other sides of the person that we may in fact like; or we judge them good and find out after interacting with them that we really do not know or like them. Our initial judgment is based on what we have observed and applied to our own codes of moral character. It sets the stage for future interactions, and taints or biases our opinion.

FYI: the more attractive we find someone the more likely we are to have a good first impression of them.

I have found that it is best to ignore most of what someone tells you about themselves the first time you meet them. Of course, this is totally dependent on where and to whom it is I am talking and about what. You would not want to use this technique at a job interview. I just do not take it personally that I sometimes get lied to; I do not commit it to memory. I like to see how people present themselves and as my friend Misha says, "You should give everyone five minutes of listening time."

I try to be open and without judgment; I also try to allow everyone his or her own counsel. All I ask is that they allow me mine. It sounds easy, but it is not. I am trying my best to walk the middle road. I have found that if I argue my opponent's side with the same zeal as I do my own, there usually is no judgment. I know it sounds utopian, but that is my goal.

In order to truly know a person, as much as possible, it is necessary to spend a great deal of time and observe without bias how they react under different circumstances. I often tell people, never believe what I say; watch what I do. I say this because I can only say what I have done in similar circumstances that I have experienced already. I can only speculate or say what I would like to do in circumstances that I have never faced.

Stress, fear, love, competition, anger, depression and happiness have a mental, spiritual and/or physiological effect on behavior. We have to observe these different and distinct behaviors, try to understand them by asking questions, listening (to what is said and what is not), and watching for physical responses and cues. Listen intently to what is said; we hide behind words. To most the truth is more a tactic than a necessity. We do not so much tell the truth, but more retreat into it instead of embracing it. In other words, we all try to conceal or make pretty our weaknesses and motives; sometimes, we even hide from ourselves. Because of this, I believe little or none of what I hear unless I have no questions floating in my head about what I have heard and because of perspective, I realize that what I see is suspect to biased interpretation.

Living together is the best way to closely observe behavior. I have been brought under the same roof with men and women through family connections, friendships, economics, love, education and military service. The intimacy experienced in the home, dormitory, barracks or ship is of a higher level than at work, in a club or on a date. You really get to see a different side of others because we cannot wear masks forever and often take off certain masks when we enter the home. Just ask anyone who has been or is married and did not live together beforehand. What surprises did he or she experience? For some, it is too much of a transformation.

When I set myself the task of bringing to light what human beings keep hidden within them, not by the compelling power of hypnosis, but by observing what they say and what they show, I thought the task was a harder one than it really is. He who has eyes to see and ears to hear may convince himself that no mortal can keep a secret. If his lips are silent, he chatters with his fingertips: betrayal oozes out of him at every pore and thus, the task of making conscious the most hidden recesses to the mind is one which it is quite possible to accomplish. Sigmund Freud

Know Thy Self

I think the absolute best way to know people is to look in a mirror. After all, we share the same experiences and think alike in most things. We have the same needs and desires. But, most importantly, we are One. So, how is it possible to judge another to be righteous or sinful, when we have all done or will do the same sorts of things in order to experience life? If you want to know why someone did something, ask, "'Y' would I do it?" Our motives are more often than not the same.

Think of children and childhood. Do you think you are the only kid to write on the wall with a crayon, or watch television when Mom said not to and lie about it? How do parents know the thoughts or experiences of their children? We did the same things when we were young or not so young. How is it possible to give sound advice about a cheating spouse or significant other? We have experience in the subject, whether through doing the cheating, witnessing it, hearing about it, or being cheated on. How is it that we know instantly a relationship will fail or be difficult at best? You have seen the signs before and you know from experience. If you do not already, you will. We are the same and have shared or will share the same experiences of life. Only the places, times and people involved change.

I do not know many people who will willingly expose the deep recesses of their minds to others. I know I have issues with honesty, showing the real me. It exposes our vulnerability as human beings and leaves our sub-conscious naked. I do not think the majority of people hide out of spite or for some hidden agenda, though in some cases we do. I think we are incapable of expressing our every thought to another because we are incapable of knowing our own motives all the time.

How many times have you done something and explained later, "I do not know why I did that?" or "I do not know what I was thinking." If you cannot explain it, then how can another know your thoughts? Whether from shame, concern, suspicion, selfishness or any other reason the conscious mind dreams up, we are secretive creatures, who do not want others to know us. Some of us do not want to know ourselves very well either. Again, if you want to be a judge, start in the mirror. Once we have judged ourselves, we will be so much more tolerant and understanding of others.

If you want a dose of perspective reality, ask someone close to you what he or she truly thinks of you. Try to see past the kind remarks that will come out of mouths in an attempt not to offend. Use the eyes and ears to interpret what is not said. You must listen and look to find the real answer to your question. Please do not interrupt with excuses, denial or reasons to why you do what you do. Just listen and try not to be hurt. Hopefully you will hear the interpretations from another's perspective. Take it in and digest it. You have probably heard it before from others and yourself. My grandmother and aunt both said I liked women too much. Once I shook off the CRS[93], I realized they were right.

None of us could live with a habitual truth teller; but, thank goodness, none of us has to. Mark Twain[94]

We are all beautiful. We see it every time someone says, "thank you', "good morning", or "you're welcome" We see it in every kind gesture, in every child born and on every smiling face. If we can strip away everything a person owns, wipe away what they have learned and see them as if they were newborns, what would there be to judge but perfection?

Enlightenment is man's release from his self-incurred tutelage. Tutelage is the incapacity to use one's own understanding without the guidance of another. Such tutelage is self-imposed if its cause is not lack of intelligence, but rather a lack of determination and courage to use one's intelligence without being guided by another... Sapere Aude[95]! Immanuel Kant

Me, Myself and I

I believe we create our own individual Gods. Pelagius believed that through free will a person could find his or her own salvation or damnation. He did not believe in baptism, sexual repression or in the idea of original sin. He fought the ideas of Saint Augustine and Saint Jerome until he was declared a heretic in 416. Augustine believed in original sin and the Catholic Church adopted Jerome's version of the Bible. Pelagius was killed for his ideas and the Catholic Church was probably responsible for it.[96]

Our Gods are whatever we choose to worship, value, or believe. There is nothing wrong with loving what you love. Love is good. Love is the center of one's passions, the target of every

---

[93] CRS: Can't Remember Shit. Term referring to convenient memory.
[94] Mark Twain (1835-1910): Samuel Clemens. American writer and riverboat Captain, famous for his wit and wisdom. Wrote <u>Huck Finn</u> and <u>Tom Sawyer</u>.
[95] Immanuel Kant (1724-1804): German Philosopher. Sapere Aude: "Dare To Know."
[96] ST. Augustine, *Church Fathers: On Lying.*

quest, of every dream. However, be aware that wealth, drugs, power, compliments, religions and sex are not deities and should not be worshipped. I have seen the way some people pray at ATM machines.

If we drop the drama, start acting for the benefit of others and unlearn the negatives we have been taught, we can look at life through new eyes. I try to look at life through the eyes of a child, always trying to learn something new. The Tarot card of the "Fool" comes to mind. Take opportunities to look around and view life with clarity, gratitude and understanding. Every experience, new and old, invites different discoveries. None of them are good or bad. They are just what we wanted, prayed for and chose to experience. Whose fault is it when these experiences are viewed as unpleasant?

I am purposely opening my closet with this work to let everyone know the things I have done; some of them I am not proud of. I call it taking the bullets out of the gun. If I expend them first, what are left are empty and useless cartridges. If anyone confronts me with something I have done, I have no need or desire to lie. I want everyone to know that I am not perfect. I do this to exorcise my personal demons and dispel future envy and jealousy. It is the confession that cleanses and the realization of a fear that makes it harmless.

When hurtful words and actions come my way, I not only want to be able to absorb the barrage, but I also want to be able to dissolve the negativity that brought trouble my way in the first place. Antagonists are usually left with their mouths open, not knowing how to react or what to say. We are not accustomed to people knowing the truth about themselves. When pleasant words and praise come my way, I want to be able to be humble, grateful and aware if I am being flattered.

All that we are is the result of what we have thought. Buddha

I have always felt as if I were on a tightrope, stretched over a cultural, spiritual and racial conundrum. I am too Black (culturally and complexion) to be accepted into the mainstream American white culture and/or too white (educated, bourgeois, middle class) to be a part of the mainstream African-American culture. I feel too in touch with myself to be angry with anyone for long. Yet, I do not want to appear vulnerable because predators view it as a sign of weakness.

I have judged myself and found that I have been lacking as a human being. Not because of what others say, but because I have come to this conclusion by watching others and, in turn, myself. How valuable or hurtful do you think your judgments of me are? I am just trying to figure out how to love you, me and us. Is this wrong? Is it right? If so, why are we not doing it? Is there something wrong with me?

Chapter IV

Right and Wrong

I have a favor to ask. Before you read this chapter, take some time to think about what you consider absolutely wrong and absolutely right and then write them down.

Rights   Wrongs

Right: being in accordance with what is just, good or proper <conduct>.

And

Wrong: an injurious, unfair or unjust act: action or conduct inflicting harm without due provocation or just cause[97].

It is so hard to do right, when it is so easy to do wrong!

There is a Yoruba story about two farmers who were friends. They owned fields on opposite sides of a road. One day Esu[98] came strolling down the road wearing a hat that was red on the left side and black on the right. A farmer on the left side of the road said, "Did you see that man walking down the road in that red hat?" "He had a black hat," replied the farmer on the right of the road. One farmer swore that the man was wearing a red hat. The other swore it was black. The lifelong friends, who had helped each other during the planting and harvesting, argued to blows. The Trickster chuckled at the sight of the now bloodied friends and then Esu showed them his hat. He was amused by the fact they would fight about something as ridiculous as the color of another man's hat, ruining their long-standing friendship in the process. Each believed his own opinion to be right. Perspective is a mother.

Who is more culpable, the person who is ignorant of right and wrong, or the person who has a sense of right and wrong, and does wrong anyway?

One day I hope we can all be right. But until then we have to exist in a world where disagreeing with someone about something causes conflict. No one likes to be wrong, or even worse, proven wrong.

Only small minds never argue. Archbishop Desmond Tutu[99]

Examine your next conversation. The moment you make a statement that someone else disagrees with, there is potential for conflict. At that moment, try to concentrate on what words precede a person's question, sentence or statement. If the first word is "But..." or "No..." they do not agree with what you have said and are trying to be polite while at the same time maintaining their position. Hopefully they will continue the debate by saying why they disagree and then offer logical supporting evidence. But more often I have experienced people who say what is convenient and not necessarily true in order to be right. Many resort to saying the same thing over and over again, as if repeating themselves makes it so. And, if we are astute enough to challenge what someone has said, the discussion may escalate to an argument.

---

[97]Merriam-Webster's.
[98]Esu or Elegba: Yoruba deity referred to as the messenger of the gods. He is known as "guardian of the crossroads" and the trickster. Some consider him the Devil. Hermes in Greek mythology. Mercury in Roman mythology.
[99] Desmond Tutu or Desmond Mpilo Tutu: South African terrorist, cleric and activist. Opponent of apartheid. First African Anglican Archbishop Cape Town, South Africa.

When people speak, four things come from our mouths. The order may change, but usually a lie, a distraction or an excuse is expelled. If we press the issue hard enough, the truth may emerge. It goes down easy; it sounds good and feels good. A lie does not quite sit right in the mind; it causes internal questioning. A distraction does just what the name implies; it distracts you. An excuse is the reasoning behind the actions in question.

"Men need guidance", she said with a smile on her face, while incorporating the social tricks that she had used over the years to sweeten the taste of the medicine she was attempting to administer. It still tasted like crap. "No they don't." "Yes they do." "Children and adolescents need guidance; full grown men have learned the hard way most times, to make their own decisions, come to their own conclusions and think their own thoughts, simply because they have come to the realization that ultimately, people control only their own destinies." That was the beginning of a fifteen-minute conversation that went all over the place. And, at the end she still believed that men need guidance. I might have shut up if she had said, "My mate needs guidance". I remember thinking, "No wonder Skip is miserable."

I was puzzled as to why people can be so stubborn on certain points of faith, sex, men, women, money, children, which direction to drive, how best to accomplish a task or anything else you can think of to argue over. I am so guilty of this that I once argued whether the sky was actually blue. Most people do not like to be corrected, told what to do or how to do it. We like to ask for help when we are in need and do not want to feel stupid or inferior for asking. We do not like to feel inferior and rightfully so. Opinions cannot be proven false. Faith is intangible. Belief is subjective.

Everyone's point of view is affected by his or her experiences and age. Immediate needs also play a role in what we consider right and wrong. We view experiences on this level of consciousness from a selfish perspective most of the time. It is only when we transcend to higher planes of thought that we view experiences collectively, mentally walking through past events in another's shoes. We are here to explore the infinite experiences of Life, and Life is what we make of it. Life is the choices we make and the lessons we learn or do not learn.

Everyone has the ability to choose one course of action over other possible options. In making a choice, I usually internalize it as right or wrong before I do it. I weigh the possible options, their consequences, the risks and the potential rewards. Then I choose; it is called risk management. I have taken several courses on the subject and realized they are teaching formalized common sense. I like to think that I will do what is considered right by my own standards, but depending on the circumstances, I may waiver as I have in the past. It seems as though need and want drive behaviors more than morals in extremely gratifying or challenging situations.

I do not think wrong or right exists independent of life.

The Hand We Are Dealt

I think that we are born with everything we need. What do I mean by that? I do not think anyone is born without the tools needed to complete a life. I know every one of us has gifts, something at which we excel and something that comes as naturally as breathing. I believe the issues in our lives arrive when we are not doing what we are born to do, but instead are exercising our free will.

I know that we are born with certain skill sets to ensure our survival. Infants know how to nurse, breathe, move their body parts and communicate without any coaching. All of these skills serve a purpose. We are born with the ability to cry because it is a way to communicate need or desire. We have to know how to nurse from the moment of birth or we die. Breathing, hearing, sight, smell and the sense of touch are all given to most infants at birth, even though they may not be able to understand their use right away.

Infants already know the mechanics of walking; their limbs just are not mature enough to perform the required movements or support the body's weight. That is a drawback from walking upright[100], our young are born more vulnerable and do not mature as fast as other animals. Still, if you hold a child erect with feet touching a solid surface, they will begin to move their legs as if trying to walk. We do not teach children to walk or how to touch their privates; they already know how. What else do you suppose infants already know how to do? Most of us have forgotten. I believe that we are born with an individual sense of right and wrong that should not be altered.

You Get What You Ask for

When I was a child we used to play a game called "that's my car". We would gather on a corner and pick which cars we wanted from those that drove by. I watched the various choices and questioned internally why certain individuals choose certain cars. Then I wished to have my choice of all of them. If you "gonna" wish, wish big and wish specific!

We have all been warned, "Be careful what you ask for. You just might get it" Why do you suppose this cliché has been passed from generation to generation?

I believe we all have the ability to get what we want and I know that well-behaved people may be good company, but they do not make history. The power of thought and spoken word touch the very fabric of creation, and start a chain of events that attempts to manifest everyone's wishes. The queue must stretch to the edges of existence. We all get what we ask for. Can you think of a desire or wish that has not been granted? I am not talking about the everyday wishes we make without even knowing it, and I am not referring to those grand wishes to hit the lottery either. Look at the wishes we made when we were young and our hearts were pure. How many of them have come into being and how many of them did not?

I also believe all of my past wishes have been granted, and those that have not will be because I have not forgotten or given up on them. They have not all been manifested (granted) the way I wanted them to be, but I got what I asked for. I have come to realize that the more selfish the motive, the more costly the wish.

---

[100] The human pelvis has narrowed as a result of walking upright. A smaller pelvis means underdeveloped and dependent infants. An incomplete skullcap is another adaptation to a narrow pelvis.

I wanted to be a pilot so bad, I became a naval aviator. But I did not get to fly what I wanted, I did not fly as much as I wanted, I was not stationed where I wanted, and it was not at all what I imagined it would be. I am grateful for all the experiences and the skill sets I gained, but I would have preferred to receive some of them under more pleasant conditions.

Getting what you want can be dangerous. The danger lies in not building what you want from "A" to "Z". You have to visualize what you want in graphic detail. You have to foresee potential issues and their solutions ahead of time. Issues are a part of life, but an issue planned for is not an obstacle, it is a contingency plan; and an issue faced a second time is not an issue; it is a review.

Here is a joke: A woman prayed for years to hit the lottery. She did all that was required of her faith to have this wish granted. For 20 years she kept her vigil. Afterwards she began to question why she had not hit the jackpot. A friend asked her if she had bought a lottery ticket. Throwing wishes to the wind leaves the path to getting them to *chance and the fates*.

When you make your wishes, think as big as your imagination. Our only limit is fear. My mother and I once had a conversation about this very subject. She told me she wanted to be a pharmacist; in a manner of speaking, she is. We both had to laugh after that realization. Starring in a movie was also one of her dreams. She did that as well. Our conversation prompted me to ask a friend what she wished for when she was a child. Her childhood dream was to be a professional dancer on television. She was. You should have seen the look on her face when I pointed that out to her. So what is it was *Soul Train*.

During the conversation with my mother, I was reminded that I wanted to be an astronaut. She remembered, "I thought it was cute that you knew what you wanted to be before you could properly pronounce the word." I used to say, "assonot." I remember from where that dream came. I watched with the rest of the world in wonder at the Apollo Missions. I saw the reaction of everyone in the room when Neil Armstrong stepped on the moon in 1969. They were in awe; I was three. That is how I decided. I wanted to be something that left everyone in awe.

I was spending the summer with my grand aunt in the country. The day's activities came to an abrupt end when the television blurted that they had landed on the moon. People in the living room were crowded around the black and white floor model television. There were people there I did not know. It was like a party in the middle of the day. One of the older visitors said that he thought the whole thing was faked. I protested pass the allowed amount for someone my age. He was wrong and I knew it, damn the consequences. I knew it because that is what I was going to be: an assonot (I have had my ass in knots; does that count?).

I wonder how I am going to get into outer space. I read somewhere that you can get on board the International Space Station by riding with the Russians for only $20 million. And, I read that commercial space flight is coming soon for $100 or $200K. Anyone want to give me a loan?

I often play a game with guests. I ask everyone to write down three wishes. Then we pass our lists to another guest and ask them to read it aloud. Afterwards we discuss our wishes and how we plan to obtain them. "Health, wealth and happiness" are mine and how I hope to achieve them is through tolerance, persistence and patience.

Socialization

Indulge me for a moment. Think about a slab of marble fresh from the quarry. Think about the sculptor hammering and chipping away for years. In the end, a figure emerges from the stone. I believe life is like that. Our experiences drive the hammer, providing the force needed for a soft stroke or a firm blow, whatever is needed for that cut. The subconscious is the hammer, driving its way into our lives. Others are the chisels, always leaving their marks and the marble is us, cut from the same quarry to be something different, yet the same, masterpieces.

It was Thanksgiving. My mother was hosting in her first home. We were renting, but for my brother and I a house was a castle and the yard was paradise, a playground to explore. My brother and I were so excited because there were family and friends in our house having a good time. It was a chance to get some attention and show everyone how smart we were. My mother hosted cozy gatherings frequently. My brother and I would sneak down stairs to listen to the adult conversations and then retreat to our room to talk about what we had just heard - sex, politics, religion, etc.

Sam was one of our frequent visitors. I liked him. He was different from my other adult relatives. He had recently returned from Southeast Asia where he had served in the military. Because he had been drafted, like most dutiful American boys who were not in college and could not get into the Reserves, he went to fight for his country. He was exposed to Agent Orange and got cancer as a reward for national service. Somehow Sam was able to arrange the shipment of a duffle bag full of Thai Stick[101] to the states. I have never seen that much marijuana in my life.

Using three and four-year-old logic, my brother and I decided it was a good idea to get the stash and show everyone what we could do. Sam had instructed my brother and me how to roll marijuana joints. It was a big hit at some of my mother's other parties, so why not here too? We had seen many of the people who were present smoke marijuana before, so we figured it could not be anything wrong. It would be a big hit.

We sat in the middle of the living room on the floor and proceeded to roll joints. Years later, my cousin told me how mad he was that we could do that and not get in trouble for it. He also said he had wanted some. My mother caught hell for that from the old folks. My brother and I were confused about why there was such an uproar. We were not smoking it, yet!

Socialization begins the moment we are born. Even though our brains are half of their adult size, during the first critical years we begin to be imprinted with social normalities just like the blank marble beginning to be chiseled. We start to learn from our environment and adapt to it. This shapes our moral beliefs into a mold that allows us to function somewhat peacefully within society. Ultimately, a person's thought processes (neural pathways) and social normality largely depend on the broadness or narrowness of their experiences during these earlier years. In other words, what we attempt to become is directly impacted by what we are given an opportunity to see and learn from our surroundings. Once imprinted, it takes years of alternative experiences to establish new neural pathways and retrain the mind.

---

[101] Species of cannabis grown in Thailand that became popular in the 60's.

I remember driving to Beaufort, South Carolina when I was a child. Our car lost its muffler and most of its exhaust system while we were crossing a bridge. We waited for the tow truck and then because there was not enough room in the truck for everyone, my aunt, brother, and I had to walk to the other side. On the way a police officer driving the other way told us we were not supposed to be walking on the bridge. I said, "Our car broke down..." My aunt interrupted with a bowed head and a resounding, "Yes, sir." She was so humble that I was embarrassed. It reminded me of the way slaves used to speak to their masters. You have to understand that this woman was a radical shit-talking black revolutionary. I have never seen anyone change his or her demeanor so fast. Throughout my life I have seen both male and female members of my family bitch-up to white people. She scolded me as soon as the officer pulled away, "That mouth of yours is going to get you into trouble... Don't ever talk back to the police!" Fuck her and the redneck cop!

Because we are born dependent, those around us have an influence over us. If caregivers usually respond to crying by comforting the child, the child will learn to expect this. I wondered for years why certain people cry so easily. If a caregiver does not respond to a baby's cries, the child does not learn that crying leads to being comforted. If alcohol or drugs are present in the household, chances are the children will do the same. If domestic violence is present, it is well documented that the children of this household will be predisposed to violence. If you are Catholic, chances are your children will be predisposed to Catholic-like beliefs.

Our natural desire to socialize, fit in, and to be loved makes our physical selves metamorph into whatever our particular society deems appropriate. Society rewards beauty and correctness, but frowns on those considered to be maladjusted or different.

Most animals that group together have a similar social structure to that of humans. Maladjusted and defective members are driven from the group. They are alienated and live on the fringes. There is no right and wrong in it; it is just the nature of animal interaction. That is how we are socialized and one of the main reasons many people live several different lives. Ever heard someone make a professional phone call? They change their voice. People I have known go from "Heeeeey, girl" to "Yes, this is she." No judgment from me; it is just an observation. We are trained to fit in and punished through various means when we do not.

Regardless of what we are taught or what the "law" says, we all know in our heart of hearts what feels good and what does not. We were born with this ability. I know I sometimes have issues with distinguishing what I have been taught from what I feel inside. I often think about some of my past choices. I find myself asking why I made a particular decision. What did I hope to accomplish and why did I pick that particular route? Was I thinking or acting from a feeling? If I thought about it, what portion of the brain did I use, the *Old brain* (Reptile/Visceral) or the *New brain* (Neocortex/Gray Matter)? What I mean is, am I reacting with a genuine feeling from inside (some call it the heart), am I responding instinctually (like flinching when startled), am I reacting with social programming (something I learned) or is my spirit screaming at me? I try to maintain a state of agreement and peace among them, but there are times when there is conflict. That is when I have issues. It is similar to being at a multi-road junction and having to choose the best path.

I know we imitate the behavior of others and incorporate what we learn into our own set of social skills. We learn normality and behavioral laws. These two lessons, when combined, teach us a sense of morality. And morals are subject to change depending on the time, the place and the overall objectives of the society.

You do not have to take my word for it that morals are subjective and change. When I was living in a foreign country, I got into repeated arguments with other expatriates about having sex with under-aged girls. Their argument was that local men regularly had sex with boys and girls under the age of 18, and the law did little or nothing about it. They wanted to be afforded the same leniency.

I do not think a person's morals should change because of location or customs. Do you think that these people stopped having an attraction to young girls and boys when they returned to their home countries? If you take the time to pick a stance, and then reverse that stance the instant there is something to gain, it is not a moral stance at all, but adherence to local custom, the law or some other external influence. The same men I speak of live in countries where the law actively prosecutes those who have sex with under-aged people. Ask former Representative Foley.

One of the men I had this discussion with, Mr. Burns, was an American who happened to have a three-year-old daughter by a local woman. After arguing the pros and cons, I told him, "Fine, Mr. Burns, when your daughter gets fifteen, I am going to fuck her." You should have seen the look on his face. He wanted to kill me. It was priceless. You think MasterCard would be interested in that concept for a commercial?

We have been taught that there are social normalities that we must follow in order to fit into society, to survive. Who says? From where do these principles originate? Are these laws of behavior handed down by a divine spirit, have they been taught to us or do they lie in our genes? I have asked myself and others these questions all my life. The conclusion I came to is that we are socially shaped by our environment. We are products of it, but we do not have to be. We can actually think and choose for ourselves. It is hard, but worth it in the long run.

We "all" must practice social normality in order for it to be beneficial and real. We can establish that murder is wrong, but murders will continue as long as any form of murder is condoned. That includes murdering for profit, for revenge, for defense or for convenience. The same is true of stealing. Everyone pretty much says, "Do not steal," when it is common knowledge that many corporations, most people and countries steal. How can we place more blame and harsher penalties on a person who loots water and food or steals a flat screen? How many times have we made personal long distance calls at work? How many times have we "borrowed" supplies? How many times have we not worked at work or taken pay for a longer than authorized lunch break? Have you ever called in sick when you were not? We say, "Do not lie", but everyone does at some time. How real is this? How can we label these things wrong or right, and not come to the realization that if doing any of the above is wrong, we have all been wrong at some point in our lives? It is an impossible situation if people do nothing to change it.

"You steal." "No, I do not." I wanted to remind her that she was sitting on my couch while doctoring her knee with makeup. She was trying to make the small bump into a photographically convincing injury. Her claim was that she had fallen while in a store. I could have reminded her that I remember some of her other frauds for money, but I did not. Who am I to convince people they steal?

Society defines wrong or right depending on the majority and what value systems are in place. We have chosen our own forms of morality in order to continue to live together. We have come up with sets of rules and laws that govern our behavior in order to profit from large numbers of people living in close proximity with each other. These rules and laws change with time, because social attitudes and morality change and so do majorities and leadership.

Euthanasia was an acceptable part of Greek culture for years, but we prosecute individuals today for aiding in suicide, and Christianity condemns it. Abortion was illegal, but now it is not; in the near future, it may be illegal again. Capital punishment was unconstitutional, but anyone over eighteen years of age may now be executed in certain states. A woman can hire an abortionist to terminate the life inside her, but she can be charged with "child abuse" if she uses crack while pregnant. What about drinking alcohol or smoking? The Jim Crow laws and Plessy vs. Ferguson[102] were laws that kept Africans in bondage, and were considered by the ruling majority to be not only righteous, but also necessary to keep the "Niggers" in their place.

Humans, although connected and affected by communal thought, were not designed like ants, termites or bees. Social programming is an attempt to make us act like them. People are walking around trying to fit in, as if they are automatons and wonder why they are not happy or why everyone who does not agree with them is crazy.

In the 5th century BC, Protagoras[103] taught that human judgment was/is subjective and that one's perception is valid only for oneself. Protagoras' thinking was along the same lines as mine. What is right for me may or may not be right for you and vice versa, but I have no right to infringe on your choices and if you try interfering with mine, I will let you know - loudly.

Happiness lies in doing what you are destined to do, not what someone else tells you. It is difficult; anxiety and fear are real and tangible concerns. We feel alone, outnumbered and insecure. Uncertainty in our own choices makes us want to be reinforced by the comfort of others. Just remember whatever does not kill you makes you stronger. And whatever does kill you was supposed to.

---

[102]On June 7, 1892, Homer Plessy was jailed for sitting in the "White" car of the East Louisiana Railroad. In 1896, the Supreme Court of the United States heard Plessy's case and found him guilty once again. Only one Justice disagreed and wrote that the Constitution is "Color-Blind." Almost 70 years later Rosa Parks did the same.

[103] Protagoras (490-420 BC): One of the Older Sophists, a group of traveling teachers or intellectuals who were experts in rhetoric (the science of oratory) and related subjects. Protagoras believed nothing was exclusively good or bad, true or false, and that man is his own authority saying, "Man is the measure of all things."

Taking Life

I think life is the most precious gift that can be given. Is taking it wrong or right? I did not ask many people this. I have watched our planet in my lifetime and read our histories for my answer. The answer I came up with is "No". It depends on whom you ask and what the circumstances are, but everyone believes that in certain instances it is permissible to take a life.

Have you ever killed anything? Your answer should be yes. Unless of course, you never stepped on an ant, swatted a fly, eaten meat or picked a flower. Almost every living thing on this planet relies on predation to live. Only plants and some very specialized organisms can live without killing something else.

Are abortions wrong? Some seem to think so. They say that fetuses are innocent and aware in the wound. They call abortion murder. Some of them are so determined to prove themselves right that they kill abortion doctors and nurses, and bomb clinics to show that it is wrong to take life.

The pro-choice camp says that it is about woman's rights and that fetuses do not have awareness. They believe a woman should be able to choose whether or not she terminates a pregnancy. Both camps have issue in cases where rape or incest is involved.

I asked my mother why she did not have an abortion when she was pregnant with me. The question came from a desire to know why she had children, knowing how expensive it is to raise them. I overheard a conversation between my mother and my sister's father about the financial issues they were facing. My mother was pregnant at the time. I naturally asked myself, "Then why are you having another child?" This led me to ask myself other questions. One of which was "Why was I born into this family?" I felt as though I should have been born to someone else at some other time in the future or the past. That is where the abortion question came from. She said, "I do not know. I guess I did not think about it". I asked her "Why not?" She finally told me she did not have the money; she had thought about it and if she did have the money I would not be here. I never forgot that.

Some years later I found out she was pregnant again. When she told me I was pissed off and did not hide it. I think I was 16 or 17 at the time and had spent almost every weekend at home because my mother made either my brother or me watch my little sister while she went out. "Why don't you have an abortion?" "I spent the money the father gave me." I cannot write what I thought of her at that moment, but "stupid witch" is not too far off.

A few days later, I heard strange noises coming from her room one night. My mother was crying. The next day while she was at the hospital I forced myself to look in a pale covered by a cloth. It contained the dead fetus. It was at that moment I knew she had given herself an abortion. I do not know if I will ever be strong enough to do something like that. I know she must feel guilty. I know I do. I think about how selfish I was at the thought of having another child to raise. That is probably another reason I do not have children.

In 2005, 1.21 million abortions were performed in the United States[104].

What about capital punishment? The Supreme Court cannot make up its mind whether or not it is constitutional. This time around, they ruled (1976) that the death penalty is constitutional. By no means does the law make it right or wrong in my eyes. The law only reflects the majority or the powerful's overall view. I have heard the arguments for and against. And, as an African-American, I know that there are disproportionate amounts of people of color on death row. In 2008, 1,338 out of 3,207 death row inmates were African-American. [105] That is 42% in a country where African-Americans make up about 13.6 % of the population. This situation exists because African-Americans frequently receive harsher sentences than their white counterparts, unless they have the money to pay for a good lawyer[106]. These disproportionate numbers and the reasons behind them offend my sense of fairness.

What about war? I examined history to answer this question. It does not seem to matter what people think individually about war. War happens and always has. Every culture and society has war and violence in its history. As a matter of fact, I dare say, "Every great civilization on this planet was spawned by war, conquest and conflict". Just ask the Army Major shrink who opened fire on his fellow soldiers at Fort Hood.

Every one of these instances addresses the same question; is it wrong or right to take life? I personally do not see the right in taking life. I have not seen the right in it ever since I killed my pet hamster. Before you go into psychoanalysis, listen to the story.

My brother and I inherited two hamsters from a college student who left them for adoption in the hallway of the dormitory where my cousin was staying. We put them in an aquarium and cared for them diligently for about two weeks. After the newness wore off, so did our interest. We did not clean the aquarium as well as we should have. A fly laid eggs on one of the hamsters and maggots appeared. They were eating their way through the head of the hamster. I resolved to end the hamster's suffering. I dug a shallow hole and placed the hamster inside. I was hoping to bury it, but he kept crawling out (not that I blame him, but he was making my choice harder). I eventually crushed the hamster with a rock. It was one of the most difficult things I have ever done; I cried. The feeling is indescribable. I learned then and there that for me taking life is not easy.

Later in life I shot, trapped, fished and killed living things and gained tremendous pleasure from the hunt. I rarely ate what I caught. Was I hunting out of malice or instinct? I have participated in the taking of life since then. I have paid for abortions. I say that I want a son and have conceived two probable sons. They both became aborted fetuses. Am I right or wrong?

---

[104] Jones RK et al., Abortion in the United States: incidence and access to services, 2005, *Perspectives on Sexual and Reproductive Health,* 2008, 40(1):6–16.

[105] Bureau of Justice Statistics. http://www.ojp.usdoj.gov/bjs/glance/tables/drracetab.htm.

[106] The length of sentences has been tied to perceptions of beauty (Etcoff). People who are considered attractive are typically receive shorter terms. Beauty has even been used as a defense not to go to prison. The logic being, "She's too pretty to go to prison. If you send her to prison, it will be like a death sentence because she is so pretty" This was the defense for a female teacher who had sex with a child. She got probation, later sent the child a video strip tease and still did not go to prison. Her sex, blond hair and blue eyes worked to her benefit.

I was in college when the first abortion occurred. I am not sure if the child was mine or not; but one thing was sure, I was going to have to support this child and his mother. The second time was with a woman who was married and already had a child that was not her husband's. The first abortion was an easier choice; I was in college and wanted to live without the responsibility of a family. The second abortion was harder. I thought I was in love and wanted a son, but I realized that I would never have this woman to myself and the paternity was in doubt.

I have come to a decision after years of deliberation. I do not care what reasons we use to justify our actions when it comes to killing other people. I think it is wrong and I hope I am never put in a position where I have to take another human life (I did not say that I will not defend myself if attacked. I will shoot someone in the foot), but this is only applicable and valid for me. I cannot speak for the parent protecting a child from an intruder. I will not speak of those in the Super Dome or in some other horrendous situation where our morals and survival instincts are truly tested. I would have to have that experience to write or comment about it. The combatants in Afghanistan and Iraq are going to have issues with what they have done.

I had this belief challenged when my cousin was killed while at work. The two culprits were caught. The woman involved was found guilty. The male pleaded guilty. The District Attorney asked for the death penalty. They asked our family and the families of the other victims to write a *Letter of Loss* to the jurors. The purpose of this letter was to convince the jury to give the death penalty. We could not directly ask for the death penalty, and that was the only restriction. My mother and aunt drafted a letter and asked me to proof it. In their version, there was a sentence that asked for death. I am not sure if it was my aunt or my mother who put that sentence in the letter, but I took it out. I also drafted a sincere letter to the jurors asking for justice. They both got life in prison without parole. They were both African-American. The incident occurred because one of the other victims owed the girl money; I think it was $400. Three lives for $400!?! What state of mind must a person be in to rationalize that? And, how did they get that desperate in America? What's wrong with us?

When I was working abroad one of my associates told me his wife was pregnant. I asked him what they were having. He said that the government forbids medical facilities from telling them the sex of fetuses because of the tradition of aborting females. In that part of the world some still do not value females as much as males because of earning potential and physical strength. I know personally that a woman can work a field as hard as a male, maybe harder, if she must feed her children or herself. I would have to give birth to evaluate that further. The males are not viewed as a burden, girls are. It is not that different in Western cultures. We try to marry our girls off and then let them come home if it does not work out[107].

Though I think the taking of life is wrong, I cannot figure out how to exist without taking the life of something. I have resigned myself to being thankful for the sacrifice made by other living things so that I may live. My debt to these organisms is to live a whole and productive life. Anything less is a waste of the energy they have given me.

---

[107] Humans are the only species that allow their offspring back into the household.

Infidelity

My grandfather once asked a male in-law, "How did a chicken as black as you lay an egg that white?" We were at the birth celebration. It was a very festive environment. My grandfather looked at the child, and said exactly what he and anyone with eyes were thinking. He was referring to how "lily white" my infant cousin was. The supposed father is dark as night. The mother is less than "paper bag" brown. Alcohol is a truth serum.

Is it wrong to have sex outside of our relationships? The majority of us say, "Yes. It is wrong". My male social programming tells me that it is wrong for my mate to do so, but I can as long as I am not caught. My instincts tell me, "Ensure the survival of your genetic line by having as many children as possible with as many healthy women as possible." That is how I explain deadbeat dads. They know that their offspring will more than likely survive without them. They do not seem to understand the difference between simply existing and living. My mind tells me, "It does not matter; it is just sex," and, my spirit loves and wants to be a part of everyone.

My experiences with women tell me that it is not wrong to have sex outside of the relationship. After you read Chapter VI: Sex, you will see what I mean.

When most males imagine sexual infidelity, our heart rates increase, we sweat and our brows wrinkle. When we imagine an emotional attachment, men get excited, but not as upset as when sexual infidelity is the issue. It is the opposite for women. Emotional infidelity, not sex, causes more intense emotional responses[108].

Adultery is listed as one of the Judeo-Christian mortal sins, but among certain people the offering of a wife to guests is an expression of friendship and hospitality. There are areas where polygamy[109] and polyandry[110] are condoned, as a necessity to ensure the survival of society. According to some sources polygamous societies outnumber monogamous ones as much as three to one.

Most of the women I have had a sexual relationship with already had men in their lives with whom that they were intimate, and the majority of the time the women knew when I had a "significant other". They were practicing polyandry. Some women expected that I would trade-in my current mate for a better model. One woman told me very bluntly, "She's not right for you." "Who said that?" "I did." I will be blunter for those who did not get it the first time. Most of the women I have had sex with were already having sex with someone else and knew I was too. I have felt remorse in some instances and I have not in others.

I once witnessed a friend pimping a female neighbor to a millionaire. The millionaire was married and the woman knew it, but she got a Mercedes for her vagina and thanked my friend from the bottom of her heart for introducing her to Daddy War Bucks. To whom do we place the blame? According to the law of the land and popular morality, it is wrong to do this, but in my experience, morals are not enough to stop the longing for, and the prospect of security or

---

[108] Buss, David M. "The Evolution of Desire".
[109] Polygamy: Marital practice in which a man has more than one wife simultaneously.
[110] Polyandry: Marital practice in which a woman has more than one husband simultaneously.

monetary gain, or the passion of attraction. How am I supposed to judge what is right or wrong based on these observations? What am I supposed to believe: what I see, what I feel, what I have been taught, or reality? Maybe we should ask Tiger Woods.

I have only met one person who said she has never cheated in any relationship, but this person has been cheated on several times.

Lying

After reading Chapter I: Lies, you know what I think about lying; it happens and will continue. Most of us have been taught that it is wrong to lie, but we learned that in certain circumstances it is quite acceptable. I have had to tell bill collectors my mother was not home when she was standing directly in front of me. When "caller ID" was invented, we no longer had to give in to the curiosity of "Who's that?" So is it right or wrong to lie? If you say it depends on the circumstances, the real answer is not to you.

We are discreet sheep; we wait to see how the drove is going and then go with the drove. We have two opinions: one private, which we are afraid to express; and another one - the one we use - which we force ourselves to wear to please. Mark Twain

Homosexuality

Gay marriage is a big issue now. It is illegal in some states and legal in others. If two people love each other is that not enough? Who among us has the right to tell another human being whom they can marry or love? It is another example of hypocrisy, repression of freedom and the pursuit of happiness. I am not going to marry a male, but I do not care if someone else does. It has nothing to do with me.

Opponents of gay marriage say that homosexuality is not natural. Many species in nature engage in some type of homosexual activity. As a matter of fact, chimpanzees, our closest relatives, engage in mock mating and other homosexual activities regularly. Who has not seen two male or female dogs humping?

Opponents of gay marriage also say, "Gay marriage will destroy the institution of marriage." The institution of marriage is already half dead (divorce rates almost 50%) and straight people killed it. I know; I have assisted in more than a few assassinations. That stems from our own sexual repression, lies and ignorance.

Opponents also say, "It goes against God. The Bible or the Qur'an says…" The Bible also condemned slavery, but it did not stop Christians from owning slaves. The Qur'an promotes peace, will someone please tell that to the extremist. Remember that the Bible and the Qur'an were composed, edited and printed by men in positions of power, not God. Regular people like you and me have interpreted these books to fit our own versions of right and wrong. Besides, I have never met anyone who has lived up to the principles of either book. Even the most avid Christian conservatives have lied. If you think homosexuality is a sin that condemns gays to hell, how do you think God will punish lying, infidelity, envy or stealing? What about judgment?

I have recently been working on a programmed response of mine. I caught myself cringing when I saw two males kiss on television. I questioned why I cringed. If I am such an advocate of equality, how can I cringe? I realized that it was a conditioned response. I learned it from the males in my life, specifically, my grandfather. He hated gays and cringed every time he heard mention of homosexual men. He would have lost his mind if he were alive when *Brokeback Mountain* came out. I idolized him and naturally adopted the same posture against what he called "Sissies".

Although I am not gay, I have no issue with their way of life. I have associated with homosexuals all my life and so have you, whether or not you knew it. They have been around since the beginning of time. Some were on the "down low" (sorry Ms. Mc Millan). And others are openly bisexual or gay, but they are here. And, for the record, most guys have had a homosexual experience, whether as a youth or an adult. The only difference is those who are Man enough to admit it.

I am convinced that the most avid gay bashers have hidden homosexual tendencies with which that they are not comfortable. They hate the fact that they have a feminine side, and show their disapproval by lashing out at the object of their own fear and confusion. I think fear is the driving force behind not only anti-gay movements, but also every other anti-anything movement. But, that is just my opinion. Ask Rev. Haggard[111] what he thinks.

Religious Right

If you believe in God, TOTAL faith is required.
If you believe humans make their own individual destinies, hard work and long hours await.
If you believe in neither, God nor Self....
If you believe in both....

There were three holy men fishing in a rowboat. Half the day passed and none of them caught anything. One of the men noticed that fish were jumping out of the water just across the river. "I have faith and a strong God," he said, and then he stepped out of the boat, walked across the water, and then threw his line in and immediately caught a fish. The second holy man decided that his religion was just as strong as the first man's, so he said a prayer, stepped out of the boat and then walked across the water. He too caught a fish immediately. The third holy man was not about to be out done by the other two, so he said his prayer, stepped from the boat and then fell in the water. He climbed back into the boat, said a stronger prayer, stepped from the boat once more and fell into the water again. This went on for some time. The two successful conduits of God, who were catching fish left and right, watched in amazement. Finally, one said to the other, "What did you pray for? "Fish." "What did you pray for?" "Fish." "What do you think he wished for?" "Probably to walk on water." "One of us really should show him where the rocks are!"

Before I proceed, let me explain why I am concentrating on Christianity in the following paragraphs. I was raised primarily as a Christian and in a society dominated by the Judeo-

---

[111] Reverend Ted Arthur Haggard (1956-): Former leader of the National Association of Evangelicals. Disgraced by relationship with a male prostitute. Haggard declared himself "cured" after three days of religious healing.

Christian faith. Although I had youthful exposure to The Nation of Islam, mysticism and the Yoruba[112] religion, the majority of my experiences have been with Christianity and Christians. I believe that everyone needs God in his or her life; I am just unsure which concept would best serve the greater good of all people.

It does not matter what religion we examine; there are contradictions everywhere. Look at the Bible and the Qur'an. They are books and that is all. They, like other books, were written and composed by people. Remember what I said about the US Constitution? What they contain is what the publishers wanted in them, and no more. Just like this book. Many hands have washed what you are reading. Religious texts contain much of the same knowledge and are good for understanding human nature and history, but by no means are they absolute or complete. Many of the principles contained in the Bible are also printed in other texts that predate the Jews. These same ideas are also present in other religious or spiritual doctrines. They all send the same basic message: "Live righteously and do no harm", or "Turn right and go straight". So, why are there religious wars? Could it be we all think we are right about God? Has anyone you know ever met, said they have spoken to or seen The Creator of everything? Did you believe them? Have you?

If the major religions of the world promote peace and love, why do religious people fight for religious causes in religious wars?

In order to prove a point, it is important that we all understand where the modern Bible came.

The Emperor Constantine[113] commissioned the first "official" Bibles. Constantine wanted to stabilize, standardize and control what doctrines were being taught throughout his Empire. Remember that Constantine had just reunited the Roman Empire and was trying to cement his power over the state. He converted to Christianity (he said he saw a cross in the sky on the way to battle that told him to fight and win for God. OK, God told him to kill plenty of people.). Constantine then made it legal to be a Christian, and then he transformed many traditional pagan holidays to Christian holy days (Sol Invictus is Christmas). He even changed the Sabbath, which was actually the festival of Sabazios[114] from Saturday to Sunday because he needed the banks (money lenders) open on Saturday for the purpose of commerce. In 331, Emperor Constantine gave orders for Eusebius of Caesarea[115] to prepare copies of a standardized Bible for use in the state churches. Constantine's Ecumenical Bible was the result.

Saint Jerome[116] was educated as a lawyer in Rome. He was secretary to Pope Damasus I[117]. He translated and "corrected" Greek and Hebrew texts to produce the Latin Vulgate. The

---

[112] Yoruba: Western African religion and culture dating back to the Nok people.
[113] Constantine (285-377): Flavius Valerius Constantinus. Emperor of the Roman Empire (306-337).
[114] Sabazios: Nomadic horseman sky God.
[115] Eusebius of Caesarea or Eusebius Pamphili (260-340): a Bishop of Caesarea in Palestine and is often referred to as the father of church history.
[116] Saint Jerome or Eusebius Sophronius Hieronymus (347-420): translator of the Bible from Greek and Hebrew into Latin. Jerome's edition, the Vulgate, is still the official biblical text of the Catholic Church.
[117] Pope Damasus I (305-383): Pope (366-383). Accused of adultery and murder.

Vulgate served as the official Bible for more than a thousand years. The Rheims-Douay Bible [118] is the Roman Catholic English translation of Jerome's Latin Vulgate.

No one knows for sure how many books or gospels existed or what was being preached, but some believe that up to 500 books were written by various Christian sects of the time. There have been so many different versions and translations published by different groups that Bibles are different. The Catholic Bible has 73 books, the King James [119] Version contains only 66 books, and there are over 50 different versions printed in English alone. The differences are subtle. This sect changes this and that sect changed that because of different interpretations and agendas.

By looking at the origins of the modern bibles it is evident that they were influenced by the politics of the times. Many books of early Christianity have been omitted from the "versions" we read today. Furthermore, the Bible plagiarized many of its stories from other cultures. The Epic of Gilgamesh is a perfect example. It contains the story of *Noah's Ark* except it was written thousands of years earlier. The Babylonian/Sumerian/Akkadian Creation Epic, *Enuma Elish*, predates the Bible as well: *"Enki, wroughts humanity out of the red earth, mingled with the red blood of the God Kingu, slain for his part in Tiamat's attack. Enlil fills his lungs with air and humans are alive"*. Genesis 2:7: *"And the LORD God formed man of the dust of the ground and breathed into his nostrils the breath of life; and man became a living soul"*. Keep these things in mind when basing a way of life upon stories that have been written many times by many different cultures.

I am not bashing religion or Christianity. I think that truly religious and spiritual people help change the world for the better. But, it must be said that true Muslims and Christians help others, they do not judge, and they definitely do not take life or condone the taking of life. Regardless of religious faith, the taking of life is hard. If you have never done it, I pray you never have to. Whether the means of death is lethal injection, beheading, an abortion or an effort to prevent the use of weapons of mass destruction, it is a decision that will be with you for the rest of your life.

Look at what is wrong with religion in general. Religion (salvation) has taken a back seat to self-interest and instant gratification. Politics has invaded the temples; greed and ambition pollute the religions of the world. Some of the most corrupt individuals ever to walk the Earth were and are religious heads or heads of state who claim to be religious. I have sat in churches and listened to individuals interpret scriptures according to their own personal experiences, training and conditioning. I have also heard these same individuals label sinners, lobby for politicians or social causes, and judge others who think or act contrary to their beliefs. I find no fault in this; we all do these things in our ignorance. Ministers, however, should be especially careful of what they say because of the influence they have. Many in the flock take what their leaders say as absolute gospel, when in fact it is just the opinion of the speaker.

FYI: Did you know that one of the easiest places to pick up a man or woman is in church?

---

[118] Rheims-Douay Bible or the Douai Bible: Roman Catholic translation of the Bible from the Latin Vulgate into English. First appeared in 1582. First mass printing in 1609. Influenced the King James version of the Bible.
[119] King James Bible: English translation of the Bible, commissioned for the benefit of the Church of England for King James I. First published in 1611.

The Popes of old were infamous for their opinions. The Borgias[120] and Medici immediately come to mind when I think of corruption in the church. I cannot help but think about priests who are pedophiles, preachers who steal from the till, and monks who break their vows. Churches throughout history have sanctioned and promoted actions to preserve and increase their own power, wealth and control. Many of the edicts of our religious institutions are not for the well-being of the member's souls, but for the survival and benefit of the religious hierarchy and institution. The Spanish Inquisition, jihads, the various ethnic cleansings and the crusades are just a few examples of when religion and regionalism have gone bad.

Religions and societies have supported slavery for eons because it was profitable, even though everything that makes us human forbids it. Biblical law made man-stealing punishable by death in Exodus 21:16 *"anyone who kidnaps another and either sells him or still has him when he is caught must be put to death."* In Deuteronomy 24:7 it states *"If a man is caught kidnapping one of his fellow Israelites and treats him as a slave or sells him, the kidnapper must die. You must purge the evil from among you."* It seems strange that the Israelites seem to have adopted the same position as others have before and after this law was written. Slavery is acceptable as long as you do not enslave one of your own, and who is one of your own seems to be determined on a sliding scale, another two-tier justice system at work.

On December 3rd 1839 Pope Gregory XVI issued *In Supremo Apostolatus* (In Higher Canon Law) during the 4th Provincial Council of Baltimore. It "condemned" slavery and the slave trade, and forbade all Catholics to propound views contrary to this. In 1838, Pope Gregory XIV [121]had condemned all forms of colonial slavery and the slave trade, calling it *"inhumanum illud commercium"* (inhuman commerce)[122]. I wonder how many Catholics released their slaves, especially those in Brazil and South America…

*"*Slavery was established by the decree of Almighty God... It is sanctioned in the Bible, in both Testaments, from Genesis to Revelations... It has existed in all ages, has been found among the people of the highest civilization and in nations of the highest proficiency in the arts," *Jefferson Davis*[123]

"The doom of Ham has been branded on the form and features of his African descendants. The hand of fate has united his color and destiny. Man cannot separate what God hath joined"
James Henry Hammond[124]

Learned Christian men made the above statements. They were admired enough to be the President of the Confederacy and a US Senator. Christians and other men and women have always made similar statements to justify what they do. I will say this: any religion that promotes, condones, or turns a blind eye to rape, murder, kidnapping, theft and lack of respect

---

[120] Borgias: Influential family in 15th Century Italy: Pope Callistus III and Pope Alexander VI. Cesare Borgia: Cardinal and soldier. Machiavelli modeled his Ideal Statesman after Cesare.
[121] Pope Gregory XIV (1765-1846): Pope from 1831-1846.
[122] http://www.catholic-forum.com/saints/pope0254j.htm.
[123] Jefferson Davis (1808-1889): Soldier, Politician (Congressman and Secretary of War) and the only President of the Confederate States of America.
[124] James Henry Hammond (1807-1864): Governor of South Carolina (1842-1844). United States Senator (1857-1860).

for our fellow human beings is not viable in my eyes. Regardless of the reasoning (excuses), these things are universally considered wrong. But many different religions have accepted inhumane behavior throughout history. Some people engage in slaving today and will continue into the future. It is like watching the same show over and over again. You finally memorize the entire sequence of events and know what the ending is because we all have seen this movie before.

Look at all the different forms of religion. Religions seem to evolve or metamorph to fit the times and the majority. Henry VIII[125] parted with the Catholic Church in 1533 and took his country with him because he wanted a son and thought that his wife, Catherine of Aragon, could not give him one. Pope Clement VII[126] would have given him an annulment, if Catherine[127] had not been the aunt of Charles V, Emperor of the Holy Roman Empire[128]. Hence, the Church of England was founded and Henry became its head.

"Truth is what the majority thinks it is at any given moment, precisely because the majority is permitted to govern and redefine its values constantly" Justice Robert Bork[129]

I remember when my grandmother asked my brother, cousins and me if we wanted to be baptized. I said, "I am not going to let Reverend Dean drown me." What did I know of baptisms? I knew it was supposed to wash our sins away. That was what I had heard. I remember thinking, "I am five; I have only been sinning for a few years. If I get one shot to wash my sins away, I'll save mine for much later." I declined; my brother and one cousin agreed to be "washed."

I remember their wearing all white and being dunked backwards under the water. I remember thinking, "Water would get up my nose." I did not like that and knew I had made the right decision. There was a lot of singing, shouting, praising and dancing. One lady was possessed, or at least she acted like it. I remember asking myself and, later that night, my grandmother, "Why did she act like that?" "She was possessed." "What is that?" "That is when the Holy Spirit enters you." "If it makes you act crazy, I do not want the Holy Spirit." "Do God and the Spirit enter the people who got baptized too?" "Yes." I could not wait until I had a chance to talk to my brother and cousin. I was very interested in the transformation that had taken place.

That night, when we were in bed, I asked them what they felt and what they saw. My brother said he felt the same and my cousin said, "I did not see Jesus in that water." More to the point, both have history with FIVE-O. I am not trying to be funny, judgmental or sarcastic; I am trying to get the point across that our salvation does not involve religion. It does involve self-evaluation and the realization that we are God and God is love. There is no separating the two and there is

---

[125] Henry VIII (1491-1547): King of England (1509-1547). Established the Church of England in 1534.

[126] Pope Clement VII or Giulio di Giuliano de' Medici (1478-1534): Pope (1523-1534). Part of the influential Medici family of Florence. Cousin of Pope Leo X. Rivals of the Borgias.

[127] Catharine of Aragon (1485-1536): Queen consort of England. Princess of Wales (married to Prince Arthur). Henry VIII's sister-in-law and first wife.

[128] Charles V (1500-1558): King of Spain (1516-1556). Co-king of Castile (1516-1555), full king (1555-56) and Holy Roman Emperor (1519-1556).

[129] Robert Heron Bork: Conservative American legal scholar and former judge. Nominated as Associate Justice by President Ronald Reagan in 1987.

no separating us from God or love. I like to think that I underwent baptism by fire. Now, I seek it by water.

Just to be fair, I think Islam suffered after the death of the Prophet Mohammed. The second Caliph, Umar Ibn al-Khattab, warred on and defeated Syria, Turkey, Persia and Northern Africa, all in the name of the "Jihad". In other words, Muslims spread the word of their God through violence. Does that sound familiar? Think about the Crusades, slavery and colonization.

Umar was assassinated in 656. His successor, Uthman Ibn Affan, was also assassinated. His successor, Ali Ibn Abu Talib, was assassinated. The man who had him killed, Mu' awiyah, became Caliph. He died of something other than assassination; but, when his son, Yazid, became Caliph, a major split occurred in Islam. Some wanted hereditary passage of the title and others wanted Ali's son, Husayn, to take his place, but he died at the hands of Yazid's army. That is basically why we have Sunnites (Sunni) and Shi'ites (Shi'a), as well as other Islamic sects today. I would not have wanted that job during those years. It reminds me of the King of Syracuse and the continuous power struggles throughout history.

The Bible says the last time Jesus voluntarily entered a temple he wrecked the joint. I wish he could visit us without the hail and brimstone or the Judgment Day effect. I want to hear what he has to say face to face. Some may say I am questioning God. "No. I want to talk to the person who was Jesus Christ. I have a few questions. I would like to ask," Not the meaning of life, I know that already - evolve or perish. I want to know what my part is and how I can help. I am not ungodly. I just know that the entity I worship, the creator of it all, existed before religions did. For the record, I do not think Jesus was a virgin. Women have always been drawn to power. If he was, it was because his mother was walking beside him with a stick.

Once when he was asked what made him most sad about the world, Confucius[130] *said, "The fact that virtue is not cultivated, that knowledge is not made clear, that people hear of duty and do not practice it, that those who know they are evil do nothing to improve themselves. These are things that made me sad". "You speak of serving gods," he once remarked to his followers, "But how shall you serve gods when you have not yet learned to serve people?"*

Religious Wrong

Jesus Wept

Who is right or wrong when it comes to religion? Here in the United States it is pretty much expected that one should be some form of Christian. I know that there is supposed to be religious tolerance, but I would not want to be labeled as a Muslim today because of the unleashed prejudice after 9/11. I would not want to be a Sikh or an atheist either.

I was once called the "Devil" because I questioned the Bible. We were discussing religion. As usual, I mentioned the Book of Job. I openly questioned why Job[131] was subjected to all sorts of cruelty because of a bet between the devil and God. The Christian I was speaking to said it

---

[130] Confucius (551-479 BC): K'ung-fu-tzu or Pinyin Kongfuzi. Chinese moral and political philosopher.
[131] The Book of Job. One of 39 books in the Old Testament.

was not a bet. I said it was and continued with, "My God does not gamble!" I rationalized, "Why would an all-knowing being make a bet?" Those present still denied that it was a bet. I wrote a term paper on the subject years ago. It was titled "The Unfair Tests of Job". I was more than prepared to defend my position against someone who had never read it. I received an "A" because I questioned the validity of the story. To me it is another one of the contradictions that occurs in the Bible. If Christians believe in God, they know that there is a plan or intelligent design and that we have free will. Following this logic, why would a benevolent God allow one of his most faithful to be tortured for no other reason than proving the devil wrong? The devil is always wrong (it is the nature of evil to be wrong, the yang of the yin, the white of the black), because if it were right, we are all screwed and I refuse to believe that. I also refuse to believe that an all knowing and all seeing God would test Abraham or anyone else by asking them to kill their children as a test of loyalty.

I do not think many really believe in God. If we did, we would not fear or pray for anything. I do not refer to a Christian or Muslim interpretation of God; they cannot agree between themselves what God said or how we should worship. I speak of God eternal, that which made us all.

I follow a God that is unexplainable. My God is forgiving and caring. My God planned all this. "It's God's way," if so, then why are so many people trying to explain God's will and why are so many afraid of dying when "paradise" waits? I believe in the incomprehensible Being who has created our reality. What this force's name is I do not know. What the ideals of this force are I do not know. What the overall plan of this force is I do not know. I know only what I see in our world and what I feel inside. What I feel inside says we are supposed to grow. Pascal[132] said something to the effect: if you do not believe in God and are right, you gain nothing. If you are wrong, you lose everything. If you do believe in God and are wrong, you lose nothing. If you are right you gain everything. What I have seen and continue to see, tell me that it is a sucker bet that God does exist.

Many believe Revelations, the end of days, is approaching. Maybe that explains the "I do not give a fuck attitude," we are witnessing. There is not going to be an end it all battle at Megiddo. If I wrote Revelations and had to pick a spot on the planet around 100 A.D. where that battle would occur, it would have been Megiddo. Megiddo is arguably the most embattled place on the planet. The Judeans, Persians, Ottoman Turks, Assyrians, Egyptians, Greeks, Israelites, Philistines, Canaanites and Romans all fought there. During World War I the British finally drove the Turks from Palestine and Syria because of a battle that occurred near Megiddo in September of 1918. Megiddo guarded one of the most important highways of the ancient world, the Via Maris that connected ancient Syria, the Levant, Anatolia and Mesopotamia, modern day Iran, Iraq, Turkey and Syria. It was a strategic checkpoint and the nation that controlled it controlled the region's trade. Today Megiddo is just a hill of ruins. If Revelations were written today, John probably would have named Baghdad as the final battle ground between good and evil.

---

[132] Blaise Pascal (1623-1662): French physicist, mathematician, philosopher and inventor of the adding machine. Wrote "Thoughts" (1670), a work that tried to prove the existence of God.

Do not let anything guide your decisions, but you. When I say "you," I mean that sense we all have inside before we get a chance to think. Any cause is only as good as its practitioners. Those who follow are foolish not to first have an intimate understanding of what they are following, and secondly have legitimate reasons why they are following. Most people I know have limited knowledge of the Bible because they have not read it from cover to cover and even less knowledge of the Constitution. More often than not, history teaches us that we are usually following the ambitions, traditions and insanity of others. Ask the Germans, who walked with Hitler, the Italians who marched with Mussolini and those 500,000[133] dead who accompanied Napoleon to Moscow, or Jim Jones' followers. Ask those sacrificed on the altars, on battlefields and in the temples of the world and through history what they think about a God that demanded their blood to be appeased.

I am not religious, though I try to remain spiritual. I pray and have conversations with the Infinite or myself. Is there anyone out there who will condemn me to their hell because of this? And, will they hold my hand when we get there?

I bought a surfboard for this wave we call life. I say, "Bring it on", and I mean it. I am prepared by my past experiences, by my God, to survive the trial. If I "believe", I grow stronger from the experience. If I do not, I go through the experience again and again. The lessons must be learned before graduation; the tests must be passed alone.

Religion is what keeps the poor from murdering the rich. Napoleon Bonaparte[134]

The Universe

The universe is infinite. No one knows what is out there. The Hubble space telescope can see only a portion of it and most speculate about the rest - black holes, dark matter and dark energy. Give me a modern day Christopher Columbus in need of a crew, or a ship and a fair solar wind. I want to know. It would not shatter my belief system if there were life somewhere else. I believe in the universe.

Capitalism

If you really think about it, Capitalism is in direct contradiction with "*Thou shall not covet...*" It is based on wanting or coveting what others have. Credit is a side effect of capitalism. I seem to remember Ezekiel 18:17 stating that money lending at interest (he shall take no usury or charge excessive interest) is a bad thing. Psalm 15:5 says, "Those who do not charge interest on the money they lend and who refuse to accept bribes to testify against the innocent. Such people will stand firm forever." I have paid interest rates as high as 28% and the majority of those who take these types of loans are poor or struggling. At the same time, our government bails out the very same lenders who are raping the people our government is supposed to represent. The average American household carries almost $9,000 in credit card debt[135]. My

---

[133] Most died of exposure. The Russian winter has stopped many a foe including the Germans in World War II.
[134] Napoleon Bonaparte (1769-1821): General of the French Revolution. First Consul (*Premier Consul*) of the French Republic (1799-1804). Emperor and King of Italy under the name Napoleon I (1804-1814) and again briefly (1815).
[135] Nilson Report (April 2009)

granddad said, "If you can't pay cash for it, you don't really need or own it." I once had someone get upset with me because I did not want to tour their new house. When he asked why I told him, "It ain't mine." I think in a nation supposedly founded on Christian morals that holds the Bible in such high reverence, money lending at interest should be against the law, but is not.

Racism

Almost everyone I've talked to says, "We're going to move to Houston"… What I'm hearing, which is sort of scary, is they all want to stay in Texas… And so many of the people in the arena here, you know, were underprivileged anyway, so this, this (slight chuckle) is working very well for them.[136]

America was founded on bigotry, sexism, discrimination and racism. You do not have to believe me. Ask the aboriginal peoples or get in your time machine, go back to 1619, and ask the first slaves what they think about the land of the free. Many of the original colonies raided the villages of their new neighbors for food. Racism is so embedded in American culture that the majority of people do not recognize it anymore. Even the original Declaration of Independence refers to the aboriginal-Americans as "savages". I have heard, "You're so well spoken," so many times it makes me sick. That is not a compliment. It says that there is no expectation for an African-American to have command of the English language. It is equivalent to my saying "Damn, you sure can dance.", "You sure can jump.", or "Your butt is so round." to a white person. I have also shown up at a new job or squadron and had people tell me with some pride that they had a basketball team. It is a hell of an assumption to think that all African-Americans are good at sports. Granted some African-Americans do excel at sports, music and entertaining, but that does not mean that one should be or act surprised when they realize that we are also capable of academic, intellectual and professional achievements as well. Not all of us wear our pants so that our underwear shows and speak only Ebonics. I admire Langston Hughes[137], George Washington Carver[138], and W.E.B. Dubois[139] more than I do any of the Michaels (Jackson, Jordan or Tyson). I aspire to be more like a Colin Powell before he lied to the UN and took one for the "team" or a MLK without the extramarital affairs, FBI investigations, or the assassination.

I know racism exists because Don Imus can call African-American women, "Nappy - headed ho's." on his nationally syndicated radio show. I am a racist of sorts or rather I have been, but I am trying to change. I tell myself that not all white folks think they are better than everyone else, but then I remember past incidents that contradict what I want to be true in my heart. I tell myself that lighter skin color does not equate to beauty or success, but then I watch television or I think about the Tuskegee airmen[140]. I also remember Strom Thurman[141], one of the most ardent

---

[136] Barbara Bush on National Public Radio referring to hurricane Katrina evacuees living in the Astrodome.

[137] James Mercer Langston Hughes (1902-1967) American writer, playwright, and columnist.

[138] George Washington Carver (1864-1943), American inventor, educator, and scientist.

[139] William Edward Burghardt Du Bois (1868-1963) American author, activist, historian and writer who helped found the NAACP.

[140] First African-American Army Air Corps pilots. The 99th fighter Squadron (the Red Tails), never lost a bomber to enemy fighters. The unit received two Presidential Unit Citations, 744 Air metals, 150 Distinguished Flying Crosses, 14 Bronze Stars and several Silver Stars.

[141] James Strom Thurmond (1902-2003): US politician, former governor of South Carolina and US Senator.

supports of segregation, who had an African-American daughter that he did not publicly recognize, but supported financially throughout his life. At his 100th birthday party Trent Lott[142] said, "I want to say this about my state: When Strom Thurmond ran for president, we voted for him. We're proud of it. And if the rest of the country had followed our lead, we wouldn't have had all these problems over all these years, either." Mr. Lott also voted against the renewal of the Voter's Rights Act and the King Holiday. Senator George Allen's[143] referring to an Indian-American as a "macaca" only fortifies my view. I suspect he inherited the term from his mother, a Tunisian born Frenchwomen. Europeans use the word "macaca" to describe African immigrants or it could be a monkey. Either way it was not meant as a compliment. Mel Gibson's drunken slur against the Jews only furthers my assertion that America is racist.

I can go back as far as I can remember and find numerous examples in the African-American community where racist and/or bigots terms were used against Latinos, Jews, Asians, and Whites. When Congressman Joe Wilson of South Carolina yelled, "You lie!" at President Obama, I knew why he did it. Despite being a "Christian" school, Bob Jones University in South Carolina (What is up with South Carolina?) had a policy that forbids interracial dating. The university's administration cited scripture to support this policy when the IRS revoked their tax-exempt status: "God intended segregation of the races and that the scriptures forbid interracial marriage."[144] The federal district court agreed, but the 4th Circuit Court of Appeals overturned the decision. President Reagan authorized the Treasury and Justice Departments to ask that the university's case be dropped and that the previous court decisions be vacated, but later reversed his position after public outcries. When Bush visited the university while campaigning for President, the public uproar caused the University to drop the restriction on inter-racial dating. That was not 1950; it was the year 2000.

I once had a fellow student naval aviator tell me, "Blacks are better athletes because they have an extra muscle in their legs." It seems some people need an excuse (remember that excuses are the tools of the incompetent) as to why African-Americans out perform their white counterparts and the explanation does not even have to make since.

I was stuck at an Air Force base over night during a cross-country flight. A caution light malfunctioned in the aircraft we were flying, and I had to wait for a maintenance team. It was early afternoon and I decided to take a walk around the base. It was beautiful, as most Air Force bases are. Tall oaks lined both sides of the roads, giving just enough shade to make the southern sun pleasant.

I noticed a formation of airmen marching down the right side of the street and coming in my direction. It was then I remembered that the base seconded as an advanced training school for recent boot camp graduates. I readied myself to return a brisk salute to the squad leader. I knew it was not often they saw a Navy officer in a flight suit walking down the street and that we, officers, did not have the best of reputations among the enlisted. "Give them a sharp salute… Show these Air Force fags how to do it." The formation passed and there was no salute. I thought to myself, "Was it the flight suit and unfamiliar insignia on my cover? Was it the color of my

---

[142] Chester Trent Lott, Sr. (1941-): former US Senator from Mississippi.
[143] George Felix Allen (1952-) is a former US Senator from Virginia. Son of former NFL coach George Allen.
[144] Bob Jones University v. The United States.

skin?" It was not until I heard several members of the formation laugh that I got my answer. I thought about bringing the entire formation to a halt and balling out the squad leader, but then I remembered that the lowest form of authority is authority by position. I would not have accomplished anything but to perpetuate the continuation of the "All officers are assholes" mentality.

Later that night I went to the Officer's Club for dinner with my co-pilot. We met an elderly woman who was there alone to play bingo. For some reason she joined us at the bar and struck up a conversation. She asked me if it was all right if she told a cute joke. If someone has to ask for permission to say something, you can bet it will not be flattering. It turned out to be a racial joke. I answered, "I prefer not to hear it." "Oh, but it is so cute," she retorted. "No thank you. I'll leave so you can tell it to him." "I do not want to hear it either," my co-pilot chimed. His not wanting to hear the joke either made me feel better. What made this woman think that I would want to be insulted? I had learned that many a true word is said in a joke, "White Privilege" at its best.

Some years later I was chatting up two females in another Officer's Club. I was accompanied at the table by one of my married squadron mates. I thought things were progressing nicely until one of the girls asked if she could touch my hair. I thought it was odd, and I do not like people touching my head for spiritual and historical reasons. I thought in quick succession, "Why does she want to touch my hair? Maybe she has never felt an African-American's hair before... What harm can be done?" I obliged. She touched what little hair I had (military crew cut). Soon after she said, "How do you keep black babies from jumping on the bed?" I looked at her as if she had lost her mind; I knew the joke. I had heard it before. How could she internally justify telling a racial joke to me? "You put Velcro on the ceiling." I wanted to slap the bitch. She is extremely lucky she pulled that on me and not an African-American woman, who may not have as much to lose or control as I did. She would have at the least got an ear full, and at most an ass whipping. I looked around the table to see not only her friend laughing but also my squadron mate. I got up and walked away. That lesson hurt, but the most valuable ones always do.

Later the same evening I ran into several other African-American aviators. There were five or six of us in the middle of the lobby talking. After we made plans to meet later and they had departed, a senior lieutenant in my squadron walked up to me and told me I need to hang out with the squadron more. "Why?" I asked. He came up with several answers, none of them the truth. He was giving me a warning. They did not like the fact that I was hanging with other African-Americans. I saw the senior officers huddled together when I was with the African-American aviators, and could tell by the way they were staring that they did not approve. I even made a joke about breaking the 'No more than three Negroes in a group' law because of the stares we received by being together. They either did not like the fact that I was more comfortable with people whom I share more things in common, or they did not understand why. They have never been a minority in anything, so they will never understand. I told the lieutenant that I was just insulted *hanging out* in the bar with a squadron mate and two white girls. And, he should talk to the other officer who witnessed the joke at the table if he did not believe me.

I did not tell him that I do not like to be around them at all. I knew how some of them really felt about me. The Command Master Chief, the highest-rank for an enlisted person in the Navy, once insulted me and every other African-American in the squadron while we were drinking with the Commanding Officer, the Executive Officer and a number of others. He said several unflattering things that escalated with, "You are an OK nigger; I don't care what they say." I looked at my Commanding Officer. I wanted and expected him to intervene, but he didn't; he was laughed. A Warrant Officer finally said, "That's enough!" to the Master Chief; I wanted to kill him. Also one of the few squadron mates that treated me fairly had already told me what was being said about me and who was saying it. I had no intention of kissing their butts to improve their opinion of me. It would have been pointless. Although I have no issue hanging out in white establishments or dancing to rock, classical or country, I prefer dancing to rhythm and blues, Latin sounds, hip-hop and reggae. I do not fit on anyone's social totem pole but my own.

I went so far as to try to explain to my squadron mates what it was like to be African-American in a society of whites. I invited all of them to accompany me to a "Black" club. Only one of them said he would go, but he never did. African-Americans have to assimilate into white culture, but many whites would never be able to fit into ours. They would be too uncomfortable being a minority and I do not blame them.

I was at the bar in an Officer's Club on a Friday. The Admiral's Chief of Staff walked up and greeted me in the following manner: he said, "How are you, Ron?" and he then proceeded to pat me on the top of my head. What went through my mind at that moment! I could have and wanted to hit him, but I did not want to end up in more trouble than I was already. I hate biting my tongue. I told him as sternly as I could without being insubordinate, "Sir, do not ever pat a black man on the head. We are not patties[145]." When I brought the incident up to my Captain, he encouraged me to drop it. Rank it seems does have its privileges. To his credit, he gave me a kind word when I needed it.

The same thing happened when I worked for a Fortune 500 company. The HR manager walked up to the group of managers with whom I was having a conversation. He said hello to everyone else then patted me on the top of my head. I tried to hide my disapproval, but that "What the fuck are you doing!?!" look appeared before I could stop it. The Navy had long diffused the "Knock the shit out of him" reflex. He stepped back and immediately apologized. Too late, you have already shown me your subconscious opinion of me. Being Jewish, he should have known better.

I loved air shows because it was the chance to travel somewhere new. The fact that the people who frequented these events, females included, were supportive of the military did not hurt. It was always a good time to be had and we added flight hours to our logbooks. At one show I was taking my turn lending people a hand as they exited the aircraft. It was a good foot and a half drop after the ladder's last step and the last thing you want is an accident. One lady reached for my hand instinctively, and then she looked me in the face and withdrew it. As I stood watching her struggle, I pondered as I have every time something like this happens. She chose to negotiate what a healthy person could do with no issue. Kids frequently tried to jump down. That is why we stationed people there in the first place, to assist people like her who would have some difficulty.

---

[145] Patty: It was once common practice of whites to pat African-Americans, regardless of age, on the top of the head for good luck.

99

She had to turn around backwards and give me a visual nightmare, her lumpy wide butt. Holding on to the railing, she slowly and carefully lowered herself down searching for the ground with the toe of her left foot. She held up the line, but made it safely to the ground. "Have a good day," I said with a smile on my face.

Her lengthy descent gave me time to think. I thought, "How could she disrespect me like that?" The answer came in a silent voice, "She's a racist". "I know. Most people are." I was in the military doing my part to defend our nation, I was in uniform, I was an officer and I WAS AN AVIATOR! "What is another word for an African-American college graduate?" "I do not know. What?" "Nigger." Sob, "Oh yeah, I forget sometimes… And I defend her right to say that." "Well then snap to; she helps pay your check." "Have a nice day." She smirked. I had to laugh because the "I showed you" face mixed with the remembrance of her big white stained in both spots underwear was funny. I could not help but think, "Yeah, you showed me and the entire tarmac."

I was standing at the valet station of a high-end hotel in New Orleans waiting for my car. A fellow naval officer and I made the five-hour drive for Carnival. He had arranged to meet a woman there. So, there were three of us talking when a guest walked up to us and stood there as if he were expecting something. "Can I help you?" "Yes, you can get my car." He thought we were valets. Before I go on, let me mention that we were all dressed elegantly and John and I were drinking beers (the "Big Easy" does not have open container laws). It did not matter to him. Our colored skin meant that we could not possibly be guests at the five-star hotel. In his mind, despite all the evidence to the contrary, we were working and drinking on the job. He must have thought, "Look at those trifling Niggers drinking on the job." I for one would not ask a valet who was drinking to retrieve my car, but that is just me.

Before I could get, "Fuck you!" out of my mouth, John barked, "We do not work here… We are all Naval Officers!" The white man was taking steps backwards by now. I guess he could see that an ass whipping was about half a heartbeat away. His female companion also had a look of stark terror on her face. He whimpered a half apologetic, half scared shitless, "I'm sorry." I said, "You should be; that was insulting!" John's friend was as embarrassed as he was; she is white.

I went to dinner with two friends, a white male and female. When the check came, they wanted to pay for their portion of the meal in cash, but I was going to use my credit card. They gave me the cash and I gave the waiter my card. A different waiter returned with the receipt for signature and handed it to the white male. I guess to him "Niggers" do not have credit. I did not have to say a word. My companions saw it for themselves, and were embarrassed by the incident. I simply said, "I'm used to it by now."

Racism exists, but it is the reaction to it that gives it, like any other vibration, power. I have encountered African-American on African-American racism, reverse racism, foreigner racism and institutional racism. I have had racism southern fried and northern disguised. I have seen racism on the eastern and western shores. It is here and it is real.

I am an American with skin color. I am not pure African, but I am labeled as "Black". As such, at the moment I was born, I was slated to a position on the United States' social totem pole.

It is my experience that white men generally come first. Educated men of color come next, if looking at it from an economic earning stance, but more often white women are typically next on the social ladder. Women of color follow this group. Finally, uneducated men of color occupy the majority of the positions on the bottom rung of our social system, followed by the real slaves of our society, immigrants.

I decided to go out alone. I wanted to see if the racism was real or if it was a figment of my imagination. I went to a popular restaurant that I often frequented. The only difference this night was that I was solo. The hosts standing near the entrance hawking for their commission turned away when they saw me. I could not get any of them to pay me any mind as I stood by the sign that read, "Wait here to be seated". No white friends with me tonight. They usually did not miss a step from the car to the table. They always got smiles and prompt service. When I arrived, the light-skinned maître D's pretended they did not see me. I was finally seated when one of them recognized me. There was an African beauty dancing her butt off. I grabbed her and we danced in the aisle. People danced in the aisles all the time. Security came and told us to stop. After I told him to "Fuck off." He left, but returned with more security. I stopped dancing, but held my partners hand, and pointed out all the whites dancing in the aisles with the whores who frequented this particular club on Monday night. One couple was only two feet away. Finally, I said, "Enough!" thanked my dance partner, and then returned to my table, which I had noticed, was in the black section. I experienced the same sensation that I had when I walked into a Denny's for a late meal after a night of bowling with relatives. The hostess walked us pass many open tables and through a partition. I noticed that on one part of the partition were all white and on the other were all colored. I sarcastically said, "What's this, the black section?" We were in the DC metropolitan area. Not two months afterward, FBI agents who had happen the same experience sued Denny's. My cousin brought an advertisement from the *Washington Post* asking for plaintiffs in the lawsuit to my attention. "We should join this." "Why Bryan, so that we can get money we did not earn?" He was quiet for a moment - thinking. "I got what I wanted: Denny's is on notice... I told you that night!"

A Frenchman who was sitting at the next table and understood English tried to explain why it happened. He said, "You were wild." He was referring to the way we were dancing. We stopped traffic! She could go! That is why I wanted to dance with her in the first place. That is why they stopped us and that is why I protested. By the end of conversation the Frenchman grabbed my wrist like I was his slave. He did because I refused to believe that racism does not exist and was attempting to walk away. He was attempting to restrain me. I looked at him like he had lost his mind. He did not respond. I pulled my arm away from him, but he did not let go, despite the fact he was seated and struggling to maintain his grip. I was shaking him in his seat. It was not until; I pointed out that he was the aggressor, and holding me hostage despite the fact that I could pound his sixty-year-old smaller than Napoleonic body (size does not matter) to dust, that he understood global racism. "Why are you holding my arm?" "I don't know... I'm sorry" "You should be! You did it because you thought you could!" That was the first night of confirmation. The next night ended in a police station.

I was pissed from the previous night's foray. "This can't be real!" The next night I chose the whitest club in town. I went to show my ass. How? By dancing well, I danced like my mother taught me, like the DC Black Repertory Company taught me. Why? Confirmation! I took over one of the three by three foot square dancing podiums and tried to rock the world. I prayed to my ancestors and my God for protection.

The first assault came pleasantly. An older gentleman asked me if his companion could sit on the square I was dancing on. I played ignorant, showed him my US passport and spoke English. "Hey, she can sit there… when I'm done dancing." That is probably the first time in his life a black male said "No" to him. As pleasant as my response was, he hated it. His facial expression went from a smile to an instant frown. Sometime later his companion sat down then proceeded to try to scoot me off the block by backing her ass across the platform inch by inch. I tapped a security guard on the shoulder and let him see what she was doing. The bouncer was "Negro". I glanced at the DJ every time he abruptly changed the music. I knew it was an attempt to get me off the podium, but I can dance to anything with a beat. I paused just long enough to feel it and then started dancing again, no matter what he played. When I stopped dancing and went to get a drink, while pointing to the podium I told the older gentleman, "You can have it now."

I did not ask anyone to dance. I danced alone. A six foot something boy fell on me deliberately. I saw them formulate the plan. The girl in the trio tried to stop them, but he just pulled away from her. Then he and his friend positioned themselves strategically in front of me and to my right. When he fell he acted like it was an accident. He then postured and when he saw no fear in my eyes, he tried to pat my head. Fuck that! I have been patted on the head before by "whites" and I know what it means, "Sorry Nigger!" When I squared my shoulders, blocked his forearm with my own, and then fingered "No", his smile turned to a frown. I was ready to throw blows now, but his friend intervened, apologizing for what they had done and why. That was after the US passport came out. "I am American. I don't put up with this shit!" The night ain't over….

I needed another drink. When I returned to the dance floor there was a group of seven guys waiting for me, boys really. They surrounded me when I began to dance again. I did a Michael Jackson, Prince, James Brown, Lil' Richard slide out of the middle of the circle they had formed and escaped. The leader looked at me with such distain and then led his troops from the field to reformulate. This night got so ugly I decided to push it further; I wanted to see. I went upstairs to the VIP area. The waiter who happened to of African descent, imagine that, the servants were "black", what has changed? He served my drink graciously. I was hungry and needed to feed the alcohol I had consumed, so I ordered my usual, fajitas. While waiting for my food, I noticed the other patrons did not appreciate my presence. The waiter told me I had to eat my food down stairs. "No! I want my food here." By the end of the night they would not even serve me my food and made me pay for it before I left. I was right, but against six 200 plus-pound security guards there is a way of making you wrong. That is how I ended up at the police station. No one can do that to me and expect nothing in retaliation; I felt like taking a flamethrower to the place. The police would not take the report until I came back the next day and insisted. They put guns in my face and used threatening voices. "No!" You are going to take this report!

"That's discrimination," is what they were saying by the time I left and had a typed letter of complaint. I went to the US Consulate. She was worthless. "What do you want me to do?" "Your job!" I then took the report to the local magistrate who told me, "I see no crime here". "You don't see a crime in my being forced to pay for food I did not get?" They did not want me to pursue the case. There was a crime and discrimination, but after visiting three other government agencies I realized that no one was going to support me because discrimination does not exist in Brazil just like racism does not exist in America.

Why is it that white actors whom receive an Oscar are elevated to instant stardom and receive huge contracts and numerous movie offers and their minority counterparts do not?

I try to laugh at those who think they are better than anyone else. Life will wake them up one day because, in truth, there is only one race. I have yet to read anything that separates anyone on the planet by more than thirty or forty thousand years - a pimple on the ass of the universe's fifteen billion years. Furthermore, there are African populations who are further apart from each other genetically than they are from white people[146].

Humans all share 99.9% of the same genes. Scientists at the Department of Energy have been working on the Human Genome Project[147] since 1990. They estimate humans have twenty to twenty-five thousand genes. If we take the number to be twenty five thousand, it means that the biggest difference between any two people is approximately 25 genes. It seems to me that racism is self-hate or better, the lack of self-love because we are the same. 25 genes are not enough to justify what we do to one another. "What's wrong with us?"

Speaking of the Genome Project, I recently received my results. I am from the Haplogroup B (Y-DNA). The marker M60 identifies me has Bantu. There is only one line from DNA Adam[148] to me. That means I am from the oldest living strand of Y-DNA on the planet. I am all for respecting your elders now... By seniority I claim my place.

FYI: There has not been an African-American elected by the people to the US Senate despite some the states having huge populations of African-Americans.

Drugs

Coca-Cola's magic ingredient was cocaine. Sigmund 'Fraud' was addicted to it. In 2002, 26.9% of the population of the United States were on painkillers, 23.8% were on antidepressants, 30.8% used tobacco and 68.6% of those eighteen or older used alcohol[149]. U.S. prescriptions for stimulants increased from around 5 million in 1991 to almost 35 million in 2007. Prescriptions for opioid painkillers such as oxycodone (OxyContin) and hydrocodone (Vicodin) increased from 40 million in 1991 to 180 million in 2007[150]. All of these are drugs. I guess it is not wrong to alter our perception of the world, if you have a prescription, or can find either a Starbuck's or a liquor store - or both.

FYI: The first drug addiction of the "New World" was tobacco.

---

[146] The Bantu of Western Africa and the! Kung of Southwestern Africa are examples.

[147] http://ornl.gov/sci/techresources/Human_Genome/home.shtml

[148] It is interesting that National Geographic calls my ancestor "Eurasian Adam" even though he is from eastern Africa.

[149] National Institute of Mental Health.

[150] http://www.mayoclinic.com/print/prescription-drug-abuse/DS01079/METHOD=print&DSECTION=all

Marijuana, cocaine and opiates are considered the illicit drugs. It does not matter that the last US President and Vice President, and the current President smoked marijuana. How many people have not? Is the drug issue another illusion? There is another bumper crop of opium in Afghanistan. If I wanted to stop the drug trade that might not be a bad spot to start, considering it supplies about 90% of the world's need, but we would upset the warlords who are profiting from the enterprise and are supposedly helping "US" in the war on terror. How long have we been there? Columbia is also our ally and so is Bolivia.

Are the illicit drugs any more harmful than the legal ones? If so, why are we allowed to prescribe children drugs that may drive them to suicide? Did you know what the best selling prescription drug is Hydrocodone? These are opiate-based painkillers - synthetic opium. Opioid analgesics, also known as narcotic analgesics, are pain relievers that act on the central nervous system and like all narcotics they may become habit forming if used over long periods. America is popping them like jellybeans. What hurts so much? I am going to have to ask Rush Limbaugh.

The Unites States is the largest user of drugs on the planet. So many people are doing drugs that I am forced to think that no one should be pointing fingers over drugs of choice. According to the Partnership for a Drug-Free America, twenty percent of teens have tried pain relievers[151] for non medical reasons. What is worse is that the source of the drugs is not some shady drug dealer on a corner; they frequently come from their parents' medicine cabinets or were prescribed by Dr. Feel Good, MD.

FYI: I consider food a drug. Food addicts are everywhere in the United States; 75% of us are overweight.

Even the CIA has changed its hiring policy as it relates to drug use. I remember when admitting using any drugs was an automatic disqualifier. Now, they require that you have not done drugs within the last 12 months. What does tell you about drug usage?

If you really want to know about drugs, and who are the addicts and big time dealers, reference the National Center for Health Statistics report that finds more than 40% of Americans take at least one prescription drug and 17% take three or more. Look at the people being admitted to the Betty Ford Clinic. Prescription drugs account for about 10% of the nation's total medical bill. Grown men are willing to risk heart attacks and blindness to get a hard on. I guess sex is a stronger motive than sight or a longer life. Look into the opium wars of China, the poppy fields of Afghanistan, go to the library and research the history of tobacco, steroids, marijuana, cocaine, LSD, speed, Manuel Noriega[152], Iran-Contra, the CIA, and The Central Bank of Panama.

In 1989 the Senate Foreign Relations Committee investigated whether the CIA was involved in drug trafficking in relation to Nicaragua and the Contras. Senator John Kerry (D-MA), Chairman of that sub-Committee, said, "There is no question in my mind that people affiliated with, or on the payroll of the CIA were involved in drug trafficking while involved in support of

---

[151] Vicodin, OxyContin, and Tylox.
[152] Manuel Noriega: Panamanian general and military leader of Panama (1983-1989). Graduate of the School of Americas and reportedly a benefactor of the CIA as far back as 1966.

the Contras..."[153]. In 1998 the House of Representatives (Maxine Waters, D-California) revealed the following memorandum: "the CIA and Attorney General William French Smith had an agreement that the CIA was not required to report allegations of drug smuggling by non-employees. 'Non-employees' was explicitly interpreted to include unpaid and paid assets of the CIA, such as pilots and informants. The memorandum dated February 11, 1982 states, 'no formal requirement regarding the reporting of narcotics violations has been included in these procedures.' referring to the procedures relating to non-employee crimes."[154] This memorandum allowed the CIA from 1982 onward to associate with known drug dealers without having to report their transactions to anyone. Also, this memorandum referred only to operations in Nicaragua (cocaine) and Afghanistan (opium). Smoking gun or not, I know the CIA did/do have a hand in drug dealing. Drug trafficking is an open checkbook without Congressional controls or any real oversight. Remember that huge crops of poppies coming from Afghanistan since the US military's arrival. We will never stop drug use until we do not need them anymore; and the feel good trade is just too profitable, but "If you lie with dogs, you are bound to get fleas."

FYI: The journalist who first reported the "Frogmen" incident that started the investigations into the drug smuggling by the CIA and the Contras, Gary Webb[155], died from "two" gunshot wounds to the head. It was ruled a suicide. How do you shot yourself in the head twice?

The moment we can stop eating when we are not hungry anymore it is a step forward. At the moment we cannot stop drinking, smoking, injecting, swallowing, excusing and playing video games, or whatever we do to distract ourselves. At the moment we put our personal crack pipes down we gain some freedom and peace.

Teaching of Creation

Many people have issue with Christian conservatives who want to teach an alternate theory to evolution. The Christians would like to have the story of Genesis presented in public schools. There is a wave of Creationism that is sweeping the country. The Supreme Court ruled that teaching Creationism is unconstitutional. Yet, there are groups who are campaigning to have it taught in schools despite this. In 1925 John T. Scopes, a teacher in Dayton, Tennessee, went through the famous "Monkey Trial" for teaching evolution and defying Tennessee's Butler Act. He was found guilty and fined $100.00, which the ACLU offered to pay. The fine was over turned on a technicality; the judge instead of the jury issued the fine. The Butler Act was repealed in 1967.

Personally I see nothing wrong with teaching alternative views to evolution. They only give other perspectives. Every religion and culture has a story about how it all began. Different societies have other stories that can be added to the mass of tales. I would teach all of these forms of Creationism. We would not want to bias children.

The proponents of creationism say they want alternative theories (plural) taught, but in reality they mean "one" alternate theory, Genesis. No one has the right to force their version of God on

---

[153] http://www.pbs.org/newshour/forum/october96/crack_contra_11-1.html.
[154] http://www.vcsun.org/%7Ebattias/cia/980507.cr.txt.
[155] http://en.wikipedia.org/wiki/Gary_Webb

anyone, especially children. They are as connected to God as we were at that age. If you want your child to know the Bible, teach at home, or better in the park or at the beach.

Terrorism

Terrorism is defined as the use of terror especially as a means of coercion especially as a political weapon or policy. By that definition, I am a terrorist and I could place a terrorist sticker on most individuals and civilizations that have ever existed. Terrorism has been around for centuries, depending on the situation and who is doing the labeling. I have used intimidation and other techniques that generate fear in order to influence behavior, so have the KKK and both national political parties.

On July 8, 1853 a squadron of four ships led by USS *Powhatan* and commanded by Commodore Matthew Perry[156], anchored at Edo Bay (Tokyo). They were not invited and were there to secure a trade treaty. After being refused, Perry destroyed several buildings in the harbor with naval gunfire. We used intimidation to open the ports of Japan to our trading fleets.

Teddy Roosevelt used warships to intimidate the locals in order to build the Panama Canal. The established power base used, and are still using, intimidation in many forms (literacy tests, night rides, etc.) to stop African-American voter registration. The only difference I see between Teddy Roosevelt's "Gunboat Diplomacy[157]", George Bush's Dubya-plomacy and "Terrorism" is the amount of profit involved and the justification.

The United States once started a war over terrorism. The USS Maine exploded in the middle of the night in Havana Harbor in 1898. They did not know what happened, but the investigation reported it was likely a Spanish mine. It was not. Naval investigators have recently determined that it was most probably a coal dust explosion. However, William Randolph Hearst[158] used the *New York Journal* to instigate and manipulate popular opinion by lying about what happened. He was quoted as saying, "You supply the pictures and I'll supply the war," to one of his photographers on assignment in Cuba who wanted to come home because there was no revolution or civil unrest occurring. Americans were outraged at the loss of 254 sailors and eventually went to war over a lie. But, look on the bright side; we got Guantanamo Bay and other territories, like the Philippines and other Pacific islands out of the deal effectively securing our place among the other empires of the world. The locals greeted us as liberators until they realized that we were not leaving. Then we had to fight the Filipinos for years in what we called the "Philippine Insurrection". "Remember the Maine" indeed. "Remember the Twin Towers" as well.

The Irgun, the Haganah and the Stern Group[159] were all terrorist by today's standards. Yet, Menachem Begin[160], a commander in the Irgun organization, became the sixth Prime Minister of

---

[156] Matthew Calbraith Perry (1794-1858): Commodore of the United States Navy who forced the opening of Japanese ports to the West with the Convention of Kanagawa in 1854, under the threat of military force.
[157] Gunboat Diplomacy or Big stick Ideology: "I walk softly, but carry a big stick." Comes from an African proverb.
[158] William Randolph Hearst (1863-1951) American newspaper mogul and publisher.
[159] The Stern Group: Zionist group later known as Lehi founded by Avraham Stern (1907-1942).
[160] Menachem Begin (1913-1992): the sixth prime minister of the State of Israel.

Israel. He organized the bombing of the King David Hotel where 91 people were killed. David Ben-Gurion[161], Israel's first Prime Minister and a member of the Haganah, knew about the plan. Yitzhak Rabin[162], the fifth Prime Minister and Ariel Sharon[163], the eleventh, were also members of Haganah. Yitzhak Shamir[164], the seventh Prime Minister was a member of Irgun. Even Golda Meir[165], the only female Prime Minister, was a member of Histadrut and ordered retaliation for the Munich incident, "Operation Wrath of God"[166] in 1972. These people were involved in guerilla warfare or terrorism, depending upon who is telling the tale, and are considered heroes today in Israel. In 1973 Mossad agents killed an innocent male, Ahmed Bouchiki, in Norway. It was a case of mistaken identity. Five agents were convicted of murder, but released two years later. How can we label anyone as a terrorist when these individuals are admitted murderers of civilians, yet have been able to rise to world prominence? I think we have given Israel three billion dollars per year for at least 25 years. The total population of Israel is estimated at 6.2 million. That equates to $484.00 per person. Why? The total aid from the United States to the entire continent of Africa was just over three billion USD last year for about ninety million people. That equates to $3.33 per person. There is something very wrong with us and for many it starts with skin color. For the record and detractors, I am not Mel Gibson; the truth is the truth.

The African National Congress (ANC) were considered terrorist, yet Nelson Mandela is a hero. I know it is universally thought that the indigenous South Africans were right, but their violence settled nothing. It was peaceful movements, knowledge and economic pressure that finally broke the back of Apartheid, not revolutionary acts that took lives.

A tyrannical minority can only hold down the majority so long and a tyrannical majority turns on itself sooner or later.

Libyan leader Moammar Gadhafi capitulated to the demands of the United States after years of giving the West the finger. He is a terrorist and has supported terrorism for years. Why would he change his spots? The 2003 fall of Saddam's regime awakened him to the possibility of what could happen in his country, and to his regime. In early 2004, Libya relinquished its nuclear parts and documents pertaining to weapons of mass destruction. Libya also provided intelligence on Pakistan's Dr. Doom, Abdul Qadeer Khan[167], who was instrumental in catapulting Pakistan into the nuclear age. Dr. Khan confessed to being involved with a network of nuclear weapons technology sales to Libya, Iran and North Korea. The former President of Pakistan, General Musharraf, pardoned Dr. Khan. United States intelligence agents could not question him about the matter. Is Pakistan really an ally in the war on terror?

A Libyan intelligence agent was convicted of planting the bomb that downed Pam Am Flight 103. That flight exploded over Lockerbie, Scotland, and killed 270 people in 1988. Gadhafi's

---

[161] David Ben-Gurion (1886-1973): the first prime minister of Israel.
[162] Yitzhak Rabin (1922-1995): the fifth prime minister of Israel. Assassinated in 1995.
[163] Ariel Sharon (1928-) the eleventh prime minister of Israel. Suffered an incapacitating stroke in 2006.
[164] Yitzhak Shamir (1915-): the seventh prime minister of Israel 1983 to 1984 and from 1986 to 1992.
[165] Golda Meir aka Golda Myerson (1898-1978): the fourth prime minister of Israel.
[166] Covert operation carried out by the Mossad (Israeli Intelligence) to assassinate everyone in Black September involved with the deaths of 11 Israeli athletes killed during the 1972 Munich Olympics.
[167] Abdul Qadeer Khan (1936-) Pakistani engineer and nuclear scientist known as the founder of Pakistan's nuclear program.

government agreed to pay $2.7 billion to the victims' families. I guess it is acceptable to kill if one can pay a million dollars per person. Because of Libya's cooperation the United States ended 18 years of trade embargoes and the United States is restoring full diplomatic relations. After 27 years, Libya was removed from the list of states that sponsor terrorism. I questioned why the sudden reversal by both parties until I realized that Libya is the 12ᵗʰ largest producer of oil in the world.

"It seems in today's world the power to absolve debt is greater than the power of forgiveness".
Archbishop Gilday, the Godfather Part III.

Luis Posada Carriles was in the custody of US Immigration. He is an admitted terrorist who was trained for the Bay of Pigs by the CIA. He was also a former member of the US Army. The Justice Department made the following statement about Carriles: "Luis Posada Carriles is an admitted mastermind of terrorist plots and attacks. The Department of Justice believes that Posada is a flight risk and that his release would be a danger to the community...."[168] Carriles has admitted that he waged a campaign of bombings and assassination attempts in a series of New York Times Articles[169]. Carriles said the Cuban-American National Foundation, an influential lobbying group, supported him financially. Carriles was also a CIA operative who worked with Oliver North to illegally supply weapons to the Contras of Nicaragua. This was after he relayed information to the CIA that he and his compatriots were planning to bomb civilian airliners[170]. 73 people died on October 6, 1976 in the one attempt that was successful. Posada was jailed in Venezuela, but escaped in 1985. He was arrested again in 2000 by the Panamanian government for plotting the assignation of Fidel Castro during a summit. He was pardoned by the Panamanian President in 2004 and then made his way to the USA. Venezuela has requested Posada be extradited, but a US immigration judge denied the request because he thought that he would be tortured. Double standards like this muddy the water in the ongoing war on <u>some</u> terrorist. I guess he must be a "good" (useful) terrorist or a freedom fighter.

A warning and a prediction: fear is a double-edged sword. The human body is programmed to fight or flee. If it runs, it runs fast and hard. If it decides to fight, it will fight for its very survival. I sincerely hope people take care and remember to bring their lunches if a scared anything decides to turn around and fight, because a cornered animal is the most dangerous animal of all. Victory does not always go to the strongest, the best, or the most righteous.

If the insurgents in Iraq were in their "final death throes" as Dick Cheney said in May of 2005, why are we still fighting them? It must take a long time for an insurgent to die.

---

[168] http://www.usdoj.gov/opa/pr/2006/October/06_ag_681.html.
[169] http://select.nytimes.com/gst/abstract.html?res=F00B16F73E550C718DDDAE0894D0494D81
[170] http://www.gwu.edu/~nsarchiv/NSAEBB/NSAEBB202/19761105.pdf

Immigration

Give me your tired, your poor, Your huddled masses yearning to breathe free, The wretched refuse of your teeming shore. Send these, the homeless, tempest-tossed, to me: I lift my lamp beside the golden door. The New Colossus by Emma Lazarus appears at the base of the Statue of Liberty.

Years ago I saw an editorial cartoon that showed an American male saying, "I wish all these immigrants would go home." Standing beside him was an Aboriginal-American with a suitcase in his hand who replied, "I'll help you pack."

This is not a new issue. America has discriminated against many immigrants. It seems people like to blame everyone, but its leadership and itself, for their ills. In 1921 the Immigration Bill, which was designed to maintain the "character" of the United States, passed. By "character" I think they meant a European-Christian majority. The National Origins Act of 1924 established immigration quotas according to the national origins system. In 1929 the act was revised to allow 70% of admissions to come from Northern and Western Europe, while the other 30% was reserved for those coming from Southern and Eastern Europe. This law severely restricted immigration by establishing a system that blatantly discriminated against immigrants from countries like Italy, Greece, Serbia, Poland, Russia, Yugoslavia, Bulgaria, Spain, Romania and Turkey, and virtually excluded Asians and Africans who were considered inferior races. It also left the southern US border open for the cheap labor of Latinos. I always wondered why the Statue of Liberty pointed toward Western Europe. The policy stayed in effect until 1965. The McCarran-Walter Act of 1952 consolidated earlier immigration laws and removed race as a basis for exclusion, but added an ideological criteria for admission. Immigrants and visitors could now be denied entry on the basis of their political views (more Cold War crap).

The Chinese in California faced horribly unfair legislation. The Anti-Coolie Act in 1862 passed because white unions lobbied successfully to severely cut Chinese migration, but then the Central Pacific Railroad needed thousands of Chinese workers to help it build its section of the transcontinental railroad[171]. The Chinese routinely outpaced their white counter parts.

The Irish and Catholics faced discrimination as well, especially during the *Know Nothing Movement* of the 1850's. 110 years later, we had an Irish-Catholic President, who is arguably one of the most popular Presidents ever.

Mexicans have been brutalized by Americans for some time. The American settlers "immigrated" to Texas, California, Colorado, New Mexico and Arizona. Under the ideology of Manifest Destiny the United States first tried to buy, and then used force to obtain these territories. In 1885 Ulysses S. Grant[172] called the Mexican-American War, "…the most unjust

---

[171] Central Pacific Railroad Company started from Sacramento in 1863. In two years they only laid 50 miles of track. There was a labor shortage because of the gold rush. In 1865 the first Chinese were brought in for $27 per month, while the Irish were paid $35 per month. If it were not for the Chinese, the railroad would not been finished in 1869.

[172] Ulysses S. Grant (born Hiram Ulysses Grant) (1822-1885): 18th President of the United States (1869-1877). General-in-Chief of the Union Army during the American Civil War.

war ever waged by a stronger against a weaker nation . . . a republic following the bad example of European monarchies." I wonder what he would have said about Iraq. The Mexicans have been second class citizens in those areas since.

I have heard many say of African-Americans, "If you don't like it, why don't you go back to Africa?" We did not immigrate to the United States; we got forced passage as cargo and still there is prejudice against us as well. Besides, what am I going to do in Africa? Where should I settle to be with my ancestors? My people were taken, much like the Jews by the Babylonians. But, I do not even know where my African roots are. I can guess they lie in western Africa, but which country, which tribe? What about my other ancestry? Would I be welcomed as a citizen in Scotland, Portugal, China, or Germany?

I once saw a guy wearing a T-shirt that read: "If I knew it would be this much trouble, I would have picked my own damn cotton." Of course, I was in the South when I saw this. I could not help but think, "No, you would not have. You would have used Mexicans, Indians or other indentured servants."

Now America is up in arms about "illegals" again. I do not think it is about illegals. I do think it is about illegal Latinos. Americans have historically frowned upon the immigration of non-whites, and those they consider to be inferior whites, unless of course there is a need for inexpensive labor or fighting men. Mexicans, illegal or no, have been welcome in the border states for years because it meant cheap labor. That was until the Great Depression of 1929 when jobs and resources became scarce. During the 1930s anti-immigrant campaign, Mexicans and Mexican-born Americans were deported in mass and denied employment throughout the Southwestern United States. The same thing is happening now; the economy must not be as good as we are being told, and history does repeat itself if we let it. People throughout history have always turned on minority groups in times of scarcity or turmoil. The problem arises because majorities want to remain majorities, and become very uncomfortable when some other ethnic group challenges their dominance over a society or culture.

The illegal alien problem is easy to fix. Stop hiring illegals. It will remove the impetus to migrate. But that would mean that someone else would have to pick fruit and vegetables; nannies and aupairs would have to be paid on an American scale; we would have to do our own landscaping; construction companies would no longer be able to pick-up day laborers; and many well off households would have to do their own cooking and cleaning. Even former President Bush was on the fence because of this issue. He wanted to support the likes of Wal-Mart[173] and Mc Donald's[174], but Middle America and border state bases were pissed. What to do?

FYI: The former President Bush's first nominee for the head of Homeland Security, Bernard B. Kerik, had an illegal domestic worker in his employ when he was nominated. How embarrassing is that? He is going to serve time himself for tax evasion and lying to the White House.

---

[173] Wal-Mart gave $467K, 97% of the contributions went to Republicans during the 2004 elections.
[174] Mc Donald's Corporation gave $197K, 86% of the contributions went to Republicans during the 2004 elections.

What does one have to do to be accepted in the United States without prejudice from the majority: be blond, blue eyed and Christian? There is one world and one race. Besides, if we keep killing the planet, animals and each other at the rate we are going, we will not have to worry about keeping America white - Save the Humans.

Even now there are non-citizens fighting in the United States military. Will anyone want to displace them after their service or will we treat them like we did many of the Aboriginal-American scouts who helped in the battles against their own kind? The United States disarmed them and then placed them on the same reservations as the hostiles.

FYI: Almost 20% of the Medal of Honor recipients were immigrants.

Traveling

Mohammad[175] once said, "Do not tell me how educated you are. Do not tell me what you do for living. Tell me how much you have traveled and I will tell you how much you know."

If you want to shock your sense of reality, and wrong and right, traveling is the ticket. I do not mean acting like the typical "Ugly American" tourist. I am referring to the willingness to immerse in another culture and learn to speak the language. Resocialize yourself. It will open up your mind to a different way of living and thinking, no matter where you decide to go or how you decide to travel.

Every male in the United States should leave the country (without the company of a female) before he decides to get married. Different cultures have very different views on male-female interaction. After experiencing some of these interactions firsthand, I could better understand the American mating ritual and see through the veil of inequality. I have learned this. A friend and occasional lover once told me that I was dangerous. She said, "You burn women." I replied, "That is true, but it is a dry heat". We both had to laugh.

Elizabeth was a cutie I met on the beach. It was my first time in this country thanks to my mentor. I was young and had a fist full of dollars. I had to be one of the youngest members of the group. He was the HNiC[176], roughly translated: CEO of the tour group. They were a group of artists. I immediately disassociated with them and, as usual, went my own way.

I ended up associating with the younger people who, like me, smoked and wanted to party. I bartered with a Rasta on the beach. I traded a biker cap for what looked like a $20 bag. We met some other Americans who had been living in the country for some time. They led us to a secluded beach to the north of the city. That is where I met Elizabeth. She was a natural beauty. Her sun-bleached hair was all over her head. It looked like a lion's mane, but was very attractive. She also had that natural Latin femininity and grace. I had to stumble through the communication barrier. I invited her to come to the hotel that night and gave her the equivalent of $5 US for transportation.

---

[175]Mohammad "the praised one" (570-632): Generally considered the Prophet who founded Islam.
[176] HNiC: Head Nigga in Charge.

I bought a fifth of rum, had Rasta weed and a date. Who could ask for more? When Elizabeth came to the hotel, we went to dinner and took in the festivities. This was my first experience with a foreigner. She insisted on ironing my clothes, which I did not let her do, and feeding me, which I definitely put a halt to. I did not want a slave; I wanted sex and nothing more.

She was raised to perform these duties much like some Southern women, and most women in the United States before World War II. If I had known then, what I know now, I would not have coupled with her. I do not think she was used to being treated well, or being seduced in the manner Western women are accustomed. I knew that she was not used to having things in abundance; she smoked and drank herself sick, and then she insisted that I give her one of the swimsuits I had bought for my mother and sister. As she slept off the affects, I sat there mad as hell. She eventually came to and wanted to have sex. I asked her to brush her teeth.

I remember the way her bottom felt. It was soft, but not flabby. It reminded me of a roll fresh from the oven. I wished I spoke the language or rather understood it. I wanted to know what she was murmuring during the act. The sex was very good. On a scale from one to ten, foreign country, tropical atmosphere, exotic woman and my youth factor considered, she was an 8 ½. It was late and she wanted to spend the night. I had no issue with it, but there was one problem, I had a gay roommate. It was a free trip; what could I say?

In the middle of the night, she woke me up with the best oral sex I had experienced to that date, but my roommate woke up and broke up the festivities. He said he was uncomfortable with her in the room. Do not get me wrong; I do not have a sexually prejudiced bone. I would be a hypocrite if I discriminated. If he wanted to have sex with a male, that was his choice, but do not hate on me for liking women, or interrupt me when I have my penis in a girl's mouth. I would be mad at anyone who protested at that moment. Just lie there and pretend to be sleep or watch; we can talk about it in the morning or after I come, whichever happens last.

Simply having more experiences with different types of people will, or rather should, have an effect on our perspectives. I am thankful that I had the opportunity to live in other parts of the United States and around the world. I am also thankful for being able to visit different places. Traveling exposed me to the extremes in culture not only in other countries, but also within my own. You can see it in your own communities. Go to the ghetto, Chinatown, Korea town or the barrio, and then go to the suburbs or uptown where the affluent live. Exposure has allowed me to see that people, minus socialization and money, are the same no matter who, what or where they are. Most of the time, I found that what I have learned often contradicts what was portrayed as real.

My plan is to continue to travel. The ancient ruins of Babylon and Turkey, the River Ganges, the monasteries of Tibet, Iye Ife in Nigeria, the Masi Mara of Kenya, the holy sites of Jerusalem and Mecca, Cuba, Thebes, the National Parks and people of South Africa are all on my list. I am sure that I will find that the people in these areas are just like me. I am sure that I will find people who want to be happy without having to sacrifice freedom to obtain it; and I am sure I will find people who are as afraid of change and perceived differences as we are.

If you ever get a chance to go somewhere else do not hesitate or come up with reasons why you cannot do it, just go. Do not let the fear of the unknown or skeptics divert you. The worst that can happen is that you will learn something.

Outside the Box

Great people live "outside of the box". They are the individuals who can see things from multiple angles and they are often able to find very simple solutions to the most complex of issues. The bravest people I have ever seen are those who take a stand for change against all odds and survive the trial. Those who do not survive are martyrs. They take a considerable risk. There is the risk of being scorned, ridiculed and even killed. Jesus was crucified. Gandhi[177], JFK[178], Malcolm X[179], Medgar Evers[180], Martin Luther King[181] and a host of others were all assassinated for going against someone's grain. Mandela[182] and many others have been tortured and jailed for their views. Geronimo[183], Sitting Bull[184], and other leaders have fought to preserve their way of life against the tyranny of the majority. At the time, they were portrayed as savages. They were not savages; they were just different. I would fight invaders as well and I hope you would too. If come in my yard, I would do everything in my power to evict you. Today that would mean calling the authorities, but what if the authorities are the ones trespassing. They already listen to our phones and have access to our e-mail without warrants.

Socrates was made to drink hemlock because his views were so controversial, even though the Oracle at Delphi[185] pronounced him the wisest male in Greece. Galileo[186] was imprisoned and tortured for hierarchy (the crime of heresy was defined as a deliberate denial of an article of truth of the Catholic faith and a public and obstinate persistence in that alleged error.) because he proved the Earth and the rest of the planets revolved around the sun, when the church's view was that the Earth was the center of the Universe (thank goodness the church is not running our government today, or is it?). He, of course was *right* to a certain extent, but when does being right matter when you are a minority voice?

---

[177] Mohandas Karamchand Gandhi or Mahatma Gandhi (1869-1948): leader in India's fight for independence from British Colonial rule. Famous for his philosophy of nonviolence. Nominated five times for the Noble Peace Prize. Assassinated.

[178] John Fitzgerald Kennedy (1917-1963): 35th President of the United States (1961-1963). Assassinated.

[179] Malcolm X, Malcolm Little, Detroit Red, El-Hajj Malik El-Shabazz and Omowale (1925-1965): Spokesman for the Nation of Islam. Founder of the Muslim Mosque, Inc. and the Organization of Afro-American Unity. Assassinated.

[180] Medgar Evers (1925-1963): Civil rights activist in Mississippi. Assassinated.

[181] Martin Luther King (1929-1968)): Nobel Laureate, Minister and Civil Rights activist. Assassinated.

[182] Nelson Rohihlahla Mandela: First democratically elected President of South Africa. Anti-Apartheid activist and freedom fighter.

[183] Geronimo or Goyathlay (1829-1909): Aboriginal American leader of the Chiricahua Apache. Warred against the encroachment of settlers of European descent on tribal lands.

[184] Sitting Bull, Tatanka Iyotake or Tatanka Iyotanka orTa-Tanka I-Yotank, born Hunkesni, (1831-1890): Sioux Warrior, Shaman and leader of the Hunkpap.Led 3,500 Sioux and Cheyenne warriors against the United States 7th Cavalry and General Custer. At the Battle of the Little Bighorn. Assassinated.

[185] Oracle at Delphi: Greek Priestess presiding over the Apollonian Oracle at Delphi.

[186] Galileo Galilei (1564-1642): Italian mathematician, astronomer, physicist, and philosopher. Supported heliocentrism contradictory to scriptors.

I remember an episode from my youth where I felt like Copernicus. A thunderstorm was approaching. You could hear the thunder and see the lighting. We happened to be in my great-grandmother's home at the time. They had recently purchased a new television with a remote control. I was examining the remote because though I had seen them before, this was the first time I had an opportunity to handle one. I was curious about how they worked. My great-grandmother told me to put the remote down because my holding it was causing the static on the television. I knew already it was not about the remote. It was about my touching something that she did not want me to touch for her own reasons.

I kept a clandestine eye on her as she watched me examining the remote. "Put that down!" "I am just looking at it." I was very careful not to touch any of the buttons. She was watching me like a hawk. To test my theory that my great-grandmother was a mean old bitch, I touched the buttons without depressing them; I just stroked them lightly. That was enough for her. She went off the deep end, yelling and getting very excited over a remote. I thought she was crazy, maybe she was, but if so, she was that way all of my life, and before.

I tried to explain to her that the static on the television was caused by the electro-magnetic interference of the lighting. My great-grandmother was half-white and looked white. She openly showed favoritism towards her lighter children, grands and greats. My grandmother, though light enough, was on her shit list and so by association so were my mother, brother and I. Some could get away with murder and others could not blow their nose without an ear beating, or her raising her voice and cane. I was slippery enough and light enough to walk the line, but the "darkies" caught bloody hell.

I cannot remember what she said to me, but it was not nice. It was too much for a child of 12. I responded in kind with, "You old battle axe!" She shut up. There was a quiet in the room like, "No he did not." Can you hear that pin dropping? "Oh shit! What is wrong with you?" my inner voice asked. "It slipped." "No it did not. We are in trouble now!!!" "I know."

My grandfather turned three different shades of red. He was not faking this time, but he was old and he was easily restrained with words. Secretly there were those who witnessed this event that were glad I said what they had wanted to for years. I was ear beaten for that, but it was worth it. She pretty much left me alone after that, and I, in turn, gave her a wide berth for the rest of her life. I must be destined for a long life.

My grandfather, my grandaunt and others in the house told me in not so nice words how wrong I was. I shut down and let them have at me. They used words to hurt, but verbal abuse is better than throwing blows. It hurt; everyone saw what had happened, but loyalty and respect outweigh right or wrong. The rule says that adults may speak to children anyway they like, but children are not supposed to respond. Animals attack when cornered. I went outside on the front porch to cool down. One of my cousins came out later and tried to explain why we are supposed to let elderly people be right and how important it was to respect them. I remember thinking how uneducated and ignorant they all were. I was right, but she was the matriarch. I kept thinking about what my cousin said for weeks. It made me question, "If she's so right all the time, how was I able to play her?"

114

If you hold a view that is different from the majority and let it be known to others, right or wrong and regardless of who the others are (family, friends, government, etc…), you will suffer the ramifications of being on a path of your own choosing and having another point of view. Ask Mohamed Ali about his decision not to be drafted to fight the "Yellow Man" or his decision to become a Muslim. He is fortunate that he had the resources to withstand the assault. He is also fortunate that promoters with political influence and money still had use of him or he would have gone to jail. Ask Jack Johnson[187] or Michael Vick. Ask Elvis about his early struggles for playing "Nigger" music and gyrating his hips. Ask Russell Simmons[188] about Hip-Hop's gangster reputation. He will tell you, "We have a gangster government"[189] Ask Christopher Columbus[190] about the children who threw stones at him in the streets because everyone thought he was crazy. It took him years to gather support and financing.

Try disagreeing even with anyone, alone or in a group setting. If you do not relent, the issue may escalate into an argument. If we cannot get along individually, what makes anyone think we can have global peace? I am not saying that we should agree on all things. I am saying that we do not like being opposed by any voice. I have almost always been in environments where I was the racial, social or political minority. I have stood up and been shot down many times, but I still agree with William Earnest Henley[191]: *No matter how straight the gate or how charged with punishment the scroll, I am (be the) master of your fate and the captain of my (your) soul.*

Regardless of the personal cost, we must climb our individual mountains and see what is at the summit. We have to face our fears. Everyone will pay a price when deciding to take a stand and be different from others. We must all understand the fact that we will become the target of those who do not wish to see our truth; it hurts too much to be wrong or see someone brave enough to do what he or she individually thinks is right. Keats[192] wrote, "Truth is beauty and beauty is truth". If this is true, why do we hate the truth so much? I think the human animal hates to see its self for what it is, and for what it could be.

Making Choices

Human life is full of decisions, including significant choices about what to believe. Although everyone prefers to believe what is true, we often disagree with each other about what that is in particular instances. It may be that some of our most fundamental convictions in life are acquired by haphazard means rather than by the use of reason, but we all recognize that our beliefs about ourselves and the world often hang together in important ways. Garth Kemerling[193]

When I was pledging one of my line brothers dropped off line on the way to a beat down. The rest of us decided to continue without him. We had all ready lost one of our comrades on the

---

[187]Jack Johnson aka John Arthur Johnson (1878-1946): First African-American Heavyweight Champion of the World (1908-1915).
[188]Russell Simmons or Rush: Entrepreneur. Co-founder of Def Jam.
[189] Said during a C-Span interview.
[190] Christopher Columbus or Cristoforo Colombo (1451-1506): Explorer and trader. First to cross the Atlantic ocean is modern times.
[191] William Ernest Henley (1849-1903): English poet, playwright and editor. The ending of the poem *Invictus*.
[192]John Keats (1795-1821): English poet. Key element in the Romantic Movement.
[193]Garth Kemerling: Author of www.philosophypages.com.

first day. It is interesting and scary that afterwards the young man dropped out of school. We were jogging in step to our destination when John stopped. He convinced us that we had to go back and retrieve this brother from the woman he was in bed with who did not want him to finish the trials. His father had done it. He paid money and wrote letters. He spent long hours practicing steps and studying hymns, poetry and history. John convinced us of that. We have a choice whether or not we leave someone behind. I saw it in a mother wildebeest that I write about in the "Survival Instinct" section of this chapter. Do not ever give up on anything you start.

I believe we make choices that we judge to be right or wrong the moment we make them. I say this because I can feel it when I do it; there is a questioning. Social pressures have an enormous influence on our choices. Politicians carefully tailor their speeches based on the target audience. On the same day a candidate may give a speech in California and another one in Montana, but you can bet that the two speeches will be different. The candidate may address some of the same points, but his or her main focus will be tailored to the social interests of those he or she is addressing, jaw-jacking.

Societies shape our choices by first introducing us to standards and normality at an early age; then society uses social pressure to help enforce this normality. Newspapers, prison, television, history, judicial systems, music, schools, laws, religion and even science have been used as propaganda to shape the way societies think. They establish social normality and help ensure it is reinforced.

I remember walking home with a group of guys from a Go-Go concert[194]. Someone in the group saw a boy walking alone. Our leader, a guy I did not know before that night, suggested that we rob him. I did not want anything to do with it, but I did not want to seem weak either. We were approximately a 100 feet away from him when the decision was made. I picked up a glass bottle and threw it at our target. It exploded on the curve not five feet from him. He was startled, but he did not run like I wanted him to. He waited until we were on top of him, too late. I watched as the group asked him if he had any money and then someone tried to take his ring off his finger. He bolted and no one gave chase. Our leader later criticized me for throwing the bottle, but I did not care. I made up an excuse. Secretly, I was relieved the guy got away. It did not feel right, but I did not have the moral courage to stand up for what I knew was wrong. Peer pressure is a bitch.

Thinking is the most productive form of physical fitness.

How many of our choices can we really make? Many of the big choices in life have pretty much been made for us. We are supposed to go to school, get a job, get married to someone of the opposite sex (sometimes we repeat this process more than once), have children and raise them in a socially accepted manner. After this we are allowed to go to pasture on Social Security and finally die. Few of us rebel against this intrusion. It does not seem like freedom to me. I guess that is why I have never married and have no children. I am not free yet and I will not bring a child into bondage.

---

[194] Go-Go: sub-form Funk music invented in Washington DC in the late 1970's.

Many times our designed experience is intertwined with the designs of others. This means that it was in our design to share the same experience; it also means that others can have an influence on our choices or possibly have the same wishes and desires. Others can also distract us from our immediate goals or interfere with the choice that seems right for us at the time. Have you ever done something that did not feel right because of someone else (think of peer pressure)?

When decisions must be made, I try to go with what feels good at the time. When I say "Good", I mean inside, not what appeals to my eye or my appetites. Unfortunately I am not always successful. I am still making some of the same mistakes my forbearers did because they have passed on what they have learned to me. I occasionally back slide and revert to thinking as they did and not for myself. Also, I still find myself giving in to of instant gratification.

Many of my choices are, and have been, directly connected to the amount of gratification I expected to receive from my actions. Gratification can be anything and is as individual as our choices. Affection, money, praise, food, sex (my biggie) or attention can all be classified as gratifying. I think when confronted with decisions we have two roads: one choice is easy and one is hard. It is easier to choose a path along the lines of the majority, whether or not we agree. It feels good and natural to be among the crowd, but what do you do when you are alone?

I have also come to realize that I get a great deal of satisfaction from giving to others and receiving recognition for a job well done. That is primarily what motivates me (I am not referring to the pat on the back bullshit one gets from an employer. Many management classes teach how to motivate employees with words of praise. I say, "Keep the praise and give me some of the CEO's salary"). I like nothing more than doing my best and having someone else confirm that I did what was appropriate. The same is true when people sincerely say thank you to me for doing something for them; it feels really good. I really have to work on that. I know that the pleasure of giving is to do it for the sake of doing it and not expecting anything in return, not even recognition.

I understand why we have all been taught or should have been taught, that we can do anything we want to; it is true. It is called free will and free will knows no laws; it only knows choices. If we choose to, we can even say no to God. The consequences are usually grave, but the choice is ours.

Two roads diverged in a wood and I took the one less traveled by and that has made all the difference. Robert Frost [195]

Natural Law

The goal of life is living in agreement with nature. Zeno [196]

There is such a thing as "Natural Law". It explains how physical entities act, and understanding it leads to a path of understanding our physical selves. To see how natural law works, all one has to do is observe nature and other animals. In this day and age it is as simple as

---

[195] Robert Frost (1874-1963): American Poet.
[196] Zeno of Elea (488-425 BC): Greek Philosopher.

watching the animal channel. Try growing something and watching the different stages of development. What do we all have in common, how do we act and why?

Natural laws are based on the basic principle of existence (survival). Every species is intended to multiply and remain within the ecological balance at the same time. If there is an increase in the number of a prey species, there is usually a proportional increase of predators. It is a system of checks and balances that nature uses to remain in a regenerative cycle[197]. Imagine what would happen if the herds grew too large. They would eat everything in sight and upset the food chain. We can see this on many game reserves.

The same is true if we put too many people in an area that cannot support their needs; they upset their environment. Pretty soon they are forced to look elsewhere for resources, or face civil unrest and a descent into barbarism. What do you suppose happens when they find the needed resources and they just happen to belong to someone else who does not want to part with or trade for them?

Infants only know natural law. Socially they are born a blank slate. Infants are conceived with what has been woven into their beings by twenty-three chromosomes and millions of years of evolution. Nature has given them a chance at survival and the ability to learn, adapt, think and evolve. Life's struggles begin at the moment of conception. Whether we are aware or not, I cannot remember, but I do know that the condition of the mother throughout has a direct affect on the development of the embryo and fetus.

Nature is about surviving and evolving with the environment or facing extinction. It is about life and death - that is all. Natural law allows a single cell to become trees, birds and every other living thing on this planet. It is a masterpiece to behold and participate in. Natural law is about perfecting and testing designs that perform well and survive despite hardship. Look at sharks. Their design has not changed much in millions of years; neither has that of crocodiles or tapers. They are perfect for their environment. I wonder how long it will take humans to reach that level of perfection or if we ever will.

Natural law tells every living thing what is necessary, not right or wrong, in order for it and its species to survive. We all want to live forever through the continuation of our genetic lines. Any choice that contradicts the body's prime directive to live violates natural law.

Think about natural law and beings with free will.

That Feeling Inside

It's easier to ask for forgiveness than permission. Grace Hopper[198]

Have you ever had a distinct feeling inside yourself when you were about to do something stupid? Have you ever said, "Something told me not to…"? For me it comes as a voice, a snap shot of something that is about to happen or an indescribable pressure under my sternum.

---

[197] The Earth is a perfect machine recycling itself over and over again.
[198] Grace Murray Hopper (1906-1992) United States Navy Rear Admiral and computer scientist.

Sometimes it comes as that feeling you get when your feelings are hurt. When I get that feeling, I know I am about to do something that is going to come back to haunt me, or whatever I am thinking of doing is going to hurt. I had the "hurt" feeling a day before the tsunami. It was a sharp pain that made me grab my chest. It hurt, but it was not a physical hurt. I told a friend that I felt something was going to happen. She asked me if it was good or bad and all I could say was, "It is going to be bad"[199].

During occasions of imminent danger or high competition it comes in the form of slowed down time. Things move in slow motion. It is an out of body experience, or a dream where you want to run faster but cannot, almost like a peak experience.[200] At that point, we have to make a split second decision. It happens so fast in real time, that we either praise or haunt ourselves for the rest of our lives, depending on the outcome of the decision made in the blink of an eye. It seems like a "what could have been". It feels like you missed an opportunity, dropped the ball or missed a signal. "I knew it," is what I usually say, and then I kick myself.

I recall an argument I had with myself. I was in my car waiting for the light to turn green. It was a "T" intersection. That something inside said, "Put your seatbelt on." "Whatever, I am a good driver. I am not going to have an accident," is what I thought to myself. "Damn, this is a long light!" There it goes again, "Put on your seatbelt!" "For what... I am not going to get into an accident!" "Put on your seatbelt!" The light turned green, I glanced in my rearview mirror to see if I would be holding someone up if I took a second or two to put on my seatbelt. It was clear. I put on the seatbelt and as I prepared to move into the intersection, a car came into sight from my left. He went through what was a red light for him. His car passed in front of mine from left to right. Had I gone when the light turned green, I would have been broad sided.

Time slowed down. I remember the car and driver vividly. The car was a gold Toyota Camry. It was well kempt or new. The driver was graying in the beard. He was also losing his hair, slightly overweight and foreign-born (I would say Middle Easterner because of his dress) olive skinned male. He was engaged in a heated conversation with two women passengers with scarfed heads. The women were waving their arms and hands in exclamations of their point of view on the subject at hand. They were arguing. The driver was distracted enough to forget what his primary role was at the time, driving. With few visual cues that he was approaching a "T" intersection and not looking forward because he was talking with his head turned toward the woman in the passenger seat, he did not see the light. No right or wrong in it, shit happens. If we had an accident, he would have been issued a ticket, but does violating the law of the land make someone universally wrong? I might have died and the law of the land would not have meant shit to me! If the law of the land does mean anything, it was wrong for a slave to run away from his or her master. I am glad that despite my hesitation, I listened to my voice that day. I prefer not being in an accident to being right. I brought the driver back to his primary role by blowing my horn. It startled him; his head snapped back to driving. "I knew it."

---

[199] The day of the tsunami, I noticed the moon looked strange. I was so intrigued that I left the balcony and walked into the middle of the street to have a full view of the moon. It was 3 AM and I have never seen the moon look so big and intimidating. It had an aura that would fit perfectly into any horror film.
[200] Oneness with the Universe.

I wish I could hear myself all the time. On second thought, I wish I had the courage and faith to listen to my inner voice all the time. It takes a different type of person to listen to the distant and whispering suggestions of the self over the screams and demands of the body, not to mention the will of others. That is why that road is less traveled. We all have to travel these roads alone and they can seem difficult. Many times there are things that we must face by ourselves and many of us are uncomfortable with the thought of being or doing anything alone.

Frequently I have heard or felt, "Do not do that!" or "Go this way today." But, there are times when fear, disguised as greed, self-interest, anxiety and conditioning (training, programming, upbringing, experiences) overrode the advice. This battle rages inside of each and every one of us every time we must make a challenging decision, but it does not have to be a battle. The body must follow the mind. It may go kicking and screaming, but it will go. Ever worked out? The body screams, "NO", but if the mind is persistent enough the body follows and benefits greatly. And, the mind should follow the spirit, which is never wrong.

I was driving back from a painting job in the suburbs. My employer, mentor and informally adopted father let me drive his vintage Corvette back and forth to the job to save time, make money and keep him from having to do it. He showed a lot of trust considering the monetary risk. I was 19 or 20 at the time. Like most boys of that age, I liked anything fast. He gave me the keys to a Corvette with his daughter's name on the personalized plates. It was a dual fantasy for me, driving a Vette and being inside of his daughter. I actually told him that years later and he replied, "You did not have enough money for her, Son."

One day I worked a little later than usual. It had rained enough to make the roads slick. The sun was setting fast. It always seems to do that close to the summer equinox. The rows of trees that lined the road, and the smell of the end of a summer's day mixed with the freshness of country rain put me in a place of peace where I felt invincible. The single lane road was curved and narrow. Visibility was limited because of the trees and earthen embankments lining both sides of the road. The highlight of the day was the drive out of that area. It was a mile and a half of pure fun. I noticed the road was wet, but I thought I knew the road well enough, and that I was a good enough driver to do my usual high speed run anyway. I promised myself I would not push it.

I heard, "You should slow down." "Huh?" My foot eased off on the accelerator. The sound of the engine revving down brought my mind back to the drive. I pushed the accelerator harder, paying attention to the visual cues so I could anticipate the next curve, dip or bump. They all looked alike. I usually counted the curves between the road signs; they are good cues. In the two weeks I was on this job, I memorized the road like professional racers do. "Slow down!" "Damn, was that the last turn before the stop sign?" "No. There is one more… I think." I took the curve as fast as I dared. The sound of screeching tires let me know that I was at the edge of the envelope. It was an uphill curve that whined to the left about 90 degrees. You could not see the end of the curve until you were at the top of the crest. After the hill there was a downgrade, a slight incline for another 75 or 100 feet, a hairpin to the right, another climbing left turn followed by the stop sign at the "T" intersection of the main road. I hated to see that stop sign; it meant my rush was over.

As I reached the top of the crest I realized that I had made a mistake. The warning sign I saw with a stop sign on it told me that I was at the "T" intersection. "Brakes!" I hit the brakes. The car did not grip the pavement like normal; it was too slick. The sound of tires sliding across wet blacktop told me I was not going to be able to stop. As the slide continued, I noticed that a car was coming from the right. Its headlights blinded me for a moment. I caught sight of a second car coming from the left. It was further away than the first, but I could not stop in time to avoid a collision with either car. I remember seeing the two cars and the trees in front of me. The next thing I remember was driving straight on the main road like I had made a left turn. I was in front of the car that was coming from the right. Their headlights told me I was 20 or 30 feet in front of them. I lost two or three seconds of my life. My hands trembled as I tried to figure out how I got there. Take my word for it; it was physically impossible for the car to have made the 90-degree left turn at that speed. I do not know what happened. I do know I should have listened to that voice. I am sure my guardian angel has gray hair. He or she may have already applied for early retirement.

At times we are afraid to trust in what we feel is right without some sort of reinforcement or guidance. We look around for someone to ask what we already know. The inner voice is always right. We do not need to gather a consensus. The Spirit has an interest in our survival as well. If you stop listening to that voice inside, after a while it stops wasting energy.

Disclaimer: If your inner voice says kill someone or yourself, that is not your inner voice; that is psychosis. Get professional help and insist on talking it out. The shrink will probably want to give you the "blue" pill, insist on the "red" one.

If I Knew Then What I Know Now

I have asked parents who have grown children, including my own, if there was anything they would do differently as far as raising their children, knowing what they know now. Everyone I have asked said, "YES." And the majority meant it.

It seems our nature allows us to learn from our personal experiences more rapidly than if someone else tells us. My elders tried to teach me through words and they did not stick. That is not entirely true. The lessons stuck, because I remember them, but I just did not believe. It felt as though a seed had come to fruition the day I experienced the things for myself. I did not want to believe the limitations that some of the lessons placed on my dreams. I thought I knew better and in certain instances, as rare as they were, I did. An older male once told me, "Black people do not fly airplanes." He told me this after he asked me what I wanted to be when I grew up. Even though I was six, I thought he was crazy and I felt sorry for him.

When I was working for my mentor one summer, an African-American journeyman carpenter told me, "Niggas do not fly," after I told him that I wanted to fly for the Navy. I think he was right; "Niggas[201]" are not good at much except excuses.

---

[201] In my opinion anyone of any race can be considered a Nigga. It is not so much about skin color as it is attitude and outlook.

After other encounters like that, I assumed most adults did not know what they were talking about, and in some instances they did not. They were simply passing on what they had learned. I also witnessed adults doing exactly what they told me not to do. I could not make the leap of "do as I say and not as I do", not after a lifetime of following instinctual programming to imitate the behavior of those around me. We cannot deny that part of us. And, that universal answer, "Because I said so," flies like a brick. Whether or not the adults in my life were right or wrong is not the main point, learning at my own time and through my own experiences is. I do not think we should tell people what to do. I think we should tell what we have experienced and the mistakes we think we made. I think we should tell each other of our, "If I could do it again" stories.

For some reason I have always had a righteous streak. I think I got it from my grandmother and grandfather. Once I took a stand I just knew what was right. As a child, I criticized my mother and her husband to their faces. We were having financial issues. There were several moments when we were unable to pay the rent, and at one point we were without running water and electricity. My brother and I had to go to a nearby park to retrieve water from a public fountain. I was very embarrassed performing this task and finally I took out my frustrations on them. I remember having to cook on a single eye hot plate because we could not afford a stove or the gas to fuel it. One night I called them, "Rent dodgers." (I already told you I must be destined for a long life). Though that one hurt, it was worth it at the time. My mouth is my weapon. My mother recently told me, "You have always had too much mouth." I wanted to reply, "Would you rather I go crazy?"

I did not understand the trials of life, why we make the choices we do, or the external influences others have on our reality. All I saw was not having the same things that other families did. By this time in my life I was associating with white children of my age. I had been in their homes and seen the outrageous differences in the standard of living. I wondered why we did not live like that. "Why you white men have so much cargo?"[202] I wondered why the only African-Americans I knew who lived like that seemed too old to enjoy it or were still working themselves to death.

All I knew was what I had been taught and seen. It did not help that my brother and I had spent years being raised by our grandparents and they spoiled us rotten. We had no responsibilities and there were little to no expectations, just get good grades, do not cause any trouble and be in by streetlights[203]. My grandparents never seemed to have issues with money. It was not until later that I found out that they did have problems, and not just with money. Grammy cooked every night or we would go for ourselves. The summers were of freedom that I have not since experienced, but am always in search of.

My brother and I were both working at the time. We sold subscriptions for a small regional newspaper and received a $1.00 commission for each three-month trial subscription. I was bringing home $50.00-75.00 dollars a week and donated half of this to the household. My mother asked for one-third of the money and I volunteered to give one half of it to her despite being

---

[202] Jared Diamond, <u>Guns, Germs and Steel</u>.
[203] Streetlights: the time when the utility lamps came on, as early as 5:30 PM in the winter and as late as 8:30 PM in the summer.

infuriated that I had to contribute anything. I guess I could see the need. My brother did the same. I do not know if he was following my example or feeling the same altruistic urges that convinced me that as individuals we were not as important as the whole.

Everyone is a prisoner of his own experiences. Edward R. Murrow[204]

I now know that my judgment in that case came from my grandfather. He told me time and time again, "A man pays his debts. If he cannot pay them when they are due, then he should make arrangements to pay them when he can." I do not know what is right or what is wrong. There are only individual choices in response to individual circumstances. Because I lacked what I thought I should have, I vowed not to want for them again. I was going to pursue the American dream with a vengeance. I was on my way to becoming a conspicuous consumer because of neurotic fears and jealousy.

Although I have earned more than most in my family, I have also spent more in an attempt to keep up with the Joneses, the Joneses being society's expectations and my own. I wanted to show success with my car, with my residence and with my generosity. I have had to pay my rent late or not pay it at all for living on the wild side, gambling then losing. I have "robbed Peter to pay Paul". I too have been judged as being wrong for exhibiting the same types of behaviors that I was so critical of as a child. Except in my case I did not have income issues;

I have a champagne appetite but a beer budget.

Competition

Have you ever witnessed how mean people can become, whenever their power or status is threatened? Paul T.P. Wong, PhD[205]

Competition leads us by definition to compete. It is the main cause of our need to defend ourselves. Compete against whom? There is enough of the pie to go around, Nash said it and Covey said it and a number of others before them said it, but we have been taught that in order to be the best, we have to beat others in some form of competition. Even when we do cooperate, when the time comes to divide the pie, we want to divide it unevenly. It reminds me of lions feeding.

Life is not a hunt, boxing match or football game. Life is not supposed to be about human competition. It is like playing yourself in chess; there is no winner or loser in life. Life simply begins and ends; the lessons learned between the two events are not accidents and should not be categorized as right or wrong. So why compete over the spoils of life? If you want to compete at something, try being the first you know to reach enlightenment or try finishing Einstein's theory of everything.

---

[204] Edward R. Murrow (1908-1965): Broadcast journalist who fought for freedom of thought during McCarthyism.
[205] Paul T.P. Wong (1948-): Professor of Psychology, University of Toronto. Specializes in death acceptance, persona; meaning, and meaning-centered counseling and therapy.

Who wins at life anyway, the successful politician, the businessman, the parent, vagrant, hermit or the guru? Does the accumulation of material wealth dictate righteousness or history? I think material wealth leads to physical comfort and no more. What happens when the wealth is gone and you are left with only yourself in the grave? Wealth does not always lead to happiness or even contentment, and often the price we pay for it is higher than we as humans can afford. I do not know anyone personally who is wealthy, but from what I see, they do not seem to be any happier than the rest of us. They seem to have the same issues with weight, esteem, and love that everyone else has.

I, like others, have been conditioned to and have a biological urge to compete and win. We are frequently taught to win admiration, attention and hopefully some sex. Many times in order to win you cannot possibly stick to the rules and many people do not. I learned this tactic by being screwed; I was not born with it. It does not matter if the competition is intellectual or physical. The important thing is to win. Winning has different affects on different people, but this is guaranteed, most think of themselves first and do not like to lose. I am no different, so I limit my contact and competition with others so they do not get mad at me for trying to win too. You win and you are right - Damn!

Corporate wars and political campaigns are perfect examples of competition out of control. The mudslinging and back stabbing remind me of children fighting over the same toy even though there are hundreds of other toys in the toy box, ask Hilary and Barak. This reminds me of my brother and me fighting over things when we were children. It is only when we want the same things that competition arises, and we always seem to want the same things: affection, attention and love.

I have competed with people most of my life and so have you. People, in general, like to compete as long as they think they have a chance of winning. The higher their chance of winning, the more willing they are to compete or take a risk. In general, men like to compete more than women at games that involve physical strength and agility (though the video game seems to have taken over). It is a genetic throwback from yesteryear.

On one of my trips home, I decided to take my niece and nephew with me on an errand. I do not get to see them that often, so I like to take them away from their home and ask questions about school and life. I was amazed at how they fought over who was going to sit in the front seat. I remember doing it and why I did it, so I told them what was passed to me by my grandfather, "The front of the car goes to the same destination as the back." They were not hearing it.

My nephew is bigger and stronger than my niece, so he bullied his way into the front seat. My niece jumped in the back seat where she complained and demanded that she get the front seat on the way home. I told her that in parts of Asia the person of honor sits in the back seat. She said, "But I want to ride in the front seat." I pulled over and strapped them both into the front seat. By the time we got where we were going they were both more willing to sit in the back seat to avoid the discomfort of sharing and sitting two in a seat meant for one.

I tried to teach them the futility of fighting over nothing. My nephew reminded me of the natural order, the strongest usually gets what he or she wants, and my niece showed me the innate sense of justice and fairness that is inside each of us when we get the short end of the stick. She was trying to appeal to fairness after she lost the physical struggle. They both taught me that having children is not easy. I jokingly call them, "Birth Control."

Those two fight over everything. They fight over the television, the computer, video games and even food. Is that normal among siblings? I remembered how my brother and I fought over resources. It made me think, "If it is normal for siblings to compete and fight, it is logical to conclude that we will compete and fight more readily with someone who is not related." I do not think it is "right", but I know I did it. It is the animal inside of us. It is the body controlling the underdeveloped brain.

I remember being sent to a Risk Management course sponsored by my employer called "Realizing Your Potential." I will not go into the fact that when I showed up I noticed that every participant was African-American. It was a week long course held at corporate headquarters. We called it the "Fishbowl". One day the facilitator, also African-American, had prearranged what looked like horseshoe pegs on the floor in a box shape. The pegs were aligned in rows of sixteen. They were about 6-inches high and were placed at one-foot intervals. They were numbered 1-16 (0 being at your feet and 16 being 16 feet away). Imagine a square 18 feet x 18 feet. The shape made by the rows of pegs represents the sides of the square, there is an empty space at each of the four corners between the end of one row and the beginning of another and they were 90 degrees perpendicular to one another. If you were looking from the ceiling, it would look like a square with the corners erased. We were given three hoops each. The hoops were about 6 inches in diameter.

The first exercise was to guess how many of the three hoops we could make on any of the pegs. For example, one could say, "I think I can make two out of three, if I aim for the number '5'." Afterwards, the participant tried to do what he said he could. We did this in four different groups simultaneously. I said I could make one out of three on the 16th peg. I made sure I went last in my group. I missed the first one, but just barely. Someone said, "Oh, close!" The second was not as close as the first. Several other people chimed in. I could feel the tension. I knew some were hoping I would and others were hoping I could not. The third hit the ground further away from the peg than the other two. There was a resounding, "Awwww" in the room, until it did a weird bounce and went on the peg. The entire room cheered. The instructor said, "It was luck." I responded, "Luck counts!"

The next exercise we had to perform was identical to the first, but this time we had to do it individually and we were supposed to adjust our estimates of what we could do based on the results of our first try. When my turn came up, I asked if I could think outside the box. The instructor agreed. I said, "I can make three out of three on the 16th peg." He said, "No one has ever done that and I'll give you $20, if you can." I smiled, bent my knees, turned my waist 90 degrees to the right and dropped the three hoops on the 16th peg not one foot away. The instructor said, "Boy, you *gon'* get hurt." and I never got my $20. I cheated, but followed instructions.

It is funny as hell to beat someone in a competition of their choosing. The big thing among the youth is video games these days. I play very little, but as in all things, practice means improvement. I once spent ten hours playing against a computer to hone my skills so that I could beat the daylights out of my girlfriend's son. He came up with an excuse as to why he lost and wanted to switch games. I reminded him that when I lost to him a few days before, I said, "I lost because I do not play, but if I practice I will beat you." Rarely will people say, "Good game." If you do not believe me, do something well. Go to the ghetto and speak proper English. Give a great presentation for your regional director with your peers present; most will focus on your mistakes when giving feedback. Many people like to search for imperfections and faults just so they can feel better about themselves. That is why we judge. It is our insecurity looking for a hug.

I once had to intervene on behalf of a very attractive woman who had the balls to wear a sheer black cat suit that showed her laced black thong and bra. She had the right body to wear it and look good, but the other women lost their minds and wanted to fight the girl because she was getting more attention than they were. One of the girls said, "Go home and put on some clothes, Bitch!" The woman who said this managed to fit her 200-pound frame in a mini-skirt. I almost said what I was thinking. Instead, I grabbed "cat woman" by the arm and led her to the dance floor. The girls kept looking and kept talking, but they stopped the physical assaults. They were willing to fight and harass her, but they were not willing to risk fighting me. While I danced with the girl, I told her, "You wanted attention and you got it. Now, go home."

How many times have we heard people talk about someone behind his or her back? One of my favorite suggestions to people who do that is to ask, "Have you said that to them?" It is called *hating* and is a tool for the insecure. Because of this type of behavior, it is necessary to defend against our own kind. Whether we are in a bar room, boardroom or at church, adults can be as petty as children. Do yourself a favor, smile at the behavior or ignore it totally with the "blank face" then watch how silly the other person looks and acts.

It was around Christmas and I was in a club. There was a male there who had three of those blinking ice cubes in his glass. One was yellow; one was green and one was red. After someone brought the display to our attention, I said, "He just wants some attention." Later in the evening, he walked by me. I said, "You look like you have a stop light in your drink." He said, "Oh, you think you funny, huh!?!" I did think it was funny, but it was not my intention to offend him. It was Christmas and a time for festive cheer. It is one of the few times of the year when you can act friendly and people do not think that you want something. He followed with, "My friends call me Knockout." "What?" "My friends call me Knockout!!" I said, "Now, that is funny." I could not help it and I had a smile on my face. He walked away. I guess I was supposed to be intimidated by his posturing and selling "Wolf Tickets[206]". The woman standing at my side later told me she thought I was going to get into a fight. She does not know me or human behavior very well.

Let me tell you a story about two female cousins. They were invited to attend a boat party. One of the cousins is barren and the other has stretch marks. They were both in bikinis. The cousin with the stretch marks was receiving more attention than the cousin who thought she

---

[206] Wolf Tickets: Fighting with your mouth, but having no intention of backing it up with physical force.

deserved it. The barren cousin said, "I do not think women with stretch marks should wear bikinis" Ouch! The other responded, "Some women wish they had stretch marks" Touché. Game, set and match to the stretch marks.

Moreover and to remove the excuses, how do we treat the individual who performs better than we do (those on the fast track at work or those more successful with the opposite sex)? The parallels are the same because we are conditioned from the cradle to be in competition with one another, and our general reactions to being anything but the winner is programmed as well. Those who receive more rewards or attention will not only invoke judgment, but also jealousy and envy from someone. I have done this and had this done to me. Many do not like being out shined by anyone. We want attention and praise to be bestowed on us, not on others. Ask Abel, or, better yet, ask Cain.

Have you noticed the competition that exists between white women and women of color? The African-American women I know hate to see a brother with a white girl (so do white men). They seem to think that there are not enough eligible brothers, and think that African-American men with wealth marry white women. It is jealousy, but we all do it.

Have you noticed the competition that exists between white men and men of color? The African-American men I have known do not like to see their women with white men. They openly question what a sister could possibly see in a weak white male. That is how many African-American men view white men, as wimps, made soft by privilege and wealth. I have mixed emotions on the subject, but it does not matter what I like or dislike, people do what they want. Because there is competition, it is necessary to be able to defend yourself even if that defense means turning the other cheek or ignoring the competition.

Having lost a dominant moral consensus, we are struggling in our courts, voting booths and even in our churches to resolve the difficult moral issues that are separating us.
Josh McDowell[207]

Defense

FYI: The White House budget for 2010 is estimated to be $533.7 billion.

I have no pity for anyone who shoots the first shot or throws the first punch. Because competition exists, we all need a viable defense.

There certain things you should not do to another person. And, there are certain people you really should not do these things to.

I remember going on a training flight while I was still a junior pilot in my operational squadron. It was a hot seat. That means we just swapped crews without shutting down the aircraft. From the moment we took off something did not feel right. There was a slight side-to-side motion. That voice inside said, "This ain't right." I told the pilot in command that I thought

---

[207] Josh McDowell: Christian Evangelist and writer. The founder of the Christian ministries Josh.org and Operation Airlift.

we had a possible malfunction. He told me I was wrong and attributed the vibration to strong crosswinds. It still did not feel right and I said so. The crew chief intervened and backed up the pilot. I shut up. We ended up causing $100,000 in damage to the aircraft because of a damper failure. We had just landed and were shutting down when the failure occurred. I lit a cigarette and thanked God we were all still alive.

There were two Boards, the Accident Investigation Board and the Safety Board, charged with determining what had occurred. I was reluctant to tell the truth. I did not want to get the pilot in trouble. The pilot said nothing about my diagnosing the problem ahead of time. I revealed nothing incriminating to the Accident Investigation Board because this could inflict punitive damage to a pilot's career, but during the Safety Board I asked, "Is what I divulge here strictly for safety purposes?" "Yes." "Is what I say here going to be passed on to the Accident Investigation Board?" "No." My voice would not let me be quiet; the information I had could save money and lives in the future. This was more important than any single pilot's reputation. I had to tell the truth to someone.

It was a night flight. We should have gone to the clinic for a physical that night, but the Executive Officer told us to go home. I went home, had a beer and went to bed. The next morning the squadron was abuzz. The cost of the accident made it a serious offense and drug tests for fault and negligence were required. That is why we had the two investigating boards. We appeared before them first thing in the morning. The squadron was playing catch up with Standard Operating Procedures. Everything happened faster than normal.

We went to the clinic. I offered to drive because I had a moral dilemma I wanted to solve. I knew what I had done and why, but I had no clue what the pilot in command was thinking or what he had said to the Boards. From the moment he got in the car he professed his innocence and how unnecessary the physical was. He did not say a word about my analysis. I told him that I did not tell the Accident Investigation Board that I had diagnosed the problem ahead of time. He said, "Thank you." I left out that I had told the Safety Board.

Someone on the Safety Board did tell the pilot I said I had diagnosed the problem during the training flight. It made an enemy of him, of his friends, and some of the senior officers in the squadron. There is an unwritten code in many professional groups which states, "You do not rat."

I paid for it dearly. One of his friends was the Senior Watch Officer. That is a senior lieutenant who assigns watch schedules. Shortly afterwards we embarked aboard ship for an exercise. I had to stand the worst watches (midnight to 4 or 4 to 8 AM) and some in the squadron ostracized me.

One night I had watch following the pilot who had misdiagnosed the plane malfunction. We were docked and I was asleep. I overslept despite having set my alarm clock. It must have been the strong European beer I had earlier that day. The pilot and the Senior Watch Officer went immediately to the Executive Officer who awakened everyone and then publicly berated me before the entire squadron. Then he threatened punitive punishment. I found out later that the Senior Watch Officer went to the Quarterdeck to check and see if I was on board the ship before he reported to the Executive Officer. They did not knock on my door. They knew I was on the ship and wanted to nail me to the wall.

Months later the pilot approached me in the squadron hangar and apologized for what he had done; I wondered why. He said that he hoped that I did not hold it against him. At the time I said it was fine and that I did not harbor any ill feelings toward him or the Senior Watch Officer. I did not see the point in giving them the satisfaction of knowing that I was so mad that I wanted to kick the living shit out of both of them. As I write this story for you, the same feelings surface, but I realize that everything happens for a reason. I was berated in front of my peers again. I felt ashamed and inferior. That was the desired effect, but there was a deeper effect that not even I could see at the time; it made me stronger.

Later, I had a watch and my relief was late, so I went to the Senior Watch Officer and reported it. I demanded he take the same steps he had on my account, but he did not. I was confronted once more with the two-tier system of justice, but I knew that ahead of time. I just wanted it confirmed.

What goes around comes around. The pilot got his. He had to leave the ship and our European exercise to go home and take care of his adulterous free spending wife. Looking at the conduct of some of my other peers, I realize that I got some raw deals. I am not saying that I was right for being late; I am saying that other people were late as well and no one reported them. It offends my sense of fairness, and I hope to meet everyone involved once more so that I can honestly discuss what occurred. I want to look into their eyes and ask them "Why?" In hindsight, I would have been more insistent on my call regardless of the other pilot's seniority, and there would not have been any Safety Board. Consensus is not better than listening to that voice inside.

I remember when the first female pilots joined our squadron. The Commanding Officer told every officer point blank that he would not tolerate sexual relationships between his officers. The women were off limits. Two showed up, one married a senior officer who once scolded me for breaking the rules and the other slept with a guy we called the "Skipper's Bitch". In both cases it was common knowledge, but because of the favored status of the offenders... you know the rest of the story. I wonder what would have happened had I dipped into either well. You know the rest of that story too. I actually left one of the women on her couch naked one night, I knew better.

Machiavelli[208] said in *The Prince,*[209] "The unarmed prophet (instrument of change or new ideas) is doomed to obscurity." That is to say, that if you take an unpopular stand or view, you had better be able to defend yourself.

The infamous Spanish Inquisition[210] was authorized by Pope Sixtus IV[211] in 1478 to combat the heretical Cathari[212] and Waldenses[213]. The Inquisition later extended its activity to include

---

[208]Niccolo Machiavelli (1469-1527): Italian Statesman and political philosopher. Wrote "The Prince" to gain favor of the Medici Family.
[209] The Prince: Novel writing giving suggestions on how to rule. Written for Giuliano Medici. The main character is based on Cesare Borgia, rival to the Medici.

witches, diviners, blasphemers, Jews, Muslims and other sacrilegious persons. In other words, anyone who did not agree with the Catholic Church would be tortured, displaced or killed. They used it to politically clean house.

I have needed a defense on more than one occasion. My high school chemistry teacher once tried to give me an "F". It was not my performance in class, or my test scores. It had to do with a lab book that counted for one third of our grade for the quarter. I tried to turn mine in a day late and the teacher refused to accept it. Before you side with the teacher, listen to the lunacy. The day we were supposed to turn the lab books in, the teacher asked to see mine. I had finished the day's assigned work early and was talking to another student, as usual. Mrs. Donaldson interrupted, "Are you finished with your work?" "Yes." "Is your lab book complete?" "Yes it is." "Let me see it." She checked the book and said it was a "B+". I then put the book under my seat. At the end of class she called for the books, but for some reason I forgot. The following day I found my lab book under my seat, and tried to give it to her. She refused. She said they were due yesterday. I explained that she had seen it, it was complete and it was a "B+" - yesterday. "I won't accept it, and your grade for the semester is an "F" without it." She was happy as hell. She hated me for consistently finishing the assigned work quickly and for engaging the other members of the class. She thought I was disruptive, but I was helping the others with the assigned work. The teachers at the Center for Black Education knew how to handle me; they would give me something else constructive to do. I am one of those who need projects. I cannot help but think, "I'd probably be put on Ritalin if I were in school today."

The Vice-Principal saw me crying and inquired why. I had never had an "F." The teacher was being mean and I was not about to let her get away with it; she was just a teacher. The Vice-Principal could not believe it. He spoke to her, but she would not back down. Then I pulled out the "BIG GUNS", my mother. She was in the Principal's office the next day. Do you remember I wrote in the Introduction that my principal said I was not properly socialized? This is when he said it. My mother asked, "What are his grades like?" He tried to justify why an "A" or "High B" student deserved an "F" for the quarter because I was not properly socialized. He said that my overall GPA would not be affected that much. "Fuck You," is what I thought. I wanted Valedictorian and they were killing that dream right there. I ended up with a "C+" for the quarter as a compromise. Years later I showed up in uniform to speak to the students. I made sure I spoke to Mrs. Donaldson as well. She confessed that she should have accepted the lab book.

Defense, we should not need it, but we do. One night I met a woman and her friend at an ATM machine. We were all withdrawing money. I flirted. She told me that she and her friend were going to a cabaret that night and I accepted an invitation on behalf of my cousin and me. We were going out anyway and this beats having to hunt. After an evening of dancing, we kissed and the deal was set. "Where do you live?" "Who's closer?" I did not want to take these girls back to my cousin's apartment; it was a dump. His bedroom closet had a hole in it big enough to

---

[210] Spanish Inquisition (1478-1834): Ferdinand and Isabella chose Catholicism to unite Spain and in 1478 asked permission of the Pope to begin the Spanish Inquisition to purify the people of Spain. They began by driving out Jews, Protestants and other non-believers.
[211] Pope Sixtus IV or Francesco della Rovere (1414-1484). Pope (1471-1484).
[212] The essential characteristic of the Cathari faith was Dualism, i.e. the belief in a good and an evil principle, of whom the former created the invisible and spiritual universe, while the latter was the author of the material world.
[213] Waldenses: the perfect, bound by the vow of poverty, wandered about from place to place preaching.

see through. I am sure he looked through that hole on more than one occasion, but we had no choice. At twenty-six years old she lived with her parents. I told her the truth and she agreed to come anyway.

My cousin was cool about giving up his bedroom. I had a bird in the hand. He had one in the bush. I wished him luck with his seemingly reluctant partner before I went into the bedroom. The other woman's attitude toward my cousin had changed since we left the parking lot of the cabaret. I was kissing my new love while leaning back on the trunk of her car. The event had ended over half an hour before, but I wanted to give my cousin a chance and time alone to persuade the other woman that there was something in this venture for her. It was maybe three AM. The very last car in the parking lot with two young men in it stopped in the driveway maybe 20 feet away. My date was facing me and I was facing the driveway. The driver said something that could not be considered flattering. I ignored him. This was my kill and I was not going to share. It would take more than horn blowing and a vulgar introduction to get her from me now. I told her, "Ignore him; he's acting ignorant." He kept badgering us. I asked her to tell him, "Thank you very much, but I am OK."

My cousin saw what was going on and thought I was in need of assistance. He made his presence known. Just like another pride male would when facing bachelors in search of mates. He roared, "What?" from my car, which was 50 ft further away. I remember thinking, "Oh no!" The rutting session started despite my nearly defusing the problem. My partner had declined her suitor's invitation three times and his persistence was waning. My cousin's outburst, which is almost always construed as a challenge, made our adversary respond as expected.

My cousin approached at a quickening pace, all the while yelling "What!" (Step) "What you say… (Two steps), Nigga?" (Three steps) The driver promptly responded, "Fuck you!" His friend sat quietly in the passenger seat with a concerned look on his face. He did not want any more to be a part of this than I did. "Oh no!" I was not leaning anymore. I made a B-line toward my cousin. I wanted to stop him from walking up to their car. There was a reason for the driver not getting out, but I needed time to figure out how to defuse the escalating competition.

It was not worth fighting because of words, and fighting at this point was not a good choice strategically either. We did not know their strength. At some point my cousin got so pissed off that he did a u-turn and ran toward my car before I got a chance to calm him down. He was going for my gun. That surprised me. I was not upset at his decision; I had been thinking of a way to retrieve my weapon before this. He just broadcast to everybody, including the enemy that he was going to get something from the car. I ran as fast as I could. I got there in time to grab my cousin's hand and persuade him to give me my gun. Thank goodness he did.

Once I had the gun I concentrated on the other threat. The Wild Card (I call the driver a wild card because it takes a different mindset to stop your car to be rude to a couple. His actions would not be easy to predict and I could not be sure if logic or reason would prevail). This had gotten way out of control over nothing. Our antagonist was exiting his car. When he headed for the trunk, I thought, "Ohhhh, HELL NO!!! Please do not show me a weapon. I will have to kill you."

My cousin was pleading for me to shoot him before I knew what he was getting out of his trunk. The headlights of the girl's car pulling off shined on him just as he emerged from the trunk (the girls had the sense to get out of the way, but paused half in the driveway and half in the street to watch the outcome).

He had something in his right hand. I could not tell what it was, but I could tell what it was not. He was out gunned. I tried to convince my cousin to shut up and get in the car. I did this repeatedly until he did what I told him to. The driver did everything he could to provoke a fight with my cousin. He did not know I had a gun and I knew he was bluffing. If he had had a gun, he would have been waving it around to scare us, or he would have used it.

His companion, who was behind him, responded to my demand, "You better get your boy." He said, "Come on, man." His friend now knew I had a gun. He heard me chamber a round. Despite this, his friend kept trying to provoke my cousin by throwing insults. He was so busy jousting he did not hear the distinctive "Cha-chink" sound that an automatic pistol makes when you pull the slide back. It is the rattler shaking its tail for me. "I don't wanna, but I will!"

I repeated, "You better get your boy!" This time he grabbed him and pulled him away. He saw me square my shoulders so that they pointed at his friend. He also saw me raise a loaded weapon to the prone position, the barrel pointed in his friend's direction. I did not want to shoot him; I wanted him to go away. They drove off with much the same types of insulting words that had begun this episode of lunacy. They even had the courtesy to say good night to the waiting ladies as they drove by. There is something very wrong with us.

I can understand why the girls were mad at my cousin. They must have thought he was crazy; I know I did. My cousin and I argued about what should have happened. He said, "I never would have let anyone walk up on you like that." I said, "I know, that is why I took the gun." He could not see the victory. No combat and we still had the girls. Well, at least I did.

Was that a good defense? No one was hurt, and we lost nothing but a little bit of false pride. There is nothing new under the sun.

Sometimes we have to defend against our own government. Remember McCarthyism[214]? We had the House of Un-American Activities Committee. As a result, many people accused of being communists lost their jobs, homes and sometimes their lives. They were blacklisted. Yet today major corporations outsource to and obtain cheap material goods from a communist country, China. It seems our hate can be overcome if the profit margin is large enough.

The Patriot Act violates civil liberties for reasons of national security in much the same way the House of Un-American Activities Committee did in the past. There are people being held in prison for extended periods of time just to be released uncharged without so much as an apology. The President can tap phones without a warrant. The 4th Amendment: *"The right of the people to be secure in their persons, houses, papers, and effects, against unreasonable searches and seizures, shall not be violated, and no Warrants shall issue, but upon probable cause, supported by Oath or affirmation, and particularly describing the place to be searched, and the persons or*

---

[214] McCarthyism officially ended when he was censored by the Senate on December 2, 1954.

things to be seized", shot to shit. It seems we have not learned from the error of our ways. Our need for security now outweighs our sense of justice and freedom.

Great spirits have always found violent opposition from mediocrities. The latter cannot understand it when a man does not thoughtlessly submit to hereditary prejudices but honestly and courageously uses his intelligence. Albert Einstein

Most people will do nothing to protest wrongs, though they know in their hearts they can do something. Fear of reprisals keeps heads in the sand. Just ask any German who was alive in the 1930's or 40's about what happened to the Jews under Hitler's regime[215]. Ask anyone who lived under Stalin[216]. His successor, Nikita Khrushchev,[217] was giving a speech when someone yelled, "Why didn't you do something to stop Stalin?" Khrushchev said, "Who said that?" The room was pin-drop quiet. "That is why I did nothing to stop Stalin." He was referring to fear. Many are happy with the status quo, and as long as they are not directly affected, will gladly accept any explanation to rationalize the wrong they do not want to see (Jews, homosexuals, immigrants, terrorism, the threat of the communist horde, the danger of racial equality or mixing, etc.). The conscientious people who voice their opinions openly are in danger of sharing the fate and ridicule of those they intend to aid.

I was once standing in a taxi queue. There was a man in front of me standing beside a sign that said, "Taxi queue starts here". A group of about twelve people arrived just as a taxi pulled up and the guy in front of me got into it. The group formed their own line to my right. Was I invisible or did I not matter? I thought about saying something, but I decided against it. Instead I was just going to take the next cab and not say a word.

While we were waiting, a male in a kilt arrived and stood in front of them. They protested and he apologized. At this point, I decided to say something to them about stepping in front of me. When I did this, a woman in the group got particularly upset. She said, "The line usually starts here." I simply pointed at the sign beside me "Taxi Queue Starts Here". That was not enough to quiet her. She continued to try to be right. She said some pretty nasty things. I did not reply until she insulted me personally, "Who do you think you are?" I thought, "A human being with equal rights, Bitch!" I looked her in her eyes and said, "Fuck you!"

Not one of them said or did anything. I got into the taxi and left. I was so mad that I could have slapped her; not because her mouth was writing a check her ass could not cash, but because she seemed to be the only one in her group who did not see the lunacy in why she was upset with me. I did exactly what they did and I was right according to the rules of fairness that they made our kilt-wearing friend acknowledge. He was obviously Scottish (Britannia) and they were Indian. If I were Indian I would hate the British too. I would remember how they conquered my

---

[215] Allied soldiers adopted the practice of forcing captured Hitler Youths and nearby townspeople to view the death inside liberated execution camps and also made them bury the corpses.

[216] In 1961, Stalin was moved from a place of honor in Red Square and then reburied inside the walls of the Kremlin among minor Soviet heroes.

[217] Nikita Khrushchev (1894-1971): First Secretary of the Communist Party (1953-1964) and Chairman of the USSR. Chairman of the Council of ministers of the Soviet Union (1958-1964).

country, and then sent my ancestors to the four corners of the earth for cheap labor. But, these were well to do Indians. They looked at me as if I were an "untouchable".

Despite my appropriate apparel, despite my position in a Fortune 500 company, I was a black person in Singapore. I learned no matter where I go in the world "black" is the bottom, until I mention "American" which many equate to wealth-class versus color discrimination. We are crazy.

I know that there is comfort in consensus, but sometimes it is a false comfort, full of deceit, mistrust and unnecessary games because of self-interest and competition. As soon as the goals of those in a group start to differ, groups splinter and former allies become present enemies. The surrounding herd gives a feeling of not being alone, but ultimately, we are. You were born alone and will die alone. We, as individuals, all have to live with our choices and others have to live with theirs. Allow them to and allow yourself to as well. We feel safe when we are with others, but depending on whom those others are, we may or may not be safe. It is a natural animalistic desire to want to congregate. We developed this in order to increase our chances of survival. We learned that predators pick easy prey and group life affords some protection.

Predators look for the inattentive, the old, the weak, the inexperienced and the solo animal. In most cultures, we have evolved enough not to have to worry about natural predation or the elements in our daily task of survival. In the human animal, independent thought is now being hunted to extinction, not by a lion or leopard, but by people. Instinct tells us the single animal is the easiest prey. And so it is, if we were animals in the wild. But we are not only animals, and though we are in the wild we can do more than just survive, if only we would listen to ourselves. Unfortunately, we now have to set our defenses not only against natural predators and the elements, but also and most importantly against our own.

I rarely feel safe in crowds unless I have known the individuals for some time, and even then I realize that competition is only one selfish thought away. I rarely get comfortable with co-workers; it is my experience that they will turn on you at the drop of a hat, depending on the prize up for grabs. I rarely feel comfortable in relationships with women; experience has taught me that the moment I dare to venture from the path she has chosen for us, she will do what she must to bring me back to my senses. If my finances wane, will her affections and interest follow? I feel comfortable with those I consider friends; they have proven their metal in the furnace of life. I feel relatively safe with family; I know them and know pretty much what they are and are not capable of doing.

It is in group settings that I find myself most vulnerable to surrender. I have surrendered more than once. I surrender every time I go against what I know to be right for me. Every time I cave in to the demands of the majority and feel that it is wrong, I surrender. I am not referring to the little things such as where to eat. I keep asking myself how much longer will I have to wait before I can stop being and acting like I am expected, and begin to live as I am meant? How much longer before we can disagree with each other and not be made to feel wrong or stupid for our point of view? When we do not have to fight, defend or surrender any more is when I know we have grown as a species.

How many people do you know? How many of them would you tell a secret?

The reed does not resist the strong wind; it bends and weaves staying firmly rooted at its base. The oak stands firm and breaks in the face of the hurricane. After a time, the reed has spread its seed and is surrounded by other reeds that protect it from the wind. It stands alone for only a time, a trying time, but not an infinite time.

According to Castiglione[218], the perfect courtier must first and foremost be an expert in all forms of arms and combat. The reasoning for this is irrational, but true to the nature of people in general. The human creature is threatened by the thought of being inferior. Most people do not like someone who they perceive to be smarter, faster, better off, better-looking or to possess any admirable quality that they do not, and because of ignorance, cannot.

People will attempt to attack, belittle and/or offend the object of their displeasure. We have all heard people criticize other people. "She thinks she's cute." If you make a statement like that, she probably is cute to someone; and the person who made the statement did so out of jealousy or to bring to everyone's attention that she or he is better-looking. If a person is not attractive to us, but they think they are attractive, what difference does it make? Why speak poorly of someone we do not know, or worse, do?

Still not convinced that you have to defend yourself? Go through your own experiences. What happens to the smart kid in school or the one who gets special attention from the teacher? "Teacher's Pet" comes to mind does it not? What happens to any child who has a perceived deformity or difference? Ugly insults come to mind when I choose to remember. Children ridicule each other and sometimes get into physical confrontation. It is normal behavior, but it does not have to be. Not if children are raised not to do that and we are insistent enough to make sure it becomes programmed behavior, like making up beds in the morning or saying "Thank you" and "Please". But most importantly, we must practice what we preach and lead by example.

I have come to the realization that most of us do not experience insecurity until we leave our households. To be more specific, most people do not hear negative feedback until they are separated from their caregivers. Our psychosis begins when other people start to leave their mark on the blank slates.

One day my gym class was being instructed in the even parallel bars. Our instructor showed us how to swing between the bars using our arms and shoulders for support. He also showed us how to dismount. He gave us two different options. One was safe; you simply sat on one of the bars and jumped down. The other was a simple dismount, where you swing your legs over the bars on the back swing, let go of the bars and land on the mats beside the bars. No one dismounted this way, until it was my turn. I was scared, but I wanted to do it. I loved watching gymnasts on television. Here I was with a chance to be like them.

I remember being on the bars. It seemed higher than I expected it to be. When I began to swing my legs, they seemed to be able to go as high as I dared push them. I got scared because I

---

[218] Baldassare Castiglione (1478-1529): Italian Renaissance writer, humanist, diplomat and courtier. Author of *The Book of the Courtier.*

thought about falling and failing. I thought about the reaction of my classmates if I messed up. I remember looking my gym teacher in the eye. He wanted me to do it. I swung my legs backwards hard enough to raise my torso almost to the vertical and pushed off the bars. My legs and body began to return to the upright position as I cleared the bar to my right. I grabbed the bar with my left hand as I passed it. So when I landed I was in a cross position with my arms stretched out to both sides with one hand on the right bar of the apparatus. I felt like an Olympiad. My teacher yelled, "Yes!" and clapped his hands. I smiled and rejoined the class. One of my classmates said, "Show off" Another said, "Mr. Perfect!" I earned the hatred of some of my peers that day and did not want to believe the reason why. This was 7th grade. My reward and defense was the "A" I got in the class. More importantly, I recognized then and there the nature of the human animal.

One mark of a great soldier is that he fights on his own terms or does not fight at all. Sun Tzu[219]

I once was in a fight with a boy named Terry who was reportedly the toughest kid in our grade. I did not want to. It was over something stupid, but I was backed into a corner. We were wrestling in gym class. I like to wrestle. My brother and I wrestled all the time. I surprised the other boys who looked at my small frame as weak by pinning my first three opponents. The teacher matched guys of equal size together. By my fourth match he had moved me up in weight and class status. I was going to wrestle the number two boy in the school. I beat him, but because I did not know that letting an opponent go gave him a point for an escape, it was ruled a draw. He was pissed. While standing in line to enter the showers I mentioned to someone beside me, "Terry got dogged." My opponent overheard and went immediately to Terry.

I was sitting on a bench when Terry showed up with his entourage. "I heard you want to fight me." "No. I do not want to fight you." "Eric said you said you want to fight me." "No. I said you got dogged out on the wrestling mat." It was true. He lost. He did not like it and neither did Eric. "I don't want to fight you Terry." I was scared now. The other boys, especially Eric, were pushing for Terry to beat my ass. They wanted to see a fight and it was going to happen. I was contemplating how to escape or how to win – fight or flight. Terry kept talking, but I did not hear him. I felt the vibration of the room. There was going to be violence; the crowd demanded it. I punched Terry as hard and as fast as I could. The first punch landed square on his jaw. He stumbled backwards. I threw punches in rhythm with his retreat. When he had backed himself out of the room and was pinned against a wall I kept punching, every blow to the face. The assistant gym teacher broke it up. I explained the situation with tears in my eyes. I told him, "I didn't want to fight." I even tried to shake Terry's hand. "Terry, I didn't want to fight you." He not only refused to shake my hand, but also would not look at me. He got his ass kicked twice in one day. His reputation was gone and so was he.

As I walked to my next class I noticed the buzz spreading and people pointing. I saw Eric telling the story to someone and felt the need to intervene. "Who won?" I asked. "You did", Eric said shaking his head in disbelief. They never messed with me again. I was promoted to the Captain of our gym class and I headed the exercise routine and all activities from that day forward. I did not want to fight and still do not. It is a waste. But, if you open a "Can a

---

[219] Giles: Sun Tzu or Sūn Zǐ (5th century BC?): Wu Dynasty era military strategists and philosopher. Credited with writing portions of The *Art of War*.

Whoopass,"[220] you had better bring your lunch, a gun or run. If someone says to you, "I don't want to fight you," do not mistake it for not being able to.

I remember walking across campus one day. We had just received the results of our Basic Computer Language Programming test. I saw two of my classmates sitting on a bench and one of them asked me how I did. I told him I got an 86. I was not impressed with the score but I was satisfied, because of the curve it was an "A". The other classmate did not like me because I had a hand in kicking him out of one of our fraternity parties. He tried to sneak in without paying. I was watching the door, and chances are I would have let him in for free if he had asked. But, he did not see it that way because he had crashed the party, ran to the bathroom, entered the last stall and then acted like he had been using the facilities. I grabbed his right shoulder from behind. "You 'gotta' go Brah." He protested and lied. My fraternity brothers showed up about that time and they were rough with him. I tried to intervene and tell them to stop trying to use force when it was not needed, but it was too late. They were throwing Jerry Springer punches by then and I was in the middle trying to stop it.

I had no gripes with this guy. He was just another knucklehead in a world full of them. My magnanimous friend did not see it that way. I was wrong and he was going to remind me of it at every opportunity. It did not help that he had gotten away with hitting one of my fraternity brothers in the mouth after his eviction. He walked up behind the principal person who was trying to assault him in the bathroom, blindsided him and ran. The University administrators forbade retaliation, so my aggressor felt untouchable and chose to forget the fact that I saved his ass from a serious beating the night he snuck into the party.

This particular day he saw fit to vent his anger at me once more with some smart-ass comment about my test grade. I was not bragging. It was a true score, but I was fed-up with his outbursts. I let him slide with too many comments before and he was gaining confidence. I had to stop it or it would only get worse. I told him, "If you want to fight me, let's go. I have a private spot where we will not be disturbed." He said many words, but declined my offer. I am ashamed that I allowed someone else to influence and control my emotions in that manner. However, he never bothered me again. It seems that many like to talk trash, but few are willing to put their asses where their mouths are, especially if the one they face is not afraid.

I was in the habit of going to Capitol Hill in Washington. It was the white area of town by then. They had not long converted the brick "row houses" into "townhouses" by simply putting a fence in the front and back. Whenever it snowed I liked to go door to door and ask if they wanted their walkways shoveled. It was quick, tax-free money. I could make $100.00 in a day or night, depending on when it stopped snowing. I was returning from such a foray about 10:30 at night (people do not like to open their doors to strangers after 9:30 or 10). I was alone because my cousin had declined to come with me. "It is too cold." "I ain't shoveling no white person's snow!" I quietly thought that everyone in the world shovels white people's snow in some form. Even now the Euro and Dollar run shit. I noticed a group of five or six boys walking towards me. I was carrying a shovel, so I was not afraid, but I knew that these boys were not going to let me walk through them without a confrontation. It was the rules of the streets. I was a stranger to

---

[220] "Can a Whoopass" (slang): angering someone to the point where they beat you for everyone they have been mad at since the last time the can was opened.

them. They had to defend their territory. It was three blocks to my destination, my cousin's house. I could have crossed the street but that would have made them think I was scared, and I had learned not to show fear and never to trigger the chase response. I made the conscious decision to walk through the group.

The oldest and biggest member of the group started with verbal jabs and threats. "Who are you?" "Where do you live?" "You got any money?" They surrounded me on three sides. I placed my back on the fence that separated the sidewalk from someone's front yard and kept the shovel on my shoulder, but my grip tensed. I remember thinking I could have incapacitated the leader and chased the other boys away, but I also thought about killing him by accident; I had never hit anyone in the face with the sharp edge of a shovel. I kept telling them, "No." and "Leave me alone." I also refused to give them money. I was giving them a warning. The leader pulled out a penknife and put the tiny blade against the left side of my chin. He told me how lucky I was that he did not cut me up. He was showing off for his friends and I was contemplating how best to get the shovel's blade from over my right shoulder to his head. I was getting mad. He was pushing. Right before I reached pressure point, he removed the knife and walked away, talking the entire time. One of the smaller boys saw fit to hit me with a snowball as a parting gift. I felt like going crazy and chasing them down the street, but I thought about catching one of them and what I might do in that state of mind. I wish I never had cause to mount a defense, but unfortunately that is not the way animal social groups function. Defense is as much a part of our lives as competition.

I keep telling myself I will to be happy. I will have good health. I will have wealth and I will not screw over anyone to get what is mine. That would make me more animal than human. At the same time, I will not be screwed either. Henry V[221] said it best just before the battle of Agincourt[222]. Outnumbered and weary from a long campaign, Henry's escape was cut off and he was asked to surrender and be ransomed. He replied, "I do not seek combat in my present condition, but I will not run from it either." The French lost. Just because someone does not appear to have a chance at victory does not mean they will not fight back, and win or die if given no other choice.

FYI: After World War I the British set their war plans, not against France or some other European power, but against the next foreseeable threat to their dominance of the sea, the United States. It is not ironic how easily friends can become foes and then friend again?

The Power of No

One of the most powerful defenses is the ability and willingness to say "No". A relative once called me. I had not heard from her in a God's minute so curiosity whispered in my ear, "What does she want?" About that time a male's voice was in the background and I asked her, "Who's that?" "My boyfriend." "Can you send me some money so I can pay the electric bill?" "Can I talk to your boyfriend?" I heard them discussing why I wanted to talk to him through her attempt to muffle the phone. "Yeah, what's up?" I tried my best to convey to him that it takes a desperate

---

[221] Henry V (1387-1422 AD): King of England (1413-1422). Would have been King of England and France had he lived a few months longer.
[222] Agincourt, France: Battle of Agincourt was fought on 25 October 1415 during the Hundred Years War.

"Man" to have his girlfriend call someone and ask for money to pay his electric bill. He tried to convey to me why I should send the money via Western Union. This same person later called and asked me if I would take her child. I said, "No." on both occasions.

No one likes to hear the word "No" when they ask for something. We are programmed socially to lie before saying, "No". It is a lot easier to tell someone that you have to think about it than to refuse outright. For many different reasons, we do not like to say no. Hearing someone say, "No!" is enough to spark the demon inside us all. Have you ever tried saying no to your children? Have you ever said, "No" to a bully, a teacher, a spouse, a parent, a preacher, a friend or a stranger? How did they react?

There are examples in our history where countries did not accept "No" for an answer, and used physical force and/or intimidation to force their will upon others. Commodore Perry to the Japanese: "Open your ports to trade or else this fleet of warships I brought with me on this mission of peace will return with more ships on a different mission." Great Britain (the Opium Wars) to China: "Let the East-Indian Trading Company sell opium in your country or we will declare war." The introduction of Christianity in the Americas: "Be saved and/or be slaves." The Unites States to Japan during the 1930's, "Stop your expansion into China or we will cut off your oil supply[223] and give the Chinese military support." If I were Japan, I would have replied, "You did the same thing in the Philippines not long ago." Great Britain to the American colonials, "Do as you are told, pay us taxes, and remain subservient or else." These are just a few examples of what happens when you say, "No!"

Children do the same thing. They learn that saying, "Please," a million times or asking for the same thing in different ways is a useful way of getting what they want. If they do not get it, they get nasty and throw temper tantrums. I constantly have to remind myself that everyone has the right to say "No" and I should not be upset or offended. I usually try to avoid asking people for anything; I do not like hearing lies, excuses or the word "No". It saves me from a lot of drama and disappointment.

Here is a situation that we all have encountered. I call it backing someone into a corner and emotional blackmail. Have you ever had people set you up so that they think you cannot say no? It usually starts with some flattery or plea to our humanity, exploitation of a relationship and/or an appeal to your sense of right and wrong. We have all had to endure some lengthy explanation as to why we have to do something for someone else. "If you care about me…" I hate it and I interrupt it every time by asking, "What do you want?" before they get a chance to make me feel guilty about a situation that I have nothing to with and did nothing to instigate.

If you ever want to get rid of a goldigger, consistently tell her, "No". If you want to keep her, say, "Yes" some times.

---

[223] The Japanese imported the majority of its oil from the United States. They had a limited amount of oil after the embargo and had to do what the United States said or find its own oil. The Japanese opted for the latter. They took raw material rich Southeast from the colonial powers.

What We Do For Money

Every evil, harm and suffering in this life comes from the love of riches. Saint Catherine of Siena[224]

Because we have isolated ourselves from natural predators and have overcome most of the issues of surviving our environment, we have become less dependent on each other and more dependent on our professions (jobs) and society. Selfishness and self-interest now outweigh human obligation. Because of this we are able to concentrate more energy trying to satisfy our need for love (esteem, attention, affection).

In many societies love is strangely associated with material wealth. We have learned that the person with more cows can have more wives. The person with more money has better living conditions, more luxury items, and higher social status and is perceived as a better perspective mate, not to mention a powerful friend. To have more is a major objective in most people's lives. I guess that is why I am a minimalist. I once told my sister, "You should never travel with more than you can carry."

It is in our nature to seek more. Unfortunately, we seek more money and status so that we may have more love. Instead of more knowledge, wisdom and spiritual balance, we want more material wealth and power. These are temporary things that can change with the winds of fortune and disappear all together after death. We seem to have forgotten that with inner peace, and balance comes all our heart's desires and that love is not only free but also infinite.

Wealth has become the prevailing gauge by which most of us are judged. Have you ever seen a beautiful woman with the dorkiest looking guy or vice versa and wondered, "What are they doing together?" Yes it could be true love, but more than likely it is all about the Benjamins[225]. I have told people, "When I am wealthy, I will not change." We will see.

Have you ever known people to boost their own social status by claiming association with someone who is rich, famous or in good social standing? My friend has a bottle of wine autographed by a barber who once cut Michael Jackson's hair. He holds on to it like it is some type of ancient artifact; I feel like drinking it. It is as if knowing someone who has fame and wealth gives you a portion of what they have. Some want autographs and photo opportunities with famous people. I understand the thought process behind it, but I do not agree with it. I do not go crazy when I see a personality and I do not want their autograph. However, I would like to ask them about their experiences.

If you have a Mercedes, you do not have to be physically beautiful. One day a guy driving a Ferrari summoned my friend to him. I say summoned because he did not even get out of the car, he just waved her over. The other women commented that he was not attractive. She said, "I do not care; he's driving a Ferrari." Would she have gone to him, if she had not seen the car? I doubt it. The Ferrari owner knew his chances of success were greater if he was associated with the car. The car said everything that his unattractiveness could not. "I am rich." "I am a good

---

[224] Saint Catherine of Siena (1347-1380): Dominican Tertiary. Said to have received the Stigmata in 1375.
[225] Benjamins: reference to Benjamin Franklin who is pictured on the $100.00 bill.

provider." and "If you have sex with me, I can take care of you." Do you most admire the beggar or the tycoon, the trash man or the lawyer? To most, money is the end that justifies the means. In actuality, money should be the means that justifies the end.

I became involved with a stripper who thought she was a player. Shaquana had arranged for someone to introduce us at a club. From the beginning I knew she wanted to be with me for one reason and one reason only; she wanted to be paid for sex. If you think about a ghetto girl trying to be classy, you have her pegged from the multi-colored fake nails and the big over done hair with sparkles to her attitude. She was low budget. She was sexy, but had little else going for her from my perspective. We wanted the same things out of life, but our methods of obtaining them were different.

The first time she spent the night together, she would not let me have sex with her. I was puzzled as to why she was naked in my bed in the first place. I made my intentions plain and she came over anyway. Why the games? I rolled over and went to sleep thinking, "You can keep the pussy! I'll get it sooner or later, if you keep coming over."

I went to see her work one night with the boys. My friend suggested it. It was boys' night and he really liked strip clubs. No wonder he's on his third marriage. We watched and tipped all the performers. Shaquana danced, but did not take her top off. She did however pay for a lap dance for me. The next night she let me have sex with her, but she kept trying to get me to take the condom off. After that first time, we did it on several other occasions. Yes, I went along with the game and took her without a condom. She now wanted me to come inside of her. I asked her if she was on birth control. She said, "No". I asked her why she wanted me to come inside of her. "Do you want to get pregnant?" She again said, "No". That was enough to confirm my suspicions. She wanted to run the "I'm pregnant" game, even though she was on birth control. The objective of this game is to get abortion money. I had been the victim of this before. I decided to play along; I faked coming inside of her.

Not long afterwards, she came over to tell me she was pregnant. I told her how happy I was and that I was looking forward to having a baby boy. I just wanted a blood test when the child materialized. She looked at me as if she wanted to kill me. I had rewritten her script and she had nowhere to go with her bullshit plan. When she departed she said, "I am going to have it and I hope it is yours." Women like this give all other women a bad name. If you have ever done something like this, you cannot judge her. She was just trying to play a game with someone who had played it before and understood the rules a bit more than she. Fear is the key to making this strategy effective. The victim has to have something to lose and believe that he is the father.

When I reunited with my father he was a permanent resident at Howard University Hospital. His diabetes and alcohol had put him there. His favorite drink was Crown Royal. I used to buy him a bottle once or twice a week. It took some effort and ingenuity on my part because I was 16-years old. I felt bad about doing this. I knew that the alcohol was not helping his condition, but I also remembered something my grandfather had said years earlier. His father had once asked for a glass of whiskey and the women caring for him refused to give it to him. My grandfather braved their wrath and gave him what he asked for. "He's a grown man… If he wants a drink, he should be able to have one; he earned it," is what my grandfather said. I asked

141

an adult what I should do. "Let him drink himself to death… He hasn't done anything for you this far in your life. At least you will get the insurance money," I had already mentioned that my father had told me of a policy that would pay each of his children $25,000.00 upon his death. Armed with that advice I continued to buy him liquor until the day I walked into his room and he was comatose. The staff was working frantically to revive him when I walked in. My heart sank when the doctor asked me if I was bringing him alcohol. I lied, but the doctor knew better and the smell confirmed that alcohol was the cause of my father's current condition. At that moment I felt small and worthless. I felt like I was killing him and never bought another bottle. If he wanted to drink himself to death, I would not be a part of it. My conscience would not allow it. When he died alone there was no insurance - another lie to his children. I felt relieved that I had not followed the advice of my confidant. They had selfish reasons for wanting Robert dead.

Peace

I now pray for peace before I pray for money. If anyone can give me a single example when there has not been war, I will stop.

What has happened to every person that has promoted peace and non-violence?

That is the testimony that will be presented at the trial of humanity.

Contradictions

My entire life I have run into situations that contradict what I have been taught was right. Sometimes I went with what felt right, and at others times I went with the desires of others. Even as a child I remember making conscious decisions that I knew were against the wishes of adults.

Parents instruct their children about what is right according to their own value system (usually what they were taught). Adults act as a substitute for the prefrontal cortex until our children's brains develop enough to properly make these decisions for themselves. But frequently the real world shows children the opposite of what they have been taught in-house. We tell our children not to fight and that it is not nice to talk about people, but they see it everywhere. We tell children that sex is bad or that it is only for married people, but the pornography we hide in the house, the sexually suggestive clothing we wear and the cinematic performances we continuously watch send a different message (show me a major movie without sex). Imagine their confusion. Actually we do not have to imagine the confusion; we can remember it. Remember the violence (verbal or mental abuse included), the lies and how rare it was to have a real friend when you were a child?

We tell our children not to use drugs and we use them ourselves. Using any drug (alcohol, tobacco, marijuana, Prozac, Valium, Viagra, sugar, etc.) to cope with daily life sends a message loud and clear. The interpretation from a child's point of view is it is acceptable to use drugs; Mom and Dad use them, even if they deny it. The only issue that remains is which ones to use. Many children get their drugs from the medicine cabinet. Regardless of what we say, if we do something to the contrary, we have lost credibility. And, do not be fooled into thinking you can hide *anything* from a child. We can send them to their rooms and lock the door, but they are aware of what goes on. If you cannot find something in the house, even if they are not supposed to know where it is, ask your children.

I remember the after church conversations I sometimes heard in my grandparent's home. They always contained something negative about someone in the congregation or some criticism of what the preacher said. I thought it was a huge contradiction. We just left the house of God where love and virtue are paramount. And here they were cackling like hens about what someone wore, who was pregnant and not married or "All My Children." I did not get it. I still do not, though I do understand why we exhibit the behavior.

A woman once accused me of using her sister. I told her, "You use two men: one you live with and the other is married." She sat quiet for a few seconds before she replied in the baby voice, "But I'm a woman." "Oh, you crazy... You crazy."

I have been trying to comprehend the fact that adolescents who reach the age of eighteen are mature enough to decide whether a fetus has life or death, go off to war and vote, but cannot buy alcohol because they are not mature enough to handle the responsibility of drinking.

The Teacher asks, "Can anyone in the class tell me what state we are in?" A student replies, "Denial!"

Another example of how we contradict ourselves is the "birds and bees conversation". Instead of explaining sex and the biological drive behind it, parents try to camouflage it. Instead of telling the naked truth about the strange urges inside of us, we stress the negative concepts of engaging in these natural desires in an attempt to scare children out of exploring their sexuality.

Mothers frequently tell their daughters, "Boys just want sex." This is true, but we should tell them why. Furthermore, girls like sex too; otherwise boys would have to rape them. They just like to get something in exchange for it. "You'll get pregnant!" is another common statement. My grandfather told my mother, "Make him wear a condom." He told me, "Make sure you wear a condom." and that was it as far as the sex conversation. Everything I know about sex came from doing it. If I had listened to the suggestions of other males, my partners would be sexually frustrated.

If I had a child, I would explain the physiological reasons behind sexual curiosity. I would take my daughter to a physician to be given some form of contraceptive, and I would show a son and a daughter how to put on a condom. If she or he is going to have sex I cannot stop them. I can advise against it or for it, but they are the ones who will ultimately have to make that decision, and they will be without me when they make it. I cannot make them do anything; there is such a thing as free will. Parents can only apply negative reinforcement to incidents they discover. In my solution, I am removing the possibility of pregnancy. I am also addressing STDs. I would not "order" a child not to have sex, but I would make sure he or she was aware of the possible consequences of sex and being in a relationship.

The fear we try to instill cannot fight natural urges. If it could, we would not have teen pregnancy, "immoral" behavior, sexually transmitted diseases or lawbreakers. What the young

143

are feeling is not new; it is natural and hormonal. We have all experienced it, should be able to accurately describe the feelings, and explain the biology and associated natural behavior of puberty to them so they can truly understand why they feel the way they do. At the least they are enabled to make informed, if not smart, choices.

Again, the decision to choose any path is strongly influenced by the society in which we live. If it was acceptable in ancient times to invade another village or community to take the women and food for your own village's survival, regardless of the reasoning, it set precedence for following generations. If our neighbor was not willing to trade with us or had more than us, if strong enough, would try to take what we wanted. We have been robbing and enslaving our neighbors for ages in order to improve our lives. Them or us, is where it began and where it remains, the strong subduing the weak. We were taught long ago that the most profitable and risky form of business (gambling) is war. No culture can call itself civilized and at the same time practice this kind of behavior. Anyone who has read about colonization knows of what we are capable of as human animals. Millions of those displaced over the eons can testify against "civilization" at the trial of humanity.

Differences in culture, sexual preference, religion, physical appearance, thinking or location are enough separation between people of the same origins to justify wholesale slaughter, abuse, slavery and bigotry. Ever heard of ethnic cleansing, gay bashing, modern day slavery or racism? If right and wrong exists, where do we point the finger of blame for such behavior?

"All human evil comes from a single cause, man's inability to sit still in a room." Blaise Pascal[226]

I have a question. Why can Israel, Pakistan and India have nuclear weapons, but North Korea cannot? By that I mean, of the countries that are not signatories of the Nuclear Non-Proliferation Treaty, NPT, and are suspected of developing nuclear technology, (India, Pakistan, Israel, and North Korea, which withdrew from the NPT in 2003), the United States has not applied the same pressures on Israel, Pakistan or India that it has on North Korea. As a matter of fact, we have agreed to sell India civilian nuclear technology and have not extended the same offer to Pakistan (possibly because of Dr. Abdul Khan's confession that he sold nuclear technology to Iran and North Korea and other countries). When the international community became aware of a budding nuclear program in Israel in the 1960's, the Israelis refused inspections by the International Atomic Energy Agency (IAEA) and placed obstacles in the way of US inspectors.

When thinking about the above question, please assume that I know what the worldview of Kim Jong-Il is. My point is that we do not apply the same sanctions or threats to all of the countries that have developed or are attempting to develop nuclear weapons, but we should have. It is too late now. Inconsistent and biased policies, do not promote cooperation from those on the short end of the stick. Besides, nothing is going to happen militarily. A law is not a law unless you can enforce it, so the United States position of "North Korea can have peace or nuclear weapons, but not both!" and "We will not tolerate a nuclear North Korea!" mean nothing. It reminds me of that scene in "Team America; The World's Policemen" when the UN representative threatened Lil' Kim with, "We will be very very angry with you, and we will send

---

[226] Blaise Pascal (1623-1662): French Mathematician, Philosopher and Physicist.

you a letter saying so." Our foreign policies suck. Instead of talking softly and carrying a big stick, we are talking loudly and carrying a twig. Not that I agree with either, but if you talk big and cannot or will not back it up with effective actions, it means nothing.

FYI: We started a war once over "WMD's", "Regime change" and "Democracy"....

I once called a female friend a "bitch". Her response was predictably hostile (if you have ever called an African-American female that word, you know what I am talking about), "Don't call me a bitch!" I responded with, "I just did." "Don't call me that!" she repeated. I retorted with, "If you stop acting like one, I will." She stood there with a look of helplessness on her face. It was an accurate look since there was not a damn thing she could do to enforce her proclamation because I was not having sex with her.

Lessons Learned

I was raised to keep white people at arm's length. That is a mild way to put it. I was raised not to trust or like white people, but I cannot go to work or school and act like I do not trust and like them. They would get offended and there are a lot more white people than African-American people in the United States. My grandfather told me, "If I were fighting a bear and a white man offered to help, I'd tell him to help the bear." Over the years, I learned trusting anyone is a chancy proposition. Am I wrong or right in thinking this way?

I was not born with this distrust; I learned it. I learned it the first time I told another boy that I had sex with a girl. He confronted the girl. She got mad. That lesson took a long time to learn. "The root cannot get mad at the leaves for revealing what it knows to the wind." If you want something to spread quickly, say it is a secret.

I learned to distrust the first time someone did not repay a loan. I do not care anymore. If I have it, you are welcome to it. The things you give always come back tenfold. A friend once gave me some advice. She said, "If someone asks you for a loan, give them twice as much. If they do not pay you back, it was a small price to pay to be rid of them."

I do not even take lies personally anymore. I have learned to live with them. Hell, I expect to be lied to everyday. When I hear the truth, it is a pleasant surprise. Watching how easily loyalties can change is a lesson we all learn early. How many best friends have turned out to be better enemies? Have you ever fallen out of favor? Have you ever been called something foul? Who said this to you? Have you forgiven them or are you haunted by desires to hit them so hard their dog bleeds? If we were all raised with a sense of right and wrong, why is it that so many people do things that make us think they are wrong?

I had to be nine or ten years old when I got into a fight with a classmate. I do not remember what the fight was about, but do remember the matter pertained to maintaining my reputation and social standing. We started fighting right outside of our classroom shortly after school. Our teacher must have heard the commotion because she intervened, let him go home and held me after school in her classroom for ten minutes or so.

She said some things to me that day that I did not actually hear until recently. I remember her telling me that I was smart enough not to have to fight. It was a moral sermon of the wrong in fighting over something stupid. I did not have the words to explain the importance of fighting and winning outside the protection of the classroom. The ear beating reduced me to a simple "Yes, Ms. Gordon."

When she let me out of the classroom there was a crowd waiting for me. They wanted to see a fight. Motivated and excited by the crowd (mob mentality), I ran after the boy. They directed me to him. I did not know it at the time, but I caught up with him in front of his home. I kicked him in the back to start round two. Round three started after his mother intervened and decided to let us continue the fight while she refereed.

It was a TKO. Despite the bias she showed as a referee, his mother threw in the towel when I was straddled on top of her son beating his face into a pulp while he grasped my bushy Afro with both hands. It seemed like all the spectators formed a procession and I was walked home with them cheering the entire way. It felt good to have the support of so many people. Their cheers made the pain in my neck and the fatigue I was feeling worth it because I did not hear my teacher's words until recently. She said, "Anytime you have to resort to violence, you are in the wrong because there is always another way."

Me, Myself and I

Doing the right thing is not always so simple. But, I believe that people do not purposely develop bad habits.

Aristotle sharply disagreed with Socrates' belief that knowing what is right always results in doing right. Aristotle thought, "The great enemy of moral conduct is precisely the failure to behave well even on those occasions when one's deliberation has resulted in clear knowledge of what is right." Aristotle thought that knowing right does not mean doing right. I agree because I can name circumstances when I have not followed my inner voice and the consequences of doing so have always come back to kick me in the butt one way or the other. Shoulda, woulda, coulda...

My nephew hit puberty at nine. He began to find reasons to enter his mother's room without knocking. This peculiar behavior seemed to occur right after she showered. When his mother told me, I almost busted a gut. "Poor boy," was all I could say. This little kid was masturbating at an extremely early age. I did not start masturbating until I was 15 or 16. It was shortly after I had my first "wet dream". This kid is nine and coming into puberty. And they wonder why he is so high strung. It is the beginning of his first "rut".

I remember seeing my mother's friend naked; I was about the same age as my nephew. I was exiting our room and made a left. There in the bathroom was Pat with a towel in her hand. I noticed her breasts looked different, they sagged. She scared me; the sight of her body did not. I thought that I might have done something wrong when she screamed. It was not until she said, "I am sorry," and covered up did I know it was "all good". I think I was making one of my nephew's moves. Was I wrong for sexual curiosity?

146

All my life I have been told to tell the truth. I have come to realize that people do not like the truth when it pertains to them, if it is unflattering. I have learned that people actually anticipate and expect others to lie. I have learned that I cannot tell the truth all the time and expect to fit in.

I was once given the charge of conducting an investigation into the cause of a damaged engine on one of our aircraft while I was in the Navy. The engine ingested a foreign particle, probably a rock, but it was my charge to prove that the engine damage occurred by some other means. Foreign object damage was viewed as preventable and reflected badly on the command. When I suggested that the damage was indeed a result of the ingestion of a foreign body, the maintenance department protested. My Commanding Officer and the Maintenance Officer coerced (threatened) me into changing my evaluation. When I would not do it, they assigned someone else who could do a more thorough job.

When I was working at a manufacturing company a plastic stirring paddle broke in one of the huge corn cooking vats. The paddle broke during the previous shift and when aware of it, I had the processors pick the visible pieces of plastic from the corn as it passed on the conveyer belt. The next day when all the information came to light, I found myself talking to Quality Assurance and the Production Manager. I told them that I was not confident that we had retrieved all the plastic. I told them had I known that the problem had happened on the previous shift, I would have discarded all of the corn in that vat and used one of the others. Despite this, they dragged me in front of the Plant Manager to decide whether to destroy two shifts of product or to ship it. I told the Plant Manager the truth. I was confident of product quality from the point I became aware of the issue and instructed the processors to watch the corn conveyor belt. They shipped all of it. The customer complaints went through the roof.

I was taught not to lie, but in both instances I was pressured not to tell the truth. I was given options that supported the team's objectives and violated my own sense of right and wrong. It hurt. It hurts every time I do what is best for the group and violate my own personal beliefs. Sometimes consensus sucks.

I remember meeting three people during Carnival. We met through a mutual acquaintance who had arranged their housing. They were fairly good people from what I could tell. Their group consisted of one male and two females, so the male had his hands full whenever they went out at night. One of the girls would get high on everything and needed to be watched constantly. The first time I met them I was sympathetic. "We want to have a good time, but we do not feel safe." I invited them to join with us. It was taxing. I ended up tying one of the girl's arms to my belt hoop, so she would not run off with the first guy who grabbed her. The real issue was they were foreigners and during Carnival many tourists lose their inhibitions. The locals have become accustomed to foreigners performing highly promiscuous acts during this time of the year. All of the people I was with looked local, except for one male, but he spoke the language fluently and lived there so he knew the routine. Despite this, his white skin attracted a pickpocket who was promptly apprehended by two of the women in our original group.

My friends did not want to be bothered with them after the first night, but the next night they wanted to join with us again. Most of the group (the black females) vocally expressed disapproval. I relayed this to the male. He assured me that the girls would behave. That was an impossible promise, but I could not say no. I liked him and one of the girls. She was cool and did not do anything to bring issues to the group. That night we tried to leave my place before they showed up, but they arrived in time to catch us.

We knew they liked to purchase drugs and go to their place to "juice up" before we hit the streets. I have no issue with this; everyone who was out and about was on his or her own personal drug, and who was I to judge. Besides, I was higher than a kite in a hurricane. I told them we would wait at the same spot as the night before. The only difference was that I would not accompany them to their spot to get high. It was in fact a way to ditch them without any conflict.

We did ditch them and I feel horrible for it. If I had it to do again, I would have stayed with them and allowed my friends to do what they wanted, with or without me. It did not help that later one of our group had to use the bathroom, and I waited for him. This friend ran into the party we had ditched. The look on his face when he relayed their exchange to me hurt. He said that the male was having a hell of a time protecting the girls and they were headed back to their apartment for the night. I think I was personally wrong for lying even though I probably saved us an evening of complications.

If you do not have your life together and want to superimpose your drama on others, imagine me holding up three fingers and saying, "Read between the lines!"

People are debating the correctness of the conflict in Iraq. My personal view is that we have no business in Iraq or any other country that has not invited us[227]. It feels wrong to me. It feels like a lie and it is getting worse. It feels like a game of global monopoly where the names of the properties and the time period have been changed. It feels like the most dangerous job bank in the world. It feels like someone's trying to start another crusade. In saying that, I have just labeled myself unpatriotic. I am a historian and a patriot. I study history and until we do something different, "It ain't rocket science". Some of you who are reading this have never served a day in military service or even fired a weapon in anger, and yet you will call me unpatriotic after almost ten years of military service. Some of you have never killed or been held up at gunpoint. Some of you have never been beaten by a group of humans acting like animals. Some have never known freedom. Some have never been a minority in anything. Most have not faced death. The assumption is not logical. Especially since some have never had to defend anything except their vanity.

I think for myself after gathering relevant data[228] and in this case, there is no humanist reason to be in Iraq. There are several other reasons, and that "Ain't brain surgery". It was a mistake that many have paid for with their lives and limbs. When I read that the VA's budget was decreased in time of war, I questioned it. When I see the Gulf Coast years after hurricane Katrina, I questioned it. When US senators, cameramen, writers, a teenager with Pelotas the size of Alaska and soldiers come back with different reports than I see on BBC or any other news

---

[227] I say this meaning the majority of the people, not the rich, powerful or puppets.

[228] My data: the history of armies that invade and try to hold foreign territories far from home. They always lose and end up leaving eventually, no matter how mighty the invader. Sometimes it takes one year, sometimes 10, sometimes 40 years or 300.

agencies that are not run by one of the US moguls with private agendas, I question it. I say our brand of freedom costs too much of everything and is gained through the toils, sweat, tears and blood of others.

No one will be held accountable for this blunder. For those of you who argue that the people of Iraq are now free, yeah right. We have just postponed a civil war, a natural power struggle that happens all the time. Look at the rest of the world and how we respond to their internal issues then ask yourself why we respond with force, diplomacy, flirting, etc.

I like freedom. I wish it for everyone, but I question the governments of Saudi Arabia, China, Jordan, Kuwait, Egypt, etc. who do not have free elections, who are ruled by kings or dictators, but are not on the United States' "Axis of Evil" list. If we are going to fight for freedom, we need to fight for everyone's freedom (at home first), not just those countries where there is the prospect of economic gain, not just to fill our gas tanks (it is better to walk than to have someone die), not in countries where we are protecting the economic interests of a corporation, an individual or ideology. But, that is just my option.

I believe that war is designed to obtain something by the use of force, and that something usually translates to profit. I also believe that countries with large military arms have to use them somewhere, somehow, sometime and on someone. We have run out of logical options of how to get what we want, so we resort to force. It reminds me of children in my kindergarten sandbox. They were maladjusted and unaccustomed to sharing anything.

I was taught not to fight without a reason. When it was time to fight, I was taught to win at any cost. "If he's bigger than you, then you pick up a stick and hit him in the head," my aunt said. I remember thinking, "I could kill someone if I hit them like that."

Later in life I learned about non-violence and what can be accomplished through peaceful means. Gandhi and M.L. King used these techniques to great effect. I read a book called "The Art of War", the oldest military treatise in the world by Sun Tzu. This book is required reading in many of the military academies of the world and in many of the boardrooms as well. The most important thing I learned from Sun Tzu with all his strategies and suggestions about what to do when outnumbered or deep in enemy territory was: *To fight and conquer in all your battles is not supreme excellence; supreme excellence consists in breaking the enemy's resistance without fighting* (Giles). In other words, ultimate victory is defined by not having to fight; my teacher's words years ago. I did not hear them then. I hear them now.

Only the fearful need defend themselves.

War is wasteful and should be used as a last resort to defend against those who have not learned that violence is destructive. And that includes our individual selves. Yes, I think a person should wait to be struck before striking. I did not say stand there and be hit; move or duck and do not be blind-sided. We have all been in situations where we became uncomfortable because of the threat of physical conflict. We can read our opponent at that moment. Pretend the opponent is your husband, wife, kids, best friend, girl or boyfriend.

149

There is a reason for the conflict; who is wrong? They are. They are always wrong. I ask how I offended them. Is there any way to diffuse this without losing face, appearing weak or being at a disadvantage? Are they going to hit me, and if so where and with which hand or foot, or with which memory? I certainly hope they do not know karate or the Jedi mind trick.

We have a right to defend ourselves, but without killing if possible. If we were as smart as we pretend to be, we would not ever be blind-sided. But it always happens and we always react or overreact. I like proactive thinking not reactive.

I am convinced that if those who decided to go to war had to fight and lead on the front lines as real leaders did, there would not only be less conflicts, but also fewer bad leaders. They would die in battle like they should. Their God seems to demand blood sacrifice. I would pay good money to see the former President and Vice-President fight in Iraq. Mr. Bush, if you want to impress me, strap on some body armor or not, and go on a foot patrol in Ramadi with a Marine unit. Mr. Cheney, keep going hunting with your friends.

It is my belief that we are supposed to be altruists. It is one of the things that separate us from other forms of animals. That is why we came together to form societies, for mutual cooperation and benefit. Competition and greed put a big dent into that idea. I tried to figure out why I feel guilty and sad when I pass by a homeless person and do nothing to help them. Is it that I feel remorse because I am breaking a spiritual law? Are these emotions built into our being to remind us of our obligations to one another? I know what some of you are thinking. "I do not give to homeless people because they can work just like me;" "I give at church;" "I cannot help everybody;" "I do not have the money to give away;" or "I give to organizations at work." These attitudes are directly related to how we are socialized.

It warms my heart to see the outpouring of donations for victims of hunger, natural disasters, disease and war. I believe we have a need to help each other. This, like crying, is not learned; it is instinctual. And, mentally or genetically damaged creatures and people are the only beings that break instinctual laws. Again, only defective animals and people violate natural laws. And, only "Human's" can violate spiritual law. Societies are forced to instill their own sets of laws in order to enforce compliance to normalities that may or may not contradict natural and spiritual law. These normalities are put into place to stabilize societies and standardize behavior. It is akin to herding cattle. Yet, if we followed the voice inside, we would not need the laws of any country, state, county or city. Instead of following what we feel inside, we continuously violate our altruistic nature and then wonder why there is crime, hunger, war and a hole in the ozone.

Every species has evolved and continues to evolve in order to adapt to the environment. Believe me; we humans have not stopped evolving. There are only a few species that have not changed over time. Into what do you suppose we are evolving? I think that we are evolving into the perfect altruist species, a species that does not get jealous if one of its members possesses more of this or that. I believe we are headed in a direction where greed, self-interest and fear of not having do not exist. I think at some point in time people who choose to stand-alone or have a controversial point of view will not be assaulted. People will become Masters-At-Arms physically and intellectually, but most importantly, spiritually.

150

We will learn to trust in our choices and feelings, and our societies will begin to raise children in an environment that is truly nurturing. Our societies will stop making choices for us. This allows true freedom and real growth. Somewhere along the time line we will no longer care about money or physical appearance, and we will give to those who are in need without expectation of reward or recognition. We will start to believe that there are no accidents and we are placed in the path of others for a reason. Somehow we must learn that unions are temporary; that every experience has a purpose and lesson. I know that one day we will be forced to act according to the natural and spiritual laws or we will join the dinosaurs.

I cannot live your experiences; I can only share similar ones. The same is true of you. Even when we witness the exact same event, when trying to explain what we saw, our stories are frequently different. I equate opinions and choices to seeing the light of the Sun. It is beautiful and magnificent. But what color is it? The light spectrum has many colors. The color you see is dependent upon perspective and filters you choose to use. These days when I take a stance, I argue the opposite point of view to see where the holes in my argument lie. That keeps me from taking many stances because there are always two sides, and the truth which lies somewhere in the middle.

Good living is harming no others, living by the internal law and being able and willing to give to others, knowing it to be a reward in itself. I say, "Right and Wrong do not, and never did exist." It is a matter of perspective and perspectives are subjective.

I will always believe that there are no accidents. Therefore every decision has a lesson or a reason for being. I wished it or it is here as a teacher. Every obstacle is a learning opportunity, and unpleasant events should not be considered as negative. No decision we make, or the consequences of those decisions, can be considered wrong or right. It was simply what we chose to do by our own design. No one complains when the tree bears fruit, so why be discouraged when leaves fall to the ground. Rake them up and use them for mulch. That is life because we are still animals trying to be human beings.

I know I have done the right thing if I have no questions, regrets or concerns after the deed.

There is no greater hierarchy than to do the right thing for the wrong reasons. T.S. Elliot[229]

We all seem to run from Destiny. But, she is more persistent than United Student Aid Funds' collections department. I have come to believe that if someone were stranded on a dessert island, eating coconuts and fishing to survive, a guy in scuba gear would emerge from the surf once a year with a collections letter enclosed in a waterproof satchel, "Here you are MR. / MRS. SMITH... Have a nice day."

Please readdress the list of rights and wrongs that you wrote down or thought about before you read this chapter.

---

[229] Thomas Stearns Eliot aka T.S. Elliot (1888-1965): Noble Prize winning Poet, Writer, and Critic.

Rights	Wrongs

Chapter V

Relationships

Relationship: the state of being related or interrelated[230].

Those who will not hear a scream will strain to hear a whisper.

Relationship Quiz

1. Ever wish your other half would disappear?

2. Ever said a foul word to them aloud?

3. Ever had a physical confrontation with them?

4. Do you have children together?

5. Do you have children separate?

6. Do you fight over money?

7. Are there long periods of time without sex?

8. Has your mate gained weight?

If you answered, "Yes" to one (1) of these questions, you must be going into the second month of your relationship.

If you answered, "Yes" to two to three (2-3) of these questions, the six (6) month threshold has been breached.

If you answered, "Yes" to four (4) of these questions, I'm going to take a wild guess and say you are married, or have been together so long, you might as well be.

If you answered "Yes" to more than four (4) of these questions, it is time for RITZ Crackers[231].

How are your relationships? Think about it for at least a minute… How do you really feel about your mother, father, siblings, co-workers, husband, wife, children and friends? How do they really feel about you? If you could vent and say exactly what you feel to everyone you know, what would you say? Pretend you are talking to a shrink.

It takes two or more to argue.

It seems to me that most modern relationships are based on the "What can you do for me" principle.

---

[230]Merriam-Webster's.
[231] Reference to Eddie Murphy's *Raw* comedy routine.

We are related and interrelated to every living thing, and made of that same material expelled by dying stars billions of years ago. We are connected to one another physiologically, chemically, mentally and spiritually. That is a humanistic point of view and one I happen to share.

I also believe in another reality, the day-to-day interaction with other humans. It is every person for self most of the time. If you are related in some way to another, they might get the occasional pass, if not "fuck you". This is the view I think most people have of our reality. But, as I said before, I think we are all related. What a conundrum!

The voice inside says, "We are one." My body says, "I am an individual." My mind questions, "Why do we have an inexplicable need to be with others?" This is where most modern relationships stand. There are too many questions that have gone unexplained.

Indulge me in what Albert Einstein would call a "thought experiment". Imagine that everyone was physically identical. How would you judge your mate then? Imagine everyone had the same accessories and possessions. What would you use to distinguish between a good potential mate and a bad one? If someone has no perceived value or subjective faults, do we associate with him or her from a stance of equality? That being said, what do we have left in our day-to-day relationships?

I think everyone should stand alone before they try to stand with someone else. Being self-sufficiency is the goal of every organism that has its basis in organic life, from the amoeba to the human. Only after achieving this, can we truly bond; anything else is a parasitic relationship. They say "God blesses the child who has his own". I tend to agree, but I have an expanded interpretation of this parable. I take it to not only mean have my own house, car or money, but I also extend it to having my own spirit, will, dreams and freedom. My mate, friends and associates should have the same.

This is a sensitive subject and I am sure I will piss off many people by stating a simple truth: the only reason we interact is that we want something that we think another person can provide. We have a need, an itch that we think they can scratch. For the most part, everyone who associates with us does so with an agenda and everyone with whom we associate is to complete some agenda. We all function this way, consciously or not.

When someone wants something from you, be polite, wash your ass and put on clean knickers because it is about to be kissed or kicked, and we all remember what our mothers said about clean underwear and going to the hospital. We stroke egos, use grooming, make jailhouse promises and sometimes beg. If these tactics work, we are happy. If they do not work, we may try intimidation, emotional blackmail, or force if it is an option. We will punish by pouting or displaying some other form of malicious behavior. We all like to get what we want.

I prefer to get to the point without the usual pleasantries. The flattery that usually precedes a request is designed to make denial difficult. I do not want to be groomed, lied to or backed into a corner to do a favor. Just ask. I have heard many stories from people seeking favors, some true, some exaggerations, and some outright lies. I have also been on the telling end. I know now that it is not necessary. Just be honest and ask for what you want, and accept "No" as readily as you do "Yes". There is no need to be mad at someone because we think we were denied. The day continues and we can try something else to achieve the same goals. Destiny just said, "Not like that."

Whenever we socialize, it is because we have a reason. We want something and it does not have to be a bad something. If you have considered only negative agendas, maybe some internal searching is needed. It could be that we enjoy someone's company or the sound of their voice; they make us laugh; or we could want advice or help with some project. It could be that it is the best sex you have ever had or you want to borrow money, or both. It could be as simple as feeling safe, wanting affection or having a physical attraction. Whatever the reason, we are attracted to those who serve a purpose or are of use. Some people go to great lengths to be of use in order to secure a mate, and this is the foundation of most modern relationships.

I believe our primary motivation and reason for socialization is to be loved and feel affection. It is built into our genetic code. It is also my belief that we not only need to be loved, adored and praised, but also need to have these things shown to us in some form that is recognizable to us as love. Our appetite for attention often leads us along paths we really do not need to travel, but we do. Children throw temper tantrums and adults often act out scenes that warrant nominations for the Academy Awards: all for attention. It makes us adorn ourselves in a certain manner, using superficial accessories to enhance physical appearance. We frequent particular areas or we congregate with a particular crowd to feel secure. Affection makes us want attention: attention being equated with love. We totally expect to be rewarded for displaying wealth; wearing expensive clothing and jewelry, driving a high-end car, living in the right neighborhood and conforming to society's defined concept of beauty. We are told these things all but guarantee attention. Feeling loved means security, and it satisfies a need that I believe none but God can explain.

The way a person interacts with others started forming the day he or she was born, through his or her interactions with the primary and/or secondary caregivers. From the crib to the grave, these are the experiences that will govern our behavior in all of our relationships[232]. Dr. Marvin Harris[233] wrote there are four biological and psychological needs that concern us:

1. People need to eat and will generally opt for diets that offer more rather than fewer calories and proteins and other nutrients.

2. People cannot be totally inactive, but when confronted with a given task, they prefer to carry it out by expending less rather than more human energy.

3. People are highly sexed and generally find reinforcing pleasure from sexual intercourse.

---

[232] In my opinion the human being progresses in three stages: childhood, adolescence and adulthood. Childhood and adolescence are divided by menstruation and viable sperm production. Adolescence and adulthood are divided by attained wisdom through experience.
[233] Marvin Harris Ph D. (1927-2001): American Cultural Anthropologist specializing in Cultural Materialism.

4. People need love and affection in order to feel secure and happy and other things being equal, they will act to increase the love and affection others give them.

According to Dr. Abraham Maslow[234], we all have physiological, safety, love (affection and belongingness), esteem and self-actualization needs.

Essentially they are saying the same thing; we need food, water, and shelter, security, sex, love and the feelings associated with them. But, Maslow carries it a step further into a more spiritual realm. He implies that there is a seed inside of everyone waiting for the right conditions (fertile soil) to sprout. After we satisfy our needs in the physical realm, we seek our destiny. He calls it self-actualization; I call it getting out of "Survival Mode".

How do we manage to eat, be active, have sex, feel secure and feel loved at the same time? To many the answer is financial independence, money. I do not think that is the answer, but it eliminates being hungry and needing shelter in our society, it often satisfies the esteem need because people like to suck rich people's dicks. However, only small portions of people who have money are self-actualizing, or happy.

Some believe working hard is the answer. I see work as a means to raise money to finance my real wants. Working for someone else consumed a minimum of 10 hours of my day and sometimes my nights and weekends. I served the greater good of the company in order to be promoted, get more money and make myself more attractive as a mate in order to satisfy my need to be loved. How perfect. Only there is a problem, I have not found the unconditional love I am seeking and I feel like a slave. Work only provides money. If you are fortunate enough to find something you would do for free and receive pay for it that is not work. That is called finding your path and I wish it on everyone.

Still, a great many others think the answer lies in religion or faith. I tend to agree, if this faith is in the righteousness of one's self and humanity as a whole, and not the form of faith being encouraged by most. True faith and love will do everything.

I think the only road to true happiness is inside of each and every one of us. It starts with loving yourself first, and then loving others can be easy. Do not get self-interest, conceit or self-absorption confused with love. If we could only look in a mirror and love what we see without physical modification, we would be on the right road. But we rarely do. We have become prisoners of our society. Others define our concept of beauty and it seems that we do not know how to think for ourselves. Look at the magazines on any news stand. Media defines what a particular society's concept of beauty is, governments tell us how to think and what is best for our children.

Cultures not exposed to multi-media define beauty within their own grouping, raise their children among the family or tribe, and have a more altruistic way of thinking. Their queens are not skinny. Their children do not do drive bys or take guns to school. Prozac, Viagra, Percadan, Valium and crack are unknown to them. They know what bark to eat if constipated.

---

[234] Abraham Maslow (1908-1970): Considered by many as the father of Humanistic Psychology. Established pyramid of "Being Needs".

157

In our culture people are lining up at Botox clinics to remove wrinkles; they are flocking to collagen clinics to thicken their lips and add shape to their butts. I remember when big lips and butts with curves were considered an unattractive African trait. Both men and women spend huge amounts of money on plastic surgery, on hair and on anything that will increase sexual arousal. There has been an invasion of Eastern philosophy. Zen masters, shamans, psychiatrists[235] and gurus are becoming rich deprogramming people because independent thought has become a casualty of conformity, and the fear of standing out has left development of the human spirit in the hands of governments, religious institutions and the ruling classes. We do not even have straightforward conversations anymore. Everything seems to be a subterfuge. Instead of working in order to live, we now live in order to work, forever chasing the carrot dangling in front of us. Civilization has come to resemble beehives or ant colonies (compulsive cooperation) more than a gathering of humans. Our relationships suffer because of it.

The Body

Our bodies have been programmed by and are subject to the laws of nature. We grow old. We have to eat and need water. We need shelter from the elements. We are essentially animals. As sophisticated and evolved as we are, in matters of the body, we are 100% animal, made that way over millions of years of trial and error. The human body, like all other bodies, is a machine. The machine is useless without an operator. There are bodies that cannot move because the brain is dead or damaged. Everything the body does originates as a synaptic signal from the brain. That being said, should we allow our bodies to control our brains or vice versa?

The brain can dream. It can do whatever it wants. It moves at the speed of thought, the only thing faster than light. The brain wants the body to comply with the contract we signed; it wants us to live up to the promise we made to experience life. The body frequently rebels. It only wants to feel good and procreate. Give it enough food, water, warmth and affection all the time and it will behave itself. Did you notice I said "enough"? Do not over indulge in food or anything else; we are killing our bodies. Would you constantly feed a fat baby?

It is in times of lacking that the body screams the loudest. *Feed me! I am cold! I am thirsty! I want to have a baby! Give me a hug! I need a drink!* Control these requirements and the body will follow the brain like a well-trained dog. After we satisfy the body and learn to control its urges, I believe it is natural to take the next step in human evolution. That step is to try to satisfy the mind's needs.

Maslow developed a theory of behavior based on needs. He was a humanistic psychologist. Humanists believe that humans strive for an upper level of capabilities. Humans seek the frontiers of creativity, the highest reaches of consciousness and wisdom. Maslow has labeled this highest level of being, "the self-actualizing person" (Dr. C. George Boeree). Others may call it enlightenment or some other term. This is his final stage of human needs. We seem to need to know who we are.

---

[235] There are two types of Psychiatrists. One will give you a pill. That is the best you will get. The other will ask you about your relationship with your mother. Ten minutes into that session, we all ask for a pill.

Our bodies are affected by instinct, desires, chemical reactions, emotions, food and water requirements and the connection we have with each other. I am trying my best to control or at least understand my body. That way I can recognize what I am feeling and know ahead of time how my body will respond. For example, when I am anxious about something I know the body will produce adrenaline. I also know that I can control this automatic response to stimuli by doing breathing exercises to slow respiration. Controlled shallow breathing calms the body. A calm body does not release adrenaline into the blood stream as an autonomic response to external stimuli.

I want to go to Tibet or Nepal so that I may learn firsthand how the Buddhist monks meditate. I figure three or four months with them should be enough time to get the basics, if they let me through the front door. I am too spoiled to live that lifestyle for long, but I want to see if I can adapt their methods to my principles of controlling the body. One thing I do understand is that the body is lazy and self-serving. It does not want to do anything that will endanger itself and it does not want to expend any energy that does not have a gratifying return.

I have said that the body will behave, if it is given what it needs. I am convinced that if we take everyone out of Survival (animal) Mode by giving them enough of everything, we would be closer to paradise on Earth. But, while in survival mode the body consistently rebels hijacking the brain in an attempt to fulfill some need. It seems even when the body has enough, it typically wants more.

I remember watching a pride of lions that had not eaten for three days take down a zebra. The lions worked as a team to set up the ambush, but when the kill was made and the feeding started, they bit and scratched each other, every member trying to get its piece of the pie. The cubs, which usually feed first, were forced to lick bones. It was not until the meal was gone that the conflict stopped. Then the lions cleaned one another to reaffirm bonds.

They can cooperate up to the point when they have to share food. If there was more than enough meat to go around what would happen? Lions gorge themselves to the point of barely being able to move and then there is no conflict. I remember thinking why do they eat like that; they overdose at each opportunity.

Animal's bodies are so satisfied by eating that they often do not know when to quit. They are following their internal programming that says, "You better clean your plate, there are lions starving in China." Lions know that good meals are often hard to come by and they need to gorge themselves. They sleep up to twenty hours a day. Why does the human animal gorge itself even when the pantries are full?

The body can survive on a lot less than we frequently stuff into it. We have been programmed to think we need three meals per day. I remember telling several ex-girlfriends that they were getting chunky and I was concerned about the weight. It is true that I was concerned for selfish reasons, but concern is concern. One said, "Doctors say you have to eat three meals a day to be healthy." I would have agreed with this if she were a construction worker who burned off what she took in, and not a student who slept more than she studied. I usually eat one, maybe two meals a day, depending on my level of activity. As my physical activity increases I eat more.

159

Also, I do not restrict myself to eating at specific times; I eat when I am hungry. Rats raised on a barely subsistence diet have an increased life expectancy of 30 to 35%. Mice on similar diets are more than doubling their life spans (Blüher, Kahn and Kahn). My ex-girlfriend weighed more than I could guess the last time I saw her; that will decrease her life expectancy. The body will cry, "Hungry" with a loaf of bread under both arms.

The body needs water, but it prefers soda. If you put equal quantities of juices, sodas, beer, wine and water in your refrigerator, which one would be gone first in your household? The body only needs water, but it will select alternatives that contain water and sugar, protein, fat or alcohol, if they are available.

The body needs to maintain itself at a certain temperature. Long ago we learned to shelter in harsh environments. Through the years we have developed technologies that allow for all sorts of conveniences. The body wants more than it needs to survive. But, for humans, life is not just about survival. The body wants food, water, shelter and to procreate with the best available mates. Why is it so hard to satisfy? If you gave everyone a million dollars would it be enough or would the bar of satisfaction rise even higher? Eons ago, the bigger and stronger males were dominant (not that it has changed much today). They received the lion's share when it came to resources. They were excellent potential providers, if being viewed by an interested female. They probably provided more security as well. Who wants to fight someone bigger than self? I am sure in the days before holy matrimony mating and rape were one and the same, unless a male provided security.

The women with the curves and appendages in the proper natural proportions[236], long healthy hair, big breasts, colored eyes and straight teeth were perceived as healthy and good mates. It is called physical symmetry. These physical attributes signal health and convey that they will probably produce strong healthy children. The Egyptians used this same ratio for the pyramids. It is called Phi; 1:1.618 roughly a three to five ratio, so common in nature that even the ancient Greeks noticed it. They constructed their temples and other important buildings to these exact proportions. The human eye, like all of nature, looks for this symmetry when choosing mates.

Over the years this concept has transformed itself into what we have today. It is the same situation as before, but with a twist. Men know that security and being perceived as a good provider are more important than being big, strong, fast or attractive when it comes to getting attention. Money makes people more attractive.

We have also learned that being pretty is more advantageous than being smart when it comes to attracting a mate or getting attention. People typically pluck eyebrows, use lip liners, eye pencils, fake hair, girdles, wonder bras and a multitude of techniques to look physically fit and symmetrically pleasing to the eye. Although most males do not care to see through these veils, women can. Spend some time in the presence of women talking about other people. Males know that sparkling things such as cars, boats, homes and the appearance of wealth attracts most women. If he is physically symmetric and good-looking as well, that is icing on the cake and is considered a "good catch".

---

[236] Examples of the "golden ratio" can be found in the natural world as flowers, pine cones, animals, the human body or seashells and in human works such as the Parthenon, Mozart's music and Leonardo da Vinci's paintings.

There is a strange phenomena dealing with the concept of physical attractiveness versus wealth and stability. According to David M. Buss[237], Ph D., when women ovulate they are more attracted to the symmetric male regardless of his financial status or their relationship status. It makes sense; why would you want to partner with anyone but the fittest looking mate around, if you are ovulating? It seems that the body still knows what is best for its own survival.

Dr. Buss also formulates that human females have hidden ovulation. In the wild, primate females display their ovulation through smells, enlarged or colorful reproductive organs and a variety of other methods. They advertise. Humans are no different, but men typically cannot tell when a woman is ovulating. I have noticed that the women I have known change behavior and are typically more aggressive sexually when they ovulate[238]. The physical changes range from swelled or tender breasts, a different smell and a little added sway in the step. Dr. Buss believes women have hidden ovulation to give them the opportunity to choose who will father their children. My grandfather has known this for years. He said, "Mama's baby and Papa's maybe." We would all do well to reign in the body and let the mind make the decisions.

Socializing

I have found that it is inevitable that in social settings someone will go out of his or her way to find something not to like about you if they view you as competition or a threat, and many will go out of their way to make you feel inferior. I hate having to defend myself from the silly little creatures that we have become.

Dr. James W. Prescott[239] states that people can have body pleasure or violent behavior, but not both at the same time. He believes they have a mutually inhibiting relation. The presence of body pleasure or violent behavior impedes the emergence of the other. He explains that when the brain's pleasure circuits are activated, the violence circuits close down and vice versa[240]. I like to think that we should keep the switch in pleasure mode. Unfortunately, many people do not like to see others with something they do not have and will go out of their way to end it. I am sure that there are things about me that get on people's nerves. I have had verbal and written confirmation of this fact. I am not mad at them; I just do not respond to what they think. Not that what others say is not important; *it is just that most people's opinions revolve around themselves. And, anyone's opinion of me is only as important as they are to me.*

Changing others to fit our mold seems to be the single most important task in relationships. If we do not submit, we are horrible human beings and do not love our mate. If we do, we are not being ourselves, but performing in a manner that pleases others in order to obtain something we want.

---

[237] David M. Buss: Ph D.: Professor of Psychology at the University of Texas at Austin. Specializes in Evolutionary Psychology.
[238] I mean women I have seen naked through period and ovulation and noticed the swelling and tenderness of the breasts, the different smells and the mood changes, the erect clitoris.
[239] Dr. James W. Prescott: formerly Health Scientist Administrator, Developmental Behavioral Biology Program, National Institute of Child Health and Human Development, National Institutes of Health.
[240] Prescott, <u>Body Pleasure and the Origins of Violence</u>.

The Social Totem Pole

I have a question... If you were walking down a crowded street and needed to know the time, whom would you ask, a man or a woman, the suit or a bum, the White, the Black or other? What would influence your choices? I wouldn't ask a white woman, last choice. Why? Even predatory animals know to go for the easy kill. "Hey, brotha you got the time?"

I think we are unconsciously and sometimes consciously slated to certain roles by society, and stepping out of these accepted stations usually leads to someone getting upset. It is like the movie *Gaticca*[241]. I definitely feel like that when I have my first face-to-face interviews. I cannot help but see the look of surprise on some people's faces when they see I am not white. For some reason my face does not match the resume. Remember, I was once asked during an interview, "But you were not born here were you?" I interpret that question to mean it is improbable that a qualified African-American male is from the same stock as the other African-Americans in the United States. When I hear comments like that I know that I am not going to get the job.

Appearance seems to play a particularly interesting role in conveying social status. It tells others where on the social totem pole someone should be. The preferred American model is white, male, tall, symmetrically attractive, well clothed and shoed. Anything less than this almost guarantees a slot lower than the top ring. Whether male or female, if someone is judged to be fat, ugly or have some other characteristic that is deemed a flaw (dark skin), they are treated a certain way and expected to act appropriately. A hot body can wear a thong at the beach, but the big girl cannot. A muscular male can wear a tight shirt, but a skinny guy cannot (If fat is so ugly, why are two-thirds of Americans over weight and 61.3 million people obese?). No wonder people diet so much. Of course, having large sums of money (finance) nullifies most of the above. The most physically unattractive person can marry a super model (male or female), if they are well off, but that does not mean they can hold on to them. Ask Donald Trump or Hugh Hefner.

I am of small physical stature. Add strong opinions and the fact that I am not white to the mixture and people get pissed. Some people see a small frame and colored skin then automatically think that I have low self-esteem or a type "B" or "C" personality. Wrong one, homey; my mother taught me how beautiful I am, society said I was not. Who would you believe? Still others have seen my skin color, darker or lighter than theirs, and have placed me above or below them depending on their own skin color. Finally, damn near everyone has asked, "What you do for a living?" They want to have an idea of how much money you make, where you stand socially and what your education level is. I once had a guy at a Christmas party ask me if I had ever shot a missile. This was after he found out that I was an aviator. "Are you asking me have I ever killed anyone?"

If I could keep my mouth shut and act as I am expected, I would get along fine. Unfortunately, according to the Myers-Briggs[242] psychological test my mental attitude is "ENTJ" (Extraversion, iNtuition, Thinking, Judgment: Field Marshal). That is why I have difficulty following anyone; I want to lead and there are people out there who have issues following the

---

[241] Gaticca: Andrew Niccol's 1997 film addressing the issue of genetic prejudice and perfection.
[242] Katherine Cook Briggs (1875-1968) and Isabel Briggs Myers (1897-1980): Mother and daughter team that developed the Myers-Briggs Type Indicator (MBTI) personality test based on Carl Jung's theories.

direction of those they deem inferior. My grandfather once told me, "Boy... it is not the size of the dog in the fight; it is the size of the fight in the dog." The PIMP movie with Terrence Howard was late.

I remember hanging out with a group of marijuana smokers at lunchtime during high school. We would chip in on a *nickel bag* and find someplace private to eat lunch and smoke. I once made the mistake of showing this group my report card; it had all A's and B's on it. The stereotype says that teenagers are not supposed to be able to smoke marijuana and do well in school. I wanted to go to college and knew grades would do it. Not judging anyone, but many are not on the college after high school track. But, I could not imagine climbing the social latter in America any other way. I was ostracized after I shared my grades with them. One of them called me, "Brainiac". It was a compliment, but it did not feel like it at the time. More *crabs in a basket*. It seems that we easily dismiss those we consider beneath us, compete aggressively with those we consider peers and either hate or try to climb on the backs or fronts of those we deem superior.

I met this physical perfection of femininity at one of those high-end expatriate clubs that exist anywhere that has been colonized. Marah was a gorgeous Arabian, twenty-one, hot body. Her roommate, Iknei, was like Malaysian nitro-glycerin. When we met she said, "Call me, 'EYE', pointing at her eye, and, 'KNEE', pointing at her knee." I thought, "I'd call you on one knee, and see her, on two knees!"

Marah asked me for $8,000 dollars while sitting around the hotel pool. I had known them for three weeks. I liked her and her roommate. Usually when we went out, I paid. To her credit, the roommate helped when she could. They took advantage of the hotel facilities and the months went on. I was wondering what this semi-frequent guest at the hotel, and restaurateur, at my expense, really wanted. She was not trying to sleep with me and the chump change for going out did not matter; I was expensing everything.

Marah set it up nicely, "My grandmother died." Iknei later told me she was in England partying with a male friend, and the airline realized it because she checked into a hotel in partnership with the airline. She was fired. Her contract required that she repay any expenses incurred during her training if she did not remain with the airline for 'X' number of years. She came clean finally, and I asked her, "Why is it in my interest to help you?" She spent the night. I told her, "I don't know you! Why should I give you my money?" She had no answer. I think that was the first time a male had told her, "NO!" Iknei was concerned because Marah was responsible for half of their rent.

She came over late. I was asleep when the call came from reception. "Who... OK!"

I won't go into the story. Do I need to? I already said, "No!" once. Her trying to convince me I was in error was like every other time a female had sex with me for gain.

163

Sometimes you have to get a couple hundred bloody noses to learn one lesson, "Free Will".

Am I Alone

We always have someone near us. People cross our paths all day every day, sometimes they cross our paths several times or for long periods of time. Because of interaction we have a habit of superimposing wants, fears and desires on those around us. We have thought, prayed and wished desires onto the matrix of the Universe just like everyone else and the Universe is trying to respond as it was designed. It is difficult to concentrate on our course in such a storm of thoughts. "Mommy, I...." "Honey, can you...." or "I need it by...." create a pause in whatever we are doing for ourselves. They are distractions from individual goals, objectives and destiny.

If you want to test my theory, try being alone and without external influences for an extended period of time. Prepare a warm bath with Epson salt. Turn the lights off; the room must be as dark and quiet as possible. This simulates the effects of the Samadhi Tank[243]. When there are no external stimuli and no pressure to adapt to outside events, the body and mind can devote its energies to restoring itself to homeostasis. Homeostasis is the normal state of balance, which our bodies try to maintain, but because of the overwhelming external stimuli it is difficult to achieve. This is a state of consciousness that promotes good health, happiness and pleasure in being alive.

If that is too much, try turning off your phones and the television. Do not do laundry and do not get on the computer for a day. Do nothing that requires contact with others. During this time alone, think, ask questions of yourself, look in a mirror and remember. I like to have the television and music on at the same time. Then I try to block them both out. I try not to hear the noise by concentrating on some thought. I can effectively turn off my ears. The eyes are easy. I close them.

Write down your experiences and make some definite choices, set some goals, and draw out specific and realistic objectives. In many cases you will find that you are not doing what you want to do the majority of the time. Unless you are financially independent and single with no children, the majority of the time we are performing activities that include or revolve around someone else's objectives and goals.

I don't have a Samadhi Tank, but I'm going to build one. For now I like to sleep in front of the fireplace. The dance of the flames relaxes me and promotes serious thought. The changing of form from a solid living thing into light energy (photons) and ashes (carbon), to start the life cycle once more in some other form is amazing to me. It draws definite parallels to human existence.

---

[243] Samadhi Tank: isolation tank invented by Dr. John Lilly in 1954. It is a dark sound-proof tank in which subjects float in salty water at skin temperature. They are used for meditation, relaxation, and healing. Lilly, M.D. (1915-2001): psychoanalyst. Specializing in Respiratory Physiology, Neurophysics, Neurophysiology, Psychiatry, interspecies communication and the nature of consciousness and the self.

Survival Instinct

If two men were on a sinking raft and only one could stay aboard and live, at the moment of this realization the bigger and stronger male would think of throwing the other off; and the smaller, weaker person would be thinking of a way to keep the other from throwing him off. I would like to think that we could come up with a way we both could survive. What do you think two women would do? What about a "Man" and a woman? I think that scene at the end of *Titanic* was Hollywood bullshit for the most part.

I remember harassing the dog down the street from my grandfather's house one night. My cousin, my brother and I were kicking the fence that enclosed the dog. We were walking and feeling full of our selves. The dog barked like crazy whenever people walked by the yard pretending to be vicious, but would not leave to pursue anyone even if the gate was open. He was just acting out his natural behavior, but we, being young and stupid, were offended by the dog's false posturing and took every opportunity to fuck with him and the owner. They lived two houses down from ours. After 30 seconds or so of kicking the fence to provoke the dog, we continued walking home. As we entered the walkway, shots were fired from the old man's house. From the left we could hear the sounds of bullets whizzing through the leaves of the tree above our heads. My cousin grabbed me by the arms from behind and placed me between him and the sound of the shots as I tried to escape as well.

We have learned to get what we want and to hell with everyone else. We have invented communities, cities, states, nations and religions to bind us in a common cause, a circle of security against the elements, predators and each other. But, depending on the size of the prize, the threat at hand or the scarcity of resources, this circle of confidants gets smaller and smaller, until it includes only you. This is the Old Brain at work. Dr. Paul Maclean[244] calls it the Reptile Brain.

Even a lioness will leave her cubs after defending them fiercely, if the threat to her own life is great enough. I saw this on one of the more useful television channels. A herd of Cape buffalo stumbled upon the den of a lioness. She had given birth a few days earlier, so the cubs were too young to be led away from the approaching danger. The den was located in a thicket of dead trees. The lioness fought ferociously until it was clear that she too would die if she stayed any longer. Nature told her that she could have more cubs so she ran.

The buffalo mauled the cubs, eliminating future predators. Though it was sad to see, there was no malice in the act of the buffalo or blame in the act of the lioness; it was just the most primitive part of their brains at work, instinct. This is why we are the way we are. We have the same primitive behaviors inside us and frequently we use this as an excuse to justify our actions. That is why I am not surprised when I hear about children dying in a house fire while the parents survived. That is why I was not surprised to hear that a woman who was carrying her two children let go of the older one when they were caught in the tsunami in Thailand. She thought that all of them would die if she did not make a choice. I am thankful for her sake that both

---

[244] Dr. Paul MacLean (1913-2007): Senior Research Scientist at the National Institute of Mental Health work involved understanding the human brain. Specialized in techniques for teaching and learning throughout the lifespan.

children survived, but can you imagine the guilt that she has because of that decision? Can you hear the released child bringing this up twenty years from now when he is angry and wants to hurt her? "You love Todd more than me."

On the other side of the coin, I saw a pack of African wild dogs attack a wildebeest's calf. Wild dogs are infamous for their stamina and tenacity during the hunt. The alpha male picks a target and the pack uses relay tactics to run down the prey. They are among the most successful of hunting animals. In this instance the wildebeest stood her ground and fought valiantly for her offspring. The struggle for life and death went on for some time, and eventually the dogs gave up. It was strange to see the wildebeest and her calf standing next to one another while one of the dogs laid down on the ground in front of them panting from exhaustion. The mother and calf were scarred, but alive, alive for another day, week or year. This is why I am not surprised when I hear of tremendous heroism or sacrifice in the face of insurmountable odds. I am no longer surprised when I hear of soldiers who throw themselves on grenades to save their comrades or fire fighters who run into burning towers or common people who turn into "Subway Superman". We all have it in us. Never give up the good fight.

Our manifestation of animal behavior begins when we are young and we start to learn the lessons of survival within an environment of people. It will be the same until societies as a whole change, for *we would have to leave this Earth*, if we wanted to raise our children in a truly nurturing environment without conflicting ideas and actions. I believe we should reverse the natural order of importance. Instead of thinking of self first, we should think of the whole first, the whole being the Universe. Everything else will fall into place after that.

Manipulation

I like to know where we are going and how we are getting there before I get on board.

How do you feel when you discover that you have been used in some way or performed as predicted? Recently I had a conversation that prompted my thinking about manipulation. I would define it as getting what you want without being totally forthcoming in your purpose. Who manipulates whom? Do children do it to their parents and vice versa? Do lovers manipulate one another? What about our bosses, families and friends? Do they manipulate us and we them? Do we try to manipulate our very existence every day? For most, manipulation is only an issue if we feel out smarted or do not get what we want.

Tears

Why do we use tears as weapons? I have had women cry on me in times of desperation. I used to respond with compassion and genuine empathy. That was before I realized that many women use tears to hijack the minds of males and to elicit sympathy. Not responding to a woman's crying is like trying not to respond to a baby when it cries. Once I figured this out, I fought the innate feelings to respond with tenderness and stuck to my guns, whatever the situation. The reactions I got both surprised and scared me. The main reaction was an instant 180°. They stopped crying, got mad as hell and usually acted like they wanted to throw punches (though most women have the common sense not to hit someone who is bigger, stronger and has more experience fighting than they do). They were acting in order to get what they wanted. Here is a suggestion to every woman who uses emotions as a weapon: stop that shit. It makes you look ridiculous and manipulative. Besides, it does not work on real "MEN". They know that there is only one real emotion. Everything else is a misinterpretation or misrepresentation of that emotion.

I cried one night in my bunk on the ship. I was alone and buried my face in the pillow. I had just returned from our brief shore leave. It was not the European woman who casually called me "Nigger". It was the van ride back to the ship. It was late and we were waiting in the final van to depart on the hour as scheduled. The Chief Warrant Officer who was in charge for the night was standing in the doorway of the van. As usual, the guys were rowdy and rambunctious. It is to be expected after drinking and freedom from the ship for the first time in weeks. The Warrant's eyes scanned the dark van and upon seeing all black faces, he said, "Settle down! This ain't Soul Train." The entire van went quiet. Not because he was right, but because he out ranked everyone on the van but me. The others were biting their tongues, offended, but too afraid to buck authority because they knew, like I did, that he would win if anyone brought the issue up as racism. Not only that, but also the accuser would be labeled and targeted as a troublemaker or be accused of pulling the "race card". "It ain't American Band Stand either!" was my reply. The Warrant looked to see who had the nerve to reply. He found me *gritting* at him. He and I had become what I thought were friends over the course of the voyage, but I guess I was wrong and now he knew it as well. He apologized and tried to explain the following day, but... "What do you call a bunch of patriotic African-Americans serving their country in a military van on the way back to the ship?" "I don't know... What?" "Niggers!" "Oh yeah, I forgot again!"

The Nest

How do women judge a perspective mate? I think most women want a breadwinner, the cream of the crop and security for herself and any offspring. This is natural, no fault there. I asked my mother what attracts her to a male. She told me a nice tall body first attracts her attention and then she looks at the shoes. She said, "You can tell a lot about a man by his shoes." I laughed because what she told me was that physique is a good thing, but he has to have some money. I remember boarding a plane shortly after we had this conversation. I caught the eye of a cutie sitting in an aisle seat in business class. She looked me in the eyes and diverted her gaze as we made contact, but as I passed I noticed she looked right down at my shoes, lizard skin cowboy boots.

A 14-year-old said she looks at faces first and then the type of clothes the boy is wearing. Notice that there is not much difference in what qualities they both look for despite the plus 40-year age difference? Physical attractiveness came first. Finances came second.

Men are attracted by the same physical symmetry. We want this symmetry for our children. Most men do not look for financial security in women, though many males do look for other forms of security in relationships. I think the quest is the same, but biological urges and social programming have distorted the search. I think the ultimate goal in any interaction is to feel loved, but who has time to know real love when you have to worry about your next meal and bills. We are too busy to be human.

The lengths to which most people are willing to go to get security surprise me. Monetary gains are replacing "Love". I have heard women say of successful and attractive men who are getting married, "He's a good catch." Sounds like a trap being sprung. Once he is caught, what do you do with him, mount him over your fireplace? What do you give in return? Please do not mention sex. Sex feels good to men and women or rather it should; it is an even trade and, if it does not feel good, if you are not enjoying it, then why do it? I practice the catch and release program, regularly tagging and throwing back the immature ones. I usually take a picture with the keepers before I throw them back as well; you can always catch them again using the same bait. I call it conservation.

Women's expectations of boys are too high. Most males would be happy in a cave playing a video game, or watching cable and scratching ourselves. This is an oversimplification, but as long as there is food, something to do with our hands and sex every now and then, males are typically satisfied. If we get bored, we will find something to occupy ourselves. We do not need anyone finding things for us to do. We do not really want the expensive car or house. We would rather spend our money on something practical, entertaining or sexual. We buy homes and cars to impress. They advertise our wealth and increase our chances of getting some attention, and hopefully some sex.

The male weaverbird attracts his mate for the season by building a nest. The female inspects the nest then either stays, or destroys it and goes. It is that simple. Build a good enough nest, get a mate. Men learned long ago that we do not need sweet talk, a big penis or physical beauty if we drive a Mercedes, live in Beverly Hills and wear a Rolex. The extras are just gravy or icing. The nest you build is going to get you laid, if you do not mess up by saying or doing something stupid.

I have a conundrum; I want to have great sex and have true pure love. The problem is the types of women who are strongly attracted to material wealth are not the type of women who I want to be within a relationship; but a well built nest attracts them in droves and most women who do not put strong emphasis on material wealth are already married or have been, have children, are self-absorbed or are past child bearing years.

Materialistic relationships are too taxing to maintain. Unless you are born rich, you have to work too damn hard just to support habits and maintain a certain standard of living. Even on a friendship basis it is hard to have a relationship with people who consume themselves with material thoughts.

Females

"No woman. No cry... No woman. No cry." Bob Marley

According to Homer, thousands died in a ten-year war for Troy because of a woman. I have one favor to ask of women. Live up to your own expectations. What I mean by that is, "Be the person you demand your mate to be," and fill the requirements you have of your mate before you try to superimpose them on someone else.

A girl I call Crazy once pulled my own handgun on me. We went away for the weekend. I had grown fond of a club in the city we were visiting. It had music, reasonably priced drinks and a pool table, perfect. My cousin, Crazy and I went there. She and I had an argument over something insignificant. I blew her off for the rest of the night by playing pool and talking to my cousin, but ignoring her. I still bought drinks and food for the group, but no direct conversation. She was very attractive and it did not take much encouragement for a male to spark up conversation with her. I had no issue with the jealousy game; I do not play.

When it was time to go, I told her she could stay with her new friend or come with us. She came with us. In the car I explained some of the rules of conduct. I said even though we were not on the best of terms, she should not have flirted with a male with the sole purpose of trying to make me jealous. I cannot remember what she said, and I admired her spunk, but it was enough for me to pull onto the shoulder and tell her, "Get the fuck out"[245].

We were on the highway and she refused. I got out, walked to her door, opened it and repeated my demand that she get out of my car. She again refused. I did not listen to what she was saying. I reached for her by the arms, but she started to swing and kick. Her arms were flailing wildly. I had to use real force to pull her to her feet and push her to the side. My cousin had already pushed the seat forward so he could move from the back to the front seat, so I left the door open and retraced my steps back toward the driver's side of the car.

She reached into my car and grabbed the weapon I kept between the middle console and my seat. By the time I knew what was happening, she had her arm extended over the roof and the gun pointed directly at my face. It was not three feet away. Right around the time the surprise receded, the panic kicked in. Fear clutched me. I had one of those peak experiences. My life started to flash before me and I thought, "Not right now, not over this, not by her." My cousin slipped quietly back into the backseat, out of the line of fire. Finally I said, "Fuck It!" to myself. I was not scared anymore; I was mad as hell. If you pull a gun on someone, you had better use it to kill them because the anger, fear and hate you invoke will make them react to save self.

I walked toward her and told her, "Shoot, bitch!" I told her, "If you ever pull a weapon, you should do so with the intention of using it, not to scare someone." By the time I had finished this speech I was in her face. I took the gun and smacked her. It is the only time I remember ever striking a woman with my hand. I wanted to knock her damn head off, but I hit her with a pulled slap, as you do when you pop your kids. I am glad I had some restraint in a moment of high emotions. I do not want anyone to think I am "Billy Badass". After the panic left, I remembered that I had not chambered a round and the safety was on. I did not see or hear her chamber one. If she had, who knows where this episode would have ended.

I drove off and left her on the side of the road, but felt guilty just leaving her there. I backed up and put her in the car. I took her to her father's and gave her money to get home, but she did not want her father to see her. Her shirt was ripped. It was silk and fragile; in the scuffle getting her out or putting her back in the car, her shirt ripped. I sympathized with this and saw myself

---

[245] It says a lot about what type of woman you are if you go out of town with a man and do not have two nickels to rub together.

having to kill her Dad. I even told her that when her Dad asked her what happened, that she had better tell him the truth so he would know why he died. Meaning when Daddy saw her torn shirt, he would assume I beat her ass and come after me for disrespecting his little girl (remember, girls are sacred to parents, and in incidents of violence the male never gets the benefit of the doubt). He should at least know the real reason he ended up in a pine box. It was not worth it. I took her back to my cousin's.

When we arrived, she called the police. My cousin and I were next door. I knew what she was going to do and was hiding the firearm. Sure enough, she had dialed 911 three times, but hung up. The emergency response operator called my cousin's house three times with no answer, we were next door and Crazy was outside. The operator dispatched a unit to the house. My cousin noticed that there were three new calls on his caller ID and they were from the police department. Here we go. I made myself a drink just in case the cops wanted to give me a breathalyzer. My cousin and I then sat down to play video games. I knew I was condemned. Anyone walking into a scene where a woman has a torn shirt and is hysterical is going to assume that I beat her. I had to come up with a plan.

The cops knocked at the door. My cousin answered and as soon as the cops asked to speak to me, he pointed and said, "Right there." It was funny the way he did it. I later cussed him out for acting like a bitch.

There were two of them, a white male corporal (oh damn) and an African-American female patrolperson (some hope). We went through the drama of he said-she said. They had already heard her side and saw her torn shirt. I told the entire story, gunplay included. I also told them I did no wrong and that she could still go to her father's and I would pay for her bus or train ticket if they would take her.

The male was so convinced that I was in the wrong that he did not hear me. The woman listened intently and had obviously experienced something like this before. She knew I was telling the truth. She made a mental picture of what really happened in her head from the two different versions of the same story and decided I was not in the wrong. They left sighting jurisdiction as their excuse for not taking me to jail. As they put it, I was lucky. Fuck them; I was well within my rights. The fact that I had a gun, that it was concealed in my car and that it was used in an assault against me were not the issues. The city's finest doing their usual best. They should have taken her ass to jail for assault with a deadly weapon, but she is a woman and they are running shit.

The neighbor who hid the gun calmed Crazy down. My cousin was having sex with her at the time, so she was willing to do us a favor. Crazy came in and acted angelic. She apologized. I remember thinking how irrational people sometimes act when they feel like they have been wronged. As humans our first instinct is to reciprocate, to get even. That is what she was trying to do.

I cried that night while lying beside her naked body. I told her that I could not understand why she wanted to see me in jail, and at the same time say that she loved me. Women are not the only ones who can use tears as weapon. I guess I was as crazy as she is.

Women have been running shit for a long time. The passive-aggressive-vulnerable style seems to work on males, even when other males use it. I have seen guys "bitch up" to avoid conflict. It is only when a person stands his ground that competition arises. I saw a couple celebrating their 75th wedding anniversary. They were asked what their secret was. The woman said, "Getting along." "What do you mean?" "Well… Agreeing and disagreeing… I agree with what I like and I disagree with the things I do not." The male partner did not get to say a word.

A girlfriend once told me that her mother said she was in school to get her BA, BS or Mrs. (Misses). I had heard this expression from an older male as well. He said that mothers send their girls to college to get a husband. I did not want to believe that. I found it hard to swallow that a parent could be so manipulative. I sincerely believed that the primary purpose of college was to get a higher education, both intellectually and socially. I did not go to find a wife or be a husband.

I once saw a beautiful policewoman. There is something about a woman in uniform. I eye balled her from the moment I first glimpsed her attractiveness. When our eyes met, she cracked a slight smile. I did not return it, but I kept the stare. I tried maintaining a neutral facial expression. It was my intention to communicate with the eyes only. Her gaze turned from interest to suspicion as I approached. I was maybe ten feet away from her when she put her hand on her gun. At that cue I cracked a smile and said, "Voce esta bonita."[246]

I once had a woman tell me, "I will be in your life in whatever capacity you will have me." This proclamation came after she was caught in a compromising situation and I was trying to end the relationship. The promise lasted as long as her memory did - yesterday. Women are no better or worse than males when it comes to relationships. Some are the most selfish creatures ever born to this planet; others are the most giving, and the rest fall somewhere in between. It depends on experiences and desires. Am I being too cynical? Have we not been socialized to "Use what you got to get what you want," or "Make him work for it"?

I have asked many women over the years if they would rather be male or female. The question is prompted by my thought that there are obvious advantages to being male. Males earn more, are not held to as high a standard of beauty and do not have to deal with menstruation, make-up, childbirth or unfortunately, childrearing. Males are faster, stronger and typically hold the majority of front positions of power. Despite these advantages, not one woman said she would rather be a male, though some have acted like it in and out of bed. I watched a popular daytime show and the four female hosts discussed this very issue. None of them wanted to be men either. This puzzled me until I asked why. It seems that the women I asked think that women have it easier than men. Before you hit the roof and start calling me a sexist, remember this is what women said. The women with whom I spoke know a startling truth, they are aware that they can manipulate men into doing what they want. It is an old maneuver called the "cat's-paw".[247]

---

[246] Brazilian Portuguese for "You are beautiful".
[247] Cat's-Paw: La Fontaine's fable, "The Monkey and the Cat", referring to one used unwittingly by another to accomplish his own purposes.

I am aware that I can have the most outstanding and envious relationship on the planet as long as I do not ever say, "No", go along with my partner's decisions (whether or not I had any input) and have plenty of money.

Women, I plead with you to be patient with males and not play with boys to the point of ruining them. It takes us boys a long time to grow up, but if we do, we turn into what women really want. When a "Man" or potential "Man" walks into a room, everyone recognizes the Silverback. His experience and confidence are hard to miss and many women think to themselves or say aloud, "Now that is a 'Man'," or "He's a keeper."

Ladies, I am going to let you in on a secret. Most men do not like the majority of women very much. And, as you and I know, the majority of women do not like men. Do you remember the way young boys treated young girls before they wanted sex? Well, the feelings have not changed that much in adulthood. Most just want sex and are willing to pay for it, and most women are willing to sell it. The male of the sex says, "I love you," all the time. Some even believe it. But, how many people have said that, and are no longer in your circle of friends? How many boyfriends and/or husbands have you had? What are you looking for in a male? Are we really dogs or could it be something else? Try to balance the scales of the relationship.

I hate when she leaves, but I love to watch her walk away.

We Need to Talk

Imagine communicating with someone who could read your mind. What would it be like? "Is silence truly golden?"

We do not need to talk. We need to communicate. If I had to pick one area that would improve relationships the most, it would be communication. Not how we communicate or whether we need to talk more, but how we need to listen. We need to listen to the other signals that mean more than words, actions tell a vivid story, facial expressions another, and stares in a moment of thought, a third. There are many other telltale signs of communication that paint a perfect picture of our relationships. All we have to do is open our eyes and look. Why do most of us pretend not to see? I think we prefer and need confirmation of what we know to be true in order to gain some type of closure, or a better sense of righteousness. I think we wear blinders and live lies as long as possible.

We frequently label issues in our relationships as communication problems because we have vocalized our desires and our partner has not modified behavior to our satisfaction. It is not about communication; it is about a battle of wills. I once went to lunch with the plant manager. It meant that he had something he wanted to talk to me about. I had no idea what it was, but it was not good. We ate lunch and talked about many things. He was very cordial. He wanted me to be careful about pulling the "race" card. Evidently my lecturing the HR manager about patting a black man, me, on the head in front of the other managers was not well received. I asked Greg if he could forget the next 10 seconds of his life. Then I put my hand on his head and rubbed his well-groomed and moussed blonde hair as he drove his customized Eddie Bauer Truck. "Now tell me I'm pulling the 'race' card... MEN do not pat other MEN like pets!" By the time we returned to the plant, we were discussing golf swings and his favorite sport, WWF wrestling. My granddad would have been proud, but I made an enemy, the cost of noncompliance.

Whether it is your manager or your spouse, the phrase, "We need to talk," is not good. I usually brace myself. We can be mean, when we do not get what we want.

In the wild, the most ferocious of most species are the females. Have you ever seen a mother fight to protect her child, or a female fight a male? I am not talking about mouthing off; I am referring to throwing blows. If you piss a woman off, you had better stand back and prepare for some sort of retaliation. That retaliation is usually in the form of vicious verbal assaults and may escalate to some other activity that is meant to make the male pay in some form. I have had women stand in front of the television during a football game just to get my attention. "Are you fucking crazy?" went through my mind. Before you judge, remember that no one has the right to superimpose their desires on another, especially when the Redskins are playing Dallas and I am in Texas watching it. Think of a male physically forcing a woman to listen to what he has to say. I have had women stand in front of the door so that I would not leave. We do not need to talk; you are trying to get me to do something I do not want to and you are going to make life with you miserable until I come to my senses.

Most everyone likes to get what he or she wants. I have had women ask me to do things that I considered unreasonable. Sometimes it was an attempt to get me to change something about myself in order to make them feel better (people's opinions revolve around them). At other times it had to do with finances. Women frequently got upset when I said "No." If "No" means I do not love you, and then there are many who do not love you. Not only did some women get mad, but they also needed to punish me by telling me everything they did not like about our relationship and/or me. We are all familiar with discussions that get out of control. They usually start with, "We need to talk". "No. WE do not; you want to say something that I do not necessarily want to hear", especially when I am occupied.

Chances are, if we have been in an argument during the last 6 six months or years, I have already heard what is about to be said and the only thing added to this conversation will be anything that has met disapproval since the last argument/discussion "we" needed to have. I have had to listen to rapid-fire complaints. It is as if some women reload their mouths with the same bullets over and over again. No one can ear beat me into submission. I know myself and I am comfortable with me. If a woman is with me, she should be comfortable with me as well or leave the relationship. Trust me; I do not need an explanation as to why someone wants to leave. Just say, "I do not think this is working out." I will probably agree. But, it usually is not that straightforward.

A woman was once got mad at me because, in her own words, "How can you fuck me on Wednesday and not talk to me until Saturday?" It was Saturday and I did not call her; she called me. She called to ask if she could come over. I casually said, "Sure." She showed up in less than five minutes. I was cleaning my carpets, so I did not notice her body language immediately. I looked up to find her with a beer in one hand, the other hand was on her hip and her right foot was tapping impatiently. "Oh boy!" "I know…" After I listened to her bitch for five minutes, I finally had to say, "Get the fuck out!"

I now listen intently and then ask them to repeat what they have said calmly and exactly as they said it before. I then go through the complaints and ranting sentence by sentence and discuss them. Usually they cannot remember everything they have said; it was not true, they did not mean it and/or it did not make sense. This is easy for me because I do what I said I would do at the beginning of the relationship. My goals were clear then and have not changed despite my partner's subtle hints, complaints and demands or good pussy.

The only time I argue is when I do not perform, react or do, as my antagonist wants. Do not misunderstand what I am saying. I am generous and giving when I am able or when I feel like it. But, I do not like solicited responses, and I do not like being told what to do or how to do it. I should not have to explain why. No one does! It is as if once we become involved, we are not allowed to say "No" or choose our own path. Is everything supposed to be done together? I am not under contract to any person and I never will be. I have the right to say no and should not have to hear about how selfish, stupid, mean, inconsiderate, unloving or imperfect I am. It is blackmail: it is vindictive and it is nasty. It is just like the monkey throwing the grape from the cage again. You are not hurting me. You are hurting yourself if you want to continue in a relationship with me. I say this because I remember what was said in moments of passion and anger. That is when most truths come out. You may apologize later, but I have already heard what was said and stored it in the memory bank. I will probably thank you for your honesty. If I am selfish, stupid, mean, inconsiderate, unloving and imperfect, why are you with me and what does that make you: desperate, manipulative or trying to renegotiate?

The moment a woman flares up like this, it is the beginning of the end. I start looking for another sex partner who does not resort to purposeful hurting when she does not get what she wants. I do not want to be emotionally involved with a brat; life is too hard as it is. The last thing a person wants is to have to fight as hard in the home as out of it. I have a long list of casualties who can testify to my resolve.

There were three bulls on a hill. One was 10-years old, one was 15 and the elder was 20. The youngest of the three, having better eyes spied a herd of heifers in the meadow below. He said, "Let's run down there and screw some of those cows." The 15-year old said, "I'm with you, but I get to choose which ones I want to have sex with first." The 20-year old asked, "Have they seen us yet?" "No", responded the 5-year old. The 20-year old retorted with, "Let's run and hide before they do."

Do not take any of this too much to heart; there is little fault and no blame. The larger portion of the blame lies with our society and the way we were conditioned to interact with the opposite sex. I also place no judgment on the way we are taught to pursue mates and interact with one another.

Hidden Beauty

I believe the quest for what is beautiful is a driving force because it induces pleasurable feelings and that what we consider beauty has to do with what cultural biases we have been exposed.

What is beauty in reality?

All things. If we think about and understand the principles of life and how things grow, we will see beauty in the absolute persistence and determination of all things that want to live. We are also innately drawn towards beauty or rather what our instincts perceive as symmetric perfection. Unfortunately our instincts developed long before the wonder bra, make-up, lipstick, perfume, hipsters, plastic surgery, hair relaxers, girdles, steroids, fake nails, synthetic eyelashes, bank accounts and hair implants. They have not had time to develop an effective defense against cosmetic enhancement. Our instincts are easily fooled by the physical refinements and material incentives of our time. We have been taught not only what beauty is, but also how to express our appreciation for it.

It is our nature to be attracted to what we perceive as beautiful. I will go further to say that it is our desire to possess beauty, which we have been taught is good. Beauty is a thing to behold. But, I have issue with purchased beauty because it gives an inaccurate picture of a person's physical appearance. Those who artificially enhance themselves are usually trying to hide something they view as a flaw. It is my belief that those who feel the need to change their physical appearance are those who are the least satisfied with themselves. I know a woman who exchanged her stretch marks for an ugly scar across her entire abdomen below the bikini line.

I do not think beautiful people are beautiful because of how they look. I have known enough physically attractive people to realize that they are not necessarily beautiful. I have seen people who are not considered attractive by popular standards carry themselves as if they were kings or queens, and be treated that way by others because they know how beautiful they are in reality and refuse to be categorized by others.

I do not think it is possible to see the true beauty in another by looking solely at what is pleasing anatomically. We are distracting the mind with the contemplation of what we have seen and deemed physically attractive, beautiful and desirable. Many times this attraction is conditioned and it is not even our own opinion of beauty, but the opinion of popular culture. We allow our choices to be made by biological processes, innate emotions and the fashion industry. I do not know about you, but my emotions have gotten me in more trouble than I care to remember simply because I was not thinking: I was following my social programming. This was a repetitive cycle that I have longed to understand. As a potential "Man", I want to know why a pretty face or a hot body are enough to distract me to irrational thought.

People do not seem to understand that we are beautiful because of our souls, what is inside of each and every one of us. The closer we get to our true selves the more attractive we become. Physical beauty and our attraction to it, leads to what Pietro Bembo[248] referred to as "Sensual Love". To the Platonist[249], even when the experience of love is sexual, love is the search for absolute beauty, the goodness that precedes everything.

I believe that sensual love or lust can only lead to folly, if the parties involved are not honest with themselves and their partners about what is required for that level of need to be fulfilled.

---

[248] Pietro Bembo (1470-1547): Italian Cardinal, Poet, Philosopher and Scholar.
[249] Platonic idealism: Theory that the substantive reality around us is only a reflection of a higher truth.

Sensual love also frequently requires presence and constant reinforcement. Those are drawbacks that must be addressed, if you want to have a solely sensual relationship. In our quest to obtain true beauty (divine love), we often seek it with our senses and desires rather than our reason (mind) and spirit. Most of the resultant relationships are just manifestations of our wanting. And, we wonder why so many relationships fail.

We are as ugly or beautiful as we see ourselves.

I saw a woman sitting at the end of the bar in one of my favorite clubs. She was dressed elegantly and carried herself well. I watched her for several weeks to be sure she was real. One night I spoke to her. After some talking, we ended up back at her place. The first surprise was when we were petting in her living room. I was about to take her shirt off, when she stopped me. Remember what I said about bedroom confessions! She said, "I had breast cancer." I noticed that she had small breasts, but I had no idea that they had been removed. Her chest was flat as a male's. Only her nipples and the two crescent shaped scars remained as a reminder that she was a female. My eyes had fallen for the *wonder* bra again.

Dr. Ray Dolan[250] suggests that emotion affects brain processes such as memory and attention. This is a no brainer, but his research showed a measured decrease in the performance of tasks when certain photos or words emotionally stimulated the mind to distraction. The increased attention that emotional events require takes away from our ability to register less striking events that occur around the same time frame. The contemplation of what we see, read, or hear and the emotional responses to these stimuli distract us. Emotion it seems is so important to us that it slows many of our cognitive processes, even when the emotion is slight.

What happens when a physically attractive person walks in the room? The stunning sight of beauty distracts others; we stare and marvel in the pleasure of contemplation or we get jealous of the attention received for being perceived as beautiful. What happens when an obese or physically ugly person walks in the room or attempts to give a presentation? We concentrate on their imperfections. We look for fault.

You may call me shallow if you like, but how would a woman feel if a male told them the bulge that was so attractive is not real but a sock in his pants? Would you want to have sex with an overweight person or would you prefer a hard body? It is just sex and I prefer having sex with someone I find physically attractive. Sex is all about the physical with me, but with many others it is about the material or the spiritual. If anyone wants a spiritual and physical connection with me, they have to have a spiritual connection to God and themselves first. Otherwise, it is a "Hoop Dream".

I remember being disappointed when a lover took her clothes off the first time; she was wearing a girdle. Her stomach was full of stretch marks and she had a potbelly. I guess that was why the lights were off. Ladies, you should not fool men like that. By the time I found out, I felt it was too late. This is another of those bedroom confessions. I closed my eyes and imagined that her body looked like what she had advertised and thought about someone else (I have found that laying pot-bellied women on their backs helps hide the stomach and makes it possible to

---

[250]Ray Dolan, Ph D.: University College of London. Head of the Neuropsychiatry & Neuropsychology Department.

maintain an erection.). Do not get mad, if you are a big woman. Some males like big girls. Find one of them or lose the weight. We can live on less food, and the rewards from the resulting sex will make it worth it.

In *Survival of the Prettiest*, Dr. Nancy Etcoff[251] points out that more attractive people have easier lives. She states that they get lower prison sentences, are promoted faster, and are generally more popular. She believes that physical attraction is innate and biologically based rather than learned behavior. I disagree with her assertion that learned behavior does not affect our perception of beauty. There were times when obesity was considered attractive because it signified affluence (money) and health. In many parts of the world, it is a fact that white skin is viewed as more beautiful than brown skin simply because of economics. The outdoor worker has darker skin and is automatically placed in a lower financial bracket and assumed to be of lower social status. I wonder where we got this idea.

Dr. Etcoff also believes that we are programmed by nature to seek out the most perfect mate. We find this perfection by looking for the physical cues. Symmetry of body parts, everything in the right place, has been found to be a common denominator across cultures as the main focal point of the human description of beauty.

Did you know that symmetry could be affected in the womb by stressors on the mother? Did you know that we are more helpful to those we consider attractive? That would go a long way in explaining why people try so hard to be beautiful. I always wondered why people would have surgery they do not need. I also wondered about wigs, weaves, push up bras, girdles (male and female), the fashion industry, fake teats, buttocks and lips. My curiosity did not stop there. I wondered why people would want to show the world a false image. I would have asked Ms. Argentina, but she died after having plastic surgery.

I cannot describe the level of disappointment that accompanies the realization of a physical falsehood. I could tell you about the time I found out about wonder bras, or the first time I put a fake breast in my mouth. It was like sucking on the breast of a grown-up Barbie Doll. It was hard and unnatural. They are great to look at, but not much to touch. I remember seeing numerous women's real finger nails after they removed the acrylic ones. The natural nails were discolored and looked deformed. I could not understand why anyone would do that before I realized how much importance is placed on beauty and good health. Fingernails and hair are excellent indicators of general health. "If she does not take care of her hands and feet..." is what I was taught. If your nails are brittle or will not grow I suggest you increase your calcium intake before you develop a hunched back. I would also suggest that you do not cover them with layers of acrylic that smother the real nail. I remember watching my shipmate sprinkle hair powder on his bald spot. I remember my grandmother's false teeth in a cup beside her bed. We try to change what we look like to become more attractive. I get a haircut for job interviews and evenings out. The beautiful and healthy have it better, but it is easier and more expensive to fake it.

Here is the downside of cosmetic refinements. They are not real and someone is going to find out. The masks have to come off sooner or later. I usually find out about the hidden physical ugliness right before sexual encounters. "I have something to tell you..." is the usual start to the

---

[251]Nancy Etcoff, Ph D.: Psychologist and faculty member of the Harvard Medical.

confession that is about to be revealed. There is a shit-eating grin that crosses a person's face when they have you in the bedroom and are about to undress. I have heard, "I have stretch marks." "I wear a girdle." "I have a skin condition." "My breasts are not real." "Do not pull my hair; it is a weave." "I had a Caesarean Section." "I had my breasts removed because of cancer." and "I had a tummy tuck and it left a scar all the way across my stomach." I have felt like I was in that scene from *I'm Gonna Get You, Sucker* and I felt lied to. The bedroom is not a good confessional. I would rather hear confessions over the phone or at least before I took you to dinner.

I once got my hand stuck in the tracks of a girl's weave during petting. I have also had a woman scare the hell out of me when she got up to go to the bathroom and left her fake ponytail on the pillow. I thought it was a rodent or some other small furry animal. Speaking of fake ponytails, I once had a date lose hers on the dance floor. Another woman picked it up and handed it to her. She ran off to the restroom to recoup. Do yourself a favor; come clean up front because the shit you are hiding always shows its ugly head. When it does become known, not only is it is as ugly a secret as you made it, but it always seems to happen at the worst time.

We even hide from the most important of the physical senses. We mask smell. Smell is the only sense that is not processed through the thinking brain. Smell goes directly to the old brain. In many instances it is the deciding factor in determining "yea" or "nay" regarding a mate. We use deodorants, perfume, body wash, shampoo, douche, scented lotion, and breath mints to mask our natural odor (it is not natural to stink, odor is a signal of bad diet or bad health). Hiding what we find unattractive about ourselves only magnifies it, and frequently leads to disappointment on all sides. "You said you love me." "I did, when I thought you were someone else."

Hidden mental defects are much more traumatic and take a lot longer to surface because the cosmetics we use on these imperfections are a lot more complex in their design. I have had to confront and comfort women who have experienced rape, incest, physical abuse and sexual molestation. I have had to deal with depression, anxiety, low self-esteem and megalomania. How about you?

American Beauty

Why would anyone not want to be considered beautiful when looking at the benefits? My issue with societal concepts of beauty is that I live in the United States, and light skin is not only privilege, but also considered by the majority to be more attractive. I cannot possibly compete with a white person if I were to superimpose the popular view of beauty on the women I choose or myself. Many people try to do just that and end up altering who they are, trying to be what others deem to be beautiful. What makes this even more insane is the fact that, in reality, the majority of people are not white, skinny, blond or blue eyed. The Nazis used a similar standard of beauty and tried to use eugenics[252] to increase this desired portion of the population.

If you want to see what a society's definition of beauty is, look at television or any newsstand in a particular country; they are blanketed with what advertisers (the pulse of popular culture)

---

[252] Eugenics: Greek roots for "good" and "generation" or "origin" and was first used to refer to the "science" of heredity and good breeding in about 1883. Reached its height around 1923 in the United States.

consider attractive. These media models help program our definition of beauty from birth using what we already consider naturally beautiful (symmetry) as a catalyst.

I was teased in elementary school for having a curly afro. Some of the white children chanted, "Ron is a sappy bear and he has nappy hair." I remember teasing others because they did not fit the mold of beauty that I was taught. I called really dark skinned people "black" as if it were an insult because I was taught that dark skin was not a desirable trait. In Africa someone called me white.

I was taught within the African-American community that light skinned people were more attractive than the dark skinned people, but even the light people were not as good as white. "Light, bright and damn near white," was what we called yellow people. In short, I thought my own skin color was not beautiful because I did not see it portrayed as beautiful. Even now the majority of successful and prominent minority actors and actresses or models are those with Arian features and "paper bag brown" skin or lighter. I feel sorry for anyone who does not see the beauty in all things, especially themselves.

Pri$e-Tag-Roman$e

"I like Americans. You all have a lot of money." That is what a foreign whore told me. I once overheard an older man in the corner laundry tell the attendant, "There are two things God never should have made: an ugly woman or a broke man," I was 13. He obviously understood the principles that govern Pri$e-Tag-Roman$e. Every male I know says, "I have paid for sex all my life." I do not care what you use to justify it or what name you call it. An escort, courtesan, concubine, whore, prostitute, girlfriend, or wives, if you are in it for the money fuck you, literally; I will consider you all whores and treat you the way you act.

A female very close to me told me, "Men should pay for sex." She never did give me a rational explanation as to why. I have done it and I have declined it. If your woman wants money up front, or she asks for it discreetly after sex, or expects it in the future, what does that make her?

A woman once spent the evening drinking champagne and flirting with me. I was watching a jazz band and one of the members introduced her to me. She made herself comfortable and was quite engaging. I thought we were getting along fine until the evening was coming to an end and she mentioned that she was a hooker and her future company would cost, "$300.00?" "What am I going to get for $300.00?" "Anything you want" "Can I fuck you in the ass?" "No." "Well that is not anything I want." I paid $900.00 a month for my house. She wanted $300.00 for an orgasm and would not consider deducting any of the check (please, do not go there). She made the playing field a paying field. Once that happens I go retro and add up everything from the moment I met you. I have yet to meet a woman who has matched my monetary generosity. "You'd have to wash my clothes by hand, cook like the "Bam" guy, clean to military specifications for a month and then let me do anything I wanted and reciprocate, to make $300.00 for sex." "I have already had anything I want and it cost me much more."

179

I was not mad at her, but I was upset with the musician. "What makes you think I wanted a whore?" Something stupid came out of his mouth that equated to "you have a penis." It was as if I was crazy for not wanting her. She was fine as hell, but there is something about Pri$e-Tags that makes my penis disappear and the woman a whore. "I pay for pussy of my own choosing," is what I told him as I left for another frustrating solo masturbation session.

I try to avoid serious involvement with most females because many of them think that showing material appreciation is the priority in a relationship. Some think that men are obligated to support them because they have sex. I can count the relationships where I have not been asked for money in one form or another. One woman asked me to pay her electric bill. I said, "No." If she had asked for a loan, I probably would have given it to her with full knowledge that I may or may not see it again. I did not give it to her because I did not want to establish a precedent. I knew, and so do you that if I gave her money once, she would be back the next time she needed or wanted something for which she did not have the money. Why should I have to pay a woman to be in a relationship with me? It is like a one sided game. I am supposed to be emotionally attached, sympathetic, monogamous, obedient and understanding as well. I was not upset with her. However, I did question the logic behind the request.

If women did not exist, all the money in the world would have no meaning. Aristotle Onassis[253]

One of the richest men in the world said the above statement. He believed it too. Do you have any idea how much he paid for Jackie Kennedy? No one should have to pay for it. The big difference between sex for money and sex for free, is that sex for money usually costs a lot less. I do not necessarily mean in dollars, but that is what it usually boils down to. American society reinforces this concept. You do not have to take my word for it, look at the advertisements that come out just before Valentine's Day. Men are peppered with gift ideas for women, but I have yet to see an advertisement with gifts for men. Look at the courtship process. Who does the chasing (on the surface) and usually the paying? How would women feel if men told them up front that he wanted to split the check on your first date? If "cheap" came to mind, you probably subscribe to the philosophy of Pri$e-Tag-Roman$e. What if he wanted to get to know you better and did not feel that he should have to pay for it? What if he extended this request to the entire relationship? I think most women would walk away disgusted? If a relationship is supposed to be equal, why are men expected to pay more? I know this is the way it has been for ages, but I think it is wrong. For the record, I am not cheap; I am very generous, but I expect the same from my partner and have rarely found it. On top of the Pri$e-Tag-Roman$e are the emotional, mental and spiritual prices that are a lot higher than the material ones. Purchasing the services of a whore often costs less when compared to sustaining a relationship that is wrong.

I have had experiences with woman who tried to hint their way into getting what they wanted. I do not like being pressured to do anything, and I do not like ear beatings or being trained either. One afternoon I was reading the Sunday newspaper next to my partner on the sofa. She kept interrupting me with these advertisements for jewelry. She was so persistent that I finally asked her why she was doing it. She said, "I am trying to give you a hint; I want a diamond tennis bracelet" I said, "If you want one, go buy one; you make the same amount of

---

[253] Aristotle Onassis (1900-1975): Greek Shipping Magnate (one of the wealthiest men in the world). Jackie got $30 million when he died.

money as I and I pay every bill in this house except the phone bill". Please try to understand that we moved in together so that she could fix her finances. She had student loans, credit cards, a mortgage and a car loan that all but wiped out her paycheck. I suggested that she move in, rent her condominium out and use the additional income to pay her bills. While we were together she bought a new car, a picture-in-picture television, a CD player for the new car, diamond earrings (I bought) and a multitude of other things. She won a trip in a raffle. We agreed that we would pay for the hotel and expenses equally. In the end, I paid for the entire trip.

We lived together for almost two years. I was relocating because of work. I let her use my relocation package to sell her place without any fees. Sometime later I asked her for $400; she gave it to me. Later she asked when I was going to pay it back. Am I wrong for thinking that she should not have asked me for anything? She also got the tennis bracelet. I gave it to her for Christmas. She took the one she bought for herself off and then put my gift on. I asked her why. "This one is real." I remember thinking, "Why would anyone ask someone to buy something for them that they would not buy themselves." That was $1,000.00 down the drain.

I have even had women call to invite me to dinner, and when the check came they expected me to pay. I was so confused that I asked other women about it. Am I wrong for viewing this type of behavior as manipulative? I thought the rule was: "If you invite, you pay."

There are women who like to change those things about males they do not like, and typically they do not have the courtesy to let males in on it. Males are manipulative as well, but at least with another male I am not subjected to tears or other forms of emotional blackmail when I decline to participate in agendas that do not appeal to me, the pri$e is often too high.

In every meaningful relationship that I have had we ended up spending too much time together. There were times I would have rather been alone or doing something else without the constant companionship of my significant other. I have had women interrupt my reading, hobby or anything else that took attention from them even though we were in the same house or apartment. I have a habit of working late into the night. I guess it is the Air sign in me. The world seems quiet after the multitudes settle down. On several occasions I have had women wake up, get out of bed and then order me to join them. I do not see the need in being with my partner whenever I have free time because I am not consumed with other people. I know this sounds selfish, but I think it is actually the opposite. I believe being with another to feel loved is selfish, a sure sign of insecurity and it carries a mentally hidden pri$e-tag that my soul cannot bear.

I remember having sex for the first time with a woman I had been seeing for about a month. I will not go into the games we played to get into bed, but I will say that she cancelled a trip paid for by another man. Yeah, she was humping someone else, but I guess local sex beats long distance booty calls. After the act, I wanted to go home. Not that I objected to staying with her, but I had not fed my dog, it was late and I had to work the next day. I explained this to her, but she was insistent that I stay. You should have heard the reasons that exited her mouth to convince me that my dog was not hungry, and that it was all right to stay the night. She suggested that I get up early and go to work. It was not until I relented by saying that I would return did I get out of the door without a major blow out. That scared me. I knew from that moment on that she needed large amounts of attention and our relationship would suffer because of it. I was right, but time taught me a lot more than her mouth could.

I cannot love a woman without first knowing her and what I want from her. I need to know you and love me before I can answer these questions. I think self-love is the most important element in any relationship. Only then can a union or reunion be good. It is not a consuming need or desire, but a mutually beneficial and healthy connection. It does not cost either partner anything. I strongly disagree with the premise that one must sacrifice in order to commune. It is my belief that we have become accustomed to sacrificing, and we now believe it to be normal and acceptable.

I have not met many people who view relationships in this way; therefore I maintain distance and try to avoid unspoken commitments. I say unspoken because many people assume that sex or any other form of satisfaction we feel with one another constitutes some form of mutual bond, gained responsibility and commitment whether the subject is actually discussed or not.

Because it takes time to know a person, I am trying not to give in to emotions and desires at the onset of a relationship. I know sex for what it is, just sex. I like to wait and see if the person I have feelings and desires for is real. Am I watching a performance designed to attract and keep my attention? If so, the act cannot last forever and the real person will emerge eventually. I like to wait and see if I like this person as much as I like the person they are trying to portray to the world. Am I superimposing my desires on this person? If so, they cannot possibly live up to my expectations, and are losing themselves in my desires in order to gain affection or something else. They are trying to be what I want them to be instead of themselves. Only time can tell these things for certain. And we have plenty of time.

There are parts of every woman with whom I have been in long standing relationships that I love, but there have always been more drawbacks to being committed than living a life without a committed loved one. There are more negatives than positives. I always hated being asked, "Where have you been?" and "Where are you going?" I stopped checking in after I left home.

Some women seem to want to train men to do their bidding or act in a certain way. I am not particularly fond of constant cuddling. I am intolerant of people who demand constant attention or look for the meaning of life in marriage or sexual relationships. I said it before and I shall repeat it for the mentally challenged, I do not want anything hard in my life. Dependent relationships with insecure women or males are hard for me. I have always felt a wanting, restlessness, a repression and a confinement when involved in monogamous relationships. Do not get me wrong; I have been happy in relationships, but it always wore off once familiarity set in, and I found that many people are not who they present themselves to be. I bought into the misrepresentation with the hope of finding it to be true, but knowing that it more than likely was not.

The "dos" and "do nots" of relationships feel too restrictive to me. It is normally expected that we cannot have anyone outside of the relationship with whom to share strong feelings - ex's, friends and family included. It is too intimidating and threatening to the relationship because most partners want all the love for themselves. I am not that type of person and I do not want to be involved with that type of person. That is a pri$e I cannot and will not pay.

What the superior man seeks is in himself is what the small man seeks is in others.
Confucius

Finding people attractive is natural. Why is it supposed to end after we enter a relationship? There are always beautiful people around us. We would have to walk with our eyes glued to the sidewalk not to see an attractive person every now and then. I find myself attracted to beauty whether I am involved or not. If I were married I would feel the same way. Not being able to look at and admire beauty openly seems too much like being forced to serve a term in public office or being sentenced to a Siberian gulag. Before you go off in judgment, listen. Married men and women do find others attractive; they are just expected to hide it and keep it to themselves. Which would you prefer, my honesty or their denial? Do not even think about having a female or male friend with whom you enjoy spending time or talking. And, we do not have to talk about the, "until death do you part" segment of marriage vows; divorce and fidelity statistics tell us all we need to know.

Every relationship I have had became hard to maintain. I was taught it takes two to argue and I do not have to participate in a discussion where someone thinks I need to do something to make them feel better. Because of this, women have tried to force conversation. Women have attempted to keep me from walking out of an argument. Women have refused to leave my residence when asked. Women have showed up unannounced and knocked on my bedroom window when I did not answer the door. Women have scaled my security gate because I refused to answer the bell. One night I watched from a distance as one woman put a note on my windshield. I was having a conversation with a friend about half a block from where my car was parked. Thirty seconds after she drove off another woman took the note off. A woman has called me at work, called my cellular, paged me, called my home phone and when all of these failed, she called my roommate's home number. Another woman bought diamond earrings without telling or asking me through a home lay-a-way program where you pay 10% up front then the balance in monthly installments. She expected me to pay the balance. She even put them under my name. I once caught two women going through my wallet. They thought I was in the shower.

I once had a woman ask me for money for her daughter. I immediately thought she was lying about being broke. While she was in the bathroom I looked in her purse; she had money, condoms and a tube of K-Y jelly. Five different women have asked me for money for abortions when they were not pregnant. A woman once called my Executive Officer to tell him that I would not return her phone calls. When he mentioned it to me, I told him I did nothing wrong and I was in no way responsible for the actions of a crazy person. Sisters have knowingly had sex with me. I have had married women stalk me. I have had sex with friends, and then listened to them degrade each other in my presence only to act the part of best friends when they were together. A woman once had a friend who lived across the street call me to see if I was at home so that she could ring the doorbell and gain entry. Five minutes after the phone call, I heard the bell. I called my friend back and asked him if she was still at his house. He said, "No." She later complained that she could not believe that I did not answer my door knowing that she and her

183

daughter were ringing the bell. I asked her, "Did you really want to come in even though I had company?"

I have never wanted anything hard in my life. Life is supposed to be easy after all. It is our right to be happy and happy does not equate to hard in my book. If happy = hard in your book, you should rewrite it and try to make it easy.

It is with our passions, as it is with fire and water; they are good servants but bad masters.
Aesop[254]

You might say I am holding out for perfection because I have come to realize that anything else is a pacifier. I am tired of women who seem to think they need to fake orgasms, and I am tired of materialistic love (Pri$e-Tag-Roman$e). If we are not completely honest about our intentions from the beginning, there is no need to proceed past the first hello. If you are in it for the money, say so, that way we can begin negotiations. If you want tons of affection, you should say so. I will respond with, "I cannot provide physical affection in abundance until I know who you are; I have been scarred too many times." If you want to be a stay-at-home partner that is something you should tell your mate. You should not have a secret plan to get pregnant and never return to work. It would not work for me because I cook, do laundry and clean better than most. In my case, a stay-at-home partner would be in the way. I have had women look in my trash can to see if I really cooked the meal I was serving to them. I have had to instruct women on how to properly do laundry.

One woman looked at me like I was insane when I told her that lemon juice works better than bleach on white sheets suffering from period stains. How many women have gone through an inspection by a Marine Corps drill sergeant with a white glove while they yell at you? I could not internally justify taking care of a healthy adult just because she has a vagina or I love her. Life is too hard for an African-American male as it is. If I had teats, I might think differently, but I have been through "the shit" and I do not want it from my mate under any circumstances. If you do not like the situation, leave! I have supported women before, but it was an effort to try to help them stand on their own. Once it became evident that they would not and did not want to stand alone, I moved on. I have had women help me out during times of need, but women always want to be paid back. No problem with that, but why is it that women have issues repaying debts, especially to males they are fucking? Every woman I asked this question said, "Men are getting something too." "What sex?" "Yes." "You whore!"

I want my partner to be an asset in all things; I consider deficits, in business or relationships, a waste of time, energy, emotions and finance. I am not a psychiatrist; I am not qualified to fix anyone's emotional issues, including my own sometimes. I am so tired of meeting people with serious emotional issues who do not seem to think it is a requirement to disclose until after we are involved. I want to know if and why my mate is on Prozac beforehand. I have made many women mad at me for sticking to these convictions. I am sorry, but when I say I do not want a typical committed relationship, I mean it. I do not want the drama, sacrifice and baggage that usually accompany them. And, please do not expect me to change my mind after we have sex or

---

[254] Aesop (6th Century BC): Greek fabulist. Wrote a total of 655 + fables. Many are still in use today "One good turn deserves another."

a pleasurable evening together. Chances are I do not know you well enough to even want to change for you. I have had good sex before and will not reevaluate the situation after you "throw it on me". No one should be upset because of it; it is just sex and most women are good at sex. I do not pay for it with character changes. I will not change my mind and I do not need anyone trying to change it for me; I am full-grown and can make my own decisions.

In my experiences, some people seem to think that they have to trick others into giving them what they want. This technique floats like a brick with me. As a matter of fact, it puts them in the manipulative category…deficit. If you want something from me, more time, attention or affection, ask for it; but be prepared for the possibility that you may receive, "No" as a reply. It does not make me a monster; it does make me clear about my desires.

It is my opinion that most women need men in their lives and vice versa. We seem to need each other as much as we need food and water. Men were designed for several purposes: procreation and security being the most prominent. I have found that when most people do not feel safe, enter a mate. Do you sleep better when there is someone beside you? Do you wake up at the slightest unfamiliar sound when you are alone? Do you feel incomplete if you do not have a significant other in your life? Do your friends and family constantly inquire about your love life? Have you been married more than once? Have you jumped from relationship to relationship all your life, only taking breaks to heal the hurt from the last one? What are you looking for in a partner and why? We should stop selling and buying ourselves. It cheapens us all. Remember this: the person who wants nothing from you is invincible to your advances and requests.

Money grows on cotton bushes… Bring on the love.

How Many Men Do You Know

If man ever finds his true strength, nothing will stop him.

I believe there is a natural progression to the development of a "Man". Having a penis means we were born male. God and nature made that happen. All males have been, will be, or shall remain forever boys, whether they are infants, toddlers, teenagers, adolescents, or adults. Very few males become men. Men have the courage to be honest. Fewer still will become human. Humans do not fear for fears sake. They love too much. They embrace their circumstances or change them. They have control of their minds and are able to regulate their bodies.

I call most males, including myself, "boys" because, as many women say, and as I have often observed, there are very few or no men on the planet. Let us do some math. Males in the United States make up 48-49% of the population. If we eliminate the males under 18 and then take into account those who are not interested in women, premature death, incarcerations, HIV, alcoholics, workaholics, crack addicts, marriage, and the mentally ill or unstable, anyone can come to the logical conclusion that eligible males are a rarity. Of those remaining, the males whom have never been married and/or have no children are rarer still. And a physically and spiritually mature male, a "Man", who is not married and has no children, is an anomaly or considered gay.

185

FYI: African-American males should be on the endangered species list. In some cases 50% of males of color are not graduating high school. They tend to end up in prison or dead. It is not a new occurrence. Sociologists and social anthropologists alike have studied this situation. The solutions have varied, but the trend continues. The cause is poverty and hopelessness. The cure is love, mentorship, a hand when needed and a slap[255] when justified.

I found it interesting that when I asked women what their definition of a "Man" was. They all mentioned provides for his family. I do not think being married or fatherhood has anything to do with "Manhood" and your family can destroy you if you tried to support them all. On the contrary, I think that resisting the early urges to bond, mate and procreate is a sure sign of probable maturity.

I have found that relationships between males can be more taxing than those between males and females. We can be more jealous than women, our expectations are higher and the competition is greater. Adult boys have not learned that we get more by cooperating, than by competing. Dr. Nash had it right. The group does profit more when everyone in the group is being fulfilled, versus competing as individuals where there is one winner. I like to avoid locking horns and still get what I want without hurting anyone intentionally.

Boys seem to want to have a cockfight to see who the big "Man" on campus is, rather than grow up to be men. These competitions lead, as they have throughout history, to conflict. We seem to need to establish a social order to associate with one another. You can have it. I have more important things to do with my time than to be distracted by the antics of people trying to get as much attention as I. And pretty please do not judge me; I have my reasons for being who I am, just as you have yours.

Pick any group of boys anywhere in the world with nothing to do and that was us. We were standing on the banks of the Anacostia River. It happened to be summer vacation. Our parents did not have the luxury of sending us to camp and unless some family member was willing to assume the task of caregiver for a fee, we were stuck with idle time and no organized activities for the entire summer.

Bryan challenged everyone, as usual, to throw a rock further than he could. He was our leader. I was maybe, six, the runt and the youngest in the group. They did not want me along, but I could keep up no matter what fence, ditch, or railroad trestle. I did what they did, followed Brian, and males of all ages like that. I began looking for the right rock to throw. Bryan tossed a lemon-size rock halfway across the river. No one had even come close to matching his achievement. "That one!" the voice said. "The white one," I questioned. "Yeah!" It was a flat square piece of what had to be quartz. It looked like a small bathroom tile. When it was my turn, I grabbed the rock by two of its corners and threw it sidearm like I had with old records to increase the distance. It sailed through the air low towards the water and then suddenly, as if caught by some invisible hand, it rose in the air and did a wide sweeping barrel roll. We were all amazed when its white form came to rest on the mud brown bank of the other side. They dared me to do it again. I was afraid to try to repeat the miracle. I did not believe it myself. I know now

---

[255] There have been times when I have been slapped harder mentally than could ever be possible on the physical plane.

that it was Bernoulli's theory [256] that gave the rock lift. What I do not know is who or what told me to pick that particular rock.

By definition a MAN is a bipedal primate mammal (homo-sapiens) that is anatomically related to great apes but distinguished especially by notable development of the brain with resultant capacity of speech and abstract reasoning, is usually considered to form a variable number of freely interbreeding races and is the sole representative of a natural family (hominidae).

We are two legged primates related to apes, capable of speech and we can breed with other humans. The jury is still out on the whole notable brain capacity and abstract thinking part. I think a majority of people have not had an independent thought or shown signs of "notable" brain capacity. Anyone can read a book, study a subject and pass a test where the general questions are given ahead of time; all it takes is study or cheating. That is my way of saying that having a degree (even from Yale) does not mean you have notable brain capacity. I think a true mark of intelligence is applying what one has learned to the goals one has set. And once accomplished, they move on to the next set of goals and challenges, being all they can be with or without a uniform. It does not matter if you have no experience that relates to the task at hand; just do it. Unfortunately, the transition from lessons learned to application seems much too difficult for the average person.

If asked the definition of a "Man", how many people would mention giving when you have nothing, being honest even if it is not to your benefit, protecting those who cannot protect themselves, taking a responsible role in child rearing, fighting the unwinnable fight, fortifying spirits, instilling and reinforcing spiritual law, and most importantly being able to teach the unteachable and being willing to learn from the most ignorant? I do not know many people who can live this way, including me.

Todd was the type of person who always managed to insult someone within the first five minutes of his arrival. Once he said, "Fuck Europe…" I was sitting beside a male from Holland and another from Switzerland. On another occasion he asked me, "Who is the new meat?" Two of my American friends were visiting and Todd thought they were locals and did not speak English.

Knowing how he was, I was prepared for just about anything that could possibly come out of his mouth except the following: "I am going to form a club. To become a member you have to have had sex with at least 100 women." I thought about it as he kept talking about his club and its members. At the end of his fantasy I said, "I'll join, but whores, and sex with anyone under 18 does not count. Plus, Viagra users cannot join." The effect was priceless. For the record, I did not know he was on Viagra until then.

For the not so "average bears" I told my mother I was going to build a castle and form a club of my own called *M & M,* The Masturbating Monks. I said monks, not punks! It will be a sanctuary, a place to get away from the social game. Our mission will be the betterment of

---

[256] Daniel Bernoulli (1700-1782): Developed an important principle involving the movement of a fluid through a pressure difference.

humanity and only boys or adult males, without a wife or child, who are willing to learn how to be men, will be allowed to enter. The objective is to train the mind to control the body. The rules are simple: be honest, perform our natural role as protectors, lose the fear, do what you say you will do (do not let someone else's desire become your own), seek knowledge, and remove sex and desires from the equation of relationships (you cannot know a woman if you are thinking with the other head, and you cannot hear what people are asking if you want something).

My mother said women from around the world will storm the walls and assault the fortifications with ladders, perfume and sexy clothing if they knew that "Men" were inside. I told her I would reinforce the troops with these subtle reminders: "Where are you going?" and "Where have you been?" When the ramparts are about to be overrun, I would do my Henry V impression, but instead of, "Once more into the breach," I would say, "Where are you going?" "Who was that?" "Why do you have to go out so much?" "Can I have some money?" "Do you love me?" and "Do you think I am fat?"

Most women seem to think males are incredibly stupid and need guidance. If you doubt it just ask a woman you trust, and with whom you are not and have not had sex (mother, sister, aunt, grandmother). Men do not need guidance; they are led by their inner voice. Men are not stupid; it takes time to grow confident enough to hear that voice inside and believe in oneself, especially for an African-American in the United States. If you have issues distinguishing between a boy and a "Man", just ask, *What have you done for someone else today?*" or ask him "Who are you?" His answer will tell you whether he is a "Man" or not. The course taken after that determination is yours alone.

When I can raise any child without hitting, scaring or even raising my voice, and have them follow my advice and become wiser knowing why the path they chose was better; when I can communicate with anyone with just a smile or a gesture; when I can extend my hand to every person without fear, I will be a "Man" by my own definition because by then I will be walking with the God in me.

Honesty

> *If you ever want to keep someone in your life, be honest with them.*

My boss, the three-star Admiral, could not fly back to home base in his private two-seat jet because his ears were clogged. Aviators risk blown eardrums at altitude, so he opted to fly home in the pressurized cabin of our military chartered flight. The entire staff was returning from inspecting an Air Wing that the Admiral commanded. His securing the number one seat, the seat behind the pilot in command, was all but assured. I usually try to sit there because I like to monitor the pilots and want to be able to give my assistance in case of emergency. I will be damned if I will leave my life in the hands of others. I ended up sitting across the aisle from him. I guess he felt an obligation to speak to me. He asked me how the commands were doing[257]. I asked, "Do you really want to know?" He said, "Yes." I told him what the "troops" in the training commands were telling me. He listened and then he commanded. The feedback from those he commanded, my superiors, was, "Don't you ever speak to him again… Ever!" I guess a

---

[257] I was one of three Pipeline Training Officers.

three-star, has some weight. "Yes, Sir, I will never speak to the motherfucker again, even if he asks me an honest question to improve the efficiency of the training command."

Every man has some reminiscences which he would not tell to everyone, but only to his friends. He has others which he would not reveal even to his friends, but only to himself and that in secret. But, finally there are still others which a man is even afraid to tell himself and every decent man has a considerable number of such things stored away. That is, one can even say that the more decent he is, the greater the number of such things in his mind. Fyodor Dostoyevsky[258]

People say they want honesty, but we cannot be honest without paying for this honesty in blood. "Does my butt look big in this dress?" A woman who was at least eighty pounds overweight asked me as she turned her rear towards me in a club. Honest answer, "Of course it does... Your ass is big and clothes ain't gonna change it." Desired answer, "No... You look good girl." Sometimes it does take a lie. Sarcastic answer, "I do not know; what does the mirror and the scale say?" Which answer do you think I gave? Those who know me also know that the honesty came out, the first one.

Would you rather have someone tell you the truth or lie? Would you want your lover to tell you that you are not sexually satisfying? Actually, they should not have to. Do you want to hear that you have picked up a pound or two, or that your breath stinks? Again, no one has to tell you that you no longer fit in your own clothes or why they are hesitant to kiss you. Who wants wrinkles? You do not want to hear about your cooking. No one wants to hear about his or her body odor. We do not want anyone to disapprove of our appearance, so many of us spend time carefully picking out what to wear and pay particular attention to how we look before we have an encounter. We all prefer to hear only good things and want to feel the same way. Sometimes this takes one lie or a lot of them.

I once had a girlfriend who had gained weight and her body was no longer attractive. I know it sounds shallow, but you are no different than I. A nice body attracts and a body that is not proportionate is not attractive to most people. I want to have "sex" with people I find attractive physically and I want to have offspring with a healthy woman, not one who will likely pass on unhealthy genes. It has nothing to do with love (except if thinking of the future children of your union). It has everything to do with natural selection and choosing the best available mate.

I asked my mother if there was anything I could do to let her know how big she was and not have an argument about it. Mom suggested that I take a picture of her from behind. She said, "It worked on me." I did this while we were on the beach. She walked down to the water and I took a sneaky shot of her from behind. When I had the shots developed I let her open and view them in private. After looking at the developed pictures, she saw the double prints of herself and frowned. I was watching through the breakfast bar. I found those two prints crumbled up under the couch while cleaning up a week or so later, but it did not work. I paid $10.75 for those double prints.

---

[258] Fyodor Dostoyevsky (1821-1881): considered one of the greatest Russian writers of fiction in the 20th century. The quote is from the "Idiot".

"May I ask you a question?" "Yes, you may… Answers are free; thoughtful answers cost $5.00; and the truth will set you back plenty"[259].

I prefer to hear the truth always, even if it is not flattering. The truth may sting, but lies, especially from those we care about cut to the soul. I remember my first gray hair. I plucked it and kept plucking it and then there were three. "Shit! I am getting old." Some years and many plucks later someone mentioned to my mother, "Oh my God! Your son has gray in his beard." I thought, "Someone else knows." I am salt and pepper gray now, and the gray in my beard has grown to streaks on both sides.

You should have heard some of the early feedback about the rough drafts of this work. I owe my editor a red pen[260]. Their honesty helped make it what it is. I am grown and I can take the temporary hurt, because I know that I can only gain from it in the long run.

Here is a dose of honesty: I want sex from very few women and honest input from all of them. Notice I wrote "very few"? I want love from everyone. However, I will not pay for sex from someone who says they love me. I will pay for love with love. If you pay someone, they are an employee or a dependant, not an equal.

I know a woman whose first boyfriend got her pregnant. I paid for the abortion. We were spooning one night and I happened to clutch her belly. It felt hard and round. I asked her if she was pregnant. She started crying and she said, "I do not know." We had been together for a month or so and we never had sex without a condom. I am glad she was honest enough to tell me the truth and not try to blame me. I borrowed money from my grandmother.

We ended up being together for two years. But we separated for almost a year. I went to visit her only to find out that she had been seeing someone. We resumed our relationship despite this and the relationships I confessed I had had. When we reunited the following year, we did not have sex for two weeks and I am sure she was curious about why. I was recovering from the gonorrhea a girl gave me three days before I saw her. When we did have sex, shortly afterwards she told me she was pregnant again. She aborted this child as well. I really did not think this one was mine either, but I would get the blame and the responsibility until I could get a blood test. How do I ask her this question "Was that second child mine?"

Here is more honesty. If women did not have a reproductive organ, would most men associate with them outside of work? 90% of straight men spend nine months trying to get out of a woman and most of the rest of their lives trying to get back in. The price some pay is catastrophic. Did that rock the boat? I hope so.

I stopped seeing a woman because I wanted to be faithful to someone else. I called her at work and said, "I need to talk to you in person." "No. Tell me now." "I cannot see you anymore; I want to have an honest relationship with someone else." She later told me that she was so upset that she had to leave work. What should I have done?

---

[259] Seriously, I like to ask hard questions that require thought. It requires time and brainpower to question ourselves.
[260] Ann, I hope that brought a smile to your face.

Another woman told me that she would like more oral sex. After three requests, each more forceful and demanding than the last, I had to tell her… "Your pussy stinks… I like eating women, but you smell bad. That's why I don't eat you… The first night you smelled good, but after that… your pussy stinks." Who would want to hear that? Who has to? You smell it every time you use the toilet.

Because life keeps me from my five or six real male friends for years at a time, when we talk on the phone or see one another, I simply ask, "How is your love life?" There is no need to ask about the last girl friend, she may or may not be in the picture or the wife. The married ones were hooked early, and cheat or have cheated. The single ones seem to want to be that way for good. I say they might as well; it seems better than cheating on someone who could take you to the bank. If you are not monogamous, do not get married; or marry a very different kind of woman and get her permission in writing, but that usually means you are going to have to put up with her stepping out occasionally. Do not worry. Whether you know it or not, it may be happening already. Kobe and Tiger know what I am saying.

I have a question. Why do men like strip clubs so much? It was the most popular group suggestion on cross-country flights. Married men have vagina "on tap" at home! Are they sexually frustrated or are they tired of eating chicken every day? If so, what are they looking for in a stripper? I get horny at strip clubs, but I am not looking for sex from a stripper, so if given a choice, I do not go. The last time I went to a strip club I was with a woman who had never been to one. I am nothing if not accommodating and curious. This club was topless only. The married couple that accompanied us had been there before and I thought they were swingers. My friend got a lap dance from a sexy woman I selected for her. She got so excited she smacked the girl on her ass. I was surprised and amused. Both the stripper and I told her touching was not allowed. So, that visit to the sin shack was worth it; I found out she likes girls.

Are women holding out? Is sex a bargaining tool? According to the boys, it is. Hey, holding out on sex is not smart; sex is an addictive drug. If you are not giving it to your partner, someone else will, especially if they are socially acceptable. If you made the plunge, make love, not war or get a divorce. Our mates are after all, what we wanted and whom we chose. If we are disappointed, it should be disappointment in the choice we made. We need to stop kicking ourselves in the ass.

It seems we can only tolerate the truth from a comedian or a minister.

Monogamy

How many people go away after the first rebuff to their flirtations? How many persistent potential mates back off after you say you are married, have a significant other or are engaged? How many times have you shared a mate (knowingly at the time or not)?

Our violation of natural law and trying to compensate for it with our own laws, usually throws things out of balance. Our society tells us that monogamy is the correct way to experience the rapture of love. If that is true, why is it that I do not know many who have been faithful in every relationship and why are so many unhappy? Why do the statistics on paternity,

191

prostitution, rape, divorce and infidelity show that attempting to impose a sexual moral code via punishment, whether the punishment be losing a mate, prison, a fine, alimony, palimony, death or eternal damnation, have no effect in stopping infidelity or sexual promiscuity? Is it because most think monogamy is a Diana Ross movie or an African hard wood?

I once invited everyone I knew and more to a Memorial Day cookout at my beach condominium. We ate boiled crab, and barbecued mammoth shrimp that my cousin brought with him in a cooler from D. C. They looked like lobster tails. I appreciated it and knew he was learning the lesson that our grandfather taught us, "GIVE". My grandfather is the only adult that I have ever seen insist that the children get a steak and not a hotdog if they wanted one at BBQs. But, there were also a variety salads and libation of all sorts in abundance.

At times I found I was getting jealous. The other males were scoring with some of my ex-girls (do not get it twisted; it was momentary insanity - I am a realist.). I even warned one of the guys, "Be careful with that one." I was referring to Crazy.

I lost my cousin. He was the type that could find trouble blindfolded when he was drinking, so I always kept an eye on him. Someone said they saw him headed for the beach. I could not see very far because there were no lights or hear anything above the sound of the waves, but, neither could they. My cousin had his face in the lap of a woman he had invited. She and a friend had followed him down from Washington. When I returned to the party her girlfriend asked in front of five or six other people if I had seen her friend. "Yes. She's on the beach getting her pussy licked by my cousin." Everyone laughed, the police came, and a neighbor pulled a shotgun on some of my guests (my cousin was at the center of it). They were smoking marijuana beside his house, my other cousin, whom happens to be allergic to shrimp, deliberately ate shrimp, I was cussed out several times and someone was slapped in the living room. My cousin later popped up out of the woods with leaves and sand everywhere looking possessed. I had to ask, "What the hell were you doing in there?" "I don't know," is all he said as he stumbled back to the party. About thirty seconds later a girl emerged from the same area… I had sex with the first girl my cousin ate, and ended up with three women in my bed. Monogamy indeed! Did I mention it was a jolly good party?

Monogamy is a social myth. Women are able to select the sire of their children by having an orgasm shortly before or after her partner. The muscular reflexes of the vagina help pull the sperm toward the cervix. Until a woman has an orgasm, her cervix is blocked by mucous. Why would nature have developed such a mechanism? We also have to consider hidden ovulation, the fact that women do not openly display fertility like other animals. I interpret this as a natural defense against forced copulation or selective breeding.

The penis is designed to plunge the sperm of rivals from the uterus. According to Britain's Child Support Agency, 1 in 6 men tested since 1998 were cleared of paternity[261]. That means two things to me. The women in question were having sex with more than one partner at the time of conception and the tested male had reason for uncertainty. In Canada it is estimated that in 10%

---

[261] David Hencke, <u>Child Support Agency forced to pay back wrongly accused men</u>.

of households, the social father is not the biological father[262]. These statistics tell me that not only are some people are not being monogamous, but also they are lying about it.

Monogamy rarely exists even in the wild. I used to think that there were certain species of birds that were monogamous (some actually stay together for life), but I later found out that the male usually ended up raising offspring that were not his. The female apparently copulates with other males whether by choice or by force[263]. The list of monogamous mammals used to include beavers, otters, foxes, tamarinds, some rodents, gibbons, and the marmoset[264]. It would appear that our bodies know that we are not supposed to be monogamous. Monogamy is a phenomenon, and humans are the only animals <u>trying</u> to practice it.

"You know damn well that if we were in the bed together you would want to have sex with me." "You'd want to sex with me too." She giggled... "Your boyfriend wouldn't like it." "What boyfriend?" "The guy you said you are fucking." "Oh, him!?!" Her voice changed from cheerful to gloomy, "He's not my boyfriend... He's just there when I need some." This is a true conversation with a supposedly Christian woman who is almost forty.

We are partly animal and have the same behavioral properties. Many people have affairs during relationships and this is on par with animals having multiple mates. Add to this that most people cannot accept sharing mates, sometimes even with family or friends, and you have a recipe for failure. Even if we do share our mates, facing it openly takes a different mindset and an enormous amount of self-security. There seems to be some type of forgiveness, shame or blame required by our society for doing what is natural. It is as if one does something wrong by following our instincts. I do not think it is really about infidelity when thinking from a woman's point of view. It is about the betrayal and lost emotional security. With men the main issue of contention is losing a monogamous sexual partner (paternity). I have lost women who condoned my having sex with other women, because of other women. They wanted to have a say in my choice of sexual partner. It had to be a woman who they thought presented no threat to our relationship. What they did not understand is that no other woman could have threatened our relationship, except them.

Imagine openly sharing your woman or man with another. Why is it such a taboo? Why do we get so upset about it? I am not condoning blind orgies, but I am condoning openness and honesty about sexual desires and acts. It seems a better option than what we have now. I am not monogamous and I do not pretend to be. Furthermore, I do not expect my partners to be. I have listened to many women say they are monogamous, but they had sexual partners when I met them and that did not stop them from having sex with me. In their defense, I do not know if they stopped having sex with the other/s after we started, but that is not important. What is important is that I had my tongue down their throat and my hands on their bodies while they had a boyfriend, significant other or husband. I do not believe the myth that women are the innocent victims of men. On the contrary, *I think women know exactly what they are doing and do not so much mistrust men as they mistrust other women.*

---

[262] Carolyn Abraham, <u>Mommy's little secret</u>.
[263] Baker, R. R. and Bellis, M. A., <u>Animal Behavior</u>.
[264] http://www.trinity.edu/rnadeau/FYS/Barash%20on%20monogamy.htm.

Why do we have to pay when we are caught cheating? I guess Kobe Bryant's wife subscribes to the same point of view. He had to pay for his sins with a diamond ring (the only ring in LA that year). I wonder what Jesse Jackson had to pay when his wife found out about his other family? I really want to know what Hillary and Bill Clinton talked about behind closed doors, and if they have been seen kissing. Curiosity demands an explanation as to why Bill O' Reilly[265] settled the phone sex case.

Bonobos, sub-species of chimpanzee and our closest relative, engage in sex with any member of their troop (although such contact among close family members may be suppressed) and use sex to resolve conflict[266]. The result is a society almost completely void of violence, that pleasure or violence switch in the brain at work.

Western society is structured so that monogamy is encouraged on the surface and most cultures have penalties for those who fail to live up to these standards. I was severely reprimanded for it, but only because both parties were in the military. Western cultures typically label promiscuous women as unsuitable for marriage. As a matter of fact, until the Kinsey Report in 1953, many Americans looked at the sexual needs of women as non-existent. Kinsey wrote that women masturbate, enjoy sex and are capable of having multiple orgasms. The country went wild and not in a good way. The same ignorance and blindness that has caused so many other calamities throughout history discredited this report because it was thought that it would destroy the fabric of the family. Does that sound familiar? What is tugging at the fabric of American society today?

In contrast, when Kinsey wrote about the sexual habits of males a few years earlier the country embraced it[267]. Men may be considered dogs if they are promiscuous but they do not face the same ridicule as women, another example of a two-tier system of justice.

Some of the more stringent cultures impose the death penalty for adulterous or promiscuous behavior. It must be selectively enforced or there would be a significant population drop. Such punishments accomplish nothing except forcing people to become more imaginative in their deceptions and more vivid in their fantasies. It is like the Romans outlawing Christianity; it did not stop the religion; it just forced it underground, just like illicit drug use.

We are animals and our relationships are a mixture of our animal instincts, the natural laws that govern them and socialization. We cannot and will not overcome our physical urges to have sex with multiple partners without evolving spiritually first. If you want to be monogamous, do so, but make damn sure your partner wants that too. Ask her or him every so often, "Do you ever think about having sex with someone else?" Make sure it is in a moment of honesty. Do not just drop it like a bomb! They may think that you want to do it.

---

[265] Bill O'Reilly (1948-): Conservative talk show host.
[266] B. M de Waal, "Primates, Bonobo Sex and Society"
[267] Kinsey Report (1948)

The Long Con

A friend became pregnant early in life. The family insisted that she have an abortion. A few years later she became pregnant again by the same boy, but there was no abortion this time because he was a star athlete in a Division I college and on his way to the "Pros". He had a very brief career in the NBA and then went to Europe to play. The dreams of big contracts and cash did not pan out. She ended up raising the child on her own.

Why is it that every woman I have known, know and probably will know is married, has been married or wants to get married? Why do most men pursue the same goal of marriage over and over again? My mother has been married five times, my grandmother three times, my brother twice and everyone one else in my family since my great-grandmother and father have been divorced or separated on again off again. I asked one of my mentors, "Give me one good reason to get married" He said, "Old age." I thought that was pathetic, so I asked another mentor the same question. He mentioned the names of his first and second wife. Almost every woman I asked has mentioned family and security. Very few people ever mentioned love and no one mentioned sex except when referring to men paying women for it.

It seems to me that every time I became serious in a relationship it was leading down the same path, the path to more commitment (increasing time spent together, living together and ultimately marriage) and I wanted nothing to do with it. This may seem like a harsh point of view, but I am fine with seeing people a few times a week or less, depending on what I have on my schedule. More importantly, I prefer to come together when it is a mutual want. Love is a drug and it often diverts us from our designated paths.

I do not think that being together all the time or on appointed days (which usually means weekends in this age of working couples) is healthy for a relationship. We do not take out an insurance policy by hoarding another's time. There is a time for one's self and a time for loving and sharing with others. I cannot be the only person who wants to be alone sometimes. It is very difficult to plan, think, watch a movie, listen to music, play a video game, write, read or play solitaire with someone else present who wants constant affection or attention. Nothing seems nicer than having a little time alone to do as I please. Ask any mother, member of a large family or a couple about "Me" time. In my opinion, defining self comes first. Only then can we know what we want from others, the role we expect them to fulfill in our lives and communicate these wants effectively. I strongly suggest that everyone *"know thy self"*.

I know I am not willing to compromise my ideals in order to have a relationship. I will no longer accept a woman who does not fit with my plans and goals perfectly, and I will not settle for anything less than what I want. That does not say that I will not continue to have relationships; it does say that I am looking for love that does not cost anything. I do not know many women who do not think that men owe them something. One thing is consistent among the adults I have told this; everyone says the perfect person does not exist. I disagree.

I know my perfect person does exist because everyone is perfect. They may not be perfect for my purpose, but they are for theirs. Otherwise they never would have been born. Because most see perfection as the lack of imperfection, they have issue with my unwillingness to compromise. This does not make anyone wrong; it simply means we look at the world differently.

I was once told that we usually do not end up with the person we love. For whatever reason we seem to substitute our need for love with financial and security needs. I will not do that anymore. If it is my destiny to be alone for the rest of my life or to have temporary relationships (which all relationships are: impermanence), so be it. I am finished fighting for what I think I want. If it is mine to have, it will be given to me freely and without effort. Just the way I pictured it in my dreams, prayers and meditations.

If you were upset with me before, you are going to hit the roof after this question. Straight males will give a standing ovation. Most females and others will boo. What exactly does a "Man" get out of marriage? Think about it for a minute and try to work past your initial response that the question generates.

According to the King James Bible, the Apostle Paul wrote a letter to the church of Corinth. In this letter he addressed marriage. He wrote, *"It is good for a 'Man' not to marry"* (1 Co 7: 1), *"But those who marry will face many troubles in this life and I want to spare you this"* (1 Co 7: 28), *"I would like you to be free from concern. An unmarried 'Man' is concerned about the Lord's affairs-how he can please the Lord. But a married 'Man' is concerned about the affairs of this world-how he can please his wife…"* (1 Co 32-33), *"So then, he who marries a virgin (good luck in finding one) does right, but he who does not marry her does even better"* (1 Co 7: 38).

I think Paul had it right. It is better for a "Man" not to marry. Marriage does not guarantee paternity. It does not guarantee love. It does not guarantee happiness. It does not guarantee a maid or a chef. It does not guarantee monogamy. It does not guarantee an equal partnership where both parties are working toward the same goal. It does not even guarantee sex. In most cases and states, it does guarantee that someone else is entitled to half of your shit when the relationship is over. So, why should a "Man" get married or be monogamous?

I knew an adult male who had numerous wives, many children, still greater numbers of grandchildren and a few great-grands when he died. As strange as it sounds, I thought, "He is going to live a long time."

I do not think most married men are happy with their wives and vice versa. I do think that most couples that last more than the average five years find some middle ground called contentment. Do not take my word for it; ask them. Do not think the typical spouse or anyone you are involved with sexually is going to give you an honest answer, unless they are mad with you. Ask a coworker. You have to be careful not to come out and say, "Are you happy in your marriage?" In most cases the answer will not be thoughtful or honest. Instead ask, "Do you think your spouse talks too much?" "Have you ever tried to use the remote control to make your partner shut up?" "Does your spouse try to make you do things you do not want to do?" "Does your spouse use sex as a bargaining chip?" "Does your spouse work?" "Does your spouse spend your money more readily than his or her own?" "What are you getting out of marriage?" Ask these questions and watch closely for the unsaid answers in their reactions.

The natural reason for interacting with the opposite sex is to procreate. Primates seem to be the only genus on the planet that engages in sex for pleasure. In fact, primate societies that do not repress affection typically have a lower incidence of violent behavior. So why is sex and affection supposed to be repressed except in the marriage? That seems contra-nature. It also implies that marriage guarantees sex.

Marriage and dedicated relationships are society's attempt at stabilizing itself. Families are more stable, predictable, take fewer risks and they typically provide their own replacements. Families simplify legal matters of inheritance and paternity (sometimes). Families establish roots. That is why insurance for the married male is lower than for single male. Being married is definitely one of the unwritten requirements for public office. Marriage fits into our society's plans perfectly, but how does it fit into nature's plan? The statistics say that married men live longer than single men. Statistics also say that house cats live longer than alley cats, but why do house cats spend so much time looking out the window?

I met Dollar Signs on a Saturday night. She was a hard-bodied cutie pie with killer legs, a butt that resembled the perfect upside down heart and a boyfriend. My quasi date noticed that I was watching Dollar Signs dance on the platform built specifically for those who were not afraid to show their wares, and sarcastically suggested that I join her. "OK, if you do not mind." I did.

Dollar Signs danced well enough to answer any question I had about sex and she was gorgeous. Her having a male when we met did not stop her from accepting a dinner invitation; though I did not find this out until later. The first night she went through my kitchen cabinets. She even looked in the oven and attempted to take over the cooking. After that, she spent most of her nights with me. We lived together for all intents and purposes. She was the first woman to give me an 8 x 10 glamour shot for my birthday, complete with a frame. She was not the last woman to do this, and it scared me. What was the real purpose of the picture, to provide me with moments of joy when I am alone or to ward off the evil spirits?

We lived together for a while. But, she did not work or look for work, so I decided to move on base to cut expenses and put my budget in order. It was during the time I gave the public financial brief because of the "rubber check" for my car. She had to get her own place or go home; I could not afford to support us both. She went back to live with her mother. Afterwards, we maintained our relationship by visiting each other on weekends.

She wanted to marry a secure educated male of some social status and her mother wanted the same thing. I was a naval aviator when we met and she admitted later thinking about how much money I made when I told her what I did for a living. Her brother was an Army officer of the same rank as I and she knew how much he made. She actually told me she thought, "Cha-Ching" (the sound of a cash register), when I told her I was an officer in the Navy. What did not occur to her was that this was a disqualifier, and I could not be with a woman who wanted to be with me for financial reasons.

Once I told her I hated braids (synthetic hair irritates my skin) and yet she asked me for the money to buy them. That threw me off. I did not understand how someone could ask another person to pay for something that they did not like or want.

We broke up over money, her taking more out of my account than I authorized when I was off serving Uncle Sam. Dollar Signs was the type of woman who expects to work and keep all of her money while the male pays for everything. It all started when I told her that I could not attend a barbecue her brother planned for that weekend. I had just returned from deployment in Europe and I had agreed to go with her previously. But, the night before the barbecue I went through my banking records for the first time in months. I tried to withdraw cash with the ATM card I gave Dollar Signs to use in case of emergency while I was gone and the machine said that I had no money in my checking account. I was not upset because it was payday; direct deposit would have money in my account by midnight. But, I was curious as to why this account was at zero. By my calculations I should have had money.

Dollar Signs was driving my car and making sure the bills got paid on time while I was gone, so I thought I could trust her. She was working and living at home with her mother. Before you start saying how stupid I was, remind yourselves that I was engaged to this woman and should have been able to trust her with finances. Additionally when the ship pulled into port, I had to ask someone for a ride home because she was not there. I wrote her every day and the only letter I received for three months was a two line note telling me I got a refund on my taxes.

I had money missing. I began to think I had spent a lot more than I thought in Europe or something was wrong. That led me to the bank statements. I had changed my mailing address to my grandfather's house while I was gone. Looking back, I had confirmation of a possible scenario after I showed the unopened statements to Dollar Signs. She was not happy. I left the statements on the coffee table until it was time to go to bed. I was waiting for Dollar Signs to tell me the truth. She never did.

As I went through three months of banking statements adding up the ATM withdrawals, Dollar Signs placed her hands over her face. Her explanation was, "I did not keep track of the money I withdrew... It adds up over the days." When I was having trouble at the ATM machine, she played dumb; when I returned to the car and asked her how much money she had taken out of the account. She told me, "I do not know... Maybe $90" Bitch! You meant $90.00 the day before yesterday. To compound the problem, I was just getting my finances in order after skating on thin ice with the Navy. She knew I had to be careful not to bounce any checks or I would have hell to pay from my superiors. I wrote several checks to the ship we were on and not all of them had cleared the bank.

The morning of the barbecue I was pissed. I did not even have sex with Dollar Signs the previous night. Considering I had not engaged in my favorite sport for a while, that was saying something. I needed a distraction. My brother came over that morning to install a new gas range, perfect. I decided to work on the stove and back out of the party. I did not feel like pretending to be happy or in a good mood. I told Dollar Signs I would take her to her brother's, but I had to return to finish the job. She was very upset. I could not understand her reasoning, though now I do understand her motives. I stood by my decision. She said some very nasty things to me during the drive and it was all an attempt to hurt me in order to get some type of reaction from me (remember positive or negative attention is the same for some). I gave her the blank face, totally ignoring her and everything she said. I even turned the radio up and began singing during the drive. She hit me with a left jab on the right side of my face. We could have crashed had I turned the wheel a ½ inch left or right and hit other cars, all because she was mad and decided to express it with her fist. Men cannot hit women, but some deserve it. That must not have occurred to her. I pulled over, straightened my sunglasses and looked at her with what must have been an intimidating face because she did not say another word until we reached our destination.

When she hit me it took everything I had not to knock her into next week. A person has to have mental issues if they strike another person who could kick their butts. A word of advice, do not do that; you may come across someone with less restraint than I.

Can you find any right or wrong in this situation? I used to, but not anymore. She wanted me to forgive her. I had made up my mind that I was not going to marry her anymore and she knew it. She was fighting to keep what she thought was hers. I was cutting my losses.

I understand that Dollar Signs had a violent streak because of the environment in which she was raised. We talked about it. She had to fight her two older brothers most of her life. Her mother worked and the boys were responsible for the house. They settled matters with their fists and nasty words. Sometime after she hit me we had a discussion about it. She told me that she told her brother about the incident. "Ohhhh, that was a good one," he had said. Dollar Signs said, "Yeah, I know and he just sat there, so I hit him." It was normal behavior for their family. They actually "got off" on fighting each other. It would take years for me to deprogram the hitting response and I did not have the time or patience to do it. Add lost trust into the formula and it spells disaster.

I could not see the sense in entering into a lifelong commitment with Dollar Signs because of her inconsideration and selfishness. I know I can be selfish too, but I did not take her money. In other words, I lost trust in her and realized that we were not going to make it. It was at this point that I started cheating. Looking back on it, I should have left the relationship instead of pretending it could still lead to anything more than what it was. The pri$e was too high and I did not fall for the "Long Con". It is a good thing that I got to know her before I made a mistake.

Have you ever heard of Synchronous Menstruation[268]? Evidently if a group of women spend a great deal of time together (work, home, etc.), their periods synchronize. While a woman is menstruating, her skin secretes pheromones, which other women smell subliminally. Once their nasal receptors pick up the scent, the pheromones stimulate the endocrine systems of other women in close proximity, which then drive their menstrual cycles into a similar pattern. Why do you suppose this happens? I think it is a direct result of our evolution. When efficient reproduction was essential to the survival of the species, it was important that females ovulated around the same time. This had much to do with the full moon in times past. The moon used to have more of an effect on women's cycles as well, but because of modern adaptations and alternative light sources, its influence has diminished. All or most women used to menstruate during the full moon. Some cultures even have rituals that promote this naturally occurring phenomenon and it was convenient since the men were usually hunting to take advantage of the light source. It makes perfect natural sense. All women menstruating during a time when their

---

[268] Synchronous Menstruation: This phenomenon was first described in 1971 by researcher Martha McClintock, now with the University of Chicago.

mates were away was a very efficient way to manage procreation. This is a global mystery, not a singularity.

Nature tells males of a species to spread their seed and at the same time it tells the females to secure the strongest male to ensure strong offspring. For males of a species fulfilling this drive requires multiple mates. There are very few species that mate for life and fewer still that are monogamous. For females, it means finding a physically strong mate who not only can protect and provide for her and her children, but is also willing to do so. I think that women want to have sex and children with Adonis, but want to have Steve Erkel provide and care for them (hence hidden ovulation and men raising children that are not theirs). How did this concept of nature turn into what humans have today?

It seems that at some point in our limited history men began to claim women as their property, just like a cow or a plow. Men can have multiple wives in many societies. I have to be honest in saying that I think women got the short end of the stick in this deal. Personally, I do not want several wives. It is impossible for me to satisfy one woman without sacrificing something; what am I going to do with more than one?

Sidebar: I have a suggestion for everyone. Before marriage have sex with the betrothed. Forget the "He won't buy the cow, if he can get the milk for free" saying. It does not make sense. I want ice-cold lemonade or a beer on a hot summer's day, not warm milk.

How does one select a cow? I would look at the hooves, hair, teeth, eyes, etc… for signs of general health. If the owner tries to cover up defects, I know instantly something is wrong with the cow. Then I would watch to see how it acted around other cows, social skills and mental stability are important categories when judging livestock. Breeding potential is a must. "Is it a sickly cow?" "What diseases has it had?" "What is the medical history of the dam and sire?" "Any offspring?" "May I see them?" Everyone wants profitable relationships and a good cow is worth an investment, but they get fat, their milk sours or dries up, and people are not cows. Nelson Mandela paid 50-60 cows for his second wife. How many cows ($$$) are you worth?

The males of most species are naturally adorned. Most male birds have the more colorful feathers. Lions have manes. Male gorillas have silver backs. Roosters have crowns. Male peacocks have a magnificent train. Only the male blue jay is blue and only the male cardinals are actually red. Human males have more pronounced facial hair. Unfortunately some women have it too.

Why is it that female human adorn themselves? Why are humans trying to be perceived as more beautiful? Are they attempting to attract the attention of females or the attention of males? I have already discussed why beauty is important in our society; those considered pretty make more money and have easier lives. I have also discussed the many ways these adornments fool the human eye. What I have not said before is that I believe we do this with the ultimate goal of attracting a mate. For most women, it means a husband; for men it means a healthy mother.

The traditional role of wife has been redefined and in many cases reversed. I have no issue with equal rights. However, I have met many women who say they want equal rights, but I have only known a few who practiced this philosophy. I would love to have a partner who carried her own weight financially and looked at sex as mutually beneficial, but not an activity essential to love. I would love to have a partner and a friend. I have known women like that, but then we had sex. After sex, something changes. It seemed as if I had to assume a more affectionate and monogamous role in the relationship. I have only known three women who were willing to try to be an equal financial partner and even then I ended up giving more. All the others assumed that men should bear the brunt of our financial needs. Yes, men do typically make more money than women, but when women go to dinner with one another, does the woman who makes more money pay the check the majority of the time? If two women live together or if a male and a woman who are not intimate live together as roommates, does the person who makes the most money pay more of the household bills or do they split them? So why is it that many women think that a male with whom they are intimate should? I interpret this as having to pay <u>for</u> something. If I have sex with a woman, chances are she will have more orgasms than I will[269]. If we are going to place a monetary value on sexual pleasure, then someone owes me dinners, drinks, movies and money.

Marriage does not guarantee love; if it did there would not be divorce. We would fall in love, get married and stay that way. Besides, ask yourself how many times you thought you were in love. Did you marry any of them or all of them?

Marriage does not guarantee paternity. With an infidelity[270] rate of 70-72% within the first five years of marriage, it is a wonder that number is not much higher. Monogamy is a sociological-religious wish. Marriage does not guarantee sex. Nothing guarantees sex except being very good at it. The only way to have continuous sex with the same person is to make it extremely pleasurable to them. Marriage does not guarantee a clean house or clean clothes or a home-cooked meal. Most women I know are not as neat or organized as I am, though you would never know it until it was too late. I will not let many women wash my clothes, especially African-Americans. Why? Because the first thing out of their mouths in an argument is, "I wash your dirty drawls." Finally, some modern women cannot cook. Anything you can put in a microwave is not cooking; and throwing together something edible is not either. A good cook is able to make all the meals they prepare taste good. Marriage does not even guarantee companionship. The divorce rate is my star witness to this fact.

My question is why anyone in his or her right mind would want to be married. Some screw it up once, and get married over and over again. It speaks volumes when a person cannot live alone and cannot live with someone else either. An important question one must ask himself or herself is not can I live with someone for the rest of my life, but can or would anyone want to live with the real me for the rest of theirs and who do you know who has done it monogamously?

I would like to meet the "Sanctity of Marriage" and introduce it to a 'whollotta' folk. Then I <u>might</u> get married.

---

[269] Assume I am smart enough not to fall for the fake orgasm. I have chased women off the bed with my tongue. After an oral orgasm, very few women can take the sensations caused by extended simulation. I also know women are capable of multiple orgasms, and are able to have satisfying sex without the resultant orgasm.
[270] The First Family Institute of Kansas. "Infidelity Facts"

Me, Myself and I

There once was a lazy bird that consistently left later than the other birds to fly south. One winter he left too late. During the flight south, ice formed on his wings and he fell to the Earth. There he laid freezing to death. A cow happened by and took an accidental dump on him. It was warm and melted the ice. The bird was saved from freezing to death, but he was stuck in the dung. A cat came by, pulled him free and then promptly ate him. What is the moral of the story? Everyone who appears to shit on you is not necessarily your enemy, and everyone who gets you out of shit is not necessarily your friend.

I stayed with relatives one summer. What mother does not need breaks from their children? My brother and I were separated. He stayed with other relatives. The only reason that I am mentioning this is because I was afraid of family again.

I was sitting between them on the couch watching television. I do not remember how or why it happened, but the woman tried to get me to suck her breast. She pulled it out and placed it inches from my face. I panicked and I tried to get away, but her husband grabbed me by my head and forced me to be still while she continued. I never told anyone until recently, but I have to tell it now. I do so in hopes of alerting parents, including my own, to the fact that you do not know what happens to your children once you leave them in someone else's care, genetic connection or not.

If you had to be a chess piece, which would you choose to be, and why? I give my answer at the end of the chapter.

My mother was angry with me one day because I told her that I do not believe in giving money as a show of love. She told me that my brother and I broke our contract with her. Her main issue was that she wants us to show her some appreciation by giving her things and money (code for love). I reminded her that I always sent her things when I went abroad and that I came out of college in debt. I did not have any money; otherwise I would not have had issues while in the Navy. I also told her that she did not mention my sister, who constantly asks her for money and never pays it back, another double standard. I went further to tell her that once I get it together for myself, she will be fine. "I am tired of promises," she replied. A week later I told her that she broke her contract with my brother and me long before we were grown. In our eyes, she reneged every time she left us in the care of someone else. Her response was, "You were all right." "No we weren't!"

I told her it did not feel all right when that teat was in my face. It did not feel that way when a grown male rolled my brother and me down a hallway into a wall like bowling balls. It did not feel that way when two over grown adolescent boys pounded my brother and me in the chest during a sick game they called, "chastising time". They made us pull our T-shirts over our heads and stand against the wall while they punched us in the chest. One of them cracked one of my ribs; my left side hurt for weeks. I did not say anything. The X-ray from my first physical for the Navy revealed the effects of the blow. The technician asked me if I had broken a rib in the past. I told her that my brother and I were taught to tongue kiss at three and four-years-old by female relatives. They were teenagers. "Why didn't you tell someone?" "For what," I paused, "We would have been called liars and been beaten... We tried being honest before and that is what happened...." I did not tell her this to hurt her. I told her so that she could know that she left her children under the care of unreliable adults and irresponsible teenagers. I also told her that I was not scarred emotionally; I just put every instance off as others being crazy.

I distance myself from others for a reason. That reason is self-preservation. Please do not get this concept confused with some sort of mental disorder involving a phobia. I am trying to distinguish myself from the estimated 22.1 percent of Americans ages 18 and older (over 1 in 5 adults) who suffer from a diagnosable mental disorder[271]. I have already found many of them in my own family. I want to know with whom I have to give allowances and whom I have to give distance. Furthermore, I do not like associating with people who are still caught up in games we played as children. I have enough trouble staying balanced by myself. Lastly, I am tired of having to remain on guard, telling and listening to lies.

One of my fraternity brothers was supposed to help me publish this work. He bragged and made grand plans as he praised my skills as a writer. After holding on to my manuscript for months, he confessed that he had been using my material at speaking engagements. "Oh, that's cool, Man." "Did you give me credit?" "I couldn't." "Where did you say it came from?" "I did not." "Send me my manuscript back!"

I do not have many close relationships, but the ones I do have are with people whom I have known for years. They have proven that they are indeed friends, and not just people who want to bleed you and move on. We have all had relationships where we thought people were our friends and it turned out that they were not at all. They wanted something that they thought we could provide. Once they got what they wanted or did not, they leave the relationship, or only communicate when they need a refill.

I lost faith in male-female relationships and monogamy at an early age. Not only did I hear and see what my mother was going through as a single parent, but also my grandparents, other family members and friends' families. As I grew up, stories about illegitimate children and affairs came out tumbling of the closets. I was told that what is done in the dark eventually comes to light, and how true it is. I was taught that marriage was sacred, but I saw that in reality it was not. I watched a husband and wife fight like cats and dogs in the middle of the street. The fight ended when the husband was kicked from the passenger door of a moving car. Relationships seemed to be going wrong and for the longest time I could not understand why.

It seems that my lost faith is not unfounded. After his separation and divorce from my grandmother, my grandfather told me stories of his extramarital exploits that made him less of a "Man" in my judgmental teenage eyes. He had a child with his mistress. I also learned that my grandmother had affairs as well, but they will never be brought to light because of the associated taboo. It does not matter that everyone knows. I watched as my mother dated males throughout my childhood. As a matter of fact, I once got into trouble because I made a comment about one of my mother's male friends in front of another male she was seeing. I did not know the game of dating or the consequences of a male's jealousy. I watched my older cousins and acquaintances change partners as regularly as clothing. I learned from my environment and learned well. What

---

[271]National Institute of Mental Health, 2001.

I was taught at home, in church and at school were utopian ideas of how life was supposed to be, but in reality things were different and they have always been this way.

I learned that we all have desires and fantasies. I learned that inhibition is largely restrained by the risk of loss, ridicule or punishment. I learned that love is easy when we are giving, successful and profitable to our partners, and hard when we deny anything. I have learned that most women, in contradiction to what I was taught, like to have sex as much as, if not more than men do. I know what thoughts and acts we are capable of committing with an attractive stranger in the mall, at a red light or in the grocery store. I know that many have cheated or been unfaithful to their significant others and deny it when asked. I know this because I have seen it, done it and on many occasions, my married or attached partners were doing it as well.

The Kinsey Report (1948) showed that by age 40, 50% of men had had an extramarital affair. The Hite Report on Male Sexuality (1980) found that 72% of men married two years or more had had an extramarital affair.

Shere Hite's 1987 survey of women found that 70% of women married five years or more had had an extramarital affair.

Having sexual thoughts of interaction with someone other than your significant other means that you have a wanting, a desire that is not satisfied by your partner; and if the right circumstances present themselves, that is, if you could have a fling with no fear of being caught (out of town business meeting, a stranger, the internet), you are more than likely going to take the plunge. The "Desperate House People" thing is true. You may or may not feel remorse, but you will or have done it already. Do not get me wrong, there are people out there who are faithful in the physical realm, but five will get you ten that every person has at least thought about adultery. When you close your eyes during sex or masturbation and think of someone besides your lover, what is that?

Dear Abby answered this question by saying it is healthy for the sexual side of a relationship to fantasize about other people. The fear of loss, punishment or guilt seems to be the only thing that reins in desire.

I am no different than you. I was taught to want the same things out of life, a *good* job that provided enough money to live comfortably and loving relationships. I know better now. Things that are ours will come to us regardless of what actions we perform. Things that are not ours will come if we will them and go because they are not in our design. In life, one must be very careful for what we ask, for we surely will have these things. Whose fault is it if the things asked for do not make us happy?

I wanted to be loved so much I wished for it constantly even though I did not know what love was. I was wishing for sex in reality. Guess what? I got more than I bargained. I attempted to make a list of every woman with whom I have had sex. I ended up naming places because I could not remember all the names. I have had sex with women only to awaken and have to look at their mail or driver's license to remember their names. I am not bragging; I am complaining.

Nights out mixing music, dance, drugs and the opposite sex often lead to coupling without regard to the consequences.

I learned early about male-male relationships from my family, my family's male associates, schoolmates and the other boys in the neighborhood. They taught me that males are very competitive and that they must establish a pecking order. I always felt more at home with older males because of this. Most of them were not concerned about competition from children, and I was automatically placed in the child category. My inquisitive nature and eccentric behavior did not seem to bother them as much as they did males in my own age group. I hung out with the kids in my age group when I wanted to play. But even then, there were times I wanted to be alone or do things my own way. Things have not changed that much in as an adult.

Being around older people taught me a lot. Sometimes they talked over my head, but I would remember what they said, and ask my mother or some other adult what a particular phrase meant. Older people readily answered some of my questions without knowing it and taught me many new things. If you want some wisdom, spend time with an elder, or someone who has nothing to gain or lose by sharing with you. People generally want to be honest, but are programmed to be defensive. People who are not threatened are often willing to part with knowledge more readily than say coworkers or classmates.

Of all the males in my life, I would have to say that my grandfather was the most influential. It is natural that I measured other men using him as a template. I guess my grandfather was the closest thing I had to a father figure. He was the "man of men" if speaking from the testosterone "ole" school perspective. When I found out he was a staff sergeant in the 2nd Army during World War II, I asked him all sorts of "What did you do in the war, Granddaddy?" questions. I remember feeling disappointed when he told me that he did not fight. He drove a ¾ ton truck in a transportation company. That is when I learned about the segregation of troops[272]. I remember how unfair I thought that was. I even asked, "Why did they separate the troops?" He told me that white people do not think we are capable of performing as well as them. Unfortunately, that attitude did not die after the Civil Rights Act. He also told me that white people were afraid of what might happen when the *colored* troops returned to the United States and had to face the Jim Crow[273] laws of the South and the discrimination of the North. I felt like I was doomed to failure in this country before I even got a chance to prove my worth.

My grandfather also drove a cab, worked in the Post Office, ran numbers, had a small hauling and moving company, played poker on Friday nights, chased women and drank like a sailor. I had no issue with his getting drunk until other children in the neighborhood teased me about it. My brother and I could get money from him more easily when he was in that condition. We thought he was funny. I learned about horse racing, sports and card playing from him. It took me years to figure out why he always won; he cheated. He taught me about taking risks and

---

[272] In 1948 President Truman signed Executive Order #9981 which put an end to segregation of troops in the United States armed forces.
[273] The term Jim Crow originated in a song performed by Daddy Rice, a white minstrel show entertainer in the 1830s. Rice covered his face with charcoal paste or burnt cork to resemble a black man and then sang and danced a routine in caricature of a silly black person. By 1900, the term was generally identified with those racist laws and actions that deprived African Americans of their civil rights by defining blacks as inferior to whites.

understanding women enough to get what I wanted. He taught me about family and taking care of home first. His generosity was rivaled only by his wit, sharp tongue and infamous temper. He never scared me; he was too nice to be scary. It was a good act though.

My brother and I had spent three or four years living with my grandparents after my mother moved west, joining my uncles in search of a better life in California. My great-grandfather died and the entire family came back home for the funeral. Soon after the funeral, my brother and I were on our way to join our mother. My mother asked us if we wanted to come live with her and we said, "Yes." Thinking about it now, I did this because I knew that if I had said, "No", it would have hurt her feelings. I did not want to go, but I knew that if we were being asked, the decision had been made already.

There are no accidents; the move changed my life drastically. We were leaving the relative safety of a family support system, friends and community. In the four years I lived in California I was taught more about human behavior than all of my previous years combined. Family no longer sheltered me. I was no longer in the neighborhood that I had known all my life. I did not have anyone outside of my mother and brother around with whom I felt comfortable. And, I was no longer in the majority.

I saw more diversity, but everyone seemed to stick with his or her own kind. The hierarchy of society did not change. White Americans were in charge and they still acted like it. Hispanics and Africans were running neck and neck to see who would take last place in society. This was my first exposure to open homosexuality and biracial couples. It was culture shock, but good for my development.

I remember the first elementary school. It was multiracial and my first up close experience with Mexicans, western African-Americans and Whites. I tried to adjust and fit in, but there were subtle differences in this society from the one I had known. I had never known racial prejudice. Everyone I knew was African-American and we had our own versions of inter-racial prejudice: skin color, education and economics, but nothing like what I went through in California. Even the games they played were different. Football and basketball took a back seat to kick ball, soccer and tetherball.

As the new kid, I was introduced to the hierarchy of my class in a variety of ways. One guy was # 1; I knew by the way the other guys and girls acted in his presence. Besides, he was the biggest kid in the class. Then there was # 2 and so forth. They earned these ranks, I assumed by size, fighting other boys, intimidation or by reputation alone. The issue was where I fit in. I was new and little. They came to test me almost from the beginning. It was interesting to witness the rutting ritual in this part of the country. The guys who thought their positions were threatened did juvenile things to instigate a confrontation. If I balked, they would think I was a push over and everyone in the class would eventually start to pick on me. I saw this happen to my brother many times over. There were fewer pitfalls by choosing to fight or at least put forth some form of protest. If I fought and lost, my opponent would be deemed superior, but I would not lose any ground, and I sent a message loud and clear that I was not afraid. If I fought and there was no clear winner, it was a stalemate. If I won, I assumed his rank.

My first test came when a kid in the class mocked putting his penis in my face. While I was sitting on a bench, he walked in front of me, grabbed his pubic area, leaned forward at the hips and said, "Blow me." I tried to choke him to death. He marshaled his troops after he visited the nurse and I visited the principal. They planned on gang banging me after school. Call it divine providence, but nothing happened. So there I was with a badge of courage and esteem intact. I must have been blessed; I was never suspended or "jumped". This experience has repeated itself several times since - every time I showed up at a new job or social circle. Everybody wants to know where you fit, and will do what he or she can to protect his or her interests if feeling threatened.

The next year my mother placed us into the forced busing program. Many parents protested the school board's compromise. The whites did not want their children in the inner city schools and who could blame them. The advocates for equal education saw the plan as a band-aid. The school board had acknowledged that there was a gap between inner city and suburban schools within the LA Unified School District, and busing students seemed cheaper than upgrading inadequate schools. What a trip, 500 students, 26 of them minorities, bused in from an hour away. It was a hostile environment to say the least. My saving graces were my African-American teacher and the Italian principal. My teacher identified with me and the principal understood my plight and the reasons why I was in his office for fighting so much. He would join his hands together by interconnecting his fingers, then place them on his desk before asking himself, or no one, or the two of us, "What should I do?" Then he would wait about thirty seconds while he thought about it. He always told me not to fight anymore and sent me back to class.

It was the same cycle as the first school, but different tactics. In my first fight at this school, I went after the head of the class or rather he decided to pick on me. What is it with the, "I am going to stand in front of you in line" bit? He did just that in the lunch line the first or second day of school. I saw him set up the plan ahead of time. He was with a group of four other children. They looked up and down the line. One of them pointed at me. I did not know what they were up to, but I knew it was not going to be good, but I was not having it, especially from a white boy. I told him that he could not jump in front of me. He responded with, "Oh, you want to fight? You want to fight?" He began bouncing around like he was trained in fisticuffs and he kept looking at his friends with a smile on his face. I guess he did not think I was going to fight him. I knew I was going to win because of the way he held his hands. He had little or no knowledge of how to conduct a proper fistfight. He could not hit me because he telegraphed every punch and I moved out of the way, ducked and countered just like my grandfather taught me. I held my fist tight and moved my hands in circular motions just like my karate teacher taught me (Wax on. Wax off.) I used his weight to my advantage like my uncle had taught me. I was about to throw a front kick Bruce Lee taught me when a teacher grabbed me. She said she saw the whole thing and said that I had started the fight. I did not start it; I just hit him first. She escorted the two of us to the office, me by the collar.

After the fight and the trip to the principal's office, we were required to eat lunch together. The kid asked me how I ducked his punches while we ate. I told him a lie. I knew he was no friend and, although I earned his respect, I might have to fight him again or he may try the same shit on another brother later in life. I was not going to give him an advantage.

The older boys picked on me and every other bused student. They always came in pairs or groups; they knew that if they came at me alone, there was the possibility that they would lose the fight. One day while on the playground, two of the more aggressive upper classmen decided that I would be their target. I often isolated myself to work on some project or just talk things out with myself. I cannot talk to myself with other people around; they would think I was crazy. One grabbed me from behind while the other touted racial slurs, punched my abdomen and spit on me. I have learned that this is the preferred tactic even in the business world. If someone has it out for you, they will try to build alliances against you through denigration and then they attack in mass. I always fight back; eventually the assaults, verbal, mental and physical, always slowed and then stopped. I learned that no one wants an opponent who will fight back. They prefer easy prey. Armed robbers use the same logic; find an easy mark. I also learned that people could be cruel, and ignorant. I do not blame them; I blame parents and society.

We only spent one year in this school, but I was spit on and called "Nigger" enough for the rest of my life. What scares me is these same people are now grown and are a part of my society. I often wonder where those kids who tormented us are today, and if they have changed their opinions or just hide them because it is not politically correct to call people "Niggers" anymore. I do not think leopards change spots; they just find better ways to cover and camouflage themselves, but I can always hope. I hope that they have changed.

The next year we went to a school within walking distance of home with most of the neighborhood kids. The transition was not as bad as being alone at a new school. Besides, they had football. During lunchtime I would play. All you have to do is be judged an asset to be picked to play football or anything else for that matter. One good catch by the new guy could do that, and it did. Things were going well. It was the first time since I left my birthplace that I felt comfortable at school. I was in the band, popular on the schoolyard, and a girl or two was interested in me although I had no idea why (sixth grade). Half way through the school year, I was interviewed and tested by a stranger. She was in her fifties and probably dyed her hair the platinum color it was. The only question I remember her asking during the 3-hour process was, "How tall is the average male?" I remember assembling puzzles while she timed me, and that she wrote many things down.

Soon after, I was placed into the "Mentally Gifted Minors" program at a pilot school. I caught the school bus in front of my old school along with about twenty or so other students. I was exposed to a number of wonderful things because of this program. I saw the King Tut exhibit. I went to San Francisco on a field trip, and had a chance to see the giant redwoods and sequoias. I had an opportunity to see whales, sea lions and otters in their natural environment. Learning was promoted and the classrooms were smaller, but socially it was no better than anywhere else. It seems we have a habit of finding a reason not to like things about each other. The trials continued wherever I went only the names and places changed. I have won some fights and lost others but I learned that there is something very "Wrong with Us", and that I have to fight one way or another for the rest of my life if I ever hoped to secure and maintain a place in mainstream society.

After another year we moved back home to Washington, D. C. I was "happier than a homosexual sequestered with large numbers of the same sex"[274]. My brother and I had finally separated my mother from her husband. I imagine she was happy in the marriage, but my brother and I were not. That made for friction between the calves and the bull of the house. I now know why the mature male lions drive the adolescent males from the pride. It was difficult to respect him because he did not appear to be the generous, kind and loving male he was before he married my mother, and he was not at all like my grandfather. I used to say, "He is so cheap that when he opens his wallet, dust and cobwebs fly out." One Christmas/Kwanzaa[275] he gave my grandfather cigars. Not a bad choice for a male who smokes, except my grandfather had given him the same cigars as a visiting gift six months earlier! He wanted respect and discipline in a household with two working adolescent boys. I have difficulty respecting anyone who does not earn it. Merely surviving was not enough to impress me. Besides, we had our system and it worked. Food was there and the utilities were on, after his introduction to the family things got worse financially, not better.

When we moved back to DC, I discovered that it was different. I looked at the city in another light and it looked back at me with the same unfamiliarity. My experiences had changed me. I had received a different kind of education, learned different customs, spoke a different language and had a different way of thinking. Somewhere in that mix I lost my sense of the city. I was not like the people I hung out with. I wanted to go to college, so I could be a pilot, then an astronaut.

Someone actually tried to convince me that college would not do anything for me. They used my uncle as an example. He went to college on a football scholarship, but quit because of an injury. The athletic department gave him the option of continuing his education, but he would have had to become a team manager. Because could not see going from a star athlete to the "water boy", he withdrew. He kicked himself in the butt for years after that decision; I think he is still kicking himself now. When I pointed that, "He did not get a degree and that makes all the difference in the world" they were stumped. That was and is the typical mentality on the streets of "Urbana".

When I was younger, things were always good at my grandfather's or at least that was my perspective. He would accept people into his house during hard times and give to people when they needed it. He co-signed loans, and gave loans but only after he gave a lecture on responsibility. I watched him become a more generous and tolerant person during this part of his life. I imagine his divorce and the fact that he stopped drinking had something to do with it. He even began to answer my questions as honestly as he could without invoking judgment. It was as if he could not wait for someone to ask him something. I could not believe someone was answering my questions honestly.

---

[274] My grandfather used to say, "Happier than a sissy in a CC camp." But I modernized than phrase in hopes of eliminating the negativity of the words.

[275] Kwanzaa (December 26-January 1): established in 1966. African American and Pan-African holiday. Celebrates family, community and culture. Celebrated from 26 December thru 1 January, its origins are in the first harvest celebrations of Africa. Kwanzaa is derived from the phrase "matunda ya kwanza" which means "first fruits" in Swahili.

He sometimes answered my questions with riddles, almost making it a game. "Think about it", he would say. I was not always ready to listen, and only by coming to my own realizations did I know what he was talking about. Sometimes it took years. He was the first person to tell me, "You can catch more flies with honey than with vinegar". He said this because of my "I do not give a fuck what anyone thinks attitude". My reply was, "I do not want to catch flies." He was right you know, but by my way of thinking, there were a lot more flies than bees, and I wanted to save the honey for the bees. I still do not care what people think of me. I will tell you, "Kiss my ass" in a second, but for more secure and meaningful reasons.

I asked him why he and my grandmother divorced. He said, "She is crazy; she's always been crazy." I followed with, "How do you know she's crazy?" "Her father was crazy. When I went to pick her up the first time there were Biblical billboards referring to Revelations in the front yard." "Her Dad thought he was the Angel Gabriel." "If she was crazy why did you marry her?" "She was beautiful." "Really?" My grandfather went into a description that was beyond me. I was captivated by the look on his face as he described what he saw in my grandmother and knew he loved her back then, and more surprisingly he still loved her. What I was thinking, and did not say, was I thought a pretty face suckered him. I also left out the fact that I was there in my grandmother's bed pretending to be asleep the last time he hit her. They were arguing about something. My grandmother said something wicked. I guess I knew what was coming next. The lack of an instant verbal response on my grandfather's part told my closed eyes what my ears could almost hear and my body could almost feel. I clinched as if I was on the receiving end of his fist. The loud pop that made me flinch confirmed my suspicions. The bloodied slip soaking in the bathtub was both psychological warfare and a sign. That was the end of their marriage. I have not understood male/female relationships fully ever since that night.

I remember he told me a story from his youth. He was raised in West Virginia. When he was about 18 he was summoned to the home of one of the older housewives to help move a rug while her husband was at work. He said she squatted to help him move the rug. With a dress on she exposed her pubic area to him over and over again. He said he moved that rug fifty times (an exaggeration I am sure) before she was happy with its placement. I asked him if he wanted to do "it". He said, "Hell yeah, but she was white and I did not want to get lynched!" I came to find out my grandmother also questioned the length of time it took to move the rug as well.

Sometime after hearing this I remember being with my uncle. He just happened to be dating a white woman. I recall the apprehension I experienced when we went outside for the first time. They were holding hands and I was waiting for someone to lynch my uncle for violating a social law. No one did anything. As a matter of fact, no one paid them much mind. That confused me until I realized that you can hold hands with a white woman or man on Venice Beach, California, but it might not be smart to do it in rural Georgia, in Alabama or in the vicinity of any "militia" camp.

I remember my grandfather's descriptions of the coal mine where he worked. It was the same one where his father worked and contracted black lung. He once got a hernia from lifting a coal car. After explaining what a hernia was he answered my next question: "Why did you do it?" "It was a bet and I was stupid." I took a particular interest in stories about the Company Store. The wives could go to this store and purchase necessities using their husband's future paychecks as collateral or they could use company script. I would not have a dime if I let most of the women with whom I have been involved have that type of freedom with my paycheck. We would have a lot of stuff, but no money. Everyone knew that the prices were inflated, but they had little choice. Going to town and using cash were not options. It reminded me of the sharecroppers.

He told me about being drafted and how green he was. He told me of his lessons in boot camp, gambling in the barracks, being busted from sergeant to corporal and whores in Sicily during the 1943 invasion. He told me about his experience with one of my heroes, General George S. Patton. "You knew Patton?" "Yep." "For real?" "Yep. I met him once…" "What he say to you?" My grandfather's words made Patton less of a 'Man' in my eyes. "He said 'Hey you black motherfucker, move that God damn truck!' " I was amazed that he admitted to having sex with whores gangbang style. He said they lined up; the women washed your penis in a basin with a rag, applied a lubricant and spread their legs. I asked him if they thought about venereal disease. He said they did not care. He had not seen a woman he could have sex with in a year.[276]

My grandfather was a boxer as well. As a matter of fact, he attracted my grandmother's attention by wearing a pair of boxing gloves around his neck as he walked down the street challenging people to step into the ring with him. I asked him if he ever lost a match. "Yep," I was amazed that he admitted it. Most people would not. He said once when he was patrolling the camp for an opponent when a little guy challenged him. He said he dismissed the tiny fellow with, "You too little; it wouldn't be a fair fight." He said the guy kept following him around repeatedly saying, "I'll fight you." By the time they got in the ring my grandfather was pissed. What he did not know was that the little dude was a "Golden Gloves Champion". He got his ass kicked. That is when he told me, "The size of a dog in a fight don't matter". I made him show me how to fight. He used to step on my feet and hit me. I would protest, "That's cheating Granddaddy!" "Ain't no fair fight on the streets, Boy!" "Oh, yeah." That's why I am good with my hands and hell on wheels in a street fight. My grandfather taught everything he knew.

"Why didn't you stay in the coal mines?" "After being around the world with the Army, Triadelphia, West Virginia was not big enough for me. I spent three years in those mines, and then took the GI Bill to go to Howard University." That is how my family left the hills of West Virginia and came to Washington, DC.

My grandfather used to drive older women to and from the places they needed to go for a fee after he retired from the Post Office. Once while we were driving one of these women to a doctor's appointment, I asked her what was wrong with her. She said, "I am old." "You do not look that old." I replied. She said I should not try to flatter an old woman. I was not trying to flatter her; I was being honest. She did not look old enough to make the statement she had. She could walk unaided, and from what I could tell she had all of her mental faculties. When she exited the car, my grandfather said, "You keep on flattering women. You will be able to flatter yourself right into their panties." How right he was. People love to be flattered.

As I grew older and began to explore life on my own, our relationship changed. I idolized him as a child. I used him as a teacher during my adolescence. He was my archenemy from 16 to 25. Though the competition and friction between us increased, I never lost respect for him. I had

---

[276] One of the highest casualty rates in war comes from venereal disease.

my own way of dealing with things and did not want to follow his *ole* school doctrine, especially the "white people" worship. Although I had adopted some of his *ole* school morals, I could not see myself living a life like his. I did not want to follow in his footsteps, so I did not want to do things the way he had done them. He criticized everyone's mistakes to the point that I did not want to tell him anything. We had an uneasy truce during those years. He had his opinions and I had ideas of my own. The difference in later years was the fact that I was a "Man" in his eyes, even though I knew I had a long way to go. I was supporting myself, lived out of town and was pretty much responsible for myself, so he could not say shit to me, although he always found something to say.

When I left the house, I knew it was for good. I would not be one of those whom he allowed back into the house so he could control their lives until he "ear beat" them out. Whenever I came home I went to see him, but rarely stayed under his roof. I only visited on long weekends or during the holidays; I could not take his telling me what to do or how to do it. If I had a question, I would ask for his advice. Otherwise, I thought I had a handle on my life. It hurt me deeply to know this strong male had become as feeble as a child before he died. I felt like I had lost a spiritual leader, confidant and companion. His death reminded me of the riddle of the Sphinx[277] and gave rise to ever-deepening questions into my own life. I was living in Texas at the time. I miss him, but know that he passed a torch. I think of him whenever I watch football on Sunday afternoons or flatter females. His influence is evident in me even today.

It may have been a coincidence, but at the time my grandfather and I began to bump heads, I had an opportunity to know my biological father. Our society is plagued with males who plant seeds, but do not want to work the soil, water the seedlings, remove the weeds or cultivate and harvest the crop. However, if that crop is good they will gladly stand up and claim a portion of it. Ask Shaquille O'Neal.

Robert was my contra role model, everything that I do not want to be (no child should feel comfortable calling a parent by the first name). Diabetes and alcohol crippled him. As a matter of fact, he was in the hospital when I reunited with him. It was strange to see him in such a debilitated state. I had not seen him since I was very young. My brother and I had to stay with him for a short time because my mother had been hospitalized after being struck in the head with a gun during a robbery. I think I was four or five years old and I remember that the three of us slept in the same bed in his aunt's basement.

From what I remembered, he had changed for the worst. His right leg was amputated to the shin and half of his left foot was gone. He looked like a teenager with severe acne. I had such contempt for him that his disease seemed like retribution for beating two wives and not supporting four children. I hated the way he bragged about my being in college at 16 to the nurses and doctors, as if he had anything to do with it. He was a sperm donor in my eyes and nothing more. Despite this, there is need to be with and to know your sire.

I had no pity. I rationalized the entire scenario. It was not like he was not educated. He had an engineering degree. I wanted answers to the questions I had. I asked him about everything I had heard from my mother and other sources. That was how I found out about the money he

---

[277] What crawls in the morning, walks in the afternoon and crawls again at night?

stole and used to woo my mother. I asked him about his infidelity and the violence. He confirmed everything including the alcoholism. I asked him why he had not played more of a role in the lives of his children. "I was too young... I did not have a good job... Your mother and I..." I do not think any person should be seen through the eyes I looked at my father with that day. They were hateful, scornful and pitiless; I wished him dead. If you want to avoid this do not have children, or take an active role in helping to raise them. You may get the same looks and be wished dead, but at least you earned them.

Robert died alone a year later. I almost felt guilty about driving past his apartment and not stopping to see him a week before he died. There was a voice in my head that told me to turn left at the light and go to see him. I ignored it twice. There was no surprise or guilt when the police officer knocked on the door and told me that Robert was found dead in his government-subsidized apartment. I paused and thought for a moment about the fact that I was not showing any remorse. I felt hollow because I could not mourn my own father.

The city and my mother made most of the arrangements for his funeral. I sat there in the front row of the chapel with my brother and my two half-sisters, wondering why I did not feel anything. When I asked, my half-sister said, "You know what? I do not feel sad or anything." There you have it; the decision was unanimous; he was not going to be mourned or missed by any of his children. We have to make contributions to others in order to be missed.

There was another male influence in my life. My first Christmas memory is of the toys and bulk beds he brought for my brother and me. During adolescence I learned from him how to process film and take pictures. I dreamed of Africa from the pictures he took while he was there. I could talk to him and get real answers. I was made aware of and participated in special city and government programs because of his contacts. I went to college because of his influence. I got jobs because of him. I stayed in college because of his help. My first overseas experience was because of him. He had a PhD and once had a job that my grandfather described as follows: "You have a job that few white men have and no Niggas.[278] "I have never known anyone so free professionally. He once told me, "I cannot wait for you to show people how smart you are." I told him, "Every time I do, I get smacked in the face or stabbed in the back," but I hope that one day I can give him what he asked for.

One of the most important things he taught me was if you want to have a meaningful relationship, have a very honest one. No one likes the truth unless it supports his or her interests, but in order to keep and really have another's heart you have to tell the truth. Realize that males naturally want more than one mate and some sense of control over their destinies. Another person does not grow inside of us. We do not know that connection and few males can remember it from when we were inside our mothers. Also realize that most women act like they want one mate, when in actuality their preference changes depending on their hormonal state and financial outlook, unless of course they already have a satisfying mate. Women just do not give in to the

---

[278] Not to be confused with "Niggers". No African-American is capable of calling another "Nigger"; it does not have the same impact. People seem to think they are one and the same word with the same meaning and use this excuse to justify their using the negative form to describe African-Americans. They are not the same. Nigga as used above is a term of endearment. It may be used in a negative way, but it is about context. I suggest that no white person ever call an African-American a "Nigger" to his or her face without back up, Michael Richards might disagree.

impulse as easily as men. I have learned that even if the relationships are unsuccessful, we are connected to everyone with whom we have had contact. At least we can become and remain friends no matter what transpires. The intimacy we share can be good, even after the sensual part of love is gone.

In relationships in general, I have found that it is necessary to guard the heart. I said guard the heart, not forbid love. When we first meet people, most of us act pleasant on the outside, but are also on guard. We do this knowing that people perform and we also know an act can last only so long. I have only known a few people who have not contradicted themselves by behaving contrary to the way they have said they are. This is not a judgment; I think people like to say what they would like to be, but cannot always live up to such standards. These are not purposeful lies. These are lapses in fortitude and we all know how hard that road can be.

I sometimes feel like I have to assume the role of a secret agent when I meet people. My mission is to find out who that person really is, and at the same time hide my true identity. Some encounters are like fencing or a tennis match. Others are like dancing. Still others are like making love for the first time. This tape will self-destruct in 5 seconds….

When I meet someone I try to keep the aggressive and competitive side in a dormant state and wait until people decide for themselves that I am not a person they need to hurt, use or lie to. When I find someone who is at least willing to try to be honest, I keep him or her close, love, and call them a friend. When I come across those whose main objective is to take and constantly try to manipulate situations to their sole advantage, I introduce them to the mirror. I just show them who they really are, hoping that they will see what I see.

I have told several people that I love them. After reading this work many may doubt this truth. But it is true. True as though I swore it a thousand times and believed it as I swore. However, my definition of love has changed over time. I know now that what most people consider love is not the type of love I seek or need. I need more of a grounded and permanent love, the type that allows a person to dismantle the cage, not fearing that what it contains will escape, but knowing that it can and will come and go of its own free will unimpeded by individual desires or wants. Love is indeed, free.

I am searching for the type of love that transcends the physical. I want the type of relationships that manifests themselves not in a hug for gain, but in positive thoughts, actions and wishes. I want relationships that are reinforced through actions for someone else's benefit. I am tired of confusing motives and sex with affection, attention or love. I have witnessed others and myself, caught in the repetitive search for love through intimacy. We often act more animal than human, following instinct more than rationale and reason when it comes to physical contact. We frequently try to find satisfaction through the physical rather than through more spiritual unions. This type of love does not last. It is as fleeting as the nice pair of shoes that attracted our attention in the first place.

I am not arguing that intimacy is wrong. There is nothing quite like being touched by someone to whom you are attracted, and I think sex is a good thing. I am saying that our desire for and the pleasure gained from touching one another is often confused with love. I am also saying that the feelings associated with intimate contact can be addictive. The most important thing I am saying is that in order to have a profitable relationship, one must open the heart to pain as well as pleasure. That is the way of present homo-sapiens socialization.

If I have learned nothing else from my relationships, I learned that we must associate with and grow from those we meet. I also think everyone has something to teach and that people are brought into our lives for a reason. The lessons learned from these encounters make us who we are, even if we do not get what we expected. They define our fear and our love. Our relationships prepare us for what is next and sometimes we succeed at them despite our best efforts.

If I were a chess piece, I would choice to be a pawn… Why? When a pawn reaches the other side, it has survived the trials. It has been used and given up for sacrifice by the more important pieces, but it can become any piece it choices, by then it is usually the end game. No other piece has this power or choice. A Queen cannot become a King, and vice versa.

Chapter VI

Sex (XXX)

Sex: the sum of the structural, functional and behavioral characteristics of living things that are involved in reproduction by two interacting parents and that distinguish males from females.[279]

The best sex I ever had has never happened except in my mind.

There was a fly on a branch hanging over a brook. In the brook there was a trout. The trout thought to himself, "If that fly drops down 6 inches, I am going to have a nice lunch" But, at the same time the trout was watching the fly, a bear was watching the trout. The bear thought, "When the trout makes a try for the fly, I'll dash out and get the trout" But at the same time the bear was watching the trout, a hunter was watching the bear. The hunter thought, "When the bear dashes out to get the trout, I'll shoot the bear and steal his hair. But, at the same time the hunter was watching the bear, a mouse was watching the hunter's sandwich, which he had put on the log beside him to prepare for the shot. The mouse thought, "When the hunter shoots the bear for his hair, I'll steal some crumbs from this heartless bum." But, at the same time the mouse was watching the hunter, a cat was watching the mouse. The cat thought, "When the mouse takes the bum's crumbs, I'll kill the mouse and take it back to the house."

Some time passed, but eventually the fly dropped 6 inches. It set off a chain of events. The trout made a try for the fly. The bear dashed out to get the trout. The hunter took a shot at the bear for its hair. The mouse went to steal some crumbs from the bum and the cat ran toward the log to take the mouse back to his house. BUT! The cat tripped on the log and fell in the brook.

What is the moral of the story? The answer is at the end of the chapter. Please think about it as you read.

I have had sex with educators, prostitutes (women who engage in sex for payment[280]), whores (women who engage in sex for money[281]), doctors, lawyers, strippers, engineers, Latinos, Asians, Caucasians, African-Americans, drive-thru and airline attendants, financial consultants, hustlers, law enforcement officers, big girls, skinny girls, young ones and older ones, from doghouse to penthouse. In short, I have not discriminated when it comes to my favorite sport. And though I have said, "No," many times, it did not matter to my partner in crime.

According to the above definition, sex only has to do with reproduction or distinguishing between male and female. The definition does not address the act itself. If you ask me what the definition of sex is, I would say that sex is the act of engaging in physical and mental interaction with another for profit, gain or pleasure. Reproduction is just a result of sex and one should not use sex to distinguish between a man and a woman. There are many other differences that far outweigh a penis or a vagina.

Sex is one of the most powerful biological motivators there is; it is one of the things that makes the world go round. Sex is something that practically everyone has done or will do,

---

[279] Merriam-Webster's.
[280] The New Webster's Dictionary.
[281] The New Webster's Dictionary.

whether alone or with someone else. It is just sex and has little or nothing to do with love. More than likely, it has more to do with gain or arousal. You do not have to believe me; look at your own life. Look at those who attracted you. Look at those you have had sex with and then ask yourself, "Why?"

This list is not totally inclusive. Some of the experiences read like repeats and some people need to be protected. Although I am ready to come clean about myself, there are some people who would be identified by my writings, and be judged. I have changed the names to protect the guilty and the innocent, as well as to protect myself from being sued or killed. My mentor said, "This is a best seller, but you are going to need dual citizenship at the North Pole after this is published." He later told my mother I was going to have to go to "Mars". I have purged myself and I have no shame for the experiences that have been placed in my path or the lessons I have learned.

Also realize that I am not a textbook womanizer. I am not 6 foot something with bulging muscles. I am not stunningly attractive and I am not rich, yet. I am 5 foot nothing and weigh a 100 and nothing with bricks in my pockets, soaking wet and I do not drive a Mercedes. One girlfriend said, "You fool people because you look like a nerd." I am a nerd, if that means I am reasonably intelligent and can deduce, but I also have Masters Degree in street and a Ph D in common sense. My grandfather's tests made damn sure of that. "Use your brain boy," was one of his favorite sayings.

Some years ago a friend of mine was due to ship out to California. I gave him the number of another friend who was a mentor to me in flight school in hopes that the introduction would ease his transition to a new area. I figured that two single Marines could find something to do in the Los Angeles area. I later heard of a conversation they had. It revolved around me. I was told they were perplexed by the fact that I was successful with women. I said, "I use the Jedi mind trick." "Huh?" "All you need to do is give women what they want or the illusion of it, listen to them, flatter them, show them affection, attention and spend some time with them and some money on them. That is what most of the women I have known seem to think love is." Add a sense of humor and security and you have a relationship headed for commitment. I know that is not love; you see what I wrote, "think." It is all about perception. My personal definition of love is contained in the last chapter of this work.

I remember watching a program where two male springbucks were fighting each other during the rut. They were sparring to establish dominance in an area that had good grazing so that they could have the best chance of fathering as much of the next generation as possible. I was surprised that neither of them saw the leopard that was stalking the herd. They were so engrossed in their competition that they did not notice the alert members of the herd had moved away. They saw the danger and passed the word, but the boys did not hear the alarm calls because they had testosterone in their ears. The fighting did not end until the leopard killed one of the springbucks. This is how strong the drive to mate is.

Sex Good or Bad

A Sunday school teacher asks her class what part of the body goes to heaven first. Susie said, "The heart." "And, why is that," the teacher asked with a smile. Susie answered, "Because God wants to weigh your heart." Johnny said, "The brain." "Why is that," the teacher repeated with approval. "Because God wants to know your thoughts," the goody-two-shoes said. Dirty Johnny interjected, "You are all wrong; the feet go to heaven first!" "Why is that?" the teacher responded with a puzzled look on her face. "Because Saturday nights when my Daddy is on top of my Mommy, her feet are straight up in the air and she says, 'Oh, My God, I am coming.' "

Is sex good or bad? I like it, but during the early years of my life, those years when I was not supposed to have sex, I was taught that nudity was bad and sex was worse. I suffered from a form of sexual repression. I liked being around girls for some unexplainable reason, but I had no interest in sex until I was introduced to it.

If we had to make a list of bad things we could do as a child, having sex was probably at the top, especially if you were a female. We put it right next to drug use and being gay. Penis and vagina were not used in my household. Every adult referred to those private areas using some cute word (pee-pee, wee-wee). I thought they were bad and shameful words. I remember being embarrassed because my grandmother told everyone I got my "pee-pee" stuck in the zipper of my shorts (long story: let us just say I took special care to wear underwear after that). Even as adults we rarely use the proper terminology for our genitals. Sex is hidden in the United States and at the same time it is a multibillion dollar industry. I typed sex into the Goggle search engine and got 105 million hits.

> *Sexual modesty cannot then in any simple way be identified with the use of clothing, nor shamelessness with the absence of clothing and total or partial nakedness. There are circumstances in which total nakedness is not immodest.... Nakedness as such is not to be equated with physical shamelessness. Immodesty is only present when nakedness plays a negative role with regard to the value of the person...The human body is not in itself shameful, nor for the same reasons are sensual reactions and human sensuality in general. Shamelessness (just like shame and modesty) is a function of the interior of the individual. Pope John Paul II[282]*

If sex and nudity are bad, why are Larry Flint and Hugh Hefner multimillionaires in a conservative Christian country? If sex is so filthy and nasty, why are we supposed to save it for the ones we love or marry? Why does the US pornography industry out sell all professional sports combined (an estimated $13.3 billion in 2006)? Why did the Most High make something so bad, feel so good?

I believe it is universally thought that sex feels good and/or sex is necessary. Life would not exist without it and it is natural. So where did we get the idea that it is wrong or bad to have sex? I know that there are risks associated with having sex. Sexually transmitted diseases are a danger, as is pregnancy. There is also the risk of getting hurt. I am not sure which of the three is worse.

---

[282] Pope John Paul II (1920-2005): Supreme Pontiff of the Catholic Church and Sovereign of Vatican City.

Sex has gotten me into more trouble and given me more pleasure than any of the other drugs I use. Yet, I am still vulnerable to the urges that lead to sex and have nothing bad to say about it. I do not think that sex is the issue. I think our actions surrounding sex are what make it seem good or bad. I think that we are uncomfortable openly discussing sex. I think we are unrealistic in our view of sex. I think we use sex as a tool. I think we buy and sell sex, and at the same time are sexually repressed. I think sex sells and it 'ain't' going anywhere. That being the case, we might as well be open and honest about it. It is just sex and not some phantom that will appear from the mirror to bite our heads off if we say its name three-times.

I would like to separate sex from the emotions that we often associate with it. Sex is just sex. It is not love and it is not affection, though we often get the three confused. Sex just feels so damn good it must be love. Sex is just a physical activity that renders pleasurable results almost instantly, if done right. Weightlifting and aerobic training take too damn long. That is why sex is my favorite sport. They say that a ½ hour of vigorous sex is equivalent to running ½ a marathon and you do not have to train or buy running shoes!

I like to think of sex as a two way street. I know I am at least going to ejaculate[283], if I want to, but I also want the experience to be pleasurable for my partner. In an attempt to do this, I often ask women what they want and how they want it. I am not one of those guys who think he can satisfy a woman by pounding her into pleasure with his penis alone (unless I'm on the bottom, and don't move or speak). My claim to fame is: "What I lack in the hips, I make up for in the lips and finger tips." I do not consider pleasing a woman orally as nasty or a chore; it is a delight to have that much control at the tip of my tongue, like words. I also know that the hands can be very useful in aiding the pleasure principle. But, the most important tool I like to use is the mental aspect of pleasure. The "right" words can stimulate a woman to orgasm. Whether she is into kinky "fuck me hard" talk or more subdued romantic phrases. Words, imagery and mental projection are the best devices for pleasuring the body.

Sidebar: She jumped me this morning. I did not mind… I was harder than a diamond cutter anyway. She knew I would be a willing victim; she bought wine last night, a Sonoma Valley Chardonnay and made me worship Bacchus.

"You ain't done…" "What you lack in the hips, you better make up with your lips." Her jaws got tired. "Bend over!" Thrusting into another from behind is an experience that women should have the opportunity to enjoy. The visual of it all, in and out… The sound of it, squisheeeee squish. But, that was not enough. The smell of it, straight primal: "ME TARZAN; YOU JANE."

She always gets horny this time of the month-ovulation or right before, after, or during her cycle. Honestly, she was horny all the time. I knew it was a set-up. I let her take what she wanted, as usual; she liked being "Zee Boss". I like feeling the different muscle contractions and strokes that females use when they are consciously trying to have an orgasm.

---

[283] Ejaculation should not be confused with an orgasm. Excluding masturbation, the male orgasm is as rare as the female's. I have not had a vaginally induced orgasm in years.

A few hours passed and because it was Saturday I reasoned that I could take her ass and she would not complain. "Lock the door... I want to eat your pussy!" Faster than a speeding bullet... the door was locked. All I had to do was position her on the edge of the bed. I was seated in a swivel chair, so I could maneuver into position. I just wanted her to bend over so I could lick.

I knew it would be a job. She came this morning. I'm snatching now, "Trying to snatch the pink out." She said, "It's yours." I can exercise my rights at any time after that testimonial. The sweatpants were gone. And the thong too... in one clean swipe. "Let me go wash it, Baby!" "Nope" "But it stinks." "I want it like that."

My neck hurt. I knew I was in for it when she grabbed pillows and propped herself up. I kept my eyes closed because I knew she was watching. Females are as visual as males. I did not want to interrupt whatever fantasy she was experiencing by watching me eat her relentlessly. From the clit to just above the other hole, while maintaining the outer lips in my mouth and at the same time sucking, searching, touching, probing those fleshy parts. "OH, she likes that."

"Don't pull away from me. I want to eat some more." "I can't take it; it's just like when you come... You're too sensitive for me to keep sucking." "OK... But, you owe me one." "I know."

A friend put it bluntly. He said that the worst moment in seducing a woman is the instant after you have the first orgasm. Many of the feelings of wanting and desire fade with the physical release. In pursuing desire we obtain nothing but physical satisfaction. It is temporary.

I remember wanting some of my sex partners to shower and leave as soon as the act was complete, the shower being optional. I had achieved what I wanted and realized it. Very few women were able to deal with this attitude. They wanted payment for their services. That is why I suggest to anyone who thinks as I sometimes do, have sex at the other person's place. You can get up and leave when you like. If payment for sex is expected, I also suggest that women keep their legs closed, become a professional, or marry every male they want to fuck.

There seems to be a contradiction when it comes to sex. Why can sons have sex, but our daughters cannot? It is another one of those two-tier standards and if you think that there is a difference between males having sex and females having sex, you are a victim of social programming and need to think about why you feel this way. Is there any wrong or right in this situation, and if so why?

That is a question I have asked myself, and one you will have to answer for yourself. I asked my mother for her input about sex and her children. She told me that daughters are off limits and that you raise girls differently. I asked her why. She said that she had not made mentally sound decisions when it came to sex and men from the beginning of menses until menopause. I agree with that, but I do not agree that you should treat girls differently than boys.

I have a question I would like you to think about. How old should a person be before they have sex? I want you to think about the first time you had sex and the relationships that followed. If you have only had sex with one person, I feel sorry for you or I am jealous. If you have two different answers for males and females, ask yourself why you have these opinions and from

221

where they came. I think we are living illusions of correctness, and denying what is real and present in everyday life.

I was driving behind a school bus one morning. There were four girls seated in the last two rows of the bus and they were waving, so I waved back and smiled. I felt good that these young girls were being friendly and probably flirting with a male in uniform. I looked at it as harmless and natural at their age. I guessed they were in junior high school. It was morning rush hour, but after living in a metropolis, I really should not have been complaining about being stuck behind the bus. Buses were the slowest things on the road at that time of morning. What made it worse is the fact that the single lane road, the oncoming traffic and the frequent stops to pick up children, made it impossible to pass. I know it is a small thing now, but when you are trying to make a briefing and lateness is a strike, your priorities change. After about five minutes of following the bus, one of the girls held up a sign written on notebook paper. It said, "I want to fuck you."

One last question about sex: how many times have you had sex (masturbation counts)?

There were three women sitting in the waiting room of the *OB/GYN*, a blond, a brunette and a red head. The red head said that she was having a boy. When asked how she knew. She responded with, "I was on the bottom when she conceived." The brunette said she was having a girl. She knew this because she was on top. The blond suddenly started crying. The other two women were unable to calm her down. Finally, the nurse appeared and asked her what was wrong. She screamed, "I'm going to have puppies!!"

If you do not want to read about the graphic sexual nature of my relationships, feel free to forward to page 279. Some may say it is pornography, others erotica and still others art, but I say it is just sex and I know you are going to read some parts of it!

Stink Finger

I became "taken" with a girl I will call Stink Finger. She was two or three years older than I. Genetic programming took over when she starting kissing me. I thought we were having sex. Then Stink Finger asked me to stick my finger in her "red hole". "OK". I would have done anything she wanted me to. The problem was that I had no idea what the red hole was. It was either her front or back. I had seen naked illustrations, but both holes looked red to me. With her help, my hand found its way to the general area. She did not have any panties, so it was easy to tell that she was wet, hot and sticky. I looked down at her pubic area and saw she had hair. I was bald at the time and remember hoping she did not want to see my privates. I rolled the dice and I stuck my finger up her sphincter - "Snake Eyes[284]". She promptly told me I was in the wrong hole.

This happened the first time we were alone; we immediately started kissing and touching. I was very excited, although I did not know why. Nothing else existed. I was totally enthralled with what we were doing. My eyes were closed and my body felt tingly all over. This was the first time I had touched a female the way I was touching her. I was curious about breasts. This

---

[284] Snake Eyes (slang): a throw of two dice that turns up one spot on each. Commonly referred to as "craps".

was the first time I touched a pair. I touched and she moaned. I touched harder; she moaned harder. When I kissed them; she moaned even louder. I remember how nasty I thought other people's spit was, not hers. She tasted like milk and honey. Her breath could have smelled like garlic and I would not have known it. I now understand how people are caught in compromising situations and how leopards get to eat horny springbuck. I eventually got it right.

I remember smelling my fingers afterwards. There was a pungent odor that made my lips curl. I did not say it was unpleasant. It was an exciting smell. I know now that the pheromones and estrogen in her secretions triggered autonomic responses in my body. I remember seeing male animals curl their lips up in much the same manner as I did while they smelled the urine of a female in heat. My nose still twitches when I think about it.

I should have known then that females like sex too and will initiate the process without any effort on the part of a male. The fact that most females want to have sex no longer surprises me. I understand the physical motives, pleasure and arousal. For all of you out there who have girls, beware; they are the same way we are and were.

The First Time

There is a joke: The Creator was bent over a workbench working on his design for people. An assistant was watching him draw something over and over again. Curiosity made the assistant ask, "What are you working on, Boss?" The Eternal said, "Reproductive organs. I designed a super sensitive nerve and I am going to place 50 of them in each model." The assistant shocked said, "But, Holy one, if you do that, people will always want to have sex!" "That is the point," said the Universe, "Because people have choice, they are going to have to endure arguments, hunger, cold, war, disease and more. Yet, they will still need to reproduce… I solved that problem with these nerves… Come to think of it, I better add 10 more to each model; I want to make it so good they call my name."

I have been told all my life that it is the male who pursues the female. Since my first sexual encounter, I have doubted this. In my experience, it is women who are the aggressors.

Vale took my virginity. I said took. It was not unusual for me to go over her house to talk, kiss and listen to music. She was a friend as far as I was concerned. I am telling you, I was clueless. The closest I had come to sex was the "red hole". I had kissed a little, but my relationships were mostly talk before Vale. She seduced me. One day I found myself on the living room floor with my penis inside of her. We had our pants down to our ankles and kept our shoes on. It was her idea and her mother was downstairs.

I was so naive and she was so open that I had to ask, "Is it in yet?" I did not know what I was feeling. There was a wet and hot sensation emanating from my penis. It was overwhelming. My breath shortened and sped up at the same time. The worry of her mother coming upstairs was replaced by something else. I asked myself, "What is this?" I answered, "Its pussy stupid!" "It feels funny." "No. It feels good." "Yeah, it does."

Something told me to move up and down on top of her. I had no idea what I was doing; it came naturally and after a time, I felt like what I can only describe as having to urinate badly. My head was spinning and I was sweating profusely. When I came, something said, "Pull out!" I withdrew from her to see a white opaque slime pulsing from my penis and coming to rest on her abdomen and thighs. It felt weird and great at the same time. I trembled, my body involuntarily convulsed, and I grunted aloud. "So this is sex!" "Yeah." "I like it." "Me too."

Vale started a sex spree that has spanned five continents, numerous countries and even more women. She taught me more than anything else that I enjoyed sex. All I had to figure out was how to get more of it.

Quick Silver is probably the most lasting relationship I have ever had. I do not know why, but I have always been irresistibly attracted to her, even now. Adolescence blessed her with a beautiful body. She said I was her first. She was not tight and unyielding but wet, and I slid right in. I wanted to continue the secrecy of our relationship; she did not. She once gave a letter I had written to her to another woman. Talk about throwing salt in a brother's game. She never did that again, although she has used our relationship as a weapon against other males and she will never like any of my mates. We still speak, though it has been years and she has two children. I wish she would lose some weight for health reasons.

Cherry was a virgin when I met her. We met thru a mutual acquaintance. I liked the fact that she was older than I. I used to ride the subway an hour in order to see her. On one of these excursions we had sex. It was like the blind leading the blind. I had no idea that penetrating a woman for the first time could be so difficult. After practically falling into Quick Silver, Cherry was tighter than airport security on 9/12! I had to incorporate adolescent K-Y, Vaseline. After that first time, we had sex several times every time we saw each other. She was my first experience with oral sex and the first hand job administered by another person. We had to work on the teeth, but it was an excellent beginning. We broke up over something stupid; I cannot even remember what it was, probably another opportunity to have sex.

It was funny, that for years afterwards, she would call my grandfather's house on holidays to see if I was at home. My family would tease me about the women from my past and their ability to clock the dates of my probable return to the city (holidays). I once walked down the street with Quick Silver, another girl and Cherry. The other girl said, "It's funny walking with a guy and two girls that all have slept with him." Throughout college and the first five or six years of the military, we would occasionally get together for little reunions. Yes, Cherry and I did the wild thing every time and her technique was much improved. As it should have been, she had had three children by then.

Time Flies When You're Having Fun

A seven-year-old asked her mother how old she was. The mother replied, "Honey, women do not ask each other those types of questions; you'll learn this as you grow older." "Well, how much do you weigh?" "Honey, that is another one of those questions you do not ask women; you'll learn as you grow older." The frustrated little girl relayed the conversation to her friend. Her friend said, "Do not bother asking. Look at her driver's license it is just like a report card. It has all the information you need on it." The little girl did as her friend suggested and snuck into her mother's purse for a peek. She did the math from the birth date and saw the weight. A few days later she said, "Mom, you are 38-years-old." The mother replied in astonishment, "You are so smart. How did you know that?" "And, you weigh 145 pounds." "You are so smart; how did you know that?" "And, I know why daddy left; you got an 'F' in sex".

When we leave the protection of the home and parental controls, we feel more free to do what we want, not what we have been told or taught. I was no exception.

When I saw her for the first time, I asked my roommate who she was. He said, "That is Patricia; she's a flirt." I told him I was going to have her. She had a boyfriend. Not a problem; he was not there. She was naïve about sex and I was her second lover. I taught her all I knew, to include, but not limited to my first time giving oral sex. I can honestly say that I learned to manipulate the female body with my tongue largely because of the experiments I performed on her. I also learned that I liked the feeling of control I experienced when eating at bush gardens. On top of that, it did not taste bad or I should say, "She did not taste bad."

Patricia was the first girlfriend to let me come in her mouth, but she did not swallow (I have a question for women; what would you think if you came in a male's mouth and he got up and spit it out, brushed his teeth and washed his face like he had been eating something disgusting?). We had sex every day and night. Her thing was to get on top and then rub my penis on her breasts while intermittently sucking. I would prop my head up with a pillow and watch.

The fates brought Innocence into my life and took Patricia out of it. Talk about killer bodies. Innocence had one. She had huge breasts, a small waist and a nice butt: a true brick house. The first time we were alone I seduced her. She was lying under me, legs open and I was about to stick my penis inside of her. I decided to check her for lubrication with my thumb. I penetrated her with just the thumbnail and she began to cry and said, "Please don't." I stopped. If I am nothing else, I am no rapist, unless you want me to pretend. "No" means "No" game. I immediately left. As it turned out, my response gained me her trust and admiration. She told me so. She had never had anyone not have sex with her. Her saying "No" was some sort of test. I passed with flying colors. My reward was to have her trust and heart.

Innocence was a good lover. She was comfortable with nakedness and loved to have sex. She lived alone. With no roommates, I could stay all night with no issues. I found out later that her moans announced to the entire wing when I was there. I would turn the radio up to mask her sounds, but evidently to no avail. Innocence had a peculiar habit of wanting to see my face when we had sex, even from behind. I do not know why, but I did my best to accommodate her.

She used to bring me breakfast or lunch if I stayed in her room late. She had early classes and I had late ones. After I ate she always mounted me. Once we were in her bedroom at parent's home and she decided she wanted to have sex. Her mother was down stairs, so I was apprehensive. In order to avoid being caught, she went down on all fours and stuck her head into the hallway. She told me she had done this before. I mounted her from behind. At some point I opened my eyes to see that she was shaking her head side to side and her eyes were closed too.

We went to a hotel one weekend. For some reason I let Innocence talk me into lying to her parents about where we were going. She told them that we were going to my home. Not that I was upset about being yelled at by her dad; since what I got in return was well worth it. Innocence had bought an assortment of crotchless panties and I made sure we used every pair.

I used a sure fire sexual position on her. It is hard to describe, so please bear with me. I call it the "Cross". I placed her on her back and laid on my side 90 degrees perpendicular to her. If you picture a human cross, joined at the pelvic region of both people, you got it perfect. Her left leg crossed over my hip. The right leg passed between my legs. My left hand massaged her clitoris and my right palmed her left breast. This position has never failed to please. If you use it, give me credit. If you have used it, you know what I mean. It was a good weekend, but she left the receipt from the hotel on the top of her dresser at home. She was either stupid as hell or she purposefully involved me in some sick game of getting attention.

Innocence and I were separated for the summer. That is when I got involved with The Reverend. We had grown close after working together for three months. That did not stop me from having sex with Innocence; it just made it more challenging. Innocence eventually told The Reverend that I was having sex with her. It was true and I lied to cover it up. I saw her once more a year or so later. We smoked a joint and talked, but the possibility of being laid was nil.

Are you getting the impression that I am a dog? I was not a dog; I have a healthy libido, and I was following the natural way. The only difference between then and now is I do not lie about being monogamous anymore. I have learned that if I do not lie there is no ammunition or guilt.

There is something strange that happens between people who are in close proximity for extended periods of time. I understand how movie stars can become attached to one another while shooting movies. The Reverend, another co-worker, and I grew close even though they had men and I was involved as well.

Before going on a break, The Reverend came to say good-bye, but she heard me having sex with Innocence. I knew that she was interested in becoming more than friends and her telling me that she heard me having sex with another woman confirmed it. I had no objection to becoming lovers, but I also knew that there would be ramifications. For one, she had a male and I had a woman. Secondly, I told her that I still loved Patricia. She asked me what would happen if she came back into my life. I said, "I don't know." Given these factors we both willingly proceeded with the seduction.

Why do women pursue a male they know is already in a relationship or allow a male to pursue them when they have another male? Why do they call males dogs? Remember, males are people and women are female people. Therefore, if males are dogs, then women are female dogs. I like to think of most women as cats. If you have ever owned a dog, you know how loyal they can be.

We finally had sex. After the first time, we did it anywhere and anytime. We had sex with the door open, in the shower and on a fitness trail. I remember doing her on the desk in my room. What made this memorable was the fact that the table was against the wall on the opposite side of the room from a mirror and placed between two windows, which over looked the front of the building. I placed her butt on the desk and placed a chair on both sides of me so that she could place her feet on them and support her thrusts. She was facing the mirror and her eyes stayed glue to it the entire time. I was watching as people outside walked by. I am not sure if anyone saw us or not; I did not care if they did. It was a turn on just knowing that if someone just looked up, they would get an eye full of us, naked and sweaty.

The Reverend had the biggest vaginal lips I had ever seen. She was always wet and inviting. Add to this that she willingly sucked and swallowed, and you have an excellent sexual partner. The only drawback to having sex with her was that she did not like to be on all fours.

Things between The Reverend and me were going fairly well. Innocence was out of the picture. I had two others on the side, but they were manageable risks. I was drunk one night and painted a proclamation of love in a public place. That sign would come back to haunt me, but for the time being it served its purpose.

When Patricia came back into my life, it was a nightmare. Even though I had confided in The Reverend that I still loved her, I was not sure what I would do about our relationship. Patricia wanted to pick-up where we had left off; I wanted the best mate I could have and as many partners as I could juggle. What to do?

I knew Patricia was the cheating type and she knew that I had other relationships, the whole campus told her. I first got a clue when a friend caught her in a compromising situation with another male. My second clue came two or three years later when we had sex and I got crabs. She was the only woman I was with at the time. I got my third clue when we were having sex one weekend a year later. She told me to tell her when I was about to come. I obliged and she quickly turned around on all fours and swallowed. I had no complains about it. As a matter a fact, I had been trying to get her to do it for five years, but I was unsuccessful. That was such a turn on and it still is. The way she performed the maneuver with such precision, let me know that she had been practicing. It is not surprising that years later we had a bad breakup; we were both cheating, but she was caught.

I did not stop having sex with The Reverend despite Patricia. I would go to her whenever I was pissed at Patricia or had a free moment and she would give in every time; she knew what she was doing. All I had to do was touch her right. On one occasion she let me come inside of her. I asked her, "Can I come inside of you?" "Yes" When I reach orgasm, I said, "Pull me inside." She cupped my buttocks with both hands and pulled me deeper than I already was. Do not ask me what I was thinking. The last thing in the world I wanted or needed was a child, but there is something about letting go inside of women. It feels so natural. Looking at it from The Reverend's point of view it seems just as strange. Was she hoping for a child or did she know that the possibility of her getting pregnant was low that night and she was just giving me what I wanted? Whatever the case, I do not know why she kept sleeping with me, except maybe we had good sex.

The final straw came when I went to her room one night and had oral sex with her. She said, "You really know what to do to turn me on" but she did not let me penetrate her. A few nights later she found out I had another woman in my place. It was Patricia. She looked at me like, "How could you!"

The Deep South

Most Southern women are different than those from the Northeast and the West. They are socialized with more emphasis on the old world view of what responsibilities a woman has in a relationship. The ones I have known actually cook, clean and assume a service like role in relationships. I do not want a slave or a trainer. You cannot get to my heart through my stomach or a clean house.

Loyalty was my first real experience with an older woman. She was smart, ambitious and honest, which is more than I could say for myself. We flirted with each other during a volleyball game and I knew I had been chosen when she smacked me on my ass, after I had made a spike "Smack", right on the left cheek. "Nice shot." I thought about smacking her back, but she never did make a good shot.

We petted three or four times before we finally had sex. I had someone and was reluctant to finish the chase. The first time I spent the night in her apartment, we had gone to a play and were supposed to go to dinner, but I had a badly sprained ankle and was in some pain, so we decided to order pizza at her place. After the meal and conversation, she said I could stay the night. I thought she wanted to have sex until she was kind enough to offer me the bed. She was going to sleep on the couch. We talked for some time in the living room. Then as I was hobbling toward the bedroom, she hit me in the back with the gym shorts she had put on to sleep in. I took that as a hint to renew the chase and told her so, but I put the shorts on my head like a hat and went to bed alone. I knew it was just a matter of time and I did not want to do any more chasing.

I remember saying, "It's too soon," the first time we had sex. It happened on her living room floor. She said, "It's all right" in a panting "Do not even think about stopping now" kind of voice while she gripped my back more firmly (I was not going anywhere, not until I was done). She thought I was referring to the time period it had taken to bed her, when in fact I was referring to my not being able to stop the orgasm I was about to have after only five minutes.

I sometimes spent the night at her place if I did not have a flight the next day. She would come home for lunch, not that she wanted to eat. I would send her back to work leaking. I told her I wanted her to think of me every time my semen found its way to that cotton patch in her panties. I was crazy about her. She would sometimes make the 45-minute drive in the middle of the night to get laid, and the first thing she did when she got in was to ask me why I was "soft" and then she would remove my bottoms and place my penis in her mouth.

She knew I had a girlfriend and cooperated. Hell, one Thanksgiving she helped to prepare the meal we all were going to share. She and her girlfriend teased me the entire night about my girlfriend showing up, but she was cool. It was my first experience with a woman who was not shy about her body or what she wanted sexually. It was also my first successful anal experience; I have been hooked ever since. We had talked about it, but I was reluctant because every previous attempt ended with my partner screaming with pain, not so with Loyalty. She knew what to do. She told me to grease up and enter slow. She propped herself on all fours and did not move. I could tell that she was experiencing some discomfort, but she tried to hide it. There was something on the other side of the pain that she was trying to recapture. We had a good time until she moved out of town.

The Evangelist was a tall, slim quintessentially good girl. She was a virgin and very religious. Add her traditional blue-collar family background and she was a "triple don't". She liked to dance and hang out, but she did not drink, smoke or do anything that would be deemed inappropriate. As a matter of fact, getting me to go to church with her was like a missionary quest. I did not go. Not because I did not believe in God, but because I did not want the pressure of being seen as a potential husband in the eyes of the congregation, many of whom I would see out on Friday or Saturday night. I had had enough of Baptist churches and overzealous, self-righteous preachers.

We agreed that she should spend the night at my apartment. It was my plan to seduce her and she knew it. I entered the bedroom to see her bent down beside the bed saying her prayers like a child. I cannot express in words the affect that had on me. I was about to deflower her and she was scared, but not even the guilt of knowing what I was about to introduce her to stopped me. Besides, she was only wearing one of my T-shirts and panties. Her long supple legs and beautiful brown skin were driving me crazy. At this point in my life I was young, dumb and full of come. I was not aware of the expectations attached to sex by young virgins, or maybe I was and did not care. I just wanted the physical stimulation associated with being inside of a woman, not the emotional and implied social attachment. Why did she decide to give herself to me?

I tried to ease her apprehension by touching her skin lightly, but deliberately with my fingertips. I watched for goose bumps to appear. Women are a lot like men when it comes to sexual stimulation. If you get the attention of the brain's pleasure centers people's behavior changes. It becomes more instinctual. If you understand that everyone likes to feel good and are able to cultivate this idea by stimulating them physically and mentally, you can have anything you want from them as long as they have a good feeling. It is the best of drugs.

I watched as her nipples slowly came to attention when I touched them through the T-shirt. Her breathing became more excited and erratic when I grasped her nipples with my teeth and purposely breathed harder than normal. The flow of hot exhales and cool inhalation passing over her slightly wet nipples made her squirm a little. I asked her, "Do you want me to stop?" "No." This had to be a consensual engagement to remove fault or blame, and ultimately commitment.

I liked her stomach. It had none of the stretch marks of mothers and no muffin top. She was young enough to be blessed with one of those attractive tight bodies that cost nothing to maintain. I touched, licked, bit and sucked every part from her panty line to her neck. I placed my face between her legs. I breathed through her panties directly onto her clitoris. I used the same technique here as I did on the breasts. I decided to look up to see if it was working. Her eyes were closed and her mouth was wide open; she was breathing heavily. Her abdomen was flushed, bloated and hot to the touch.

Sex has a way of bringing out the animal in us. I felt like one of the big cats; I felt I was stalking her. I felt like she was prey and I a sexual predator (the good kind). She was more than legal and had made her decision the moment she lied to her parents about where she was spending the night. I wanted to know if I was right about what I was sensing. Was she as physically stimulated as her body was signaling? I used my finger to search for moisture. I went through the side of her panties and found what can only be described as nectar. She was soaked. I used the excretions to spread the moisture to her external parts, at the same time probing for her sensitive spots. When my finger penetrated her she tensed. She felt tight. I found her hymen with the tip of my finger and remember thinking, "She really is a virgin." I began massaging her G-spot, that little knot on the roof of the uterus just before the pelvic bone. At the same time, I introduced my tongue to her clitoris. When I licked her clitoris she sat straight up in the bed and then let out a weird screech. "Do you want me to stop?" She could only shake her head "No" as she descended.

The break gave me a chance to take her panties completely off. I was especially attentive to her reactions to these advances. I wanted to see if she would assist me by slightly raising her hips while I was taking her bottoms off. She did. That was the final clearance. It was harder to get inside of her than it was getting into my first virgin. I wanted to be gentle, but her walls were so close together that I had to force entry slowly. The sun was coming up when I came. It was the most work I had done for one orgasm in ages. I went to sleep with The Evangelist in my arms.

I met her cousin, Twin, at a house party given by a friend maybe two or three weeks before I had sex with The Evangelist. I did not know they were cousins. It was boys' night out and we were tying one on. We ended up in an after-hours club and I gave my car keys to one of the boys who was ready to go. I was staying the night with a friend and was in no condition to drive. My other companion convinced two girls to give us a ride. That is how I met Twin.

Twin was the opposite of The Evangelist. She was reasonably good looking. I was so drunk that I got aggressive with her in the back seat of Flirtatious'[285] car. I was touching and kissing, and she did not mind at all. By the time we got to my friend's house, I was done and passed out in the guest bed as they cooked breakfast. I came to the next afternoon. My friend drove me home and gave me Twin's number. She wanted to see me again.

Twin liked being on top; this is no surprise, considering the fact that most women who need to feel in control are more comfortable and have more fun in bed when they feel like they are using a male for pleasure. She would bounce up and down so hard just before she was about to come that I frequently got scared. I kept thinking about the possibility of my penis coming out of her on the up stroke, and her snapping it in two on the down. I found the way she came and collapsed on the bed humorous. Because even though I witnessed her expending a huge amount of energy, I knew she was not done. I was going to demand a bit more from her fatigued and depleted body.

There was nothing special to our relationship and I probably would not even mention Twin had I not been put in a situation where I was with her and ended up going to The Evangelist's house. It was a holiday and I went over to Twin's. She said the entire family was going over her cousin's house so I went as well. When we entered The Evangelist's neighborhood, my heart dropped. When she told me to stop in front of the house, I could not breathe. It was one of my

---

[285] Flirtatious was 16 or 17 at the time and I did not know it. She slept with several people whom I knew and frequented our social gatherings. I slept with her 5 years later.

most embarrassing situations. The mothers seemed to enjoy it as much as everyone else. One of my friends was there as well and he felt bad for me. But I lived through it, and although Twin and I never hooked up again, but The Evangelist and I did.

I wrote The Evangelist a sexually explicit letter and she called to tell me how lucky I was that I was not in town. The way she said it let me know that she wanted to have sex again. We arranged to meet in a city half way between her home and mine. What was strange about our last encounter is that it occurred on a weekend that she was on a church retreat. She went to the conference and then came to my hotel room. I arranged candles and flowers around the room, and played a compilation of instrumental music made specifically for the occasion. It was for relaxation and sex. I gave her a shower and laid her on her stomach with her head at the foot of the bed. I put her in this position because it is easier to give a massage while standing and I wanted an excuse to rub my pelvis on her face. The massage oil I brought came in handy. From head to toe I rubbed her. I was slow and gentle; kissing her body parts every now and then to remind her of what was coming and why she was there. We made slow love. Of course I gave her the oral treatment. Her reactions were the same. She was still that shy girl whom I bedded some years earlier. I did come inside of her, though when I said I was coming she squirmed under me as if trying to make me withdraw. I asked her what was wrong. "I have never had a male come inside of me." I reassured her that the birth control would do its job. She left for home the next day. Last time I saw The Evangelist she preparing to marry a naval aviator. That is what she wanted and I hope it is all she desires.

Remember Loyalty? A few years passed and she was back in the country and called to ask me to meet her at Carnival. We had a romp in the backseat of my friend's car. We snuck out and drove behind a school. The spot was dark and no one could see the car from the road. I told Loyalty to get in the back seat and to take her bottoms off. She said she had not had sex in a car for a long time. I opened the sunroof so that I could stand up and had her get on all fours facing the back window. That was a good night. She finished by sucking me and I reciprocated. When we got back to the party, my friend asked where we had been, and then opened the back door, put his nose on the seat and began to smell back and forth like a drug dog. It was very funny. Later on under the light, I noticed she still had a little dry piece of "come" in the corner of her mouth; I gently kissed it away. The sex was as good as it has always been.

I want to pause and address a concern. I was single and young. I was into hard bodies, pretty faces and physical pleasure. If a woman was not willing to do what I wanted in bed I would find someone who would, just like most of you who are reading now. I suggest to anyone who has sex with a male that you let him come wherever he wants. You do not have to do this, but if you want to keep him sexually satisfied, interested and aroused, you should or the result will be the same as when a woman is not sexually satisfied.

For you men out there who think it is disgusting or unmanly to give a woman oral pleasure, keep it up and I hope another male who does eat at the "Y" will meet your woman. She will not be yours alone for long. The penis is not enough to satisfy a woman all the time. Men typically have orgasms before women. Men had better do something before or after he is done to stimulate their partners to orgasm, because although women can experience sexual satisfaction without the accompanying orgasm[286], they do want the experience.

I was awaiting orders, so I moved out of my apartment and then moved in with Sweet Bread for a few weeks. I knew her through two of my fellow students. I had slept with her several times before, and she had no issue with putting me up in her spare room for a little while. She was a total slob. I cleaned her place from top to bottom and paid rent. Her friends commented that they were glad I was there. She had a penis in the house and took advantage of it whenever I was willing.

She was not pretty by my standards, but she had a kicking hard body. It was symmetrically perfect. I have always been able to find something not proportional about a woman's body (one breast slightly larger, an eye a little different than the other, etc.). Sweet Bread had no such imperfections. I used to ask her to stand naked and do slow turns just so that I could watch. Da Vinci would have drawn her. We had a weird relationship. I lived in her apartment, we had sex sometimes and I was able to pursue other women without any issues. I even brought in a few women.

Fooled Me was one of them. I met her through a friend a year or so before. She was built like a super model with a butt. One night I bumped into her at a popular club and I spoke to her in a suggestive way for the first time. By the end of the evening, we had progressed enough that I walked her to her car and got her number. She was so fine I thought I would have to go overboard with the chase. I arranged my first picnic basket for her. Actually it was for me, but that is cause and effect. It was Sweet Bread's basket and she helped me arrange it. I found out later that Fooled Me was suspicious. She had discussed it with a friend and concluded it was too perfect, that I had done it before (I have had women look in the trashcan of my kitchen to see if I really cooked the meal we had eaten).

I took her to the beach, spread a blanket, and lit a kerosene lantern. We had grapes, a nice bottle of wine, two types of cheese, bread, strawberries, whipped cream, pepperoni, peppered olives and Prosciutto ham. I also brought music. She did not have sex with me that night, but she did sit on my face right there on the beach. I imagine some people got a kick out of our silhouettes. I knew it would not be long. She was impressed and I knew it. It was just a matter of time. The first time we had sex, she stopped me from undressing her to explain that she had Vitiligo[287] (bedroom confession). I asked if it was contagious.

I had never seen her without braids. With them she was off the scale, but I caught her in transition one day. Her head was half done. The natural half was unhealthy. No, let me explain in detail, so you do not think I hate nappy hair. I have never seen hair that looked like this. It was uneven, split ends everywhere and she was bald in some spots. Truth be told, she never should have let me see her like that. It eliminated her from serious contention. She was too sick.

---

[286] I have met women who have never experienced an orgasm. And felt compelled to help them out.

[287] Vitiligo is a pigmentation disorder in which melanocytes (the cells that make pigment in the skin) create white patches on different parts of the body.

She and Sweet Bread became close. They were a trip together, always scheming. One day they decided to bust in my room and attack me with pillows. I was naked. Fooled Me stopped Sweet Bread from entering the room. After she had ushered Sweet Bread down the stairs she came back in the room, then dropped to her knees. She was good, but not good enough to make me come. I bent her over the window seal that overlooked the living room and had sex with her while Sweet Bread looked on from downstairs, after about 5 minutes Sweet Bread left the apartment.

One night we tried anal. Sweet Bread had company and Fooled Me was making so much noise she had to put her face in a pillow. I ended up stopping, and after cleaning myself, I reentered her vagina. She said, "There you go." All is well that ends well. Another night we were out and she asked me to drive to a park. She performed extended oral stimulation on me. I could not come, so I asked her to exit the car. I walked her to a nearby gazebo, had her grab the table and pulled her pants down far enough to enter her from behind. Right after I came, a woman came by walking her dog. She had to know what we were doing by the way we were rearranging our clothing.

Fooled Me knocked herself out of the box. I learned that she had slept with her fair share of student aviators before me. I had a conversation with the guy who introduced us. He said, "Fooled Me can suck a golf ball through fifty feet of garden hose" She had neglected to mention this to me, even though she knew that he and I were close.

A Different Kind of South

I noticed that as one moves North, women seem to become more cosmopolitan. They "act" more sophisticated and worldly. They better fit the model of the modern urban woman. The number of professional and degreed women seems to rise proportionally with latitude.

Remember Dollar Signs from Relationships? She told me that she had never had sex like we were having. "We do it so much, I might get pregnant." "Birth control is 98% effective; you better not." She liked to be on top most of the time. The routine was to put her legs on the outside of mine then grind hard in small circles. She liked to have my penis continuously in contact with her clitoris. At the same time she cupped her hands under my butt cheeks to ensure I applied pressure when she wanted it. I am sure it was a control thing, but I did not mind just lying there conserving my energy for what I wanted.

When we had sex in the missionary position, all I had to do was penetrate her as far as I could and then be still. She would provide the motion needed for her climax. She moved her pelvis in small circles, again, keeping constant pressure on her cervix. I was more than happy to oblige by doing absolutely nothing except prevent my body's weight from restricting her movements. I always got mine anyway; why not let her enjoy it too? I always thought Dollar Signs had a homosexual streak. She was open enough about sex and had several sexual experiences with women. If she was gay, she is the male partner.

One night I was driving the ninety-minute ride to her Mother's home. She started fidgeting in her seat about 30 minutes into the drive. She then began fumbling with my seat belt. By now I knew I was going to get a treat. "What are you doing?" "Trying to get your seatbelt off," "Why?" "You smell so good; I want to suck your dick." "Yes!!!"

It is funny now to think about my sleeping on the couch in her mother's living room because we had sex in the house all the time and everyone knew it. We had a routine. Her mother always answered the door. "Where's Dollar Signs?" "She's in her room." I would go upstairs and have sex with her or she would have sex with me, depending on who was the horniest. We would even do it on the couch watching television. She would put on these elastic "Daisy Duke" gym shorts and turn her back to me. To the innocent eye, we were spooning with a blanket over us. In reality, I was having sex with her from behind in full view of any who wanted to watch.

Late one night I asked her to get on all fours on the living room floor. I mounted her in a standing position with my knees bent slightly. I wanted the house to wake up and know I was killing it from the audible noises she emitted. She said, "You are trying to get me in trouble." This was the first woman to make me come solely from oral stimulation. It took forever, but she was persistent. I remember we once exchanged oral favors in the back seat of my car driving from Atlanta. It was late, my sister was asleep and my cousin was driving. She came and it was my turn. My cousin turned on the interior lights just as I was about to…

She called me on a Sunday. I know it was Sunday because I was watching the Redskins play and someone's wife was giving me oral sex. "What are you doing?" "Getting a blow job." "Don't say that!" "OK" The conversation was going fine and so was everything else, except the game. The Skins made a fumble and I yelled, "Shit!" My instrument of affection questioned me loud enough to be heard on the other end of the phone, "What is wrong?" "Who the hell was that?" I spent the next twenty minutes trying to convince Dollar Signs that she was hearing things. I think it worked too, but after expelling the woman, I called Dollar Signs and confessed. Have you ever heard the sound of a relationship dying?

I was so distraught that I decided to pay an unexpected visit the following weekend. I walked in to a lukewarm reception. I figured she was still pissed about the phone incident and blew it off. She did not immediately take me upstairs to satisfy our biological urges; instead, she went upstairs alone. I followed shortly afterwards to find her hanging up the phone. This set off red flags… "Danger Will Robinson" She sat on the couch and told me that someone was coming over and that she had tried to call him to cancel, but that he was already on the way. I could hear, "Who the hell was that?" echo in my brain. The guy came and was dismissed with, "I am sorry; my boyfriend's here." Have you ever heard the sound of a dead relationship? I remember having sex with her once more, but the purity of the union was not there. It was just sex and we both knew it. I have not communicated with her since.

The Mrs. was married. Women are a trip. One day she came over by herself uninvited and unexpected, but I knew what she wanted. Women know just what to say, "Can I suck your dick?" Is that a trick question? The Mrs. is the woman who had her mouth around my penis while I was talking to Dollar Signs. She had two children and a husband. Eventually I decided to cut her off, but not before I got the number of her husband's twin sister. I had seen her picture and wanted to meet/bed her. I did both and got my own 8 x 10.

Accommodating was like chocolate and strawberries. She was the most beautiful charcoal woman in the world and had very defined East African features. I cannot remember where we met, but I am glad we did. She was a country girl, simple in every way but she had a classy disposition. Her body was Venus in human form. We had great sex and a good relationship. In the years I lived in her city, she did not trip too much when I had other women. She even slept with one of my friends. It was a double revenge tactic. She wanted to hurt me and so did he. I licked his baby's mama. She had men on and off during our time together. What made her special was the fact that she did very erotic things.

Once she came to my home in an ankle length leather trench coat, CFMPs[288] and nothing else. I got suspicious when she would not let me take her coat. I thought, "I was going to get a treat." She was there for the sex. I had not seen her a while, new boyfriend. She straddled me on the couch and half fucked me. She had her eyes closed and was shaking her head side to side. What was she saying "No," to? "Give it to me," I protested. "No!" she said. "Come on, you can't save it all for him." It took a half an hour about she let go eventually.

Accommodating was pleasing in bed and I was more than happy to reciprocate. She did not like to do it on all fours or from behind. She said it hurt. I thought it was supposed to hurt, sometimes. She also did not mind taking nude pictures. I still have them and she still turns me on. We communicate once or twice a year. She has a daughter now and has never been married. She confessed to me recently that she wished that we could have had a child. I thought about it once or twice as well, but Accommodating was not college material; I would always out earn her and this is a point of contention in many relationships.

Mental caught my attention while bending over to get something out of the back seat of her car. How animalistic is that? I told her that much later, "I saw that ass and had to get to know you." We had a plutonic relationship for almost two years. I liked her honesty and zest for life, not to mention that I knew she was hell in the sack. The way she moved told me as much. She was like a cat, graceful, proud and noble with just enough attitude about her to keep the flies away. She also had more courage than most males I know.

Frequently she would cry on my shoulders about the male in her life. I was patient and would give advice, if she asked, but mostly I would listen. At first I did not know what she wanted, and then I waited for confirmation. She would always tell me, "If you know the things he made me do..." Then she would get this blank look on her face. It was spooky. She had a demon inside of her and I knew it.

Isabel was very attractive. She had the body and the looks to dismiss the strongest restraint, but she did not have much formal education. A fellow college alumnus, Married, brought her over my house one weekend. I was forever entertaining and this weekend was no exception. My only question was why did she bring a beautiful woman around me? It was like a preliminary look before a decision had to be made. I got confirmation when Isabel and I locked eyes. They do not lie. She flinched a little and smiled approvingly. I smiled back. There you have it. She thought I was nice looking and knowing my qualifications before hand, I was "In like Flynn." if I did not screw it up.

---

[288] CFMPs (come fuck me pumps): high heel stilettos with angle straps.

Mental was at the house when they arrived and introductions were made. I was completely taken by Isabel. Because I dated almost exclusively African-American women, I thought of her as a treat. "Come to me said the spider to the fly." I guess Mental got wind of the flirtatious atmosphere, because she attacked Isabel. Her verbal witticisms went from heritage, to wanna–be "Sista", to "Chiquita Banana". I was shocked and tried to play referee, but it seemed the more I tried to stop her from attacking Isabel, the more salvos she released. It was the first time I knew for sure that Mental wanted more than just friendship (there is nothing like competition to spur people on). I thought blows would follow, but Married and Isabel left before it came to that.

Married and I talked afterwards and she told me that Isabel asked her, "Would you fuck him?" "What did you say?" "I said I would" "Did you tell her you had?" "No!" "Ask her if I can have her number." "She told me to give it to you." Isabel and I met at a club a few nights later. Isabel and I flirted over a game of pool. When a woman does not know how to hold the pool cue on purpose, am I not obliged to accept the invitation?

I followed her home that night. I was intrigued by the fact that she said, "I have never had a male induced orgasm." It may have been a challenge or an invitation, but who cared; I was about to be "knee deep". She got her orgasm after about 40 minutes of oral clitoral stimulation but my neck was a wreck for two days. I got my man. [289]

Isabel had a freaky side. One weekend her bisexual friend came to visit. That night the girlfriend drove as Isabel and I had sex in the back of her topless jeep. I had Isabel take off her bikini before we left. All that was left was this shear beach blouse. Her pink nipples showed right through. The effect was perfect. I do not know how many accidents, pregnancies or arguments we caused that night, but it was easy to see that every car or truck that passed us saw exactly what we were doing. It is hard to miss a woman straddling a male with her breast in his mouth, or two legs perched on the back of the headrests with a head between them. If that was not enough, the fact that the driver was not paying too much attention to the road put it over the top. Isabel was fun, but we had no future together; she did not fit my profile. I would have to carry her and I was struggling to keep up appearances as it was. Besides, she was seeing someone else as well.

Mental and I finally had sex when I invited her away for the weekend. She told me later, that she came with the intention of "giving me some pussy". Was it a coincidence that this happened after Isabel came into the picture? We picked up her friend, Narda, a Somali beauty and lawyer. My cousin tried his best, but he and I knew she thought she was out of his financial league. After a night of debauchery that started at Tacoma Station, got wild at Republic Gardens[290] (where we were treated to the velvet roped because of the beautiful women who accompanied us) and ended with me dropping Narda off at her place, Mental and I ended up having sex on my cousin's living room floor. I lay there next to her trying to sleep, but my penis would not let me; I could not lie on my stomach. I rolled over three or four different times trying to get comfortable. To make matters more unbearable, the sounds emanating from my cousin's bedroom did not help

---

[289] Got my man or got his or her man (slang): referring to bounty hunters and rewards.
[290] Popular night Club in northwest Washington, D.C.

the situation. He had knocked on his neighbor's door when we arrived and she obliged[291]. By now they were making enough noise to be heard.

Mental and I began to fondle. I went down on her or tried to. She said, "No" I asked, "Why not?" Her answer both shocked and delighted me. "Because you're going to want some pussy afterwards." I was thinking, "You damn right I am." I remember having to bite the inside of my cheek to keep from laughing aloud. That initial "No" held me off for about 30 seconds. Her body language betrayed her mouth. The primal side in me responded to the more ancient language being spoken. There are not that many men who willingly give oral sex and fewer still who enjoy it. Furthermore, there are not that many who are good and she was not about to miss an opportunity to answer the questions she had about my performance in bed.

Afterwards, she said that we could forget the whole thing if I wanted to, but I knew that would have flown like a brick. I should have paid the price right then and there by saying, "OK", but the sex was better than I expected. On a scale from one to ten, first time being factored in, it was a nine. She liked to raise her legs and rock back and forth. Besides I wanted to know what her ex-boyfriend made her do that she was so ashamed. She loved to hang out, party, talk shit and she was a freak. I remember watching her play with her exposed breasts while I fingered her privates. Did I mention that we were on Interstate-95 at the time? I wish I had a video camera.

She was blunt as hell, orally gifted (but would not swallow) and on many occasions tried to throw salt in my game. I remember during one of my parties she went around and asked each woman in the place if she was involved with me intimately. She then proceeded to try to get me to sit down to talk with her and one of the women who had said "yes." I was having sex with a number of women in the party but no one else was causing a scene. "No. 'WE' do not need to talk!" I declined graciously and went about my business, which was to stay the hell away from her.

Loyalty ended up being stationed in the same city as I. She came to a couple of parties I had and saw that I had several girlfriends, but she still showed me quite a bit of attention. We did a few things like horseback riding, but I was not interested in playing the courting game. We knew each other well enough to jump in the sack at will. She came over one sunny afternoon because the sun had ruined her car's paint job and I swore to her that I had a product that would restore the color. I used a rubbing compound and then colored wax. It took the better part of the day to do the job, but Loyalty was a friend, so I did not look at it as labor. Later that night we ended up talking about the past over drinks. She was straddled across the arm of the couch and I stood in front of her. Her head stood level with my chest. She looked like a cowgirl balancing herself on a saddle. My shirt was off by now. The dying fire provided just enough light for me to see its reflection in her eyes. Somehow and for some reason, we kissed. She did not want to. I stopped, just like I had on several previous occasions that night, but then she kissed my nipple. "Do you have a condom?" When I relocated, we lost contact, probably my fault. I do not know where she is, but would love to get back in contact with her.

Back to Mental: our relationship was marred with other women. Isabel actually knocked on my door the morning after to retrieve her workout shoes. I saw them after she left the night

---

[291] The same neighbor who hid my sidearm during the Crazy incident.

before and thought at that moment, "Take these shoes to her now" That first inner voice is never wrong. Instead I put them in the closet beside the front door because I did not want Mental to see them when she arrived.

The next morning I heard the doorbell, but was shaving. I asked Mental to answer the door. She came back and said, "Someone is here for you." I went to see who it was. Isabel was standing behind the closed door. She retrieved her shoes without a word, but the look said enough. It was the look of a relationship dying. I bought her an onyx and diamond ring trying to perform CPR (I did not have Kobe Bryant's money).

Did I mention how crazy Mental was? Once I had to call the police on her because she would not leave my apartment. What would you do if someone would not leave your apartment? I was not about to put a hand on her. That makes me wrong on many fronts and that is what she wanted. Our justice system and moral codes say it is wrong to use force against a woman. I could see through her plan to hurt me, and it involved getting me so upset that I struck her. What she would do then, no one but she knows. She was pushing all the right buttons. Some of you out there know. If you have saved negative observations for a particular moment, then came out with both barrels blazing, you know to what I am referring, *the straw that broke the camel's back.*

Do not become upset with me. I am not married. That was my domicile and sanctuary. No one has the right to make me feel uncomfortable in a place where I bear full responsibility, unless they are my partner and share that responsibility with me because "we need to talk". "You heard me the first time: G-e – t t-h-e f-u-c-k o-u-t!"

The dispatcher on the phone could not believe that a male was calling 9 1 1 on a woman. I was not afraid; I was covering my ass, beating her to the punch. I told him, "I have an irate woman in my house that will not leave." "What is the problem, sir?" "I said I have a crazy woman in my house that will not leave." … "Can't you hear her?" … "OK, she's leaving now" Because the carpet was wet and she was stomping, she slipped and fell out the door. I know it sounds strange, but her hate and anger manifested itself through acrobatics. She went totally horizontal and fell on the landing just outside of my condominium. She looked like she was lying in bed on her side if you forget the way she bounced off the treated wood.

I could not help but let out a laugh. It was funny as shit, but I really did not mean to laugh aloud. I actually put my hand over my mouth to stop from being heard but it was too little, too late. One audible chirp came out and she went ballistic. "Oh no. She's coming back." She tried to come at me but I was using the couch as a go between. She looked at the dining room table. I stacked CDs, a television, stereo equipment and other items there while I cleaned the living room. She tried to push them to the floor. "Thanks for your help, operator." "No problem. I'm glad it worked out." "Me too." This is the same woman who later interrupted a video game competition between my cousin and me with, "Hurry up. I want to suck your dick." My cousin looked at me as if to ask, "What you gonna do?" I looked back at him and I said, "You win."

By far her most memorable moment with me was in front of the fireplace. I tied her up. I had her spread eagle with each limb secured to a piece of furniture. The blindfold hid the fact that I had retrieved a vibrator, a feather and some lubricant. The gag in her mouth made it impossible for her to speak or protest. She gave me prior permission to do whatever I wanted to. She later told me it took her three days of washing her hair to get all of the come out. She always makes reference to that night whenever we talk of sex. What is it about romance, seduction and eroticism that spark interest in the female psyche? I wonder if it is the same as for men.

This is the same woman who once came to visit me (after all of the above) while my live-in girlfriend was out of town. We crossed the border that weekend, bought Cuban cigars, were caught by customs trying to smuggle them back into the US and had sex at every opportunity. To give you an idea of what she was like, I suggested that we return the next day and buy some more cigars; she was game if I was. I hurt her so many times that I cannot remember. It was not on purpose. I just did not want to be married or monogamous. I have this strange ability to maintain emotional distance and still have sex. She could not do it. She was starting to confuse good sex with love. One night she was on top of me. She was not on birth control so I always withdrew. This particular night I told her I was about to come and that she needed to get off. She said, "No." I had to push her off. She was ovulating. That scared me.

I have known Cotton for years and I never looked at her as a sexual partner until we were brought together later in life. She was delicate emotionally and willing to please anyone who showed her affection. She needed much more than I could give her so we never got past the sex. A memorable moment came the night she sucked me until I came. She is one of four women who have done that. I was driving her home and she decided that she was going to give me a treat. It was good, but we arrived at her house before I reached climax. I told her where she was; she stopped sucking long enough to say, "Keep driving. I want to finish." I drove around the neighborhood very slowly. She drained me dry, but she did not swallow-disqualified. When I last saw her we went out, got drunk and did a threesome with Quick Silver. The funny thing about it is that neither of them was my primary target that night: I was after someone else, but two birds in the hand are better than one probable. The three of us ended up in my bed.

As Quick Silver laid drunk on the bed, she began calling my name over and over. I was busy rolling a joint. I even told her, "Shut up; I know what you want." She repeatedly kept calling my name. It was getting on my nerves, so I went to the bed and in one quick motion, pulled her elastic band shorts and panties completely off. The look in her eyes was classic: surprise mixed with arousal. She looked at Cotton then back at me. "What are you doing? There's someone in the room." was what she was thinking. I was thinking, "So what; you called; I am here." Cotton said, "If you two want to be alone, I'll leave." "No. Do not go anywhere." was my reply, "I am just going to give her what she wants."

I kept switching positions. I started with missionary, then straight oral, then "69". While I was licking between her legs I felt a hand on the back of my head moving forcibly in circles. It took a minute for me to realize that it was Cotton's hand and not Quick Silver's. I thought, "Helloooo nurse!" I went to the bathroom, but stopped long enough to ask Cotton to take off her clothes. Quick Silver helped her. I came back to many a male's dream, two naked women waiting for me.

Picture this scene: one woman propped up by pillows supported by the headboard. Cotton was lying with the back of her head between the breasts of Quick Silver with her legs open.

Quick Silver was behind her fondling Cotton's breasts with one hand and massaging Cotton's genitals with the other. I tried to suck the pink out of Cotton while my partner in crime sucked her breasts. It was a good night even though I did not have an orgasm[292]. I have not seen Cotton since then, but I will.

Somebody Love Me Please was a friend of a friend. She had huge firm breasts and a matching ass topped with a small waist, but she had husbandry and children on the brain. I met her on an all night booze cruise. Men kept buying her drinks[293]. They fattened up that frog for another snake. I thought she was drunk, but she was not. I wanted to make sure I was not taking advantage of her, so I asked if she was sure she wanted to have sex with me that night. She responded by putting her tongue down my throat. Guess what? She had a boyfriend.

Somebody Love Me Please was from a well to do family; I got along with both her mother and father. I really could not understand why she had worked as a stripper. It did not make any sense to me, but I was reaping the benefits-provocative gyrations. Young and easy to control, she liked sex and once complained, "I am using my vibrator more than you are using me." I had been neglecting her because I had three or four other romantic interests and she knew it. Once she burst into my bedroom after one of my parties to find me in bed with three other women. She said, "I thought you said you were going to sleep with me tonight" Everyone in the bed looked at each other and we then simultaneously burst out laughing. Did I mention I was stimulating one of the girls with my finger when this happened? Did I mention Quick Silver was in the bed as well (Quick Silver and two other women who happened to be sisters)? Did I mention that my cousin and one of my fraternity brothers did the same thing ten minutes later? They did not think it was fair. I asked, "You guys want them in here?" They said, "No." almost in unison.

I liked to use half penis thrusts on her because she would always say, "Please don't tease me." in the most sincere sweet voice. My ego heard, "Put it deeper." I also liked to have sex with her outside on my patio. She would grab her ankles while standing and allow me to try to find China. Why did I let her go? She was not going to stay thin forever, and more importantly, wanted to get married. She did get married – twice, and has two children to show for it. She will probably marry again.

Remember Crazy, the gunslinger, from Chapter V? She was a young, thin, high "yella" wanna-be-hustler. I was giving a party and was out inviting female talent. She was one of those who chose to come. This is the same party where Mental acted up. Crazy wore a pink cat suit and I knew she was going to stay the night. When the party was over, she stayed to help clean up along with two other women. Crazy stayed the longest. We attempted to have sex that night, but I could not get an erection. I drank too much alcohol. I told her as much and she took the condom off. It did not help, but not to worry; I made it up to her the next morning with a condom.

Our relationship was based totally on sex. There was no girlfriend/ boyfriend thing. Though she tried to convince me that she was the one, there was always an ex-boyfriend in the picture mad at me. She had other men, and I had other women and she lived on the generosity of men. I

---

[292] It is not necessary that I have an orgasm to feel satisfied during sex. There are times when I only what to play with women. As long as they come, not all women give a damn if I do or not.
[293] Women have it good. You all can go out broke, eat, get drunk and get laid.

was on a selfish quest of pleasure and her being very limber helped me find just what I was seeking. I enjoyed placing her in the *full baked chicken*[294] and listening to her scream, "Yes." It was a power trip really good for the ego. I looked around for someone to high five that night. We came together when we wanted to be satisfied physically. She was fun to be with, but she shot herself in the foot when she asked me to pay her bills; disqualified. I do not do "Pri$e-Tag-Roman$e". I have no idea where Crazy is now, but last time I sexed her she was driving some guy's pimped out ride.

I know what some of you may be thinking, "You are a dog," or "I would do the same thing." I may have several partners at the same time, but I do not claim to be monogamous, and I certainly do not flirt with women when I go out on a date. I do not care if my sexual partner has sex with someone else. As a matter of fact, I assume that women have more than one prospect and that not all are honest. I know it sounds pessimistic, but experience has taught me that women often lie first, faster and better than men.

Almost Perfect was the poster child for a good girl. She was cute as a button with the body of a cheerleader. The short Catholic schoolgirl skirt that she was wearing showed off her long athletic legs. All I could think about was the full baked chicken. I wanted her the first time I saw her. She stood out from the other girls standing with her arms wrapped around herself as though she was bored with the whole scene. She was tapping her toe impatiently. Her friend was dancing and having a good time; she was not. It looked as if she really did not want to be there. My fraternity brother knew her, so I insisted that he introduce us. We started dating and eventually had sex.

Good girl spewed from her every pore. Her enjoyment of sex seemed limited to the missionary position; she hated doggy style. She said her cervix was misaligned somehow. The "Full Treatment" was code for oral sex and she gave it like a present on my birthday, Christmas and maybe New Years, if the champagne flowed freely enough. She gave me an 8 x 10 of her and 50 smaller professional photos. I thought that was peculiar. I do not have that many photos of my mother. I was not impressed sexually, but stayed with her nonetheless. She was giving, thoughtful and honest. She had a corny, but funny sense of humor and I loved her smile. I guess I satisfied some dark urge she had. I had to be like a walk on the wild side for her.

Once I asked her to drive on the return end of a weekend trip. It was summer and she wore shorts that showed off her long legs. I took my seatbelt off and hers as well. Ms. Goodie-Two-Shoes was about to get a treat. There is something very exciting about having or inducing an orgasm while driving, be patient. We had a three-hour drive and I was bored. I thought I would play with Almost Perfect's privates until she told me to stop. I did not think that she would let or could take my tickling her clitoris while she was driving. I not only underestimated her, but also misdefined "good girl", again.

It was she who suggested she take her panties and shorts off. She just did not know how to do it without having not to pull over. I showed her. "Put the cruise control on" "Move the seat back;

---

[294] Full baked chicken: sexual position where you pin your partner's knees on both sides beside their head. You do this by placing your hands behind their knees and supporting your weight using the resistance of their legs for support. The more limber your partner, the better the sex. It resembles a baked chicken.

I'll drive from my side, but keep one foot on the brake and your eyes on the road" You can imagine the rest. At one point, I had to stop and question why she was driving over those small reflectors that warn you to get back on the road. "You alright?" "Yeah." "Concentrate." I looked up; we were doing over 90 MPH when she came.

Our sexual moment of glory came on a weekend I flew to her town with a student. I landed on Friday night and she was waiting on the flight line with a six-pack of Corona in a cooler. That was a welcome sight after a ten-hour flight day. During one of our many couplings that weekend, I laid her on her left side. I placed her outstretched left leg between mine and put her right leg at a 90° to her torso. I was on my knees. Her right hip pointed to the ceiling and her left hip pointed toward the bed. If you can picture a position somewhere halfway between on all fours and missionary, you are on the right track.

I was vertical from the waist up and resting my body weight on my legs, which were folded so that the bottoms of my feet were touching their respective buttock. I placed my right hand on her right cheek and upright hip, as I would grip a football or a basketball and my left hand behind her right knee. As I pushed and pulled with my arms, I applied additional pressure by pushing forward and withdrawing with my pelvis in synchronization to the rhythm my arms provided. This caused her body to rock up and down and back and forth at the same time. Remember I am sideways. The longer we went, the faster the pace. By the end, I felt like I was in the home stretch of the Kentucky Derby, nothing left to give, but the prize was so close if I could just hold on one more minute. When I was done, I sat slumped and at gravity's mercy. She only pivoted her neck to look me in the eye, "You the 'Man'." I slid sideways to the bed and fell fast asleep.

I spent the entire weekend in bed. All we did was have sex, sleep and bathe. We also went to see *Phantom of the Opera* and ate (tray service in bed); I guess that is why I was there. I saw her mother once the entire weekend, when I said hello. She was in the house, but I guess the bedroom was out of bounds. She accompanied me to my new duty station. We drove down and she stayed for two days. We tried to maintain a long distance relationship. Well, she did. I was having sex with everything that moved and she probably knew it. It would be no different in any other city.

The last time I saw her was when Career Crasher came by the house, unannounced, knocked on the door, then the bedroom window and caused a scene because I had company. She was delivering a birthday present. This woman was married. Almost Perfect had seen enough. She took a taxi to the airport while I was at work and I have not seen her since. I am sorry I hurt Perfect. She was a good woman, but was not the marrying type and I needed a better sex partner or a more understanding one.

I Have a Good Job

What is it about a nice car and a well paying job that makes a male more attractive?

Bell was a Southern girl who wanted nothing more than to be married and loved. She was not exactly my type, but I had sex with her anyway because she was so pushy. It was a mistake. She acted like she had never experienced what I like to term "good lovin'". What is up with males?

There are too many unsatisfied and sexually repressed women. The moment she told me she had never had an orgasm, I knew she was in trouble and I would have issues leaving the relationship.

Why? Because I make two guarantees if I sleep with a woman: I will not do anything she does not allow and she will reach climax. She was hesitant about letting me eat her the first time, but she came in spite of her apprehension. I asked her, "Why not?" "I do not like that." "Have you ever tried it?" "No, but it's nasty." "Lay back and if it feels bad, tell me to stop." After that, getting her to open her legs was as simple as making a phone call or being in the same room. She confused love with good sex. She was one of those girls who liked to suck long enough, but did not want come in her mouth. She never said it, but actions speak louder than words.

One night I went over to her apartment. This particular evening, it was the central meeting spot. Bell was running late as usual. She had not even showered by the time the last of our party had arrived. She went to take a shower and I jumped her in the bedroom while she was still wrapped in a towel. I laid her on the bed, ripped off the towel and began to eat her. She whispered with some anxiety, "The doors open!" I replied, "So what!" After she came, I said, "Too bad I don't have a condom or I would finish." She instantly produced one from under her pillow. I left to rejoin the rest of the group. I am sure someone saw what I did, but that was exactly what I wanted; it only added to the fun.

Bell and I were never girlfriend and boyfriend. We were more like sex partners. She knew that I had other sexual interests. The city was small enough and the African-American community was even smaller. She once wrote whore on the back windshield of my car because she saw it parked in the lot of a rival's apartment complex. She admitted as much later in the relationship. Another time she came over my house very late and was drunk. It was a classic booty stop (no preceding phone call). She went into my bedroom and then she laid on the bed with her legs open (she had on a mini skirt). I was more than willing to service her, but I was in the process of ascertaining why I had unexpected sex when a knock came at the front door and then at the window. It was Career Crasher. She obviously saw Bell's car in the driveway.

I told Career Crasher the truth about what was going on and asked her if she wanted to stay the night. She said, "Yes." I demanded that we have sex and that she spend the entire night. She agreed. I told her to have a seat on the couch and then I went to the bedroom to ask Bell to leave. She was pissed. I have never seen a woman sober up so fast. When she passed Career Crasher, she said to both of us, "You are going to get into trouble fucking around with married women." There was serious venom in her voice. I should have known.

How right she was. I now think she and her friend, the one who introduced me to Career Crasher, instigated the issues I had with Career Crasher's husband. During my Admiral's Mast[295], statements from Bell and the woman who introduced us were not read, but I read them. They both screwed me. Bell's motive was revenge. I was no longer having sex with her. I never did figure out why her friend screwed me. It was entirely my fault, I showed bad judgment because of sex, but I learned that women or people in general, will go out of their way to get some payback. I do not want anyone to get the wrong idea. Bell was a good person. She helped

---

[295]Admiral's Mast: Similar to a trial without a jury except the ruling officer was an Admiral and not a judge. I was on an Admiral's staff; therefore he presided over my trial.

me out when I was in a tight spot. I am only sorry that I could not give her what she wanted and thought she needed.

I was introduced to Anytime-Anyway in the VIP lounge of my favorite late night hang out. It was the strangest introduction I had ever had. We shook hands and she ran off. I do mean ran. I was thinking I had done something wrong to her or one of her friends in the past and not remembered. Later in the evening I cornered her and then asked what the problem was. She told me she had to leave before she wet her panties. "You had to go to the bathroom?" "No." Damn! This was going to be fun. I definitely had to get her number so that we could pursue this invitation further.

I did, but she told me she was living with her boyfriend. I told her to call me when she had time to talk. That was code for call me as soon as you can so we can get this show on the road. She did. We had phone sex. I told her everything I wanted to do to her. I started with a hot bubble bath and candles and ended with my penis in her mouth. Her heavy panting told me she approved of my plans and would be in my bed soon enough. I hoped that maybe, just maybe, she was touching herself. It was perfect; she had a mate. To me that meant no commitment or drama, and that my function was to be her boy toy, a role I was quite comfortable with. Let the games begin.

She finally came over and I fulfilled my verbal promises of foreplay to the letter. I bathed her and massaged her afterwards. I made sure it was slow and deliberate. I grazed the sensitive areas lightly as if by accident. It was a seduction after all. I kissed her from neck to toe before licking the right place until I thought she would burst and then I entered. I was careful and treated her delicately. Time seems to fly when you make slow love. She turned onto her stomach, placed pillows under her tummy and perched her butt in the air. Face down, ass up; she was following the script as perfectly as I was. During the phone sex I told her to flip over when she was ready to be "fucked".

Time to have real sex; she wanted it and so did I[296]. I separated her cheeks as far apart as I could to make sure I was going as deep as nature would allow. Right before climax, I withdrew. "Come on." I guess the sense of urgency in my voice accurately conveyed the meaning and the urgency. She was no stranger to this. She did not swallow; instead she massaged me and simply allowed my discharge to fall from her outstretched tongue onto the bed. I thought, "Damn, now I am going to have to change the sheets. You should have told me you were going to do that; I would have had a towel."

We continued our affair the entire time we lived near each other. She came over whenever she felt like having sex or being intimate. One night she drove me to a private waterside hideaway and did what I can only describe as "humped the shit out me". It was in the front seat of her car (I usually have to come up with ideas like that). I had never had a woman do me like that. She took one leg out of her pants, pulled her panties to the side and mounted me.

---

[296] Sex, love making and fucking are different. You can have sex without making love. Fucking is selfish sex and some people like to be fucked or like doing the fucking. A single sexual encounter can contain all three. I usually make love to women I am fond of, but it usually turns into sex near the end of the copulation because I know that I have satisfied my partner and I have to fuck to reach climax.

The things that came out of her mouth almost scared me. "You want this pussy?" When I answered, "You know I do." It was so humble and soft I felt like the woman in the relationship. She gave me a vicious stroke with every syllable she spoke "You (up) bet- (down) - ter (up) act (down) like (up) it (down) then (up) and (down) fuck (up) me (down) good (up)" I have never had a dominant woman experience quite like that. Imagine the original "Exorcist" without cuts or the devil. I have had some women fake it and pretend to be dominant, but this was the real thing. She was not role-playing; she was throwing it on me and did not care. It was the first time a woman fucked me! She was being selfish and commanding, doing what she wanted. I enjoyed it. I wish more women were that sexually liberated. What made it so memorable was the total reversal of her usual subservient role.

I called her once just before Perfect's flight landed. I told her I wanted her to come over and give me some before my girlfriend came to town. She was in my driveway 10 minutes later. I started undressing her as soon as she entered the house. Anything less would have been out of character. I really liked Anytime-Anyway. She was straight up and honest. She asked for what she wanted and did not change her objectives midway through our relationship. We did not have any drama. That is a lot more than I can say about most. We could talk about anything and frequently did.

She always said, "Please do not come inside of me" when had sex. The look on her face was almost begging and her voice was like a child's. It freaked me out the first time. I could not figure out why she always did that; I think I have a clue, but I am not a shrink.

I had been spying Silky Slim for months. She did not come out much, but when she did she was nicely dressed and carried herself with a sense of elegance and grace. Silky was built like a model and being just as symmetrically perfect in the face. Her smile could melt butter and her long legs gave birth to impure thoughts. She was the type of woman who looked like she liked to make men choose her and then made them work for it.

I ended up in her bed Christmas Eve. She would not do anything but touch for hours. I was ready to leave and spend Christmas where I had accepted an invitation earlier. She wanted to touch me in all the right places, but restricted my touching to above the waist and anywhere but the breasts. I reciprocated, "Don't touch my penis."

What kind of game was she playing? She kept touching my penis anyway. I had to tell her four or five times not to touch me. She would stop for a moment and then start stroking my already awake and interested penis again. Fine, if she wanted to play, I was the one. I let her play with my penis as much as she wanted. Pretty soon she was rubbing it against the lips of her vagina. "Do you want to stick your long shaft in my pussy?" That sounded like it came from the script of some B rated porn movie. I told her, "I just want to stick the head in."

After I got inside of her completely, I noticed that she was watching us in a full-length mirror angled to overlook the bed. I looked in her eyes through the mirror's reflection and told her, "Now tell me to stop". She kept watching me with that blank face and searching eyes. That was kinky. I think I did her four times that day, always with her looking in the mirror. It did not matter if I returned her gaze or not. I came outside to find "*whore*" written in the thin film of dew

245

that had formed on the back windshield of my car. Oh well, you are what you eat. I suspected something was amiss because Silky Slim's phone kept ringing that morning. Whoever it was would not say anything and had the smarts to block the call so that no one could *69 them. I found out later it was Bell.

I slept with Silky Slim on and off. Her claim to "fake" was she did not do oral sex. It is a strange thing about small towns; you get to know a woman's reputation before you ever meet them. Somebody before you had probably already been there. Males like to talk about their conquests. Silky Slim told me with some sense of pride, that she had dated a guy I knew, but "I did not suck his dick!" That just gave me another mission to fulfill. I went so far as to tell her this. She said it would not happen.

I ran into her in a club one night and we ended up leaving together. She was tipsy. While I sat on her couch she knelt on the floor in front of me and began to play with my zipper. She laughed and said, "I almost sucked your dick." Then she stripped down to nothing, took me out on her balcony and we 69ed. I told her later, "I thought I heard you say you don't suck dick." She just smiled. Silky Slim was one of those women for whom you had to pack a lunch when you went to have sex with her. She would go as long as you wanted to and as many times as you dared.

One night I decided to up the ante. I had her get on all fours facing her mirror. My tongue went up her butt and she let out a banshee sound. After 30 seconds or so, she fell forward on the bed and told me she could not take it. I misinterpreted what she meant and replied, "We do not have to have sex." To my surprise and delight she said, "I did not say all that. I am not ready for your tongue in my ass; it's too much" What is that about? I thought the objective of sex was to feel good. How can it be too good or too much to take? I only stopped having sex with her when I moved out of town. I only regret not allowing her the opportunity to live out a fantasy she had mentioned. What was it? Nothing special, it was a control fantasy, a power trip. She wanted to tie me to her headboard in a seated position and have her way with me.

Career Crasher was a natural beauty who had a killer smile and really nice breasts (real). Her (real) long flowing hair was icing on the cake. I was hooked. It did not matter that I was involved with Bell, Shaquana, and Perfect at the time. I wanted her right then and there.

An acquaintance of Bell's introduced us. By the end of the night, we were kissing. She told me she was visiting from out of town and was a college student. Later that night, the same woman who introduced us told me she was married. I remember saying, "I do not give a fuck." She told that to the investigating officer of my Admiral's Mast. This contradicted what Career Crasher told me. Bell made it a point to reconfirm Career Crasher's marital status. "Damn she's married and did not tell me," is what I thought to myself. I had a decision to make. She was married and did not want me to know it. Why? I surmised that she was interested. I wanted her, but should not risk having sex with a married woman because the Navy frowned on such behavior, especially from its officers. What to do?

I did not see her for another month and a half, but when I did, we sealed our fates. She was married to an enlisted sailor. I knew better, but as I said, I was hooked. I committed adultery again. I looked at it as just sex. She was married, but she crossed the love line and became possessive. That is what I deserved for knowing so much about the female anatomy and being too passionate.

Career Crasher was so sexually repressed that she was shy about taking her clothes off and said she did not perform oral sex. When I pinned her arms to the bed and forced my tongue on her vaginal lips, her body said something different. I am no rapist. If I lick a clitoris and the vagina begins to discharge fluid, it likes what I am doing. My tongue never met a clitoris that did not like it. I do not care what a scheming mouth says, bodies frequently betray them. The body speaks untold truths when your tummy quivers. The little bumps that form around your nipples tells me the body is aroused. The rising temperature of the abdominal area does not lie. The skin in that same area overflows with blood. It swells. I have seen the transformation many times; it is sexual arousal. The symptoms are clear. So please do not tell me you do not like it. Comments like that make me think you have issues with sex and then I want to know why? I am not a shrink and it is just sex.

Career Crasher sometimes came to my home unannounced to see if I was alone. Another car in the driveway was easy to see and she usually knew to whom it belonged. If there was a car, it did not stop her from knocking on the door and if I did not respond at the door, she would bang on the window of my bedroom. She did this three times. Once she followed me to the grocery store and acted as if she wanted to run me over in the parking lot because I was with another woman. She followed me and waited until I had finished shopping. When I exited I heard higher than normal revolutions of a car engine getting closer, I looked up to see her car coming straight at me. She applied the brakes about 5 feet from me. I looked at her through the front windshield and saw that she was crying. That scared me. Not the fear of being hit by a car, but the fact that she was so attached that she would do something like that. It was an indication of her misinterpreting and not listening to what I wanted, or a mental disorder. I would have been a pancake had she not stopped. I did not even see it coming. I was not as mad with her as I was with myself for not foreseeing this turn of events.

Damn, not another one! I reminded her that she was married and that I was not. I saw that she did not care if her husband found out. There were several other guys who wanted to sample this jewel. Some of them knew her husband, but that did not stop them from trying. She was that attractive. The only night I kissed her in public, they saw me, and the word got to her husband. The word had been getting to him from various sources and for various reasons. Thank goodness I was being transferred.

That could have been the end of it, except I told her where I was being stationed (she called me from her home phone at the Officer's Quarters to my new duty station and it was used against me) and wanted to see her again. The night before I left, she mounted me and fucked me for the first time. Before this we either did it missionary position with me practically fighting for the sex or she would get on top and hold back. Remember I said she was repressed. This particular night she got on top and rode me like a pro. She said, "Ohhhh, you ain't going nowhere", let out a scream and said it again. Who was this? That was the best sex I have ever had with her. She sat on my pelvic area. The only part of her body that moved was her hips. They moved backward and forward, maybe four inches total. I had to stay in a half way in position (back arched so that she would not obtain total penetration on her down stroke) because she had a shallow vagina.

247

Once she told me, "It's not that your dick is big, it's just so long." She placed her hands on my stomach then leaned forward a little bit using this contact point as leverage to balance her gyrations. I felt the tip of my penis touching the bottom of her uterus. She liked the pressure provided by bouncing the head of my penis off the walls of the deepest part of her vagina. She called out to God and mumbled some other inaudible phrases. What a turn on. I asked myself why she was trying to make it so good. She even sucked me for the first time that night.

We saw each other whenever I was in town. I had to come back about once a month for business and she would pick me up from the airport. Once we met half way. During this visit I tried to convince her that we should end our relationship. I was seeing Housewife and she was married. I could kick myself.

I got a phone call at home on a Saturday; Housewife answered it. It was Career Crasher's husband. He acted pissed off. He said he wanted to meet me "Man to Man" to settle this. I told him he had his chance to confront me the day he followed his wife to my hotel room. I reminded him on that day he was the one who turned and walked as if he was doing something wrong.

I had gone outside to smoke shortly after Career Crasher left (I know, cigarette after sex). I noticed a male walking towards me on the landing. When our eyes met he looked at me like I was a ghost then turned and walked in the other direction. His behavior seemed so odd that I followed him, but he disappeared around a corner and down the stairs. I let it go even though that voice inside said something was wrong. My "spidey-sense" was blaring "red alert". It was her husband, but I did not know it at that time. The voice inside is never wrong.

He had no intention of settling it like a "Man". He wanted to set me up. I found out later that he had already reported my transgression to his Commanding Officer so it would not have made any difference what I did at that point. I never figured out why she turned on me, but surmised that under pressure of evidence the that her husband had gathered, she finally told that part of the truth that made me the bad guy and I had to pay for what we both did.

I want to see both of them again. I want to give her husband a fair fight, and to ask her why.

Is It Worth It

I got up to use the bathroom and my girlfriend asked me to retrieve her glasses from the bathroom counter. I used the toilet and then placed her glasses on my penis. I placed the bridge on my penis and then wrapped the temples under it and over my testicles. It looked like Mr. Potato Head. I was wearing pajamas, so it was easy to pull the elastic waistband below my testicles and still have the bottoms stay up. My top was long enough to hide the joke. When I came out she did not see the glasses in either hand. I saw the confusion on her face and knew she was going to ask, "Did you forget my glasses?" "What glasses?" She looked at me like I was crazy. "I asked you to…" I then pulled up my top. I watched her eyes traverse from my eyes to my midsection. Once she saw the glasses, it was over. She laughed so hard she cried. "You are crazy!" "Like a fox."

I have seen a mixture of women. Some think of only themselves. Some want to be paid. Some want to pay. Some genuinely like sex and others do it out of necessity. Some are afraid. Some are confused. Some are belittled. Some are used.

The southwestern United States is a cultural mixture of Hispanic, African-Americans and Caucasians that has evolved over hundreds of years of coexistence. But, like every other place I have lived, the races were divided for the most part living in defined areas and dating within their group. It was interesting to live in a society where Hispanics outnumbered even the whites.

Housewife was good looking, but I could see future weight problems, especially after a child or two. Attractions for me were her career, intelligence, honesty and sensitivity. I met her at an organizational meeting. Half the other males there were hitting on her and I was too. We were in "Few or No Black Women Land".

At the end of the meeting, she reached into her purse and pulled out the only business card she had at the time. She gave it to me through the gauntlet of outstretched hands. It was funny to see the nervous looks of five guys waiting to see who would get the card, competition at its worst. I got the card and I guess that meant I was going to get the girl too, if I did not screw it up. This is proof positive that woman pick men; after we are chosen, men can either shut up and get laid or talk themselves out of sex. I engage women. Most of their questions have little to do with you, but more to with what you can do for them.

Housewife wanted more than anything to feel safe. She said she had issues with sex and men because of an incident in her past. But, she was seeing a Marine Major[297] and I still had a lingering relationship with Career Crasher. She said she ended hers; I did not end mine. She turned out to be sexually repressed until we did a bit of experimentation. After we became confident in each other she did a presto chango, a complete sexual 180°. We did videos (she still has the tapes, I hope) and role-playing.

Her favorite was to dress up in something erotic and wear a mask. She would pretend that she was a gift from a friend (I should have such friends). I would always ask if I could do whatever I wanted, and, the programmed answer was always "yes", so I frequently did.

Picture a woman in CFMP's, clothes so freaky you have to order them through the mail and tools or toys (call them what you want). I asked her to please herself while she lay on an ottoman that I placed in front of me so I could have an unobscured view of how she touched herself. A few minutes later, I asked her to use a vibrator on herself. She asked, "Where do you want me to stick it?" I remember thinking, "If you have to ask, I have an option." "Stick it in your ass." She asked "How far up my ass?" I kept thinking, "This is getting good." I answered, "All the way."

Are you familiar with the sound that a vibrator makes when the batteries are not new and it enters a tight crevice? The motor strains to maintain the demanded setting, you can hear the frequency lower. It is like shifting to a higher gear.

---

[297] She had sex with him and he had sent her an airline ticket to get seconds.

After she prepped herself, I replaced the vibrator with the real thing. I asked, "Do you like it?" I got a labored, "Yes" in response. "Then tell me to do it harder... You're not convincing me at all. "Do it harder." "You do not mean that! You're just saying it because someone paid you?" Trying to be more convincing, "I like it; do it harder." By the end of the session, I was thrusting rather forcibly and I hope she liked it. We repeated that fantasy several times. And, every time, my visitor was dressed in a different outfit, leather, feathers, veils, masks and thongs. So I guess I was doing something right.

The end of our relationship began the night we were discussing threesomes. I started it when I bought a whore for us. It was part of our plan; the main reason we went out of the country. I did not want a professional. For me it would have been more of a fantasy with a female who wanted to do it for free and I did not see any issues getting one. Remember, this was before I figured out that women are more threatened by emotional attachment than by sex. Several other women have confirmed this fact. I can have sex with a whore for money, but I cannot have sex with a whore for free. Why? Women know other women well enough to know it "ain't" usually free.

Sex for free and for pay are physically the same. I do not pay a whore for sex. I pay them to be quiet, give me want I what at that moment physically and to leave when we are done.

Housewife was shy about it at first, sitting there in a chair as I performed oral sex with the whore on the bed, but by the end of the session, I had to fight to get some attention for myself. She was so turned on by the entire trip that I caught her rubbing her privates in a restaurant the day we were leaving. I am serious; I looked and she was rubbing her vagina through her shorts. She said that she needed to excuse herself to go to the restroom to finish. I was not going to miss this and had to accompany her to the bathroom. We were having sex a few days later and she asked me if I was thinking about our whore. I was not, but, "Yeah." "Good, fuck me like you did her."

We broke up two years later, because I was having sex with another girl. At least that is what I told myself. In actuality I overheard something that I should not have. She must have accidentally hit the send button on her cell phone while we were living together. What I heard was her contradicting the plans she and I had made to stay together.

She told me she wanted to relocate to her hometown so I got a job there. She told someone else that she planned to go overseas. This was something very different than what we had planned. I decided then and there to divest emotionally. She ended up doing just what I overheard. By far the biggest concern I had with Housewife was the fact that she was not as emotionally stable and secure as I would have liked. She cried over things that did not seem to warrant tears. Sometimes she would come home from work boohooing. Our relationship was coming to an end. I have come to recognize the divergence of individual paths. I now accept it and often welcome the change.

Housewife was going abroad the following day. We went out the night before and she wanted to do a threesome. I had no clue that she had wanted to do this and asked her why she was being so friendly with a girl she was meeting for the first time. Housewife attached herself to this woman I had spoken to in the same location several times but I never made a move on her.

She was the good friend type, but not for me. Whether or not she was interested in me, I do not know. I felt on several occasions that if I had pushed the issue, we would have end up somewhere else talking or more. When I questioned Housewife about her strange attachment to this woman, she said, "I want to do a threesome." After realizing what her plan was, I came straight out and asked the girl if she wanted to have sex with the two of us. She declined, but there was something in her eyes that I have never been able to decipher. Either she was appalled or she was very interested.

We went home and Housewife kept on talking how much she wanted to do a threesome. I asked, "Do you really want to do a threesome?" She said, "Yes!" She put two and two together, after I went out and came back with a half dressed woman. We had sex with her and my semen slid into Housewife's mouth from the other girl's vagina (use your imagination). She was hurt that I had sex with the other woman without a condom. She did not even see me do it. That was how into it she was. It was her idea to pick-up a girl that night and since we were unsuccessful at the bar, I went upstairs and grabbed a friend. I gave her what she wanted.

She insisted that she was not mad about my having sex with another woman, but my not using a condom. Their goes that brick flying again. She was pissed because I was having sex with someone else without her permission, and the condom had little or nothing to do with it. She told me, "I did not know you came inside her until your come slid down my throat" She had no issue with me having sex, but not using a condom.… When I pointed out that she had just eaten the girl and that any numbers of STDs are transmitted orally, she did not have a leg to stand on. It was not the condom. It was the infidelity, the emotional threat to her security. She did not take into account that she lied to me and was leaving the country for two years. It was over and I knew it long before she divulged her plans. I was fine with her leaving; life goes on and I was prepared.

By my way of thinking it did not get any better than that. In my eyes it is fine to have sex with anyone once the door is open. You cannot tell me with whom I must have sex once you tell me it is ok outside the relationship. When did she do this? When she told me she knew why I wanted to go out of the country and she was willing to let me go alone. I asked, "Why?" She said, "So you can fuck some foreign babe." I could not deny it. In her eyes, I was being unfaithful because she assumed emotions must have been involved for me to sleep with someone else regularly-not! It was just convenient sex. Housewife really needs to take a page out of another friend's book. This other friend told me she had an erotic dream about my calling her while I was having sex so she could listen.

Our time together ended when she left the next day. She was so distraught the night before that she demanded that I take her to her mother's home. I complied. The next morning her mother brought her back. I have no idea why; we were done as a couple as far as I was concerned. I was civil, considering all of the less than flattering words that came out of her mouth the night before. That was the last time I saw her, but we have kept in touch. I even asked her to review this work. She told me she gave up on me too soon. I already wrote that it takes a long time for boys to mature!

Sometimes, even I am ashamed of my actions when it comes to women. I met an island bombshell. Calada worked at the register. I happened to be in her line one day and she initiated general conversation. No biggie, people can be friendly and it was part of her job. The next time I purposely chose her line, she gave me a five-finger discount[298]. She did not scan all the items I had on the counter. As a matter of fact, she did not scan the most expensive item. I thought the bill was too low, but I did not say anything. I knew what it meant; she was interested and doing me a favor to let me know.

I got involved in a nightclub venture and was bar tending (I needed the money because I was supporting two people) the night she and a friend walked in. I spoke from over the bar and she did an Anytime-Anyway on me. I recognized it this time. Her eyes got big and she giggled as she ran into the bathroom with her girlfriend in tow. I guess I just got confirmation of what I knew already; I was going south of the border. She already told me she was interested at the register. I saw the ring, but I also saw her eyes. We were going to have primal sex. Calada was drunk (imagine that, I was the bartender) and stayed until we closed. I walked her and her friend to their car, but had a hell of a time getting her to get in. She wanted to have sex.

Admittedly, I did too, but I did not want to do it with her the first time while she was in that condition. It was not a hard decision, despite her grabbing my crotch and saying in front of her friend that she wanted to suck my privates. I had Housewife in bed waiting for me, and it was 3 AM. Another factor was that she was married. I graciously declined, but I gave her my phone number, stupid.

As soon as I lay down, the phone rang. It was Calada and my girlfriend was pissed. I had to lie and tell her that she got my number off the roster that hung by the bar. To be honest I did not do anything wrong yet, and I had not expected her to call me that night. I should have known right then and there that she was the type of woman who did not care about disrupting a household.

I had Calada page me. It was nothing unusual to be called or paged at any time for variety of things. I answered the page and told Housewife I had to go. I did go, but I went to Calada's house, not my job. That particular night, her husband had to work. We were in her living room on the couch talking. She was wearing a long T-shirt. Knowing this, she laid on her back with her crotch facing me. It was not an accident that I saw her panties and there was a wet spot.

It reminded me of the story my grandfather told me about the married woman who wanted him to help her move the rug. I immediately reached for her crotch and she stopped me. "Here we go again." I guess she was going to make me work. I asked her why I was there if not to have sex. I asked her what kind of game she was playing. After some discussion on the matter, I put my finger inside of her to test for smell (It is important to know the different smells of a woman. Today the wrong smell or signs of disease can kill you). She was slippery wet, no bumps or lesions. I had sex with her on the couch with her two kids upstairs. She kept saying, "Oh yes, Poppy." I had to remind her to keep the noise down. Before I came I asked her if she was on birth control. She said her tubes were tied. I came inside of her and then went home. I could not

---

[298] Five-Finger Discount: Slang for stealing.

believe that she wanted to have sex so bad that she did not think about her children coming down the stairs.

I made sure I stopped to get some gas on the way home. This is an old trick for those who have women with sensitive noses. You just sprinkle a little gas on the ground and a drop or two on your hands and then step in the gas. When you get home you smell like a gas pump, not sex and your partner will probably insist that you take a shower. I just outted a bunch of men, especially the one who taught me this trick.

She and I would meet like that once or twice a month. Sometimes she would meet me at my house at lunchtime. It was on one of these occasions that I broke her in anally. I asked, "Have you ever had anal sex?" "My husband and I tried it, but it hurts too much." I told her the first time it always hurts. And true to form, she was in some serious pain for the first 5 minutes or so. I had to massage her clitoris to distract her. She lay squirming under me, fighting the urge to say stop and the desire to experience something new. I decided to end the pain by giving her one hard thrust to break the barrier. I knew it was going to hurt her, but I figured that she could hurt for 20 minutes or for 10 seconds.

I gripped her by the hips and pushed as hard as I could. She screamed in pleasure/pain and then came the "POP". She was wide open now. Gone were the "ouches" and "go slower". She was becoming quite fond of it. She began to push back against me. I took this as an indication of wanting more penetration, so I obliged. She had her first anal orgasm. I was surprised to hear her chanting, "I am comin'… I am comin'… I am comin'." She told me later that she had her husband do it as well. I was thinking that her husband had to know that someone else was doing his wife. He had to wonder, "Who taught her that trick?" or "Why was it so easy this time" After all, you do not just come up with the idea of being penetrated anally after years of marriage.

I did her in their bed one night and came in her mouth and on her face. I must have stuck my penis too far down her throat because she gagged loudly. Shortly afterwards, her daughter knocked on the door. I had to lie by the side of the bed away from the door until she put her daughter back to bed. I am sure the little girl heard us well before the gagging incident and came to investigate what was wrong with her mother.

She called me once to tell me she was pregnant. I hate these conversations, "What, how can you be pregnant and your tubes are tied?" "It can happen." I thought, "Shit! Here we go again. What was it this time, money or attention?" Of course she was not pregnant; she was crazy. Calada moved because of her husband's job. I was happy to see her go; she was becoming a little too forward. One night at the club she was being frisky. I told her Housewife was there and she continued. "Danger, Will Robinson."

She called from their new location once to ask me for money. She said her husband had beaten her and she wanted to catch a bus to her parents' house. It was a lie. When she called she knew Housewife might be at home; it was Saturday morning. When Housewife answered the phone Calada should have said she had a wrong number, but she was too bent on her goal. I sat there trying to speak in code as Housewife sat down and listened to my conversation. The moment Housewife was out of ear shot I told Calada how wrong she was for doing this, knowing

253

my partner was present. She did not care. She said, "You did not say that when I was sucking your dick." Housewife did the typical woman thing, "Who was that?" I did the typical male thing; I lied.

The Prostitute was a whore who did not want to be considered one. I met her while in a foreign club. 99.9% of all women in that club were working girls. It had been years since I was there, but it was the same and different. It was different because I was looking at it through more mature eyes; not with the fascinated eyes of a boy who was out of his country for the first time, and I was with a woman.

My partner and I frequently returned to the hotel room around midnight after dinner, a show or dancing. Then I would go out hunting, with the understanding that I was shopping for two. Hunting, as I called it, was not that at all. It was an ego boost. Walking into that particular club would do that for the most insecure male on the planet. The girls grab and fight over men, or rather potential income. I asked The Prostitute if she was a "puta". She cried like a baby at the insult. She really did not consider herself one. As far as she was concerned, she was raising money to support her family. It was either a bad job or a good act. I did not care; my fantasy was waiting.

It reminded me of many women in the United States. They want men to give them money, but they do not want to be considered whores. I saw her several times in the club after our first encounter and invited her to our hotel during the day. When she arrived, I had my partner go to the lobby to retrieve her. I was preparing myself. She was visibly nervous about being with the two of us and she eased her apprehension by downing two or three glasses of champagne quickly. I instructed my partner to go into the bedroom and get the video camera and vibrator ready. I remained with The Prostitute. As soon as my partner closed the door, I was on my knees in front of our guest.

I opened her blouse aggressively and pulled her right breast from its cradle. I really like nice breasts (real ones). I sucked hard to see how she would react. She liked it. I bit her nipple medium-hard; she flinched and let out a slight cry of pain (I was trying to loosen The Prostitute up and give the other time to accomplish her mission and prepare herself). My hand found its way inside her panties. It was very wet. I must have played with her clitoris and vagina for 10 minutes before I stood up to take her in the room. When I did, she reached for my belt buckle. She looked me in the eyes then undid my belt and the top button of my pants. At that moment I wanted to let her, but I also wanted my friend to see her do it, so I pulled her to the room.

When we entered, Housewife was in a fishnet nighty, candles were lit and she was seated in a chair across the room. The video camera was facing the bed. I laid The Prostitute so that the angle could be appreciated later and took off her clothes. I gave her more libations before I indulged myself by pleasing her orally. I do not know why, but I always liked turning women on more than being turned on by them. I guess it is a control thing or it is my confirmation that no woman can please me as well as I can please myself.

I fed for about five minutes then stopped short because I did not want her to come. I wanted her to come for my partner. Switching positions, I laid down beside her to caress her breasts in my mouth. Across the room, my partner was watching intently. I watched her touch herself as I was performing oral sex. The Prostitute asked Housewife to join us on the bed. She then asked her to take the nighty off. I went a step further and told her to lick between The Prostitute's legs. She said she did not know how or what to do. I told her, "Do what you like to have done to you."

The next hour was spent performing to my commands. They both wanted to concentrate on me, but I kept their attentions on each other. I had them try various positions: 69, missionary and made them kiss, lick and touch each other while I watched. After a time, I did not have to say a word; Housewife straddled The Prostitute's face. She liked to sit on my face, but there was something very exciting about watching women lose their sexual inhibitions. Housewife's eyes were closed as she moved her vagina back and forth over The Prostitute's open mouth and outstretched tongue. Housewife was sitting on The Prostitute's face and playing in her hair. "HELLO!" I joined in.

The Prostitute had her second or third orgasm of the night while I was eating her. I found a condom and penetrated her while she was still negotiating my partner's vagina in her mouth. That sound women make when touched in the first uncomfortable moments of penetration is so satisfying. It is somewhere between "ouch" and "yes", or maybe both. She was astute enough to check to see if I was wearing a condom with her hand.

When my partner came, I was able to concentrate on trying to tickle The Prostitute's heart from the bottom. She was receptive, slowly raising her knees skyward as I plunged deeper. Needless to say, it was not long before I reached climax, despite interference from my partner. I withdrew; Housewife removed the condom and manually stimulated my penis all over The Prostitute's tummy, breasts and a drop on the chin. It seemed to last forever. I would have to rank that orgasm up there with Hiroshima. The Prostitute showered and seemed reluctant to take payment for her services. We saw her later that night looking for another customer and found out that her reluctance to be paid was not reluctance at all; she wanted more than the going rate because there were two of us.

Confused was a local girl who had the opportunity to travel a bit because of the military. I met her while playing pool at a club. She was wearing a mini-skirt that complimented her legs perfectly. I have always been a sucker for athletic looking women and Confused's legs looked like she ran track. I asked her as much. She said she had never participated in any organized sports. I thought, "You should have; those legs scream use me for something other than walking."

What her exact classification in the Navy was I do not remember, but we can all sleep better at night knowing that she is on guard. She was naive, religious, a Southern belle, high-strung and a bit crazy. All of these factors aided in creating a confused woman. Confused liked to party, but wanted to live like a "cook book Christian." She loved rough sex, but did not want to be considered a freak, not even by the male who was doing the freaking. She mentioned wanting to share a child with me, but she already had a seven-year-old daughter who was being raised by a relative. I had to go to bed with Mother Teresa. Once there, I had to have sex with Linda Loveless. After her religious and physical needs were satisfied, I had to try to communicate with Scarlet O'Hara. It was different, but I could wear as many masks as she.

255

I would lie in bed next to her and anticipate her throwing a leg or an arm on top of me. That was her signal that I could initiate sex. If I did not respond, she would hint more. If I were patient enough, she would end up on top of me all together. It was as if I had to start the sinful act of having an orgasm to ease her conscience. Once I just laid there. I had made up my mind not to respond to her advances. She kept up the touching and cuddling until I went to sleep. I was tired of hearing about God and the sin of sex before we hit the sheets, only to fuck like true heathens after. I am not exaggerating. The following morning was always filled with guilt. "We should not have done that."

Confused liked to be tied up. I used to tease her, "I am going to tie you up and beat you, if you do not stop." "Promise!?!" was her sure response. She liked oral sex. One night I was driving home. I undid my belt and she asked, "What are you doing?" I responded, "Taking my dick out so you can suck it." I was embarrassed as hell when I dropped the white linen pants off at the cleaners. Confused's red lipstick had stained the crotch area. The Asian drycleaner held up my pants, looked at me and asked in her broken English, "What this on zippa?" I am sure I was blushing and laughing after I whispered, "Lipstick." If I was not blushing, I had reason to.

Another time, she came to my place. I offered her a seat, stood in front of her and pulled out my penis. I simply said, "Come here." Afterwards she told me, "I like getting right to it." She was my kind of girl, but she had a religious streak that was contrary to her nature. I cannot recall the number of times she told me she was not having sex with me anymore for religious reasons. I respected that, but she should not expect me or any other male not to have sex with her after she massages our testicles or kisses our nipples. There is not enough restraint or blood in the male anatomy.

The last time I saw her was the morning after she and her cousin pissed me off. I ran into them near the pool tables of a club. I asked them if they wanted something to drink. They both said, "Yes." I took their orders and when I returned they were both gone. Confused showed up at my place around nine AM the next morning. I asked her what she would do if I had done the same thing to her. She said, "It would be over between the two of us." I think it was King Solomon who condemned himself like that because of Beersheba. She passed her own sentence. I fucked her giving no consideration to her feelings, and despite the fact that she was not on birth control I came inside of her. Then I got up, showered and asked her to leave. From her own lips we were done. Moving to another state ended that bizarre affair. Our last contact was a Fuck-U-Gram sent via the Internet. I did not even bother to read it.

Barbie was a divorcee. I met her at my favorite Friday night watering hole. It was in one of the more affluent parts of the city. We ended up standing next to one another at the bar. She had a date. I asked politely if it would bother her if I smoked a Cuban cigar. She said she liked the smell of cigars. That was the extent of our conversation. She later slipped me a business card (realtor) when her date was not looking. I had mixed emotions. My first thought was, "Trifling Bitch." My second thought was, "Easy Pussy." See! Women do choose. No need to ask which thought overruled which; and there is no rule against having sex with trifling bitches, if there were, the population would drop significantly.

You would not be reading about her, if I had sense and I have decided not to write about any near misses. I shall save that one for another book because whether or not you realize, there is a method to my madness; I do not sleep with every woman who opens her legs. I have turned down more sex than I have had.

I called Barbie just to see what would happen (as if I did not know). I figured that I was in a win-win situation. The worst that could happen would be my being laid. After the array of usual and obvious questions, we agreed that meeting in the same bar would be safe for both of us. I was sitting at the bar when she arrived. We ate at the bar and had drinks. By the end of the evening, we agreed that I should follow her home. I did not talk myself out of the sex. I knew from the way she pulled out of the parking lot that she was intoxicated. Here I was following a drunken divorcee home. We were lying on the couch opposite of each other. I put my foot up her dress and massaged her crotch with my toe. She had no objections. On to phase two: get the panties off.

There is nothing like the promise of a good licking to get a woman out of her knickers. I moved her panties to one side and after I licked her one time, it was not hard for me to remove them all together. Let me check my math: fifteen minutes of toe play, ten minutes with the tongue. She was ready. We started on the couch missionary style. We were eye to eye. She did not blink and had this strange unmoving smile. She looked like the Joker. I told her I wanted to finish on the bed. It was our first time together, so I felt I had to put an exclamation point to the evening and this particular couch was not big enough for the proper taking of a woman.

She had to come first. That way I would not have to apologize for my orgasm or how I got it. I gave her all the control she was willing to take. I let her do whatever she wanted. It is like a job interview with emphasis on practical application. I put her on top. She knew all the tricks and performed them in the same order as most every other woman does when on top: oral sex until it is hard (a few minutes usually, but when it gets interesting most stop, but women know that) and then mount. But, I was impressed when she squatted over me and did the knee bend bounce. You know the move. For those of you who do not, you should learn or have it done to you. There is just something about that visual picture that does it for me. Crazy was the best I ever had at this move.

I was hooked when I saw the black adjustable speed dildo. I was about to enter fantasyland and wanted to collect as many prizes as I could. She kept it in the top drawer of her nightstand, right beside a revolver and the motion lotion. I thought, "Be careful, Freak, and Thank you," at the same time. The 12-gauge Remington shotgun in the corner reminded me she was Texan. Barbie either came or got tired, but my turn came. I used my newly acquired tool to probe her while I used my tongue to play with her clitoris. I tried sucking her breasts, but it was difficult to control the urge to bite her nipples with my teeth. Her breasts were not real and she had no sensation. I like to suck nipples and to stimulate my partner, but there was no point with her. Besides, I did not want her to spring a leak and I doubted if biting was covered under the warrantee.

I asked her what type of sex she liked and what she wanted me to do. She said, "You can do whatever you want to". "Anything," I questioned with raised eyebrows. She replied with more

257

confidence, "Anything!" That opened the door to all sorts of possibilities; I have an over active imagination. I knew my affair with Barbie was going to be fun, turbulent and short. Barbie and I had dinner several times, went out for drinks and went gambling. There was no love in the relationship; it was strictly about selfish gains. I asked her what Mom and Dad would do if she showed up on the farm with me. She tried to put it as mildly as she could, but the answer was, her mother would hide the silverware and her father would call a shrink.

I went to the same bar where we met one Friday. I had arranged for a late night rendezvous with Confused, but I had a couple of hours and wanted to have a drink. I ran into Barbie and a friend. They were doing the girls kissing in public routine and were drunk as skunks, so you can imagine where my mind went. Barbie was mad at me for not calling her more often. I acted unconcerned about her bitching and not threatened by her affection for her friend. I was turned on and wondered if I could have sex with them both and still have enough in the reserve tank for Confused. You only live once. After it was clear that I was not getting what I wanted out of the deal in time to get to Confused at a reasonable hour, I decided to leave.

Barbie and friend came out shortly afterwards and said they were going to another club. I told her I was expecting company and I had to get home. The valet brought my car first. Before I knew what was happening, these crazy drunk women jumped in my car and drove off. I had been "Hoe-jacked" by two poster child blonds. I waited for her car and then drove it to her apartment; she was not there. I called her cell. There was no answer. I finally went home.

Imagine, I am home in bed with Confused and Barbie called my cell phone at 2 AM to tell me that she was at home if I wanted to come get my car. By the time I got there, she and girlfriend were wasted. Barbie wanted to do a three way. I said, "I just want to watch" but girlfriend was not having it.

When we got back to the condominium Barbie was frisky. I told her, "I know what you want" She said, "What?" It was not what she said; it was how she said it. She used body language and eye contact that almost dared me to do her. I pushed her to the nearest wall, pulled her panties down and entered her. There was no resistance on her part. Some women like it when you are a little forceful. After five minutes against the wall I herded her to the bed, doggy styled her, and then came in her mouth. Barbie said, "I cannot believe you made me do that," after she returned from the bathroom. I just smiled and thought, "I can. You said anything I wanted." I got dressed and went home to Confused.

My contact with Barbie was like that, hit or miss. She called me once to say, "You can come and get some pussy". If I was not doing anything, I sometimes went. The routine was the same and I soon got bored with it. Boredom in bed makes you push limits that were not intentionally offered. I found myself in this predicament while looking from behind at Barbie from behind on all fours. She was dutifully taking the pounding I was trying to give her. The thought of anal sex came to mind. I remembered the contents in her top drawer. I used the oil she kept by the gun and dildo to lubricate her rear. My finger was first. I used it to push inside of her, ensuring the oil was evenly spread. It was the type of oil that caused a warming sensation. She did not even flinch, so I followed with my penis.

There was some resistance. She was in some pain, but she did not say stop nor stop moving. The pain turned to pleasure after I felt the head of my penis passing what would have been her popping point, but I was not the first to do this to her. Our rhythms were matched and I was deep inside of her. She screamed, "Oh damn, I am comin', I am comin'" her whole body vibrated violently and then she fell flat to the bed. I readjusted my position so I could finish. Her contractions increased the pressure exerted by the anal canal on my penis. I soon joined her in that blissful post orgasmic state. That was the last time I saw her. I would frequently get notes on my car windshield or scratches across the hood to remind me that I could always go back. One of the notes on the back of her card read, "Do you want to come out and play?" "No. I don't."

Business and Pleasure

Do you remember the manager who tried to seduce me from Judgment "Who Are We"? Trixie was a revenge tactic I used to get back at my immediate manager. People hate rejection. I was on thin ice with Trixie's mother, my manager, after I rejected her advances the night I came to pick up an old evaluation. One day she asked me to pick up her daughter from work at 3 PM. What kind of manager calls her employee during "off time" to do anything? I thought this was a bit unusual and unreasonable. My shift was over at 6 AM, but I rarely made it home before 9 AM. My shift started at 10 PM, and I was usually there an hour before it started. I was especially intrigued since I had asked my manager her to introduce me to her daughter shortly after I told her how cute I thought she was (the first time I saw her). Why was this woman giving the key to the chicken coup to the fox? A fox cannot help being a fox. I had to take a chicken or at least a few eggs and she knew it. She had seen me in action. I once hit on a Christian Revivalist in her presence. I could not help it. The woman had perfect breasts and the T-shirt they were all wearing had words printed across the breasts. Her shirt was a couple of sizes too small. I knew what I was doing and so did she. I was reading the words and looking at her teats at the same time and she knew it and liked it. "Oh, this is just my boss," is what I told her when she asked, "Who is this?" "Don't say that," my manager said and continued with, "We work together." The women were jousting. Translation: "I like your shirt." "I like you, but who is the woman and why are you wearing a ring?" "She's just my boss and I am not married. I wear the ring to keep women away." My manager not only threw salt in that game, but later she also tried to take advantage of an unfaithful male.

It was more innocent than that. I picked her daughter up several times and did not do anything. One night Trixie said she needed a place to stay; her mother was having a male guest and wanted the house to herself. I imagined it was much like the night I went over for the evaluations. "Get out bitch! Mamma gonna get a roll tonight" Why did she call me? Was this a booty call? I said a prayer for the guy whom Mommy was going to ravage and "yes" to Trixie. I should have my head examined. I knew a relationship between Trixie and me would be the pig that flies as far as her mother was concerned, but I said yes anyway. She begged. I refused five times with reasons why, but she came over anyway. Remember what I wrote about going against one's own voice? Her admission ticket to my home lay in between her thighs.

I did Trixie on my couch. She was shy about her body. I guess it was youth or first time jitters, but she followed my lead more than anything else. I started with a massage. That got her out of her shirt. I undid her bra while I rubbed her back. I told her to turn over. If she kept the bra, I had work to do, if I wanted sex; if she removed it, I was going to get lucky. She rolled over and removed her arms from the bra straps. It took me the better part of an hour to get her down to her panties. Once there she let me take them off without a word.

It was a slow orchestrated dance. I have suspicions in my older age about her feelings, but I realize that I was clueless to her real motives, except I knew she wanted someone to love her and her child. Good luck, there are many women who want the same thing. I licked her clitoris and simultaneously stuck one finger in her front and another in the rear. I would not be satisfied until she broke out of her armor. I assumed that she knew what passion was. It was not a far-fetched hypothesis; the main evidence for my conclusion was the eighteen – month-old child asleep in my bed. It did not take long to produce small but noticeable gyrations and low verbal responses. She had some interest in sex after all. I pulled her as far forward on the couch as I could. Her butt maintained a precarious grasp on the edge of the sofa's cushions, but they were leather; sweat, skin and leather stick like glue.

I was on my knees between her legs praying to Aphrodite for success when I entered her. It was not bad sex; there is no such thing. It just was not up to the standard I was accustomed. Remember, I was having sex with Barbie, Confused, Ready Made and Housewife at this time. They all enjoyed it or at least acted like it. There was a point of hope during this first exchange of body fluids. Trixie began to spank my cheeks softly with both hands. It was more like a pat than a spank, but I could always hope for more.

Later in our relationship I told her, "Sex with you is like fucking a dead fish." I asked her if she enjoyed sex, and then, if she enjoyed sex with me. Both received positive acknowledgment. I finally asked her what she wanted from me. If she said, "I want a safe place to get away from my crazy mother." and "I need a financially stable male." I would have believed her, but she rendered nondescript answers that led me to believe she did not know or did not want to tell me. I did not believe her. That is my main issue with people, too many lies to see the truth.

It was not until later that I realized she answered her sexual calling on top. She turned into a stripper when I gave her the reins. It was an amazing transformation. Imagine a naked hot body on a mechanical bull and the motions necessary to stay centered and then slow it down to "Six Million Dollar Man" speed (mentally add the sound effects).

By now her mother knew that she and I were doing something. She never said a word to me about her daughter, but the situation at work got worse and she began to communicate with me through her daughter. Trixie would tell me about the arguments they had. Her mother would remind her that I was married, or say "Why don't you go stay with him?" It did not seem important that I was married when she tried to seduce me. At one point her mother kicked her out of the house and she needed somewhere to stay. That someplace was not with me, although she and her girlfriend both called me to see if I would volunteer. I ended our affair after I quit my job because of a sexual harassment complaint. I was innocent. There were a few women at work, whom I found attractive, but work is for work and I do not like spending that much time around anyone with whom I am having sex.

TIMEOUT: I do not want anyone to think it is safe to engage in unprotected sex. I have done it and consider myself lucky for only having had gonorrhea and crab louse. It is important that everyone know that if you gamble and have unprotected sex, do so after inspecting your partner (these days I would ask for a medical report; we have the time to wait for results). I have looked inside of women for sores and anything out of the ordinary, but herpes flares up when it wants to. I make sure I am near usable water, preferably a hot shower or salt water. Secondly, try to urinate immediately afterward. For guys, an alcohol wipe afterwards would not hurt.

If you engage in anal sex, it is imperative that you disinfect everything that has come in contact with feces. Do not contaminate your lubricant by double dipping. Common rubbing alcohol is the most economical way to disinfect body parts. Bleach and water works for toys in the short term, but repeated boiling water dips are a necessity between partners.

Ready Made was a short, attractive mother of three with a killer smile and please help me attitude. She had a semi-live-in boyfriend who was a wanna-be thug. It all started rather innocently enough. I saw her on several occasions and, being human, I noticed that she had some pleasing assets. Being a predator, I waited for the appropriate moment to strike. One day while I was walking to the community mailboxes, I saw her. It was a perfect opportunity to acknowledge her without risk, but how. What to say? I waited for the signal. It came in the form of her eyes rising to meet my waiting stare and the smile that followed. "How are you?" She let out the biggest smile, "I am fine." "I did not ask you how you look; I asked how you were." She kept walking without another word. I stopped and turned to see if she would look back. She did and giggled like a busted schoolgirl when she realized that I was staring as she walked away. I recognized this. That was it.

The way she smiled was enough of a signal even for the densest male. After that, we flirted on and off for months. She admitted to me later that whenever we happened to pull up around the same time, she would rush or slow down, so that we would have an opportunity to speak or just see each other. I was not hunting; I was being hunted and she had a male. I knew it already, but why was she after me?

If we are canines, and men are dogs, what are women, wolves or dingoes? If I had to describe myself in the canine genus, I would be a fox. And one thing about hunting a fox that you have to keep in mind is that foxes do not run home when being chased and they do not view themselves as prey. They lead their pursuer/s away from where they feel the safest and then ditch them. I finally asked Ready Made to meet me at the same upscale bar I used to frequent for dinner and dancing. She was reluctant, but a ½ hour after our scheduled meeting time she was there looking yummy. I immediately thought I was going to get a treat. I can tell by a woman's appearance what her intentions are. The new above the knee cocktail dress, fresh perm, cute hairstyle, manicure and pedicure, the new shoes and the sweet smell of "help me" perfume said it all.

It was partly my fault. She had asked me three days prior where and when. It gave her time to do reconnaissance. And, she had seen me on my way out on enough weekends to know what the expectation was. Secretly I thought, why is a single mother of three whose living in a one bedroom apartment and working part-time spending this much money to go out with me? I

261

acknowledged her efforts by asking her to do a slow turn around to let me look. "Very nice." We had dinner, drinks and danced to the Latin band from Canada.

At the end of the night, we stood at the stairs negotiating the terms of having sex. She had the option of entering my apartment or climbing the stairs. She opted to go. I said fine. She came down to my apartment later that night in a long T-shirt, her version of a nighty. We petted a bit, but she said, "No," a second time. What was the point of coming down to my apartment so under dressed and exposed; tricks are for kids, you silly rabbit.

The next morning, she rang my doorbell in pajamas. They were the type with the rabbit feet. "Hello, nurse!" I did her on the living room floor. I did not even ask what she wanted. After kicking her out the night before for playing softball, she was there to close the deal. I wish I had the foresight to have known she was coming back that soon. The night before I masturbated and I did not want any sex.

It was obvious to me that boyfriend was not licking or sticking the way he should have. If he were, she would not have been naked under me on my living room floor or maybe she would have. I was a nightshift manager at the time and she liked to call me at work and talk dirty over the phone. I once told her to come to my apartment wearing a flowery summer dress I liked. I was specific, "No panties."

She remembered the dress because once I flirted with her while she was walking up the steps, "Hello… Nice sun dress." She stopped on the steps between flights to talk and I could see the red thong she was wearing. I am not a pervert, just very sexual. I told her that I could see her panties, as gentlemanly as I could. I even turned my head for a moment, until it was evident that she was not embarrassed or going to move.

I was very explicit in my instructions. I said I would be home between 7:30 and 8:00 AM. She had to get her children to school and was free at 9:30 or so. I told her the door would be open and I would be asleep. Her mission was to wake me up orally and once I was aroused, she was to mount me with the dress still on and slide up and down on my penis until I went inside of her without any assistance. I was very specific about that, no hands! "Get me excited and work your way on, but you cannot use your hands." Ready Made had a pierced tongue and I encouraged her to use it. One day I openly accused her of teasing the penis just long enough to get it hard. She knew I was right.

I decided to take her away from her children for a night. I got a room at a casino two hours away. We gambled a little, had dinner and went up to the room. I seduced her in the Jacuzzi size bathtub with water jets, rose petals, bubbles and mirrors. I had her assume the "frisk me" position and washed her like this. I made sure to watch her in the mirror as I performed this cleansing ritual and I made sure she watched me, it's just foreplay.

The clock starts ticking the moment a woman decides she wants to have sex with you. If you cannot make a woman have an orgasm between that moment and the moment you come, you will have issues. I dried her with soft pats of a bath sheet. Then I soothed her drying skin with oils. I like rubbing a nice body. There so many maneuvers that one can perform that may be interpreted as both therapeutic and sensual. It serves a definite purpose, to relax your partner and stimulate as well. I figure I need to give my partner a mental and physical head start if women take an average of 15 minutes to have an orgasm.

I might whisper a naughty nothing in her ear just to see how she reacts. I might ask her to give me her tongue so I can suck it. If she is receptive to that, I might ask if I can taste it. I like to ask personal sexual questions without reservation so that I know, without a doubt what my partner likes. After gathering this information, I try to come up with a firing solution that is different, yet still gives her what she wants. If women are honest about their sexual wants or fantasies, I do my best to satisfy them. I am not afraid of sex and "it ain't rocket science".

When I do something like this, I am attempting to seduce the old part of the brain. You remember, the part of the brain that speaks without thinking, that same part of the brain that makes one blink or flinch automatically. It knows how to have sex without the baggage we have learned to carry into the encounter. I like to do this until my partner practically begs to be taken anywhere pleasure will go. You can smell the anticipation, the pheromones coming to a boil like ripe fruit that needs to be eaten right away or it will go bad. "Fuck the consequences and fuck me; I don't care anymore," exited one lover's mouth before the act.

The sex part was not as important or satisfying as playing with the body. It never is. Near the end of the encounter, I asked her if I could come in her mouth. "Yes", came from her in a voice that indicated her mouth was dry from breathing heavily. From all fours, she was summoned. I told her, "Don't waste a drop!" as she began to suck. When I was done, I showered and returned to the tables. She was sprawled across the untidy bed full asleep.

I returned early the next morning to find her writing in her journal. "What are you writing about?" I asked, knowing full well that journals are private matters usually best left alone. She smiled and said, "Don't waste a drop..." Mission accomplished. I wanted her to feel good. I wanted her to remember what I had done to her for the rest of her natural life and beyond. See, I am not always selfish. After that, I would sometimes go up to her place for a quickie, then leave. Sometimes she would come down stairs, but her kids always knocked on the door shortly afterwards.

Do not think I did not take the kids out. I did Dave and Busters, restaurants and brought snacks. Three kids were too much for my income and lifestyle: too much attention, too much love, too much money and too many priorities before me. I think a person's children should be first, but they are not mine. They are the result of past choices with three different males. A woman asks a lot when she says "Take me and my children." "Ball and chain" takes on a new meaning when the children are not a result of your loins. Women will say that they will raise a man's children. If they have children of their own, which children are going to get preferential treatment? Many animal societies function in the same way.

The night Housewife and I had the ménage a trois with her, Ready Made saw us leaving for the evening and asked me, "Can you handle all of that?" She was referring to Housewife's body size (I said her bottom was getting big: Ready Made just confirmed it by asking, "Why you with the fat girl?" The same question I was asking myself). Ready Made waited until I closed the passenger door before she said it. She was standing with two other women in the parking lot of our apartments. Women are a trip. The Caldron was a collection of would be mates. When I got in the car, Housewife asked me what she said and why I was laughing. I told her verbatim what was said and what I thought she meant by it. Housewife was not amused. She probably knew I was having sex with her at that moment.

"You really want to be with another woman tonight?" "Yes." After we returned from the same bar I had taken Ready Made on our first date, I went up stairs and kidnapped her. She was in a long T-shirt and nothing else. I served her up to Housewife like a good meal. I was carrying her in my arms and laid her on the bed next to Housewife who was licking her lips by now. Picture this: it was 2 AM when I went out for ten minutes and brought back a semi-naked woman. Would you get mad now or later?

Ready Made and I faded with time. I knew she was not going to fit the bill, three children at twenty-eight, lovely or not, scream huge financial responsibility. I purposely began to ignore her. Friction increased; she eventually moved in with her real boyfriend and I moved out of town.

It was going to be a fresh start and I promised myself, no more drama… Do yourself a favor and do not make promises.

The other side of the Pacific Ocean brought culture shock to a new height. But no matter where I went, there were Westerners and we congregated in the same locations, those that catered to foreigners.

From Russia with Love was a Ukrainian living in Seoul. She was a whore, but that meant little or nothing to me at 7 AM. She was good looking and I was horny. I met her while out dancing. I remember the sun was coming up when we exited the club. I had convinced From Russia with Love to come back to the hotel with me. She said that she did not want to have sex, but after a shower and the equivalent of $90.00 USD, she was in the bed naked. She let me do whatever I wanted, though there was some friction about penetrating her anally, she eventually said in her broken English, "OK. Go slow." I saw her damn near every day after that.

After the initial exchange of cash, she did not want anything except dinner and sex. I quickly found that I could not work affectively and have sex with her too. She was an all night experience and in this particular country, they think it is normal to be at work until 9 or 10 PM. One night I was dead tired. I left the hotel at 7:30 AM and did not get in until 10:30 PM. From Russia with Love showed up without an invite. All I wanted to do was eat, shower and sleep. "You sleep, I suck," was her reply. Needless to say, I did not get much sleep that night. I ended up standing beside the bed with my hands on her head fucking her in the mouth.

On another similar occasion, "No fuck, no sleep," was her reply; again, no sleep was the outcome. Though she was physically draining and a major distraction from what I was supposed to be doing, I have to say that I enjoyed her. I have spoken with her several times since then, but I have not seen her. If I go back again, regardless of the occasion, I will call her up and dip into that well again if she is willing.

I worked until 10 PM one night and was dead tired when I reached the hotel, but as a great manager once said, "If you want to see the dead come back to life, come around here at quitting time." Two other expatriates from my company were on their way to a club and had two girls with them. I ran into them at the hotel entrance and got a glimpse of the girls as they got in the taxi. One of them looked like a Hawaiian calendar pin up. I declined going at first; I told them they had two and I would be a fifth wheel. They insisted that I come. I relented and told them I had to shower and would catch a taxi to the club later. That was how I met Tropics.

Tropics was one of those girls who had learned that Western men were more generous with money and treated women differently than the Taiwanese males. She and her friend caught a train from Taipei to where we worked, about a three-hour trek. The return trip would not be until the next day. I call that, "A long distance booty call". I danced with Tropics several times, but I felt as though I was intruding, until one of the guys told me he had her the night before and did not want a repeat. I kept thinking she was not about to have sex with me, not right after she did the guy sitting beside me. If she did… You make the judgment.

We ended up in my suite drinking and listening to music. At some point, Tropics said, "I need to go to Toni's room," to her girlfriend. The two of them left and returned with Tropics' overnight bag. She had gathered her belongings and was relocating. I was going to have sex, if I wanted. Wait a minute, who said she could stay? When we were finally alone I did a strip tease for her. It ended with me in my underwear giving her a face-to-face lap dance and her licking my chest. It was a race to the bed after that.

The first time I ate her, she stopped me five minutes into it, laid me on my back and said, "Let me take care of you."; my kind of woman. The next morning her American boyfriend called her on the cell. It was a long conversation and I got bored listening to her say she wanted to move on and his trying to talk her out of it. As they spoke on the phone, I sat in a chair in the middle of the room and undid my bathrobe. I motioned Tropics to my side. I began to massage her genitals, trying to get an audible response. Her respiration did get faster and she began to speak as if slightly winded.

I guided her by the waist to a position that straddled my outstretched legs. I began to enter her while she was breaking up with her real boyfriend. This guy cared about her enough to have brought her to the States. She showed me pictures of them in San Francisco. She finally said she had to go and hung up. I was full inside of her by now. I picked her up and laid her on the bed without exiting. I pushed her knees up to her breasts and finished the deed standing by the side of the bed. This is a variation of the full baked chicken.

The first thing we always did was to have sex. Tropics had a body that made me want to be inside of her all the time. Most of the local girls had issues in the T&A department. Tropics had a nice quantity of both. She also had unusual skin color. It was a light tan; that is what made her look Polynesian. I do not want you to get the idea that I like really big butts or really big breasts. I do not discriminate. I have had women who are fat and I have had skinny minis.

I always stayed at the Hyatt and Tropics often stayed with me. She liked to go out to eat, drink and dance like most every other person I know. The hotel had one of the best Western

265

clubs in the city. The high-class hookers and socialites hung out there on Friday and Saturday nights. I have to admit, I could not tell the difference between the two. After the hotel, we always headed for an afterhours club a few blocks away that played hip-hop. It was funny and motivating to see Asians rocking to Hip-Hop music. I remembered thinking of a conversation I had with a professor while in college. She said rap music was not going to last, but there I was, 6,500 miles from home listening to rap's child, jazz's grandchild and the ancient rhythms of Africa's great-grand being played. Not only that, the crowd was rocking!

The next time I saw Tropics, she was in the company of my roommate. He had e-mailed me about a freak he met. From his description, I figured it was Tropics. I was due to return the following weekend, so I arranged to meet my roommate and his new found love at the Hyatt. I asked that he not tell Tropics I was coming. The look on her face when she realized that I was his roommate was priceless. It told a thousand stories and revealed what no confession could. I did not say a word or judge her actions; she did that all by herself.

Psycho was an Australian-Indian expatriate and my lover for two years. Her beauty was only surpassed by her vanity, jealousy, insecurity and insanity. She was the most confused woman I had ever met and the most sexually liberated. She was beautiful on the outside, but torn apart on the inside. She shared with me the experience of hiding under the bed as a child while her mother cheated on her father. Family members had also sexually molested her; I think it was one of her brothers and her father. What made her bearable was her sheer openness and hunger when it came to sex. She was married to an older male and had a child whose paternity was in question. She was constantly in and out of affairs and therapy. She was too much of an emotional roller coaster.

Psycho was arguably one of the most physically attractive women I have known. The first time I saw in a Singaporean nightclub her I had to do a double take. Fine is not enough of a word for her physical appearance. She did have two drawbacks: a flat butt and bony knees, but I did not know this until I took her clothes off. I already said I do not discriminate, but I prefer curves and proportion, especially in the rear. Those are my love handles.

Psycho once convinced the staff at a hotel to let her in my room because I would not answer the door and she knew I was in the room with another woman. She dismissed the girl and we made a baby that day; it was Friday. She lay under me and said, "Give me your son." She aborted the child and never forgave me.

She lived a privileged life and suffered class-consciousness. They had a maid/slave who worked 6 ½ days a week. This beauty looked down on almost everyone. We got into a huge argument one day when she laughed about drinking champagne in the penthouse, while the people rioted for freedom and equality in the streets below. I could not afford to keep her in the luxury she knew, and this would lead to future problems. Three times I tried to leave the relationship, but "let" her talk me back into it with blind promises. Since she lived abroad and we saw each other every other month, I knew she would not be faithful. I found evidence of this in her e-mail. She had given me the password and evidently one of her male friends sent her an e-mail while she was en route to see me. I confronted her with the discovery when her plane landed. I asked her to check for a return flight immediately. It would have cost me an additional $700.00 to send her back the next day, so she had to stay the entire week.

If I had the money, I would have kicked her out then. I did not speak to her for two days. She finally broke down and asked, "Please do not treat me this way." We talked for a long time and she promised, "I will be in your life in any capacity you want." I remember thinking, "No woman could ever do that." But, I was going to see.

She satisfied all of my sexual needs and then some. We had sex all the time and experimented with all sorts of things: threesomes, role-playing and a strap-on. Sorry I need to interject a point before your imaginations fall off the edge. Do not get it twisted. I said we experimented with a strap-on. I did not say she used it on me. See!

Honestly, she did use it on me or rather she tried. She had no idea what to do. I let her think I was experiencing similar feelings that she had when the roles were reversed. In actuality she did not penetrate. I was on my back, the same way she liked it. I would tighten my gluteus maximus so that she would have to thrust like a male to enter; she could not do it. She was humping pillow and bed, but without physical sensation to tell you if you are where you want to be, it was flying blind. She always came just from the visual and mental picture. There is something about women and a male's ass. It seems to give them a feeling of control and an imagined role reversal.

Every time I let a woman stick her finger or tongue in my butt, she always wants to get something bigger to stick up there, a vibrator, strap-on, etc. What does that signify? Is it penal envy or a control issue?

Psycho and I were busted in the restroom of an airplane. The flight attendants knocked on the door several times, but I was not going to stop. I always answered, "Just a moment." Psycho had to squeeze my come out of her. When I emerged alone and I sat down one of the attendants asked me, "How was it?" "How was what?" "The wine." he said. We had a conversation earlier about the wine selection. "Like I said before, the Chardonnay is good, but I prefer the Riesling."

This woman was as wild when it came to sex. Psycho loved porno, written or visual, and wanted me to have sex with another male. On several occasions I had to remind her that she was sending her XXX-rated excerpts to my job e-mail and I could conceivably be fired for her indiscretions. Additionally, I do not like pornography, so the homosexual porn that she constantly sent went unread and I told her so. She also liked to photograph our sexual encounters (no facial shots), only to masturbate to them later and then delete the pictures. She was crazy about mirrors and watching me masturbate. Once she showed me a picture of her in a Catholic schoolgirl outfit sitting on her husband's lap. She looked really young and her husband really old. The picture was taken at a Halloween party they attended.

The picture had the desired effect; I asked her to dress like that for me. One night she brought the outfit with her in an overnight bag. She went into the bathroom as a mature 30 something and emerged as a teenager. The thoughts that went through my head made me question whether I am a pedophile. She completed the illusion by putting her hair in two ponytails and wearing white knee-highs and black patent leather shoes.

It was during one of the schoolgirl occasions that I said, "Make Daddy happy, Baby." Her reply both shocked and turned me on. She responded in a child's voice with, "Is Mommy coming home soon?" Not quite what I meant, but I went with it. I know that sounds sick, but I had the mother-in-law of all orgasms. The mother of all orgasms came again when we played rape, or when she acted like a whore and asked me to treat her like one. When I came on her face the first time, she screamed, "I need more come." I gave it to her five minutes later.

Once, she sent me an e-mail saying, "I just finished masturbating with two fingers up my ass. I just had to tell someone." That was after I finally broke her in anally. I wish she had sent a picture. We had sex everywhere, in cabs, on the beach, in an elevator, at an amusement park in a gondola and on a bench at a beachside bar. She traveled with me all over the world and her husband even called my cell phone several times to speak to her. She was constantly worried that some overzealous immigration official would search her bag and find her sex tools: two whips, a dog collar and chain, a riding crop, a variable speed vibrator and an electronic strap-on.

I am mad that she would never let me tie her up. I tried to the first night. She somehow ended up in my room wearing a red lace bra, matching thongs and pumps. She chased me all over the room. I even went into the bathroom to get away from her. As hard as it is to believe, I was trying to say no, but she was too beautiful and too much trouble at the same time. I finally said, "Fuck it!" and gave in to her wishes and mine. If she wanted it that bad, she was going to get it.

I succeeded in securing her right arm, but when I tried to do the left, she freaked out. I do not know who did it to her, but I suspect that it was a family member. Remember, I am not a shrink. Whenever we were out of the country, she would encourage me to pick-up whores to play with us. As long as she could pick them, I could have them.

Picture this: I am standing while a Thai woman, seated on an ottoman, was performing oral sex on me. Psycho was on the bed masturbating with a string hanging from her vagina (that is the only reason you are not reading about our toy eating her; she did not mind, I had heard her stories.) and watching me have sex with this girl's mouth. I could not hold it any longer after Psycho gasped and spasmed announcing the arrival of her orgasm. I ejaculated in the girl's mouth. Halfway through, she removed my penis and then rubbed the head back and forth across her breasts - instant pearl necklace.

I introduced her to anal sex. In the beginning she would bitch and moan about the pain so I gave her a distraction. I told her to masturbate. This works well for those of you who want to try it, but have a low threshold of pain. In the end, she did not even have to masturbate anymore. "Oh God, I am going to come just like this," is what she said when I put some pillows under the small of her back, lifted her legs in the air and I went in her butt without any pain for the first time. I asked, "You really like that?" "Yes, it is so unnatural." It did not end there. I made her lick my anus for who knows how long one night. Afterwards, she said, "I liked that," with the most surprised look on her face.

She was the type of woman who would wake me up with oral sex or a hot moist played with vagina. If it was oral, she stayed under the covers sweating her ass off until I came. If I attempted to relieve her suffering she would protest, "I want to sweat." She did not have a perm to worry about. They broke the mold when they made her.

We broke up over another woman. Psycho hacked into my e-mail and found a sexually explicit note. This was after I had discovered and forgiven her for being with other men. We are funny creatures. I did not even remind her of her pledge "in any capacity". Humans have a habit of judging others at a higher standard than we ourselves are able to maintain. We consistently perform acts that are equal to or worse than the acts of others, and conveniently forget our trespasses when the same things are done to us.

I adopted a billiards bar was in the Boat Quay district; it was not a tourist hang out. Young locals hung out there. After I ran the pool table for three hours while drinking a half a bottle of Cuervo 1800 one night, they adopted me as well and I became a regular, regular enough to have dinner with the bartender and his sister, China Doll. I have always had a thing for tall women. It is rare to meet a six foot Chinese, but she was well proportioned. She was not a beauty queen, but she was no dog either. I think I wanted her because she took the initiative.

I had given her brother my business card and said that I always stayed in the Ritz-Carlton when I was in town. My phone rang one Friday afternoon and it was China Doll. She was taking high tea at the Raffles hotel up the street and asked if I would like to join her. Was that a booty call? What is a single male supposed to do? A woman calls and practically says, "I want to fuck you."

Shall I spell it out to you? I went for tea; yeah, right! I had a Stolichnaya martini. We talked about how to heal the world's ills, not. We were both trying to figure out how to get into my bed without violating any of the social codes of mating. She finished her tea and I finished my drink. Who do you think paid? She offered though, which is always a plus. "Would you like to come to my hotel?" "Yes." I spent an hour and twenty dollars to do what we could have done for free. I offered her a beverage, took a beer for myself and joined her on the couch. We were snuggling. I took my shirt off because it was being wrinkled and I wanted to have less on just in case.

Knock, knock?!? I thought, "Who the fuck is there?" Psycho was at the door. Shit! I ignored her pleas to open the door. "I know you are in there." "Open the door this minute or I will go away and never return." The noise subsided for about five minutes, and then the door opened. Psycho had the staff let her in my room. She then asked China Doll to wait in the bathroom while she proceeded to chastise me. She then went into the bathroom and asked China Doll to leave. She said, "He'll call you later I am sure." as she closed the door. I promised I would not. I found out later that someone at the hotel told her I had just gone to my room with a woman when she arrived. She was a frequent enough guest and a good enough liar that the staff thought nothing of allowing her in my room.

Believe it or not, China Doll called me back (I did not break my promise; that is how I rationalized it). I apologized for what happened the last time we were together and assured her it would not happen again. She came directly to my room a little later. I had taken measures to counter Psycho's initiative this time. I turned my cell phone off, instructed reception not to disturb me for the next two hours and put the internal lock on the door. There was no way I was not going to have a taste of China Doll.

She was wearing an appropriately long dress that said "good girl." I closed the blinds then managed get her to the bed, lifted her dress up enough to expose new panties, pushed the panties to one side then stuck my fingers inside of her while I licked her clitoris. After a minute or so she sat up in the bed and grabbed me by the face with both of her hands; "You are going to drive me crazy." "Going to?" is the question that immediately came to mind as I raised her dress over her arms and exposed her beautiful long body with no resistance what so ever. We did it twice.

She lay on the bed very still and quiet between sessions. I remember that she was very deep. I guess it had something to do with her large frame. It was very basic sex, but it was also very innocent and very satisfying. She showed her approval in the same manner a novice might, letting out soft involuntary moans, hugging me with slightly animated arms, and returning my kisses with physical and emotional responses. I wanted more time to explore what I could have had with her; I wanted to see how she would react to the more serious and stimulating aspects of sex, but business took me elsewhere. My two orgasms to her one were all we would have, not fair.

After years of lost contact, Somebody Help Me Please reappeared in my life. I was stationed so many different places in as many years that it was difficult to keep up old relationships when the new ones occupied so much time and energy. She got married to a male she did not know and had a son. I imagine their divorce is final by now. We saw each other right before I went out of the country and we had sex. She said, "The ball is in your court now." That scared me. I say this with full knowledge that I am not what she wants and I was leaving the country. I was just good in bed and professionally qualified, for many those qualities are as close to love as they will get. "I did not want to be married," Update: she has read this work, has another child by another male and is divorced again.

Life of an Expatriate

Before I entered her I said, "I know it's wet." "How do you know?" "I can smell it… I have smelled it all day… I smelled under the sheets this morning… You must be ovulating." Pheromones wreak havoc on the male physiology.

I was right. I slid in without the usual friction between vaginal tissue and penis, "See, I told you," as I touched bottom in one continuous stroke. I went slowly like she likes. I did it to make her come. "I already came," was her way of telling me she did not want to made love to. I went deeper harder and moved faster. The grasp of her palms on both buttocks jerking me towards her told me I was right. I sprinted then slowed. I pulled out except for the tip and then moved it inside and out. "You playing with me." "No, just your pussy."

I like it when a female opens her thighs as wide as possible, grabs her angles or thighs and points her toes skyward. She is opening up. This was not Love making; it was fucking. "Where do I come?" "Anywhere you want to." "I know." I did have a choice with her - multiple choices. I withdrew and placed my penis on her abdomen. She grabbed it immediately. The quick and deliberate motions of her hand made me release the hot contents of my testicles on her stomach. "There's more," I told her. It was all I could manage to let her know that I was not done. Ten seconds later, I came again the eruption made it up to her neck. It was her heavy breathing and the look on her face watching the semen leave me that was a turn on. I left her in the bed with, "You're nasty." She smiled, "So are you."

You can visit a place, but until you live there, you do not have a clue about that society. You can read as many books as you like, but personal experience is the only way to know a location.

Chris was my first sexual experience since returning to Brazil. I picked her up on the street one night and after negotiating down to $20 USD, I took her back to the hotel and had my way with her. That was the last time I gave her cash. From then on, it was food, drugs and the high life. One night I was feeling full of myself. I had beautiful scenery (the balcony that overlooked the Atlantic), a willing partner and a warm tropical breeze. What to do?

I lead Chris to the balcony. I had the forethought to place a tube of K-Y in an accessible place beforehand. You got it! I did her in the anus. It was a different kind of penetration though. Up to that point in my life all but two of the women with whom I had dared to penetrate in the rectum gave some sort of resistance, even if it was just a finger. You women are familiar with this resistance, if you have ever tried to play in your male's butt. Tell you what; any qualified woman on this planet who wants to play with my ass is more than welcome (no toys). I might even buy her flowers afterwards.

But, back to Chris, she bent over the railing. After seeing the K-Y she knew what I wanted and allowed me to lubricate her without as much as a peep. I remember thinking, "This is going to be fun." I knew she was a professional and had done this before, but I got a surprise when I made first contact. She was tight. I had to go slow or risk waking the building. She asked for more K-Y. I obliged. To see a woman take a finger sticky with lubricant and put in her own butt is such a turn on for me. Am I a freak? Do not answer that.

It took a good 15 to 20 minutes to get inside of her. By the time we got to the "it doesn't hurt anymore point", she was making so much noise that my neighbor came out on the adjacent balcony, watched for a minute and then called security to complain about the noise. Whether or not she was raising the roof for pleasure, or pain, or the paycheck is beyond me.

Chris was a nut, especially, when she was under the influence. She also began to get on my nerves because she would always bring her girlfriend with her. One night after she wigged out, I slept in the other bed with her girlfriend. Chris awakened me with oral sex. As I lay there enjoying the scenery, I thought I could get lucky with the girlfriend as well. I began rubbing her legs. She became hotter than Texas asphalt in the summer, and began to respond to my finger movements with those infinitesimal body gyrations. Chris got a clue and put a stop to it by smacking her friend on the thigh and moving me to the other bed to finish. How do I get myself into these situations?

I most remember her licking my butt like it was a blow pop one night. I was with a friend on his nightly hunt. She happened to be on the corner that night. "I am not paying." "You don't have to pay amore." That was the last time I saw her, but she still calls every now and then to give me the "I love you" pitch. The last time she said that she was no longer a prostitute. "I saved up enough money to buy a home and only trick on Fridays and Saturdays."

My landlord dropped The Pro in my lap. He knew that I was upset about his bad management of my apartment and sent her as a peace offering. She was gorgeous, young and sexually unquenchable. When the doorman rang to ask me if The Pro could come up, I had no idea who it was. I finally understood what she wanted after 30 minutes of trying to communicate using a translation dictionary. She came over to ask if I needed someone to clean. That is what she said. I think she and the landlord had made a deal: she gets a fresh gringo and I get off his back.

The Pro looked surprised when I answered the door because I was African-American. The landlord told her my name and that I was an American. She interpreted that to my being white. Her first thoughts of me were that I was one of the many gay males who moved in on the tourist. When sexual tourists first arrive, the hookers, homosexuals, and the children (professional and amateur), compete for new "Johns". She asked me if I was Ronaldo in a disbelieving way. She later told me it was the pursed nipple. We were knocking boots four hours and two bottles of Chardonnay later.

I enjoyed and used her for my own purposes for a year or so, and she used me for status, money and sex. She was not that much of a sexual experience, but she loved to do it, all the time, and her Brazilian beauty was off the charts. She could eat, drink, sleep and have sex more than any woman I have ever met. Anytime-Anywhere was close. All I had to do was motion, hint or think about sex and she would assume the appropriate positions.

It is funny that, if she initiated sex, she always did the same routine in bed as most experienced women do. It started with oral and then she would get on top. She would bounce, gyrate, squat and turn around backwards. After 30 or 45 minutes of that, she would switch my position from her front to her backside without any artificial lubrication and continue the dance.

What she wanted in return was to be around *all* the time. After all, I could not find another if she was there. She once stayed with me for three days without a change of clothes. That was not a big deal; she was very clean. What amazed me was the fact that I dressed to go to the beach and she wanted to go with me in a skirt. If I convinced her to go home for a few days, she would make sure the "tank" was on "E" before she left, and she always found a reason to return as soon as possible, even if I had company. She came over one Sunday morning with her aunt and I had two women in my bedroom. They were all surface polite. I was cleaning when they rang.

The Pro liked to be beaten. I have only one other experience to compare to the level of violence that she wanted inflicted on her butt. I doggy styled her one day and decided to tap on her right cheek - 'smack'. "Mas," is what she said. "You want more?" went through my mind. It was just like the other time years ago. I hit a woman in much the same manner and she said the same thing, though in English, I got the point. I hit her again, harder this time. "Mas forte… Mas forte!" My Portuguese was not all that, but I understood her saying, "More force" or "Harder" to mean "Hit me harder." I hit her so many times and so hard that my palms were sore the next day. I now know how conga players feel.

She gave me a memory with oral sex on the balcony during a beautiful sunset. Of all things, I got embarrassed and moved the show inside. The crowd of men forming on the street below made me uncomfortable.

Once I could stand on my own, I had to back away from her. Not because she was a whore, but because she was not willing to grow. She just wanted to stay in the house all day sleeping and watching television, go out every night drinking, have sex and clean the apartment. I would study Portuguese a few hours every morning then write for a few hours, or read, or work. She blamed Dani for our upheaval, but it was more her lack of initiative than anything else. If I wanted a ball and chain, I could get one in the States.

After me, she moved on to other foreigners. We saw each other three or four times a month after our official parting. We had sex and she would leave after asking me for money. One day she and her sister, Café Latte, came to the beach. Café Latte's hello after not seeing me for months was a sexual dance in public. Picture a five foot ten, nineteen year-old, bronze skinned, gift of genetic diversity with hazel eyes shaking her moneymaker in my face while wearing Daisy Dukes and a bikini top. If I did not get enough attention from that, here comes The Pro looking as scrumptious as a ripe mango.

They played this strange game of you throw sand on his crotch and I will vigorously brush it off. You can imagine what happened when the rubbing began. It seemed that everyone on the beach was watching me be seduced. Logically, we all ended up going back to my apartment. We had drunk quite a bit and the girls did not stop their flirtatious ways when we left the beach. Realize that I my having sex about it. Although I did not know what The Pro knew or did not know about her sister and me, I pushed the limits.

I dared to put my hand between Café Latte's legs. Do not blame me; she was dancing sensuously not two feet in front of me while she was smiling and staring in my eyes. "You are hot down there." The Pro hit me softly on the arm in protest, but she was smiling. Not much punishment for such a trespass. I turned the conversation to oral sex. We talked about how to do it. What women like and what men like. At some point I dared The Pro to perform oral sex on me. Her only concern was that Café Latte would see. I said, "She won't look."

The Pro looked at her sister. "Close your eyes." The sister closed her eyes. The Pro positioned herself between my legs, pulled my penis from its resting place and put it in her mouth. After the initial physical and emotional adjustments one must make when being stimulated orally, I tapped Café Latte on the shoulder. She looked me in the eyes like she had learned her lesson, but she watched none the less. I placed my hand on The Pro's head so that I would know if she decided to look up and to encourage her to keep going. Women who like to please men orally also seem to like it when you rub their heads as they do it (be careful of tracks in America).

I was being satisfied physically, but I needed a mental additive. I stared at Café Latte. Her eyes rebounded from The Pro, and then back to me. Café Latte began to squirm in her chair. She was already hot; I imagine she was a flaming inferno by now. I was having a tug of war between physical pleasure and mental pleasure. It is like rubbing your head and patting your stomach.

273

I stopped The Pro and motioned to the bedroom. When she was out of sight, I raised my still exposed and now erect penis to Café Latte and asked her to kiss it. She gathered her lips together and placed a gentle kiss on the tip. That night I moved from the bedroom to the living room and back again. I serviced them both twice. Last I heard The Pro was in Italy using what she has to get what she wants. I imagine Café Latte is not far behind.

Dani is Swiss. She was not beautiful, but she was attractive in her own way. I liked her giving spirit. Her body was thin; the six-pack was pleasing, add a nice butt for a white girl, and the fact that she could dance, and you have a good sex partner. She also had a heart of gold and I was comfortable around her. She was independent, strong willed and had no problem paying her own way. She should write a book on how to fuck a 'bratha'. She had the European attitude about sex. She showed me a clean bill of health sheet before we did anything. I was seeing The Pro at the time and confided in Dani the concerns I had in my relationship; she was a true girlfriend and I have never had better advice about women than from another woman, except when that woman happens to have hidden motives. The Pro had placed her birth control pills where I was sure to see them. I asked Dani, "What the fuck does that mean… Am I supposed to take the rubber off?" "Be careful; she wants to get pregnant." "I know." Dani always squirmed away, if I pretended I was going to come inside of her, and then she started taking the pill.

All she wanted was affection, at any cost. She told me that she was accustom to picking up any man to have one-night stands when she was horny. "It was just sex." She would make him give her affection in the form of hugs and kisses, and then, "He could do whatever he wanted to." Her desire for affection was a strong driving force. My biggest mistake was in giving her this affection knowing that I could not sustain it; it was like a drug to her. When we hugged, she would sway gently from side to side and bury her face in my chest like a baby or child.

I remember the first time I hugged her for real. We had gone out and she spent the night at my place. We got in at 5 or 6 AM and she had to be at work at 10 AM. I did not feel like driving past my apartment to her place and then doubling back. I was drunk and I was tired from the night's activities. I assured her that I would drive her to work the following morning. She said, "Don't you try anything." Women are a trip. If I wanted to try something, it was four drinks ago. I let her sleep in my bed while I slept in a hammock in the common area of the apartment. After a few hours Dani came to awaken me. She stood over the hammock for a few minutes watching me. I know because I was awake. She looked as if she was trying to make a decision. When I opened my eyes in earnest, she was surprised. I reached out my hand to her and said, "Come here." I pulled her gently towards me.

She seemed nicer, sweeter and more understanding, experienced and opened minded than most. She was well traveled and spiritually attuned, even though she was an atheist. I have already said that she carried her own weight and on occasion even paid for me. That is a big surprise to most men and attractive as well. I took it as kindness.

She once called a locksmith to open the door of my apartment one morning. I was in the bed with another woman. It was my fault, but she had no right to do that. She wanted what so many seem to, confirmation of a suspicion. I had kicked Dani out of my apartment before the other woman arrived. She showed up 30 minutes before I was expecting company. The woman was always was punctual, so I had 30 minutes to get my unannounced horny company out. How do I know she was horny? She had walked a mile at 8:30 PM unannounced. I lied to get her out and she knew it. The phone started ringing at 4:00 AM. I turned it off. Around 7 AM I heard the familiar sound of keys at my door. When I opened it, there was Dani and a locksmith. How she convinced the building management to let her do this is still a mystery to me.

I was amazed that she had repeated the behavior of Psycho. After this, I remembered that people will do whatever is in their best interest and frequently disregard social normality in such situations. She crossed a line and I knew it would only get worse if I did not do something to stop it. I decided to withdraw from seeing her.

One night she came over without an invitation, spent the night and then did not want to have sex. No problem. I do not need sex from a woman. I had to show her that I could please myself better than she could. I had hoped that this would make her realize that she could not do the affection for sex thing with me, but she had an orgasm watching me masturbate and asked me to tell her when I was going to come (I was going to get a treat); this led to even more of an attachment.

Dani used to get upset because I would not have an orgasm solely through oral sex. She once asked me in the middle of her first attempt to satisfy me orally, "You do not want to come in my mouth?" She had been going at it for a while and fatigue had begun to take its toll on her jaw, lips and neck. I confessed that it took a lot to make me come orally. She responded with, "I am usually pretty good at making men come with my mouth." I was not upset with her for that. It showed experience and willingness to please and be pleased. Besides, who am I to judge sexual acts and histories?

I once made the mistake of coming before she had. It was the first time we had anal sex. She said, "You didn't wait for me." I responded as sincerely as I could with a pathetic, "I did not know you could have an orgasm while I fucked you in the ass." This was one of the few women who admitted to enjoying anal sex. "I am sorry; it won't happen again." After that, I waited and then I would tell her, "It's my turn." At that prompting, she would tuck pillows under her torso and prepare herself for whatever I wanted to do. Most women act like anal sex is the ultimate sacrifice. But she would request it. I always got a clue when she wanted it. "Ronaldo, my ass misses you," once or twice a week, like clockwork.

Dani only came four ways: on top, orally, from visual stimulation, or anally. When she was on top, she frequently asked me to stick my finger in her unoccupied hole while she played rodeo on my pelvis. Talk about the neighbors knowing my name, and the people downstairs knowing she was riding! The bed would get so loud I felt guilty and tried to stabilize the headboard with my hands, so it would not squeak and bang against the wall so loudly. She would get into this rhythm, up and down really fast and really deep. Her tempo would increase and then with a resounding, "OH, Ronaldo." she would be finished. She often laid there on top for a few minutes. I would let her rest for a moment then say, "You're not done." She would slowly begin to move again, but her fire was out. I had to put my hands on both cheeks and use my arms to rock her body to the rhythms of my upward thrusts or switch positions. If I wanted it long, I left her on top. If I wanted it fast, I would switch. Sometimes I would let her go directly to sleep or cuddle.

Once she said, "Oh Ronaldo, More!" What was that supposed to mean if I am having anal sex with someone? I asked, "You want more dick in your ass?" I had to ask because I usually have to hold back when going into a woman's backside. She said, "YES." I told her, "If you want more, come and get it." Then I positioned myself as stiff as I could with my penis sticking out as far as it might and allowed her to administer her own pleasure. She could go as deep or as shallow as she liked without any participation from me. She elected to go deep, really deep. What a turn on. She got her man that day. Anything I did after that was gravy. Oh yeah, she had no issue with spanking either.

One day when she entered my apartment I led her straight to the couch, bent her over, lifted her skirt, pulled her panties to the side and entered her. She kept asking me what I was doing, but she did not resist. As a matter of fact, she was laughing and giggling until I was inside of her and spanking her bottom.

I came into issue with Dani because she crossed the "Do what I say," line and became even more possessive than before. I had to kick her out of my apartment several times because she refused to leave when I did not want to kiss her goodbye. I am not big on kissing mouths; I know where they have been and I am not referring to my penis. I also I do not kiss people with whom I have just argued; it takes time to switch back into pleasure mode.

Dani and I parted when she headed home for good. We had memorable sex the night before she left. We are still friends and I hope to see her again when I go to that part of the world. Besides, I miss her ass and I hope it misses me.

Horn Muffin had the type of butt that you could put an ashtray on one cheek and your drink on the other. I expected her butt to change shape and sag when her jeans came off; it has happened before. But unlike many of the other big butts I have seen, hers was firm as a body builder's biceps, a true blessing (I think it was the walking that. If you want your butt to firm up, try walking).

I met her at a beach party given by an acquaintance. She was very forward and deserved several penalties for vaginal blocking throughout the night. She was attractive, but I had several other prospects that I wanted to explore at that moment. I had been working on one particular person for months and another advertised openly that she was the one going home with me.

A few days later Horn Muffin called the guy who gave the beach party and made it a point to have him invite me to her birthday party. I was bored, curious and hungry, so I went. She was more forward at her party than she was the first time we met. I accidentally left my ball cap and went back the next day to pick it up. When I got there she accurately recounted everything I did the night she first saw me. There were more than enough other distractions at the event. Anyone that interested has an intimate curiosity. She wanted to have sex with me too badly. It was a definite yellow flag, but when it comes to sex, the prevailing thought is why let an eligible one get away. She also admitted to telling another woman that she thought I was "hot". That was a mistake that would come back to haunt her.

Horn Muffin thought she was competing with her, when in fact this female and I were just continuing a long flirtation. Horn Muffin went so far as to say, "The only reason she wants you is because I do." If that is how women operate, thank you for the good word. The night's preliminaries ended with her saying, "Let's make love," just like she planned it. No male would have been disappointed by her performance. I would have given her an 8.4 solely based on enthusiasm.

When on top she always shook her head from side to side like she was signaling "No". It looked like some internal battle between opposing forces. I would lift my midsection an inch or two higher when she did this to tip the scales in my favor. But despite how good the sex was, I knew I was not going to be with this woman the way she wanted. I wanted sex; she wanted a man. I was single; she had a 1 ½ year-old child and an American boyfriend.

The most memorable sexual moment with Horn muffin was the night she said, "My ass!!!" while bouncing up and down on top of me. I interpreted this, as she wanted to have anal sex, so I asked, "You want it in your ass?" "Yes!" I told her to prepare herself and me. She used baby oil to lubricate herself first. I watched as she applied the oil to the tip of her finger then penetrated her anal canal. She let out a low moan. She then oiled my penis by stroking it up and down after applying more oil to her hands. After this she squatted over me and stuck my penis in her rear. I did not move; I lay there listening to her moan, groan and say things like, "slower", when she was the one in control and doing all the work. It was hilarious. I let her do this for a while. Then I asked her to switch her position to all fours; I was done playing. The icing on the cake was when we were done. She said, "That was my first time." I said, "Me too." Oh, it gets better!

I was done with her when she asked me for money to pay her phone bill. Horn Muffin's lived in Los Angeles. I was sure if he visited, I would not be allowed to call or come by. She did not tell me this and neither did her family. I noticed she had several very expensive electronic items in her home, all with American manufacturing tags. She had never been in the States and her income would not explain the computer, digital camera or washer. Someone from the States had given them to her. Finally she told me her little secret. I was looking at pictures on her digital camera. I came across a photo of a male sitting at the computer in her living room. He was in shorts and holding her child. She explained that it was her real boyfriend. I was relieved that she had someone else, but thought, "Damn, not again, the lies. Even after I decide to become honest Abe, I still cannot find a woman willing to tell the fucking truth." I asked her if she was trying to double dip from the American fund and I gave her the money anyway, about the equivalent of $13 USD. It was money well spent for two weeks of sex.

She called me one Monday to say that she thought it was better if we did not see each other anymore. I said, "OK." She wanted to go into why, but I cut her off explaining that it was not necessary. She said, "I'll call you back." I said, "For what?" It turns out that her friend saw me on the beach with another woman the day before and she did not like it. Somebody tell me why someone with a mate would get mad about my being on the beach with another woman? It is illogical, but not an unfamiliar scenario to me. Career Crasher did the same thing and so did almost every person who wants something. What selfish and greedy little creatures we are!

Do you remember Patricia? She came to visit me after I had not seen or heard from her in 13 years. She was 100 lbs heavier. I was facing a nightmare again. She came with one thing in mind, to get a husband. I know this because I received an e-mail by accident that all but spelled out her plans for coming. I told her I received the e-mail by accident and verbally told her I knew what she was planning; I "read" her over the phone and she hated it. I do not know if it was her biological clock or the desperation of being 35 and unwed. She did not realize that I could never trust her to be faithful again. She was the type of woman who needs constant companionship.

She even told me she has a "fuck buddy" who she cannot stand, but keeps in her life. All I wanted was her friendship and some closure. I told her that I had questions that needed asking in person, a hole in my heart that needed filling. She was the first woman with whom I had been in a long relationship and I loved her. In the months that we spoke she never asked me about another woman. She did not have to. One passage stood out in the e-mail. Patricia was responding to my writing, "The most beautiful women in the world live here." in a previous e-mail. Her response contained the following passage, "After reading about the women, I didn't want to go, but after reading the rest of the e-mail, it's Brazil or bust." She arrived to find out my girlfriend was visiting at the same time. I had told my girlfriend the entire story before and she was just as curious as I about the outcome.

Patricia came to my apartment that first night in town to find it occupied with another woman. She was visibly hurt. Well not hurt, but mad and confused that her scheme was foiled. I was surprised that she did not get off the plane wearing a wedding dress with her two sisters carrying the train. I was curious as to how far she would go to please and obtain what she wanted. She had not taken into account that I was older and more experienced. I told her I wanted to have a son and be with a queen. She had the solution. She would give me a child and be my queen. She went further to say my current girlfriend was not right for me.

Do not judge me! I told her that I needed to see her to close a hole in my heart. I needed to find out what went wrong with us. I accomplished my mission somewhat. She said she needed the same, but had concealed motives. She brought a photo album filled with pictures she and I had taken throughout our relationship. She showed it to my mate before she showed it to me. I knew what she was trying to accomplish and so do you, but my mate was older than both of us and knew what was going on as well.

I was born yesterday but I stayed up all motherfucking night.

One night while alone, Patricia and I kissed and I briefly sucked her breast. I told my girlfriend about this and she was not mad. Honesty is best always! I do still care for Patricia, but she and I can only be friends. That being said, the fact that I had another woman in town was irrelevant because she had a mate at home whom she failed to mention and had lied about her motives. Here is the key to me; come straight or do not come at all unless you want to get your feelings hurt. I am not stupid or naive and I do not fall for the same trick twice. I do not care how good you look or how I feel about you or how convincing our lies are.

Insanity: doing the same thing over and over again and expecting different results. Albert Einstein

This list does not include the near misses, probables, nor could haves. I have also left out many one nighters and the encounters that read like repeats of each other. Actually they "all" read like repeats to me. Meet girl, seduction (me seducing her or her seducing me), sex, more or less commitment, and then the breakup. The only difference is the length of time, places and people involved. All around the world it has been the same. I did my own scientific research using my diary as the lab book.

What is the difference between good sex and great sex? Everyone can have sex and it can be good. You have to practice to be "Great" at sex.

One day an elephant got a thorn stuck in her foot. She tried for the longest to remove it, but was unsuccessful. A mouse saw her predicament and offered to remove the thorn in exchange for sex. The elephant thought about it for a moment then said, "OK" The mouse was ecstatic. He removed the thorn and mounted the elephant. While the mouse was doing his thing, the elephant grazed. She could not even feel the mouse. The mouse, on the other hand, was really into it and thought he was doing something. A monkey who had witnessed the entire affair was laughing so hard he fell off his perch in a coconut tree. While grasping for a branch on the way down, he dislodged several coconuts. They hit the elephant in the back of the head in quick succession. The elephant screamed with pain, "Ouch! Ouch! Ouch!" Upon hearing this, the mouse said, "That is right bitch… Take it!!! Take it!!! You whore!!"

What is the difference between a good man and a Great one? A Great man can resist the flirtations of a beautiful woman and has the courage to be honest.

Me, Myself and I

Notice any patterns? Does it start to read like a laundry list, like the encounters did not matter? If so, when did it start to sound like that to you? When does it start sounding like I am on "My Soapbox" or bragging? Did you read the entire section or did you skip to the "juicy" parts? When I looked back, I realize that the pattern started with "the red hole". I tried to cut this chapter short, but ran into difficulty because of the interconnectedness, and impact. I did not take "artist privilege." I wrote as I saw it knowing there are two sides to every story and the truth. Here is what I have learned after reviewing sex as a whole:

1. I am a horny springbuck. I like sex, especially uninhibited sex and I do not want drama after an orgasm.
2. Every relationship I had came with a Pri$e-Tag. Sometimes I paid it and at others I did not. Sometimes I made the female pay.
3. I noticed that the higher I went up the social latter, the more attractive a prospect I became and the more access I had to women.
4. There were few instances where finance did not play a key factor in my relationships. Most women wanted a husband or at least help. The prominent expectation is that men are obligated to help women, and if she has children, them as well. My thought is that I

279

should not be held responsible for anyone's choices. "An emergency on your part does not constitute one on mine!" And, it has nothing to do with love.

5. I repeatedly confused good sex with love (I kept trying to find love in the arms of women or rather between their legs).

6. My lost faith in relationships has led to pain and needless suffering. I also learned that by manipulating situations to my advantage, I have caused harm to others. Usually before they could do it to me.

7. I have been fooled by external beauty (cosmetic symmetry) over and over again.

8. I have not bridled emotions and passion, favoring instant pleasure over long-term goals and objectives.

9. My definition of love has changed over time, but the sex is the same everywhere. Even the techniques for pleasing a male did not change. I looked all over for something new under the sun and did not find it.

10. I can satisfy the physical needs of a woman, but have issues with the emotional and spiritual. It is my belief that I am not responsible for anyone's well being, but if have sex, I am responsible for her physical gratification; it is just sex. If observed from a humanistic point of view, I know that I am responsible for everyone, but how many share this belief?

11. Most of the women I have been involved with had a mate, and they were willing to trade his ass in for another model or share themselves.

12. Most have had sex with someone or will soon enough.

13. Women choose with whom they mate most of the time.

14. Women have the same sexual desires as men.

15. Women are more concerned with emotional attachment than physical pleasure.

16. Men are more concerned with paternity and fidelity than emotional attachment.

17. Humans are as monogamous as most other animals.

18. Foreign women have more realistic expectations than most American women.

Suggestions, if you want to have sex, have great sex. Go all the way and give your partner what is wanted and more, or your partner will seek it somewhere else consciously or not. This is also a sure way to guarantee seconds.

Even if your partner does not know what is wanted, ask about previous experiences and likes, what was done and why, then give it. Use your imagination and your partner's fantasies as a guide. If your partner is afraid of sex, more than likely there are other issues as well and you might do well to run. Sex is a natural process and should not be traumatic or repressed.

I once jumped one of my partner's bones at 4:30 AM. Before I did the deed I laid there debating whether or not to do it. I knew she would be awake in an hour and a half because the alarm always went off at 6:00, but my "stiffy" argued for immediate action. I had a debated with myself for five minutes. "She's tired." "She said you can have sex whenever you want it; remember when she said, 'I like to fuck." "You can wait until she gets up." "Last time you did not do it and she said, 'You should have. I don't mind.'" "She said, 'Sex gives me energy; it makes me feel good afterward.' " In the end, I decided to do it. I looked to see what type of bottoms she was a wearing - pajama shorts secured at the waist with a string. I could not do the "quick snatch and enter" before she knew what was going on. I turned her over by grabbing her waist. I had to get to the knot. She woke up. I said, "Shut up! I just want to fuck you; you said I could." She cooperated. When I got the shorts off I laid her on her belly. She instinctively opened her legs and arched her back. I was already harder than Chinese arithmetic, so it was easy to penetrate her. She was dry on the outside, so I went slowly. I used my left hand to massage her clitoris as I pushed my way inside of her. After a few minutes I could feel the moisture and heard the distinct sound of my penis plunging inside of a wet vagina. Her gyrations helped. It was good. How do I know? When I was done she said, "Thank you for fucking me." My kind of girl; "You can go back to sleep now."

In my lasting relationships, I often have put more emphasis on sexual performance, social standing and appearance than on the other qualities that I now consider important. It was an attempt at obtaining beauty and perfection, an adaptation of social programming, and at the same time fulfilling my natural desires to mate with the best available subjects. It is no wonder that these relationships did not last. They were based on selfish desires and social acceptance. I wanted a beauty queen with a brain and a job, who also happened to be my closet freak without children; and I wanted her to be honest as well. This has not changed, but I also now want someone who knows herself, what she wants and is in touch with the universe.

I not only wanted the people I associated with to say, "Damn, she is fine", but also wanted them to know that I had chosen well. I was looking for social status confirmed by the quality of the woman on my arm. There seems to be a given premise, the better looking the woman, the more successful the man and vice versa. I was looking for a "good catch". The bottom line was I wanted to boost my own social standing by having what others perceived as a high quality mate. Do not judge me too harshly; people do it all the time. We look at physical attractiveness and then look at what kind of shoes we are wearing or ask, "What do you do for a living (translated: how much money do you make)?"

That it is very usual for directly sexual impulsions, short-lived in themselves, to be transformed into a lasting and purely affectionate tie; and the consolidation of a passionate love marriage rests to a large extent upon this process. Freud

What happens when the sex starts to decline or becomes less pleasing? After all, I like fish, but I do not want it every day, if beef and chicken are also available... Sex with the same person all the time often turns a Ritz into a Saltine.

I have grown to know the difference between love and sex. And, I have always needed more than just sex. I have not met any one woman who was able to satisfy my emotional, financial, physical and spiritual needs. Guess what? I never will. These are things that I have to provide for myself. My perfect person is me and always has been and you are your perfect you. Everyone is perfect. All we have to do is discover what we are perfect at.

I have not been willing to give myself over to anyone completely. Nor do I believe you or I, were meant to. There are issues that I must resolve with myself before I can truly share, and so do most other people. Though I try, I do not trust myself to act appropriately all the time and I trust others less. How am I to trust someone else to do what I am incapable of, loving unconditionally?

If I knew then what I know to be true now I would never have had sex with the impression that it had anything to do with love. I would have looked at it for what it was: physiological gratification, social necessity, psychological substitution, needs displacement and spiritual connectivity. I no longer engage in such folly. After all, folly is forgivable in youth, but abominable later in life because if one repeats the same mistakes, the lesson was not learned.

Hell is repetition. Cecilia Sidenbladh[299]

If that is true, then I see hell all around me.

Sex has many purposes. The most obvious is procreation, but sex also has a healing effect on the human body just like a hug or any other form of affection. Sex has little or nothing to do with love. Until we all realize this relationships will continue to fail over and over again. Women will continue to call men "dogs" and men will continue to call women "bitches". Our bodies are not designed for monogamy. I abstained from sex for some time. That is right; I was celibate. I do not want or need the headaches or heartaches sex causes. I said it before; sex is for making babies and nothing more. We like sex because of those super sensitive nerves that trigger an explosion of chemicals in the brain. Who does not enjoy the bliss that follows an orgasm?

Females know what males want. I have always said, "If you know what someone wants, you control the interaction." The control comes from being able to dangle the carrot in front of the horse. Most have dangled the carrot of sex, and a few men have had the sense to dangle the promise of security. I have. That is how I obtain sex. I remove the implied value of the all-important vagina; it is just a sex organ, not something to worship. Have you ever seen the way some females react to not being hit on? Have you ever seen how a female acts when she realizes that a male she wants does not want her? How do people react to rejection?

I tell every new encounter, "You can keep your pussy until you are ready to give it to me." The operative word is *give*; not sell. I now understand what an old man meant when he said, "You are making the price of pussy go up." Many will criticize me for sleeping with whores. My answer to them is that I always had to pay for sex in one form or another, as most other males have. The only difference is paying up front (a clear Pri$e-Tag) or paying after (hidden Pri$e-Tag). Besides, if the CIA, Congressmen and lobbyist can do it in Watergate, so can I.

If you act like a prostitute (want payment[300] in exchange for sex), or a whore (want money in exchange for sex), I will treat you like one. You do not have to believe me. I dare you to ask any honest male if they have had to pay for women all their lives or not, gay men do not count.

If you act like an equal partner, I will treat you like one. I am not pointing fingers at people; I am pointing at the main issue of contention between males and females. We are in competition with one another. I was not exploiting women. They were trying to exploit me. Most women think they are superior to men and that we are stupid. That is bullshit. If you believe that, then

---

[299] "The Ice Maiden" late 19th century play based on the Diaries of Victoria Benedictsson, called the "Big Book".
[300] Payment can be anything. If a woman or man expects anything in exchange for sex, "anything except money", it is considered payment. Attention, affection, love, gifts, paying of bills, dinner, etc. you are by Webster's dictionary definition a "prostitute". I call it Pri$e – Tag Roman$e.

you deserve the trained monkey that you will attract. I refuse to pay the hidden charges or play the mating game by rules that favor anyone but me.

I looked at the incidents I used to see as problems that I have had in my life. At the base of most of them was a woman. I resigned my commission because of a married woman who said she loved me. I left a Fortune 500 company because I was accused of sexual harassment. I neglected my position at another Fortune 500 company because of a woman. I have lost women because of other women. I was distracted in college by women. I have spent money I did not have because of women. I have had to fight because of women. I know that I am ultimately responsible for my actions, but before a boy gains dick control (some never gain it, they just lose the ability to use it), he is at the mercy of his anatomy and women. Women know this and use it to their advantage. Do you know anyone who has pimped a male for a dinner? Ever heard of a woman pulling up her skirt or opening her top button just as the policeman approaches the car to issue a ticket?

I have learned to be patient, and not pursue or pay for sex. I have learned not to give into "Female Privilege". I watch for the physical cues that announce interest (lowering of the eyes and head, neck exposure, a smile with the head slightly tilted, the hair fling, etc…). I return these cues with cues of my own (a returned smile, posturing and flaring) if I am just flirting and ignore them when I really want to have their attention, am really interested, and want some sex, but sometimes ignoring a woman is real and I do not want to be bothered.

The interested woman usually acts in the same manner as a three month old when their caregiver ignores them in the Face-to-Still Face Paradigm experiment. They become more aggressive and forward in their attempts to solicit attention. If competition is added, the intended usually ups the ante and becomes extremely forward or, depending on the competition, gets an attitude. They want me to know without a doubt that they are interested. If I continue to ignore them, do not respond appropriately or do not try to fuck them the normal response is, "He must be gay."

I thought I would add The Rapist to list for sheer humor and impact. She was a big woman who raped me one night. I was drunk as a skunk and she lured me to her room with the offer of a cheese steak. I passed out after eating. When I woke up the following morning, The Rapist was lying beside me with a smile on her face. I was naked and had to ask what happened the night before. She told me she mounted me. "What? I was passed out. How could you think I wanted sex?" She said, "Your body responded." What if I had done that to a drunken woman? Would I be a rapist? Of course I would be, but in a two-tier system….

Oh! I almost forgot. The moral of the joke: when I first heard it, the orator said, "A fly has to drop 6 inches before the pussy will get wet." But I changed it over the years to "a lot of shit has to happen before the pussy will get wet" (Page 217).

Chapter VII

Fear

Fear: to be afraid or apprehensive.[301]

Our deepest fear is not that we are inadequate. Our deepest fear is that we are powerful beyond measure. It is our light, not our darkness, that most frightens us. We ask ourselves, who am I to be brilliant, gorgeous, talented and fabulous? Actually, who are you not to be? You are a child of God. Your playing small doesn't serve the world. We were born to make manifest the glory of God that is within us. It's not just in some of us; it's in everyone. And as we let our own light shine, we unconsciously give other people permission to do the same. As we are liberated from our own fear, our presence automatically liberates others. Marianne Williamson[302]

Think about the worse days of your life. Now think about the best days of your life. What is the difference? I put my answer at the end of the chapter, but would like you to think about it for a second.

I remember the longest walk I ever took. It was the walk from a bus stop to my great-grandparents' house. It was about a mile, 20 minutes on a good day. That winter night, it seemed to take forever. It was cold and the wind was blowing. I was dressed for the occasion, so the weather did not bother me much. The ice that had formed from the thawing and refreezing of the snow presented a challenge; it was slippery and I had to watch my step to keep my footing, one unnoticed ice patch and I would end up on my backside.

I had to walk uphill and negotiate three corners before I would reach my destination. It was downhill for a half block after that. Mentally I usually divided the walk into two sections to make it easier. I also distracted myself with songs in my head or thinking about something. There was a warehouse on the right at the first corner at the top of the hill. I had finished the longest part of the journey and made the right that placed me in front of the warehouse. There were several loading bays divided by cylindrical support columns. I would say there were eight to ten of them. I was on the side of the street closest to the warehouse, maybe twenty or thirty feet from the first bay. It had floodlights that stayed on all night to discourage theft.

I noticed a shadow behind the second column. It seemed strange, but I thought maybe someone was taking a leak. I took the precaution to cross the street. If the guy was up to no good, I had put enough distance between us to have time to make an evaluation, fight or flight. He stayed behind the column until I had passed. We were 50 feet from each other when my heart sank into the abyss of fear. A second shadow emerged from behind another pillar further ahead. I knew then that it was going to be a robbery attempt. My heart began to race and my brain struggled with the chemical reactions to come up with a solution. I thought about running, but the ice would make it difficult to keep my footing and a fall would ensure my being caught, not to mention trigger their chase instinct. In the middle of this thought, a third would-be-assailant appeared from another column and the trap was all but sprung.

My crossing the street did give me a short lead on them, but they were converging quickly. The last one tried to cut off my escape without letting me know it was a trap. I kept thinking, "Let me make it to the next corner." I could make a run for it or speed up once I was out of their

[301] Merriam-Webster's.
[302] Marianne Williamson (1952-): American spiritual activist, author, lecturer and founder of The Peace Alliance.

sight. I hit the corner 30 feet ahead of the third person. It was a three and a half block run to the house. Damned ice! I could make it, but I could also be caught. Not another person was in sight, it was dark and the street was quiet. It was early, but during the winter the sun set as early as 5:30 and the predators knew it. It was too cold to be outside without a good reason. The summer crowds who sat on their porches to keep cool were nowhere to be seen. There would be no help from concerned citizens; I was alone.

I picked up my pace at the corner and glanced over my shoulder as I did so. The three had become a group of one and my lead had diminished. Evidently they had quickened their paces as well. They were close enough that I could hear their feet crunching the ice and snow behind me. The increased pitch of the sound told me exactly how far they were and at what pace they were stepping, damn near at a trot. My brain was in overdrive, still working on a solution to the problem and still fighting my instinct to run. They had closed to within striking distance and my adrenaline levels must have been at a peak, when I turned around to face them, unzipped my coat and placed my right hand inside of it. It was a bluff. I wanted them to think I had a weapon… No. I wanted them to think I had a gun: "God made men; Sam Colt[303] made them equal" and to reinforce the ruse I walked straight towards them.

It was a gamble. I was truly rolling the dice. I concluded that they were unarmed. Armed robbers do not tend to work in groups of three and they do not set up funnel ambushes. Can you imagine the look of surprise on their faces when I turned on them? The game's rules had changed and they had no idea what to do about it. I hoped they were scared now. In those moments of uncertainty, no one was sure who was predator and who was prey. I thought my heart would jump out of my chest, but I showed nothing but the meanest war face I could muster as we passed each other. I split the group down the middle, staring the biggest of the group in the eyes as they approached and passed.

The pinnacle moment was when they were so close that our shoulders could touch one another simply by leaning left or right. They still could have grabbed me and beat me to a pulp. I would have fought back, but three to one is pretty good odds in their favor. They parted and provided a pathway for me and nothing happened as we passed each other. I kept an eye on them by looking over my shoulder. I gave them a head start before I back tracked and began to follow them. It was amusing see them start to walk even faster, like I was chasing them. The game ended when I reached my great-grand's street and made a right. They kept walking. As I entered the house I said my hellos and joined the other males for our ritual bonding. I never told anyone what had happened that night. I did not see the point. All I would have gotten in return was a lot of second-guessing and comments about how stupid I was. Besides, I doubt if anyone would have believed me anyway.

I still get scared, even though I know that outcomes are usually a lot less severe than our imagination. The difference is I know that I can control fear with a tremendous amount of energy concentrated on a real solution and not on the imagined probable outcome. I often ask myself, "What is the worst that can happen?"

---

[303] Samuel Colt (1814-1862): the inventor of the Colt revolver and founder of the Colt firearms company.

Fear can paralyze reason and temporarily stun the mind's ability to think. It grips like a python, increases respiration and heart rate. It momentarily freezes cognitive thought. It makes "men" wet their pants and the smallest of animals turn into the most vicious of beasts. It is, in my opinion, one of the most powerful emotions and instincts because even love takes a back seat to fear in most cases.

No passion so effectually robs the mind of all its powers of acting and reasoning as fear.
Edmund Burke[304]

Too many dreams fall into oblivion because of fear. The fear of failure or ridicule murders dreams in their cribs. The thought of flying scares many, even though statistics show that flying is by far safer than driving. Fear and its son, Doubt, stop people from trying out for the football team, starting a business, traveling, telling the truth, or running for student government. Fear makes us afraid of the dark, prisoners in our own homes and it makes us surrender freedoms in exchange for security.

Many times just sharing a thought with others is enough to stop the creative process. People have a habit of super imposing their fears on our ideas. Try telling someone of a dream to go into business for yourself or do something adventurous. Usually you will be bombarded with cautions and doubts instead of being encouraged and supported. Even if we are not successful in our endeavors, we learn a great deal more than by sitting secure in a 9 to 5 job where someone else dictates our lives; and we have a rare chance to live life the way it was meant to be, without fear.

We go so far as to instill our fears in our children. "Do not climb that tree; you'll break your neck." I like climbing trees; it is fun. I even taught my sister how to do it. I remember encouraging her to keep three limbs planted at all times, and then you could advance yourself with the free limb. She climbed as I guarded her. If she slipped, I had her. She was scared, but I kept talking to her and she kept climbing. We ended up in my chair at the top of the tree. We sat there a moment to view the world from a different, higher perspective and then we descended. I know why mountaineers climb the highest peak, because it is there. A friend would not even allow her daughter to take out the trash without watching her. Because of this her daughter was afraid to go outside alone; she was twelve. I remember staying out all day and going on mini-adventures when I was that age. I am not saying that there are not threats to our safety, but many times we exaggerate the danger.

I remember my family turning off all electrical appliances during thunderstorms. When I asked them why they were doing it, they really did not know the answer. They actually thought turning off electrical appliances would reduce the chances of the house being struck by lightning. I might have bought into it if they lived on a farm, but Ben Franklin[305] had solved that problem years ago. They lived in a row house in the middle of a metropolis. That particular fear was a carryover from the old days before circuit breakers and grounding. We should stop passing fear to our children. They will turn out to be just as afraid as we are.

---

[304] Edmund Burke (1729-1797): British statesman, parliamentary orator and political thinker.
[305] Benjamin Franklin (1706-1790): Invented the lightning rod. Diplomat and statesman. Among the founding fathers of the United States.

What are the odds of someone being a victim of violent crime? How many people do you know who have been victims of crimes? Compare that number with the number of people you actually know and that will give you an idea of what the odds are. If you take away those who went to an ATM at midnight in an isolated spot or those who were engaged in shady activities, the odds drop even further. I lived in a country famous for its crime and one of the two times I was assaulted, the police did it.

Violent crime rates have declined since 1994, reaching the lowest level ever recorded by National Crime Victimization Survey[306]. 2002 statistics show that minorities who live in Western states and urban areas are more likely to be victims of violent crime. 87% of murders are committed by an acquaintance. In 2002, 53% of incidents of violent crime occurred between 6 a.m. and 6 p.m. And the perpetrators were almost always acquaintances. Almost two-thirds of rapes/sexual assaults occurred at night between 6 PM. and 6 AM.

Police and correctional officers, taxicab drivers, private security workers and bartenders were the most likely victims of workplace violence. This being said, unless you are a minority dope dealing female cop who moonlights as a bartender and lives in Los Angeles and have a psychotic friend, your chances of being exposed to violent crime are about as good as hitting the lottery. So why are we afraid?

70% of our fears are influenced by environmental factors. Jeanne Wehner[307], Ph D. and Lorraine Flaherty[308], Ph D.

I remember walking across the street one day. There was always a long line of cars waiting to enter the inspection station around the corner. The line was so long that it often extended around the corner, pass my school and a block or two further. It was lunchtime and many people used this time to get their yearly vehicle inspection done. I just happened to cross near the car of a white woman. She looked at me, locked her door and rolled up the window. I do not know what she thought she had to fear from a kid in broad daylight with people everywhere. I have also had women cross the street when I was near them, or clutch their purses and then move away from me in elevators. This is the real America from the perspective of a minority. Why are you afraid of us and everyone else?

These examples of fear had a negative effect on me as well. They made me angry because I knew why they behaved the way they had. It made me fear the future and feel angry because of the stereotype that was applied to me. I knew that these were not the last instances when I would encounter prejudice because of stereotypes and fear. People have a habit of fearing what they do not know. Instead of investigating and rationalizing the unknown, many invent or listen to falsehoods that lead to incorrect conclusions. We then pass these falsehoods on to others. Before you know it, we have invented an urban myth or a stereotype. All African-American men steal, so grasp your purse close when they come near you. Actually, whites commit more crimes than

---

[306] National Crime Victimization Survey in 2002 (Department of Justice Statistics). The crime index rate decreased 1% from 2001 to 2002. From 1993 to 2002 the rate fell 25%.

[307] Jeanne Wehner, Ph, D.: Professor at Colorado University at Boulder Institute for Behavioral Genetics.

[308] Lorraine Flaherty, Ph, D.: Adjunct Professor; Office: The Genomics Institute Rensselaer Polytechnic Institute

all minorities in the United States combined. They just get lower sentences and less press coverage.

Do not go to South Central Los Angeles; there are gangs and rampant crime. I went there and I saw a nice neighborhood with nice people, not at all like the media portrayed it. These are falsehoods, but many people believe these myths with no concrete evidence.

Fear is the main source of superstition and one of the main sources of cruelty. To conquer fear is the beginning of wisdom. Bertrand Russell[309]

Fear is and has been used by tyrants, religions, governments and terrorist organizations throughout history. Governments and tyrants have used the knowledge that we want to feel safe to systematically remove liberties as well as, exercising cruelty on certain segments of the population while lulling the others into submissive behavior. McCarthyism, the war on terror and the Nazi movement are perfect examples of how governments use fear.

Terrorists use the most basic fear to their advantage, the fear of indiscriminant death. They hope to scare enough people so they can get what they want, the logic being that people will do anything to feel safe. That is one of the reasons the Taliban came to power. The Afghans were tired of constant fighting. The Taliban brought brutal peace, but peace nonetheless. Those who have an intimate understanding of how the mind reacts to fear can effectively manipulate, not only the behaviors of others, but also accurately anticipate popular reaction. It is like a global chess game that, over the eons, has exhausted its combinations.

I once scared four friends. There were three adult females and one 12-year-old. The host of the evening's festivities lived four flights above my apartment and we had planned to order pizza, drink wine and talk. I was delayed downstairs and was to join them later.

I scratched lightly on Silvia's door with my fingernails. I knew the women were sitting in the living room and would eventually hear the sounds, even over the loud cackling. I listened for footsteps and placed my finger over the peephole. I heard them discussing what they were experiencing and knew that someone else would come to the door to investigate. When she looked out the peephole, I put my eyeball close enough to be seen. I heard whoever looked explaining that she saw an eyeball. The pitch of her voice was high, and I could hear and feel the others getting nervous. Someone else approached the door and I hit it with my fist just before she reached it. All I heard was screaming and panicked footsteps on the other side of the door. I laughed so hard I cried. Needless to say they got mad at me, but it was worth it. More to the point, others have used fear in much the same manner as I did. The results of which can be seen in the behavioral patterns of people.

Where Fear Comes From

I was once locked in a closet. It was the most terrifying situation I had experienced to that point in my life. I have no idea what I thought would happen to me in that small enclosure,

---

[309] Bertrand Arthur William Russell (1872-1970) was a British philosopher, logician, essayist and social critic, best known for his work in mathematical logic and analytic philosophy.

especially since I was not alone. My brother and two girls were with me. For some reason we could not open the door from the inside. I cried and screamed until we were rescued. Strange how I like confined and dark quiet places today.

Scientists now believe that they have isolated the fear emotion or what controls the fear response. It is located in a primitive[310] part of the brain and is called the amygdala. It controls, in part, our fear factor (fight or flight). Our ancestors used the amygdala as a central alert system, a warning of predatory dangers. It works hand and hand with the central nervous system. This system has been perfected over millions of years of experiencing different fears. It has been programmed into our genes. Some fears are so basic that we are not aware of them.

There are basic fears that are common across cultures and present in many animals. An unexpected loud noise startles us; and threats, real or perceived, trigger the freeze or fight reflex[311]. Once the source of fear is removed, our bodies attempt to return to homeostasis (a state of relaxation)[312]. Learned fear is more influenced by culture, experience and environment. It also tends to be more localized. A child in a "primitive" society is less likely to be afraid of animals than an urban American. On the other hand, these same people will probably be afraid of an elevator. Inner city children's fear includes poverty and death, while suburban children may fear not getting into their college of choice.

When our senses relay information that is perceived as a threat, the amygdala sends out signals to the other parts of the brain that trigger defensive behavior: rapid heartbeat, raised blood pressure, a diminished capacity to feel pain, an exaggerated startle reflex and the production of stress hormones. In animals that have consciousness, these physical changes are accompanied by the emotion of fear.

As civilization progressed, the way in which we dealt with our environment evolved and so did our fears. Our genes already hold the automatic fear responses mentioned earlier. Animal attacks were still a minor possibility, but our neighbors, acquaintances or family are more likely to do us harm. Hence, we became afraid of people. This is quite natural. We are often forced to compete with them. If you have ever seen animals compete over resources, it is not a far leap to know of what entities with choice are capable.

Fear is an innate response, a natural occurrence. It causes the brain to short circuit our cognitive reasoning mechanisms. Irrational thinking or slow cognitive processes are the result. Ever seen a police chase and wondered, "What is he or she doing?" They are being chased and are not thinking; they just want to get away. Ask O.J. what he was thinking when he was driving all over Los Angeles; I know Johnnie Cochran did.

One way I have learned to combat the effects of fear is to practice thinking under stressful situations. The military gave me plenty of practice. They train recruits to the point where desired actions under stress are as automatic as the fear response. You cannot be afraid and think at the same time. The military has gained this knowledge through centuries of experimentation. They

---

[310] The most primitive part of the brain sometimes called the Reptile brain or Hind brain
[311] The sympathetic division of the nervous system controls the fight or flight reflex.
[312] The parasympathetic division of the nervous system controls relaxation.

bark orders, short concise messages that are designed to elicit a team response. Physical trials fatigue the body. Mental trials fatigue the brain. After a month of this, the ground is fertile for planting new ideas. After three months, 75 people can march, eat and think as a team. Strangely enough I realized this in the shower. I noticed that when I my head came into contact with the shower caddie and my eyes were closed, I would jerk my head backwards. It is a reflex. Just like touching a horse on its flanks with a rope will make it bolt. Its brain says a predator is attacking. The natural reflex is to run. Even when I consciously tried to stop moving my head backward, the moment the thought left my head, I found myself jerking every time my forehead touched anything. I finally had to convince my reptile brain that it has nothing to fear in the shower and then I repeatedly touched the shower caddie over and over again until the reflex was gone - personal deprogramming.

I remember riding my new bike through a nearby nature trail for the first time. I knew every inch of that park because I had played and walked in it for years. It was a dream of mine to race through those woods on a bright red Mongoose. At $150.00, it was very expensive. I asked my grandfather if I could have one the first time I saw it perched high on a display rack in JC Penny's. He said he would help me buy it. If I raised half the money, he would put the remaining half on his credit card, and I could pay the rest in installments. I had to cut grass and do odd jobs like wash cars and clean up people's rooms. I landed my first contract from my mother, $5 for one cleaning per week. "Need a haircut granddad?" "Hey Mr. Jones, I'll wash and wax your van for $ 10." After three months of toil we returned to the store to find that the bike I wanted was not on sale anymore. It was back to its original price - $185.00. I pleaded with my grandfather to purchase it and promised to get the rest of the money to him as soon as I could. He refused. I got mad as hell at him. I could not understand why he would not front the extra $35.00, but I do now. I compromised. There was another bike in my price range. It was a Mongoose, but not the top of line model I yearned for. I assembled it myself. I test rode it up and down the street and around the block. The other children asked me if it was my birthday. I was feeling pretty full of myself. My baby was ready for the road.

I was imagining a race. I was in the lead and trying to fend off my competitors. I do not know why; they never won (it was my imagination and in my world, my story, I always win), but it gave me an imagined reason to push harder and go faster. I rounded a corner and found myself facing a downed tree limb. I had to break hard and slide sideways to avoid a collision. "That was not here a week ago." The branch had broken from the huge walnut tree that was growing beside the path. "Jump it." "Nah; it's too high." I lifted the bike over the barrier and continued my ride and quest for the freedom of daydreaming. "You had better remember that branch is there on the way back." "I will!"

Where was I? Oh yeah… back to the race. I had to fight to get back in the lead, the unexpected pit stop had cost me valuable time, but I could still win if I pushed as hard as I could. No sooner than I was in the imaginary race again, I ran into about ten boys (there may have been only seven boys, but give me the creative license to add yeast) headed in the opposite direction on their bikes. I almost had a head-on collision with the leader. "This ain't good," is what I thought. "I know," is what I answered.

The closest member looked me up and down, "Nice bike." That was code for I like your bike and I am thinking about taking it. "Where do you live?" That was code for we do not know him, but he could live close. "Right around the corner," I pointed in the general direction of home. It was ¾ mile away. "What are you doing here?" "I am racing." I said, "You guys want to race?" I turned my bike around and began pedaling as fast as I could. I had worked too hard and long to get this bike and to fulfill this dream to have some punks take it because they outnumbered me.

They were in hot pursuit. I think I caught them off guard by bolting, but by now they had caught on. I was not racing now; I was fleeing and it was real. The dirt bike is not made for breakaway speed; but the curves, hills and my knowledge of the terrain helped me stay ahead of my pursuers. I looked over my shoulder and saw the looks on some of the faces; they were not happy. They looked like a pack of wolves on the hunt. Mr. "Nice Bike" was in the lead. He looked to be the oldest and was the biggest. He also had a ten-speed, a bigger and faster bike. The chase instinct was in full effect and I was the rabbit.

I was scared, and running more on instinct than logic. "It's just another race." "No, it ain't." "You always win." "I'm scared." "Remember the branch!" "OH SHIT, the branch!" It was just ahead, around the next bend, but they could not see it. I thought about going around, but the branch stretched from where it limply remained attached to the walnut the tree to the gully on the opposite side of the three or four foot wide path. I could not stop to pick-up my bike; they were on my heels by now. "Jump it there!" "Feet please do not fail me now!!!"

I had done it before, but never anything this high or with this much at stake. I turned the corner as fast as I could. I had a few seconds to aim for the lowest part of the obstacle; there was a dip in the branch that resembled a "U". I aimed for it. A few feet in front of the branch I yanked back and upward on the handlebars as hard as I could. The front wheel rose almost to the vertical. "Now!" I pushed forward and upwards with the same desperation. I thought I would dislocate my shoulders. The bike leveled itself about 2 feet from the ground. I felt a bump as the back tire grazed the top of the branch. I landed safely on the other side. I was surprised, amazed and happy as shit. I peeked over my shoulder to see the pack in a pile-up on the other side of the branch. Some had stopped in time, but those in the rear crashed into them. A few of them were smiling, but most were pissed. I saw Mr. "Nice Bike" at the front of the pile up staring in disbelief at what had to be a huge smile on my face. A few more seconds and I cleared the park. The checkered flag waved; I won again. The crowd went absolutely wild and so did I.

Our subconscious mind develops defense mechanisms in an attempt to keep us in a relatively happy state. The mechanism asks, "What can I do right now that will make me feel safe?" Esther Giller[313]

Our defenses often keep us alive and out of harm's way. They make us look both ways before we cross the street. They let us know when we are about to be hurt. They let us know something is wrong. The problem with some people's defenses is that they are running all the time. This happens when we have to respond to chronic and repetitive experiences such as childhood abuses, social neglect, combat, urban violence, concentration camps, prison, abusive relationships, or enduring deprivation.

---

[313] Esther Giller: President and Director, the Sidran Foundation.

When the body stays in a state of heightened alertness, the effects can be devastating. Most people who develop these types of fears suffer from a form of Post Traumatic Stress Disorder (PTSD). Their high state of alertness lulls their defenses into a low state of arousal. Eventually, our phobias become harmful and the thought of changing our behavior is terrifying, because it is all we know. The majority of us live with this disorder all of our lives, and end up taking a drug to subdue the effects.

Reality Check

Imagine the most frightening thing that could happen to you. What do you fear the most? Is it the fear of being raped (losing control), losing your job (losing income), going to prison (losing freedom), bankruptcy (losing money), not knowing love (losing life's force) or being involved in armed conflict (losing your life)?

I asked a few people that question. A friend said the pain she would experience if attacked by a wild animal. I had to laugh because she lives in the city. I asked her about death. She said her views of death had changed and it was not one of her primary fears anymore. I tend to agree. Another friend said being shot, going to jail and being without money. A waitress told me she feared her boyfriend cheating on her. I had to clarify that she meant infidelity. I then asked her if it was loss that she feared. She said yes. "Financial loss or losing intimacy?" "Intimacy" The fear of losing love is as real as the fear of spiders, but much stronger.

My sister said the fear of being alone. She had always had someone close to her. Going out on her own was traumatic for her even though she had a strong support system. I remember the experience as being uncomfortable as well, but it was not traumatic. I was happy to be out of the house and away from controlling adults. My mother said it was the fear of being without money. She said her age is the main reason for her concern. As she ages, my mother thinks more about not being able to support herself and she thinks that her children cannot or will not do it. That is a sobering and disappointing thought. My mother has been a "free" spirit for as long as I can remember. She was never been one to work a 9 to 5. Maybe if she had worked more, she could have saved and provided for herself, but she did not and now it is haunting her and residually, me.

My fear is not to live up to my own expectations. I want to be financially successful and I want to be able to love everyone and fear nothing. But, I am afraid that I will die before that mission is complete. I am not fearless. However, I do not scare as easily as most. A gun in my face is review. The police in any country are not a problem. Posturing and gum flapping are typical responses that I have come to recognize and I try not to respond, but usually I cannot help but laugh.

Another way to approach fear is from the perspective of trauma. Part of our learned fear comes from our own experiences and has nothing to do with our ancestor's experiences. If an experience is viewed as traumatic, it will be remembered as being bad, something to avoid and to fear. My perspective of trauma is probably much different from yours and vice versa. A soldier who has been in combat views the taking of life differently than someone who has never faced similar circumstances. A rape victim has a very different view of life. The military programs its

293

combatants in such a way that taking the life of an enemy is considered the lesser of two evils. The military builds and reinforces a matrix of programs that allows a human being to function under extreme stress with the sole purpose of "making the enemy give his life for his country".[314] And, even then we have to be rotated from the frontlines to recalibrate our internal gyros because the body can remain alert only so long before there is damage to the psyche. The body can only stand so much stress or trauma before it begins to break down.

Habitual criminals do not consider prison as traumatic an experience as a first time detainee might. My childhood friend had a ritual of committing petty crimes when the weather got too cold to stay on the street so that he could get "three hots and a cot" for the winter.

Whores often find that rape is just another part of doing business. I am sure they cry, but it does not drive them from the streets or the profession. I saw a documentary about prostitutes. One of the girls told of her experience with gang rape. A "John" kidnapped her at gunpoint and made her perform sexual favors for a group of eight men. I wondered if she had been paid to do the same thing if she would have considered it traumatic, profitable or even fun.

Carpenters live with the fact that they may get a splinter. My ex-girlfriend got a splinter once and she made me stop everything and attend to her needs immediately. You would have thought that the world was coming to an end. Our experiences desensitize us to certain traumas, but the fact remains, we all experience trauma on some level. The difference lies in how we react. I have been laid off, robbed at gunpoint, beaten up and without money most of my life, but I feel rich for having the experiences. I have also been behind bars and experienced what would be considered inappropriate sexual situations as a child. Life goes on and it is not an excuse. My initial reaction to each of the stimuli was much the same as anyone else's but not now.

Looking back, I know I created the fear that made the events traumatic. If I were to face the same experiences again, my reactions would be very different. I would look at them as a review of the past and not a new trauma. Not just because of the way I was socialized, but also because I am in a different mindset. No fear for fear's sake.

I was sitting in the back of the bus. It was a day like any other except for the fact that "Big Rob" was sitting five feet away. I did not know him, but I had seen him before. He was a bit of a street celebrity. He and his crew, the "A Team", were infamous around the city. It was during a time when gangs were first becoming prevalent in the inner cities and DC had the highest murder rate in the country. I must have stared too long because he noticed me. "Let me see your ring." I was wearing a gold class ring. It was not mine. I found it, but it was gold and he knew that. "If you give him the ring, you might as well kiss it goodbye." "I know." "Well, what are you going to do?" "Say 'No' " "He is going to kick your ass." "I know he is going to try."

"NO!" I noticed the looks of the other passengers who knew what was happening. There was surprise (he did not just tell that gorilla "No"!), excited anticipation (we are going to see someone get beat down.) and there was avoidance (I do not want to see what is about to happen.). I was supposed to be scared enough to hand over the ring without protest. I was afraid,

---

[314] Gen. George Patton: "No bastard ever won a war by dying for his country. He won it by making the other poor dumb bastard die for his country"

but I had been through this before. The person was different, but the objective was the same - take by force or intimidation. The last time I "loaned" a bully $ 1.00. He never paid it back, nor had he intended. I was not big enough to make him pay me back. That episode still haunted me.

"No!" I said with my bravest war face. I braced for the fight that was sure to come. He outweighed me by 100 pounds and was a foot taller. When he did nothing, I was shocked. He just sat there and stared at me. I got off the bus at my appointed stop and so did he. "What is he up to?" "I do not know, but there are plenty of people here and he probably won't try anything in public." We looked at each other from opposite bus stops until he boarded another bus headed in the opposite direction. It took some time for my body to return to "all systems clear". I had mixed emotions about the incident. I refused but the heart pounding in my chest told me I was still afraid. How do I stop the fear?

Nothing is to be feared, but - fear itself. Michel de Montaigne[315]

I do not like to lose income, but I know there are other ways to make money and I will survive. Being in a situation where I could lose my life is not a comfortable one, but when the situation involves humans, I try not to lose my composure; I usually lose what I am willing to give the assailant. I am used to not having money, and losing whatever I have in my pocket is not worth crying or dying over. The sexual lessons of childhood, limited to kissing and petting, do not generate hatred or remorse. It happened and I lived. I was behind bars for 10 or 15 minutes; it was enough to let me know I do not want to return; but if I do, chances are I will not die. Whatever does not kill you should make you stronger and whatever does kill you was supposed to. There are no accidents.

It is the subjective experience of the objective events that constitutes the trauma...The more you believe you are endangered, the more traumatized you will be...Psychologically, the bottom line of trauma is overwhelming emotion and a feeling of utter helplessness. There may or may not be bodily injury, but psychological trauma is coupled with physiological upheaval that plays a leading role in the long-range effects. In other words, trauma is defined by the experience of the survivor. Esther Giller

Many experience severe anxiety, depression and difficulty concentrating or sleeping after a traumatic experience. They also dream about what happened, have inappropriate guilt feelings and emotional numbness, or we are irritable, have flashbacks, nightmares and extreme fear after experiencing situations that others might find amusing. PTSD is a common problem when a traumatic event takes place. I am not saying that the events were not traumatic. I am saying we all have the strength to overcome them, if we stop being afraid and start understanding the way our bodies work.

I went to Griffin Park in Los Angeles with my mother and brother. It was some kind of African festival. I really cannot remember; I do know I was in the fourth grade, so that would have made me ten years old. There were people everywhere. Live bands played on stage in front

---

[315] Michel Eyquem de Montaigne (1553-1592): French Renaissance writer who made essays a popular genre. The quote was made famous by Franklin Roosevelt (Thirty-second President of the United States from 1933-1945)in his 1932 inaugural address.

of where we had placed our blanket, right in the middle of my mother's friends and their children.

Sidebar: I noticed it then. Whenever we went to events like this, I saw women and their children. The fathers were few and far between. I still see that now, especially as the economic resources lessen.

With my mother distracted, a park this large was about to become something else. I was there long enough to have explored every attraction and booth. I was bored with my brother and the other kids, imagination time. I tried to turn the park into a battlefield. Our army's mission was to rescue the princess. In my imagination, the people moving about were engaged in the confusion of combat. I have since learned that the proper term is "the fog of war", but what does a ten-year-old really know of war. Those lying on blankets were the wounded or dead. The booths were tents with banners embroided with various coats of arms flying high. Two huge armies had come together this day to do battle. I darted and weaved. How I would like to fight, but I was charged to not be seen today. The King needed a spy to find a way into the enemy's castle. I surveyed the territory to get my bearings, a tree - perfect. I climbed the tree and imagined watching the carnage below.

When you do not have toys, you have to develop an imagination to play poverty games. I ended up behind the stage, which was the enemy castle in my fantasy. How do I infiltrate the castle? Security guards that looked like Magilla Gorilla blocked both sets of stairs. For some reason I got an idea that I wanted to shimmy hand over hand the length of a pipe that extended from one end of the stage to the other. I grabbed the pipe with both hands and began my journey. I think I made it 10 feet when the contact of my right hand on the pipe caused my entire body to convulse (I know now that I touched a live circuit. There was probably an exposed wire inside the pipe). I remember thinking, "What is going on?" in the middle of the most excruciating pain I had ever felt. I tried to scream at the top of my lungs, but nothing came out. I could not hear anything. "Let go!" "I can't." I tried. My hands would not do what I told them. My body was shaking violently as I dangled like a dying bird that had landed on an electric fence. Panic set in. I could not let go; I could not scream or they could not hear me over the music. "Can't anybody see me cooking?" "Turn the power off!!!" I remember thinking my mother was going to be mad at me for dying - "HHHHHeeeeelllllppppp!"

I do not know how the power stopped, nor did I care at that moment. I fell like one of Mike Tyson's early opponents. It was a three or four foot fall to the ground. I could not even stand on my feet despite landing squarely on them. Instead I fell forward into an empty room under the stage and laid there. "Thank you, Jesus." While recovering, I thought someone had to cut the electricity. Someone saw me and will be here soon to help" "What if I am dying still?" "Where are they?"

I do not remember how long I lay there, but it was somewhere between recovery and trying to figure out how to milk attention if I had to go to the hospital. No one came. I was so embarrassed I sneaked up the stairs to see if anyone had even seen what happened. No one did. I rejoined my family.

The next day I did not feel well. I did not have to fake this. I was weak all over. I only wanted to lie down and watch television. I thought I was about to die at ten. I do not know the outcome of the battle; I had to retire from the field after being struck by a bolt of lightning caused by an evil wizard's spell, but I survived and lived to fight another day.

Fear's Disguises

Whenever we become angry, it is the result of a fear manifesting itself. We fear not having enough so we become greedy. We fear being ridiculed so we hide our true feelings. We fear being rejected and hurt so we avoid real relationships. We fear losing what we have so we do not share. We fear being alone so we put up with unsatisfactory relationships or compromise ourselves out of happiness. We fear showing our intelligence because many people do not like anyone who is smarter than they. We fear our own happiness so we become jealous of those who are happy and go out of our way to prevent them and ourselves from being so. We fear doing what we feel is right so we adopt the consciousness of the herd. We fear living because we have been conditioned to feel inadequate. We fear death because we do not understand that it is a conclusion to a mission. We have to recognize that most strong feelings have fear at their root. Knowing this is more than half the battle.

How to Control Fear

Remember Abraham Maslow's hierarchy of needs? The second level of human needs was safety. We do need to feel safe and work really hard to achieve it. Most people in Western cultures do not live in conditions where their actual safety is threatened very often. We are not in the Middle-East where car and roadside bombs are a daily threat. Nor are we in parts of Africa, Asia or South America where famine and disease grip the population, but many of us spend too much time feeling unsafe and afraid, even when we are safe. This is where our brains start the destructive fear process.

We are born able to feel safe. As long as caregivers provide the nurturing needed, children's amygdales remain normal sized. As children, we should learn that painful or fearful events do not occur very often, and when they do there is someone nearby to help deal with the issue. For example, children learning to walk often fall down. Pain is often associated with this event and the child will look around for nurturing, someone to make them feel that everything is fine. This type of learning involves trust. It is essential that children learn that the pain is not the result of a purposeful act. Pain, fear, hunger and cold, are naturally occurring incidents that are temporary and will pass; we need to know and believe this as children and adults.

If we learn this, our amygdala remains normal-sized and the brain does not over react to the fear stimulus. But, if we do not learn early that we are relatively safe, the opposite happens. We over react because our amygdales are super-sized and over active. Incidentally, if there is consistent fear stimulus anytime in life, the amygdala becomes over grown and produces more reaction to a fear stimulus than wanted or needed, the results are phobias and stress disorders that can cripple rational thought.

When the amygdala becomes enlarged, it sends persistent fear warnings to the other parts of the brain and body and then fear becomes a normal part of life. I know many who have never felt safe. That is how it feels if your amygdala is operating in over drive. You are always afraid and your body is trying to make everything feel all right, return to homeostasis. After time, over drive becomes a situation of normalcy. The physical and psychological effects, though varied in severity, are harmful nonetheless. We cannot turn this part of our brains off. It is too ancient and embedded to be nullified all together. Furthermore, we cannot pacify the amygdala by over compensating with money, friends, food or sex. Only the absence of fear stimulus or unlearning (reprogramming) societal (taught) fear can slow the natural reactions of the brain. The brain keeps asking the same question and acting the same way. It keeps protecting us against the threat that is not really there.

Protection is exactly what we need when there is real danger, but it can be catastrophic when there is no threat. Our bodies were designed to react to threats and most of us do it just fine, but when our alarm is going off constantly, we mistakenly stay at a heightened sense of alertness. We are safe, but we never learn to feel safe. Protecting yourself from the outside will never let you feel safe on the inside. Protection does not allow the feeling of safety to emerge because protection is predicated on fear. Only by experiencing fear and the reality that we are safe despite the fear, can we come to trust ourselves.

The subconscious is very efficient, but it is not very rational when it comes to the body. It does not think beyond the moment. It will use whatever is available to gain a feeling of safety. That is one of the reasons we find it difficult to think clearly when we are afraid or under extreme distress. The subconscious will use sex, drugs, extreme sports, denial, lying, anger or fleeing to feel safe and good. Have you ever wondered why some "fall in love" so easily, feel better in crowds or when we have money? Have you ever thought about why we become religious fanatics or drug addicts? These are defense mechanisms and they require fear to exist.

As I said before, there are real threats in the world, but they are few and far between in our society and most can be avoided. The truth is we are as safe as we feel. There is no boogieman in the closet or under our beds; he exists only inside of us. There may be a terrorist with a bomb strapped to his or her chest, but I know I am not the target. There are thieves in the world, but if you stay away from areas where they are known to frequent, and do your best not to look like an easy mark, chances are they will not bother you.

Whatever happens is not an accident and there is no way to predict or control the future. All we can do is roll with the punches and accept life for what it is. Then learn from and accept every new experience as it comes without taking it personally. With the realization that all is well and will be, the brain returns to the "all clear" state and is able to more effectively detect real threats because it is not being bombarded with chemical signals triggered by the fear response. We can think again.

32,000 suicides occurred in the U.S during 2005. This is the equivalent of 89 suicides per day; one suicide every 16 minutes.[316]

---

[316] http://www.cdc.gov/ncipc/dvp/suicide/suicide_data_sheet.pdf. This rate will increase as the wars continue.

It takes time and practice to master controlling fear because there are also biological factors at work. It has been shown that the pathways (neurons, dendrites and axons) from the cerebral cortex to the other systems in the body are weaker or slower than those from the hind brain to these same systems. That means the amygdala can communicate with the body's systems a lot faster than the thinking brain can. The amygdala screams, "Threat" and before the forebrain can react to the threat; we freeze, run or are startled. A split second later, the cortex's signal registers, "Wait a minute? There's no threat; that was just a car horn." I am not sure if there is any way to reconstruct the pathways, but I do know that unlearning environmental fears lessens the number of fear signals from the amygdala, and that we can strengthen pathways by using them more frequently.

Did you hear that? I said, "If we think more we can strengthen our neuro-pathways." The truth about life is that when shit happens, it's temporary and will pass. Unless there is a life-threatening situation (e.g. you are walking in front of a speeding bus), there is no need to hit the panic button. Even if someone puts a gun in your face because they want your wallet or your body, it is not cause to lose your mind (think of a solution).

Give them what they want or do not give them what they want; the choice is yours. It may take some time to get over the feelings associated with the trauma, but we always heal. Trust me on this one; I had a guy rob me at gunpoint for $5. It was my fault; I was out late at night trying to buy marijuana from people I did not know. My uncle and I went to a corner that was usually reliable, but at this time of night it was 50-50. I knew before I left the house that we were not going to get anything, but my uncle and others were insistent enough to persuade me to go and try.

We arrived at the corner and two men were standing there. I rolled down the passenger window and asked, "Yall got nickels ($5 bags)?" "Yeah, get out of the car." I got out. The one who answered me walked toward the back of the car. I thought he was reaching inside his pants for his stash, but also thought it strange that he was walking so far from the car. My uncle got the same sensation and began to back the car up. When the dealer turned around, there was a .38 caliber revolver in my face. I kept trying to see if there were bullets in the chamber and if the gun was real, but it was dark.

"Give me the money." The irony is I was not afraid and I said, "No… You're going to shoot someone over five dollars?" "You gonna die over five dollars?" His partner reached for my pocket. I instinctively pushed his hand away. The streak of pain on the left side of my face and the star burst in my head were the first indications that something metal had struck me. I did not even see it coming. I looked at my assailant and threw the five dollars on the ground "There it is." They collected their bounty and ran off. I was mad as hell about losing five dollars and getting a dislocated jaw, but felt good about keeping my wallet and the $700 in it. I said, "Just give them what they want." Even though my actions saved the rest of the money and my ego was intact, my jaw was throbbing, but it could have been much worse.

On another occasion, I was robbed while working at a gas station. I did the same stupid shit. This time it was not even my money, but the result was nearly identical, except I was hit in the head this time. I lived and the guy got away with $40 instead of the entire night's haul. The ironic part is that I had seen the guy earlier and knew he was up to no good. If I had to do it again, I probably still would say, "No." for pride's sake, but not enough times to provoke a physical reaction. It takes time to live in reality and with clarity of mind, but once mastered it makes life worth living. I think that life is what we make it. If we look at a situation as bad, it is and if we are afraid of something, we draw that something to us whether it is real or not.

Perspective is important when viewing anything. An extremely successful businessman enduring hard times once saw a homeless person. At the time he was in serious debt. He said to his daughter after seeing someone give the bum $1, "That man has $20 million more than I do." Many times I have listened to the issues of others wanting to say to them that they do not have an issue because from my perspective they did not; but I have since learned that these traumas are as individual as we are.

We all deal with stress, fear's surname, differently. I believe that needs play an important role in defining how we handle fear and stress. If you have never been hungry, you have never had to face the fear of not having enough to eat. If you have experienced this type of deprivation, your perspective of hardship will be very different from those who have not had the same experiences. In my opinion, as difficult as it is to put into practice, every experience should be treated in the same manner.

As a child, I remember wishing it would snow enough for school to close. As an adult I hated it. Did the snow change or did my perspective change? I now laugh about some of the experiences I have had in my life. At the time they were occurring, I thought life, as I knew it was ending; I had entered a black hole from which there was no escape. I could kick myself in the ass for the wasted energy I spent fearing the outcome of uncertain events.

I have been faced with the fear of professional disgrace. I was distraught for a long time until I realized that it was a small thing and that I would live. What did I learn? Do not have sex with another male's wife. I was accused of sexual harassment at my next job when I did nothing wrong. I was stressed out once more because I thought my reputation would be tarnished and I would have to find another job. I ended up with two year's severance pay and a reference. I accepted a better paying position at another company, but the three months between the two events was self generated trauma. Being accused of something I had not done hurt, but it was a blessing in disguise; after I left I realized how unhappy I was working for a manufacturing company on third shift. Not only was I working long hours for little pay, but I also disliked working in an environment where you could not tell the truth or do the job because of politics and other people's fear.

I grew up in environments where defending yourself was not only a way to survive, but it was the only way to live without constant harassment from predators. I am willing to take an ass whipping, but I know that most other people are not. As my grandfather used to say, "You have to bring some ass to get some." Most bullies, muggers and predators in the wild want easy prey. Sometimes just showing you are not afraid is enough to back them down or at least make them think about their next course of action.

In order to really lose fear you have to overrule the most primal of instincts, survival. For some the fear of dying is the greatest fear of all. If we realize, know and believe that we die at our appointed time, then the fear of death is gone. It has taken several life-threatening experiences for me to come to this realization. I have had car accidents, fallen through a ceiling, been robbed at gunpoint, shot at, beat up and almost died twice in aviation incidents. It taught me that I am not going anywhere before my time. If you do not believe me, ask someone you know who has faced a situation where they almost died. They will tell you the same thing. Of course, all the above is advisory. Most of us have found other ways to deal with fear.

I was wading in the shallow end of the pool; it was three feet of water. I could not have been much taller because I remember the water came to my chin. There is nothing quite as nice as cool water on a hot summer afternoon. It was not our pool, but my uncle and his co-worker installed pools, so for this day we were having a party in "our pool".

I was the only one in the figure eight shaped pool. It was not that big, but it was deep enough to have a diving board. I do not know how I lost track of where I was, but I walked my way out of the shallow end. I was balanced precariously on my tiptoes to keep my head above water. Those types of pools have steep drop offs and I was slowly slipping toward the deep end. I could not swim.

When I could no longer feel the bottom, I panicked. I went under. My feet touched the bottom and instinctively I pushed off toward the surface. "Hel…" I did not have enough time to get the entire word out. The attempt cost me half a mouth full of water. I went down again. The water in my mouth only increased my anxiety. The bottom again, "Push!" I broke the surface with a gasp for air. My arms were flailing and causing tremendous splashes. "Help… Help," I remember thinking, "Why are they just looking at me… Help damn it!" I saw the faces of four adults smiling and laughing. "What are you laughing at? This shit ain't funny… Help!"

I held myself above water as long as my little arms and pumping legs could. I was going down again and this time I had a strange feeling that I would not be able to come back up under my own power. I was exhausted. Strange thoughts come to mind in moments like this. I thought about who was going to rescue me from the bottom, and I thought about mouth to mouth. My eyes were open, but I was seeing images that were not real. "Ahhhh man; I do not want to die."

My hand hit something solid in the liquid tomb. I grabbed for it again. It was a hand. When I broke the surface in the shallow end, I saw that it was my brother who had stretched out his hand to me. As you read this, know that I love my brother above all because he saved my life and I am in his debt until I save his. The adults thought I was joking. Some people should not be put in charge of children.

I have had a fear of water ever since. It took a girl at a pool party three or four years later to get me in the water again. Even though I swim like a fish, (one test in the Navy requires that you swim a mile in a flight suit and boots), but the fear was still there. When I go to the beach, the fear of sharks adds to the anxiety, but I fight it and swim because I know I am not going to drown. I can swim four different strokes perfectly or float if necessary because of training. And,

I have convinced myself that sharks do not eat black people; they had their fill during the Middle Passage. We are saltines to them and they want Ritz.

Some years later, I was wading in the water at the beach. The bottom suddenly dropped steeply; it was a sinkhole hidden by the murky water. I was nose deep in water and sinking. "Do not yell or panic. You remember what happened last time!" "I won't." I had learned to "dogpaddle". I turned 180 degrees to reverse my course. I used my arms and a sort of modified breaststroke to pull myself up the slope. When I was out of danger, I thought about that day in the pool again, Post Traumatic Stress. I think I conquered a fear that day. Thank goodness, I needed all of my wits to pass the Navy's water survival course that eliminated more than a fair share of brothers years later.

I'd rather be feared than loved, because the fear lasts longer. James Todd Smith[317]

Believe it or not, one of the most frightening moments in my life came with a woman. Surprisingly, no guns, emergencies or fights scared me as much as having to tell someone I did not want to be with her anymore; "I do not love you anymore." It had nothing to do with love. It had everything to do with the relationship not fitting in with *my* long-term plans. We had been together for three years and she thought marriage was on the horizon. We lived together and worked in the same field. I loved her, but paths cross and divide. It was time for me to piss or get off the pot. I got off. It was time to move on. I came to realize that she wanted our lives to head in one direction despite saying the opposite beforehand. I still had the same objectives and goals I have always had and the two did not mesh. It was as though she expected me to compromise my dreams to be with her. I spoke to her recently; she said she gave up on me too soon. I do not know what that means.

I am serious. I felt as though I had been honest about my wants and desires. I wanted a loving relationship with good sex, and honesty - no more. I told her that I did not want to get married. Though we discussed marriage, I always said I was not ready. I was not and I still am not. She did not care what I wanted and I do not blame her; I cared about her desires, but I was not going to do something just because she wanted it. It would have been disastrous, like most other marriages.

Although there were things about her that I genuinely liked, there were more things that I did not want to deal with. The problem with letting go was we had shared so much together. We had shared intimate secrets, and having to let go was frightening. I can only imagine what a divorce with children must be like.

While living in a foreign country, I had my life threatened by the police. They were friends of my landlord. I owed her money and she did not believe me when I said that I would pay her when I could. She called in two goons who just happened to be federal police. They went through the motions of badge waving and making threats when I opened my front door. They finally asked, "Why don't you want to pay your rent?" I knew then that this was a shake down. I was supposed to be scared and I was unnerved until I figured out what they wanted. They

---

[317] James Todd Smith or LL Cool J: Rapper and Social Activist.

searched everything and found nothing except a picture of a friend smoking what could have been a joint. They left with a bunch of threats and finger waving. "Pay the landlord!"

I was so pissed that I wrote the landlady a note. It said I have the money, but I needed the full names of the two officers for the United States Consulate. It would have been easier to just pay the lady the money I owed her, but I do not like being pushed. I came to find out later that they knew they were in the wrong; it was illegal to enter someone's home for rent money. They got scared enough to pay me another visit later that day. I had been to see the urban pharmacist by then, so I was caught with illicit substances. The Miami Vice wanna-be walked through my open door with a different partner to find me smoking a marijuana joint in celebration of scaring my landlady. This time the handcuffs went on and they went through my things more thoroughly. They found nothing of value. I was taken with the drugs to Federal Police Headquarters.

I thought it was odd that we entered through the back door. I sat there in the office and meditated in a semi-lotus position awaiting my outcome. They had me for being an illegal alien, big deal. The drugs could pose a problem, but I had the out of illegal entry. That was my silver bullet. I saw an opportunity to use the training I received in Survival Escape Rescue and Evasion school (SERE[318]). I engaged the officers. I asked them about their weapons. Boys love to talk about guns. There was a map of the world on the wall. I asked if I could look at it. I pointed out all the places I have been. I assumed most of them had never been outside of their country. I explained the out of Africa theory of human migration. One of the officers even asked me to explain why people have different skin color. I even faked a diabetic seizure and had "Miami Vice" go outside to a street vendor and buy me candy.

By the time the magistrate showed up, they were giving me advice on how to obtain legal residency. One of them suggested that I marry a local or have a child with one. I told him that was worse than prison. They all laughed. The two who brought me in never mentioned the drugs as I sat in an audience with the magistrate. He told me to come back on the following Wednesday to be processed out of the country. I had a reservation to leave on the 15th of that month and the maximum time to stay after notification of deportation is eight days. So he did me a favor. "Come back eight days before your flight." is what he said to me.

"Miami" escorted me out the front door. Standing in front of the station, he said, "I am not going down for this!" "There you go threatening me again." "I am not threatening you." "I did not call the Consulate and I will not." He gave me my money, minus what I owed the landlord and my passport back. I asked for the portable humidor that contained my drugs. He paused. I said it was a gift and important for sentimental reasons. "O.K. Meet us out front." I waited for them outside the gated parking lot. Sure enough, they drove by and gave me my humidor. I looked inside to find half the green stuff gone, but the white stuff was still there. "Taxi," I picked up some beer on the way home to celebrate my victory.

Me, Myself and I

The hardest thing for me is convincing myself that I am safe.

---

[318] Two-week training course given to military personnel to simulate survival and prisoner of war scenarios.

I have faced death many times and it does not scare me anymore. I look at death as a graduate degree. But by far the greatest fear I have had to face is the fear of myself. I still scare myself sometimes with the things that I am capable of doing in moments of necessity or want. I have looked at my life and found instances of which I am ashamed. I have stolen money from family. I have lied to save my own ass, get some or to gain favor. I drank excessively just to deal with the feelings of failure and inadequacy. I have encountered people who thought it was their personal mission to put and keep me in my place because of their own fears. I have looked for love and affection in the arms of women who I knew wanted more out of the relationship than I did because of fear. I cannot remove myself from accountability by being clear in my intentions, when I knew my partner would eventually want more than I was willing to offer. I have used people to my benefit without reciprocating. I have also baited people into performing as I wanted them to; all the while letting them think that they would gain from the exchange. I prided myself in fucking people who had the same intentions, only to wake up one morning only to realize that it was they who had been bent over without so much as a *reach around*[319].

I now know that fear is a strong motive in my behavior and I have to stop if I want to evolve into a true human being. When I am afraid, I have a tendency to strike out in anger. I usually find someone or something to hurt in order to make myself feel better. I have been afraid and believe that I will be afraid again, even though I take measures not to be. I now ask myself, "Of what are you afraid," whenever I experience any feeling other than love.

What has happened to the gentle voice of reason? What has happened to grace and kindness? In the endless competition, most people have come to believe that might is right. They are afraid that showing kindness may expose themselves to attack and harm. Fear has driven away love!
Paul T. P. Wong, PhD

Love, especially self-love, is healing. Our trials are usually self-generated because we cannot see the path we as individuals should be traveling, or because we do see it and refuse to follow it because it seems difficult. We get distracted and many times we cannot see the forest for the trees. It is easy to travel through the woods and take a well-beaten path. That is how dreams die. It is harder to be off trail, to be in the vanguard.

Gandhi, Jesus, St. Francis, both Martin Luthers and later in life, Malcolm all figured it out. The shortest distance between two points is a straight line. How stupid is it to travel a path that we know leads to unhappiness (the one most travel over and over again). Every known civilization has declined or is in decline, whether from internal rot or external pressures. By modeling current societies and relationships on old ones, we are keeping the cycle of fear and human failure alive.

We know there are racists, bigots and sexists. Some Muslims do not like Christians. Some Hindus do not like Muslims. Some Catholics do not like Protestants. Most men are suspicious of and in competition with each other. Many women often look for their wealth and security in men. The majority of men look for their worth and esteem in women. We know the weak are manipulated by the strong. We are aware of injustices, and most importantly, we know that we

---

[319] Reach Around: masturbating your partner while penetrating from the rear. It is a derogatory metaphor referring being compensated for putting up with being "fucked in the ass".

have found more than enough reason to hate and fear one another. We all have looked for love in all the wrong places and found fear at the root of our search.

What fear? The fear of believing in one's self and the fact that accidents do not occur. I shall go further and state that we are afraid to believe in God. If we truly believed, we would not fear anything. We have two choices in our lives, the high road or the low, love or fear. The high one leads out of the drama and allows us to not sweat the small stuff. The low one keeps us in a repetitive cycle.

I know why men treat women with contempt and vice versa. So at whom do we point fingers? I know whites are empowered, but others have had their turn at the helm and will have it again. What will they do differently? Will they share the wealth? Will they care for the sick, the young, the poor, the disadvantaged and old? Will they protect the weak? Will they exorcize humanity's demons?

Do not wrestle with pig; you'll get dirty and pigs like it. Cyrus Ching[320]

I know life is hard, but we made it that way, ever since the first person teased us and made us insecure about the way we look, how much money we had or the way we dressed. We were made perfectly, but for some reason we cannot escape the reality that so many go out of their way to prove we are not. Humans created the set of standards by which we judge imperfections. This is fear manifested in human form. The Infinite One meant for us to live in a perfect world. It was and is our choosing fear instead of love that fucked it up.

I am trying my damnedest to choose love always. It is hard because there is always some asshole that will push you to the point where you wish bad things on them or worse, give them the "ass *whooping*" they justly deserve. If we could get 10,000 people to love everyone regardless of who they are or what they have done, we can change the world.

I have one last suggestion on fear. Try to stop fearing death and start enjoying life. I believe that we die at our appointed time, so why fear death? If you believe in destiny, if you believe in the Book of Life, you should know that death is nothing to fear, if you have lived right. As a matter of fact, death is sometimes courteous enough to pay a visit before the destined time. Try to remember that we were born to die and began doing so from the very first breath. I believe the true measure of a person is the way they meet death.

I was walking home with a local and an American after a typical day on the beach. We were talking about nothing in particular. I happened to notice an exchange between a poor black teenage boy and a rich white teenage girl. The boy whispered a sweet nothing at the girl and her friend as he walked by. He kept going and thought nothing of it. The girl was visibly startled. Shortly afterwards, three boys joined the girls. One of the boys asked her what was wrong. She was crying by now. I remember thinking, "Why are you crying? He did not do anything except flirt with you."

---

[320] Cyrus S. Ching (1876-1967) Canadian-American director of the Federal Mediation and Conciliation Service.

I do not know if he was her boyfriend or brother, but he and his two compatriots took off running after the poor kid. In my mind the words rang clear, "This ain't gonna be pretty." "I know, but what can we do about it?" I watched as the clueless boy was blind-sided from behind by the leader of the group. The other boys joined in after he hit the ground like a sack of potatoes. The crowd wondered why the three boys who appeared to be in good social standing were beating this poor kid. They said, "He stole our cell phone!"

The only thing the crowd needed to turn into a mob was a viable excuse, a spark. I was explaining to my companions that I saw the whole thing and it was a set-up. I was pissed that by-standers were so eager to beat someone they did not know for any reason. I was offended by the lack of justice, stereotypical prejudice and privilege of wealth and color. "I have to do something." My companions, "You could get hurt." "It is not your business." "Stay out of it!" Something in my heart told me it was my business. We were watching thirty people beat one person who did nothing and no one but the boy's mother was defending him.

"Hold this," I gave my backpack to the local. I cannot describe very accurately what happened after that. I do remember fighting my way to the center of the crowd. Once I got there, I saw a kid who could have been my brother or your son being kicked and hit by the circled crowd. He was in the fetal position trying to protect his vitals. "What are you going to do now?" "I do not know." It was as though something or someone pushed me into the fray. I know no one touched me or pushed me, but I felt a force move me. I ended up putting the kid in a fake chokehold. "Relax," I whispered in his ear. He did not resist. "I have him… Call the police!" The crowd stopped beating him, but was past the point of control. When a sole policeman did show up, he had to pull his weapon and point it at the crowd to keep the boy and his mother safe. He even waved the gun at me. "That is enough; he's safe."

My companions and I eventually reunited at my apartment. They told me how crazy and stupid I was. It did not matter what they said. I had a sense of satisfaction that I have never felt before or since, but know I will again, the moment I have the courage to stand up for another against the odds. I now know that I am not placed on this Earth for selfish reasons. I am my brother's keeper and so are you.

You know you are wise when you can think about good events and bad events in the same manner as an eager student views his or her next lesson. The difference between a good day and a bad one is the way you look at it; in reality they are identical and should be looked at with the same face. I now know that LIFE is precious and good; it is we who fuck it up. I love LIFE, I love US and I love GOD! Something inside of me says that they are one and the same. I am no longer afraid of trying to be myself. That is how I am going to lose my fear and help explain *What's Wrong with Me?*

Press on,

Nothing in the world can take the place of persistence.

Talent will not.

Nothing is more common than unsuccessful men with talent.

Genius will not.

Unrewarded genius is almost a proverb.

Education alone will not.

The world is full of educated derelicts.

Persistence and determination alone are omnipotent.

Calvin Coolidge [321]

This is so true. I say damn the "excuses" and full speed ahead, accomplish those dreams no matter how fearful failure may seem. "Success is failure turned inside out..." and it is never too late.

---

[321] Calvin Coolidge (1872-1933): 13th President of the United States.

Chapter VIII

Love

Love: strong affection for another based on kinship or personal ties.[322]

If I knew what love was, I would be omnipotent.

If I were God, I would make humanity like me.

I'd have people care more about themselves than for their self.

I'd kiss every newborn and elder, imparting a part of myself to them, for them and for myself. Welcoming them into the world and blessing them for surviving it.

I'd be selfish in my motivation for self-perpetuation, implanting the seed for evolution and individual growth, giving each and every part of myself the freedom, true freedom, of choice.

I would not judge what I have made, but glow in the marvel of what I have created and learn from my children as they learn from me.

I'd understand that humanity is what I made it, an ever expanding and growing thing, searching for more than what was given, searching for me in the matrix of existence.

If I were God, I'd know that there is nothing wrong in what I have created only different manifestations of myself.

I'd love the murderer as well as the saint, I'd comfort the addict as I do the Madonna, I'd see value, valor and purpose, realizing that nothing that exists on the earthly plain matters much when compared to the universe that I have created for my children.

And, I'd wonder at the diversity capable in the double helix of a DNA strand.

If I were God I'd give my children the wings of angels and the horns of demons, the sword of truth and the shield of lies, the ecstasy of love and the fever of hate, the muse of inspiration and voice of reason, the despair of failure and the faith of hope. I'd give imagination and dreams to these most precious of my being, these most important of my parts. These most favored among all.

I'd give humanity infinity. I'd give them me, to do with as they pleased. Because, they are my responsibility for as long as they cannot stand on their own.

I would not give my children money; I'd give them the ability to acquire knowledge. I would not give them a job; I'd give them a mission. I would not give them false security or righteousness; I'd give them a mind and the tools to accomplish dreams. That's what I'd do if I were God.

---

[322]Merriam-Webster's.

My very first memory was a feeling of constraint. I felt restricted and pinned in. I wanted to go forward, but an obstacle was in my way. I struggled, but the obstacle remained. I questioned, cussed and swore to God, but still challenges knocked on my door and invited themselves in.

Finally, I made a pact. I said to myself in a mirror that I will evolve or die. I will try to learn from my past, from the past of others; and I will try to be patient. I will ask the right questions of myself and wait for the answers. I will finally know love or... I turn to myself and realize that that I am my only obstacle. Me! Anything else is an excuse, a distraction or a lie to myself. I apologize to myself for not loving me and everything else. Interaction with other people made me this way, but love is my salvation.

True Love is a noble theme. I guess that is why so many authors have written about it. Science has gone to great lengths to explain it from both the physical and psychological perspective. I guess that is why religions have equated love with perfection and God. We are all looking for the same thing. In my opinion love is the most powerful need; it can lead those in search of it to behave in weirdly constrained or maladaptive ways. The love of one's mate, religion, country, family or material concerns often drives people to perform acts that vary from heroic to barbaric. And to many, true love is the ultimate sacrifice.

Love is the difficult realization that something other than oneself is real. Iris Murdoch [323]

My question, and evidently the question of many others, is why is love so important to us? I have asked many people this question and after many different answers, the only common ground is that we really do not know.

Why do we need affection past childhood? Why do we sacrifice so much of ourselves in order to associate with and be liked by others? Why do we perform dramas and tell lies to obtain attention? Why is acceptance so important to social health and tranquility? Why do we care what others think? Why do we intentionally hurt those we say we love?

I have said it before; I believe all we want is to be loved. It satisfies a need that I do not understand. It gives security, esteem and a feeling of well-being. It is akin to saying, "You have seen the real me and you still want to be around." I do not believe anyone knows what love is. The closest thing I have seen to love between two people is the relationship between some mothers and their children. And I think even this attachment is selfish deep down. It is an investment in our futures and an attempt to live forever.

According to Dr. Maslow (hierarchic theory of needs), all of our basic needs are instinctive or the equivalent of instincts in animals. Maslow believed humans start with a very weak disposition that is influenced by experience as we grow. I believe the opposite. We are born strong and grow weak because of external influences. We learn from the surrounding environment. If the environment is "right", people will grow to become the person meant to be.

---

[323] Iris Murdoch or Dame Jean Iris Murdoch (1919-1999): British writer, university lecturer, prolific and novelist.

If the environment is not "right", and usually it is not, we will not live up to the potential that is in each of us (George C. Boeree, Ph D[324]).

Beyond these, Maslow believes that higher levels of needs exist. Maslow theorized that once the lower levels of needs are met (food, water and shelter), then we seek satisfaction for the next level.

Our *Physiological Needs* are biological. They consist of the need for oxygen, food, water and a relatively constant body temperature. These are the lowest and most primitive of needs. They live and breathe in the oldest most primitive part of the brain. If deprived of any of these for a prolonged period of time, the human organism cannot survive.

Our *Safety Needs* seem to be more individualized or more acculturated. Adults living in Western cultures normally have little awareness of their security needs except in times of extreme stress, an emergency or periods of social disorganization. Children, on the other hand, are often more open and aware of their need for security. Many display the signs of insecurity and the need to be safe openly without regard for social etiquette.

Our need to conquer loneliness and alienation gives birth to the *Needs of Love, Affection and Belongingness*. This involves both giving and receiving love and affection. It also involves the sense of belonging to the society as a whole, fitting in.

Maslow labeled the next level of *Needs as Esteem*. As humans, we need a high level of self-respect (self love) and respect from others. Individuals who have high self worth and perceived worth from others feel self-confident and valuable. When these needs are frustrated, the person feels inferior, weak, helpless and worthless. Keep in mind that the above needs are realized within the first few years of life. If any of them are not met, people tend to fixate on them and typically over compensate for this lack. Psychologists call this condition neurosis. For example, those who experience hunger during childhood may over stock their cupboards and those who did not have financial means fixate on money.

Needs for Self-Actualization is a person's need to be and do that which the person was "born to do." "A soldier must fight, an athlete must play and a composer must compose." These needs make themselves felt in signs of restlessness. The person feels on edge, tense, lacking something; in short, they are looking to satisfy some need that does not fit into any of the other categories of needs. If all of a person's lower needs are met, it is difficult for an outsider to know why they are restless. It is not always clear what a person wants when there is a need for self-actualization, but they seem to want more of something and they will seek it out feverishly. I have experienced this firsthand. It is a longing. I want to spend time alone to think about life and there is an insatiable urge to learn and explore new horizons. It feels as though some unknown force is pulling me to do something that has yet to be revealed. It is like destiny calling.

I took a peek at my life and noticed that every action I perform is an attempt to satisfy one need or another. The need for love and acceptance were always more prominent than the others, because I have not really lacked many of the basic necessities of life. I have not had self-esteem

---

[324] George C. Boeree, Ph D: Psychologist at Shippensburg University. Long time colleague of Dr. Maslow.

issues, though others have tried to superimpose theirs on me. When all my primary needs were met, love became an unquenchable thirst for money, to get attention, praise, sex and affection.

Life's greatest happiness is to be convinced we are loved. Victor Hugo[325]

Some of us are so starved for love, it does not matter what kind of attention we receive, good or bad, it means the same thing; it equates to affection and caring, which in turn = Love. I count myself among them. Ever wonder why we stay in abusive or unrewarding relationships? I did, so I looked at my relationships in reverse and saw that I am in search of my perfect love. If we look closely at our behavior and the behavior of others, we will find that it is a search or a request, for attention, affection and ultimately love.

That is why we strive to excel, for praise and reward. We misbehave for attention on the other end of the behavioral spectrum. We associate with others for the physical and mental feelings associated with love. We lie and brag to make ourselves larger than life, and more attractive. That is why we want to be on the football team or the cheering squad, to be the center of attention and be popular. That is why we dream of saving the day. We care what others think, because we want to be liked. We want everyone to accept us and to love us. Unfortunately, not everyone understands these basic principles.

Science is now beginning to understand that there are real biological needs for affection and touching. However, during the 19th and the first half of the 20th Century, the prevailing thought among child psychologists was to limit the amount of affection given to children. This philosophy produced aggressive, unaffectionate and independent adults. This attitude toward child-rearing did not begin to change until the 1940's and 50's. Imagine the number of children who were raised using these draconian methods. Imagine their children. How do you think they turned out? Do you think they are loving and caring parents or do you think they are in therapy and on drugs? Now science knows that infants require affection (physical contact) and rocking (movement) to develop proper brain functions and acceptable behavioral patterns.

Love is hard, and soft.

Dr. James W. Prescott was convinced that touch deprivation is harmful to an individual's physical and psychological development[326]. This view is shared by anyone who has studied the effects of isolation or served time in solitary confinement. So what happened to the children raised under the "limited" affection regime? It will take centuries of love to undo centuries of neglect.

Dr. Prescott also asserts that handling and body contact are "nutrients" for the developing brain in humans as well as in other animals. With more touching and affection, the brain grows in a natural fashion. Depriving infants of physical affection can result in neurological dysfunction that produces abnormal and sometimes harmful behavior. How do you suppose

---

[325] Victor Marie Hugo (1802-1885): French romantic writer. Novelist, poet and dramatist. Wrote *Les Misérables* (1862).
[326] James Prescott, "Alien of Affection".

adults with the same affliction act? Look around; they are everywhere. Infants deprived of caregivers do not grow normal physically, mentally or emotionally and in many cases they die.

Doctors touring the Romanian orphanages after the 1989 fall of dictators, Nicolae and Elena Ceausescu[327], found that the majority of the children were underweight and underdeveloped socially. This was a direct result of the government policy promoting women to have five children or more. Many families responded to the demand only to find that they could not afford to raise the children. The unfortunate ones ended up in orphanages where the caregivers were overwhelmed, often caring for twenty or more children or they ended up on the streets. The children did not have the individual attention they normally would have and suffered from a variety of physical and mental aliments. [328]

Many showed behavior similar to Harry Harlow's isolated and touch-deprived monkeys[329].

Harlow separated monkeys from their mothers shortly after birth and substituted wire mesh mothers with a bottle feeder. He noticed that the monkeys began to cling to cloth that had been placed in their cages. He then placed two fake mothers in the cage, one with cloth and the other of wire mesh. Regardless of which mother held the bottle, the monkey spent most of its time with the cloth-covered surrogate. Harlow went further to make the cloth mothers vibrate harshly, make loud noises, and some even had spikes. The infant monkeys still preferred the surrogates to being alone.

The isolated monkeys were at times apathetic, at times hyperactive and exhibited outbursts of violence. Raised in isolation, they were socially maladjusted. No one taught them how to act. They often held themselves and rocked like autistic children. He also isolated baby monkeys completely for 30 days in enclosed cages; they saw nothing but the hands that fed them. When taken out, they were "enormously disturbed". Some refused to eat and starved to death. Those that survived were extremely dysfunctional.

How is it that a male who was so knowledgeable about monkeys could be so clueless about humans?

Harlow was in some ways an unlikely crusader for love. He admitted once that he had been a lonely child; he struggled himself with relationships. And yet he taught us irrefutable truths: that love alone is the foundation upon which we build our live or it should be. Deborah Blum[330]

Later studies by Dr. Prescott suggested that during the critical periods of brain growth, sensory deprivation, such as the lack of touching and rocking, resulted in incomplete or damaged development of the neuronal systems that control affection (for instance, a loss of the nerve-cell branches called dendrites).

---

[327] Nicolae Ceausescu (Elena): Communist leader of Romania from 1965 until he was overthrown on December 22, 1989. He and his wife were captured and on Christmas Day and executed by a firing squad.
[328] Beth M. Matschullat
[329] Harry Harlow, Ph D. (1905-1981): Psychologist famous for studies on Rhesus monkeys and love.
[330] Deborah Blum (1954-) is a Pulitzer Prize winning journalist and author. Excerpt from "Love at Goon Park".

Dendrites are the tentacles of neurons that spread out to receive and transmit chemical messages from and to other neurons. If these fibrous strands are underdeveloped, they do not communicate the chemically transmitted signals as efficiently as normal dendrites. Communication is impaired and behavior is affected. Children who experience touch deprivation are often unable to experience certain kinds of pleasure because there is malfunction along the neuro pathways. They tend to be predisposed to apathy and violence. I remember children like this from school. They were always alone and did not talk much. The other students seem to know that something was different about them. They either teased them or kept their distance.

Did you know that the brain almost doubles its size during the first year of life and that the brain does not fully develop until we are in our mid-twenties? It makes me wonder why we can join the military, get married, legally have sex, vote and drink at such immature ages. The result of not giving our children enough love/affection is that they become predisposed to violence. Societies where the children are nurtured and their emotional needs are promptly met have a much lower incidence of violence and rape. Unfortunately, we have to go to the jungle or bush to witness these societies up close. Few exist in the United States or Europe.

In 1983, Ed Tronick, Ph D. [331] and Jeffrey Cohn, Ph D. [332] devised an experiment to answer the question, "What if an infant could not elicit a response from their caregiver no matter what they did?"

They devised the "Face-to-Still Face Paradigm." In this experiment they instructed the mothers of three-month-olds simply to go blank for a few minutes while staring at their children. The test only required that the mother show no change in expression, a total lack of response. No anger or threat, no humor or love. "Infants almost immediately detect the change and attempt to solicit the mother's attention." When a mother still refused to respond, babies tried self-comfort. They sucked their thumbs and looked away. Then the babies tried again. They tried a variety of learned techniques to engage their mothers such as smiling or gurgling. If the mothers did not change their expressions, the babies would comfort themselves again and then try to elicit a response again and again. Babies somehow knew this was important. They were very persistent. But after a while, when confronted with only that blank face, each child stopped trying and began to comfort itself (thumb sucking, hugging, rubbing, etc.).

Children grow up to be adolescents and, eventually adults. We do not change our behavior along the way; we only modify it to suit our surroundings unless there is some life changing experience. We all displayed the same type of basic behavior as children. We all want and need food, shelter, love, touching, affection, security, attention and interaction. The only difference in adults is the complexity of our solicitations. Our job, car, house, learning, clothing, footwear, jewelry, conversations, expressions, and mannerisms are developed to elicit responses similar to that of a smiling or frowning caregiver. The approval, praise, attention, affection, and admiration received from doing well can easily be transformed into love. If we have the right kind of job,

---

[331] Ed Tronick, Ph D.: Director, Child Development Unit Children's Hospital Boston. Developed the Still-face paradigm.
[332] Jeffrey Cohn, Ph D.: Professor of Psychology and Associate Professor of Psychiatry at the University of Pittsburgh and Adjunct Faculty at the Robotics Institute, Carnegie Mellon University.

car or house, we are judged to be successful or rich and that alone is enough to feel loved in many cases. Just realize that it is just the physical manifestation of what the spirit wants.

Try taking the material and physical concerns out of the relationship. Try to communicate spiritually where we do not need words. I call it mapping. If we do not or cannot bond here, we will not be happy in our relationship; we would be working at it and we work enough at our jobs.

I challenge anyone who reads this to try ignoring or blank-facing someone who is trying to communicate with them. The effect must be complete; no changing of facial expression, no eye movement and no responses what so ever. The reactions will be varied, but one thing will certainly be true; most of what they do, after realizing that they are being ignored, will be done to get your attention. Whether they say, "Fuck you", repeat themselves several times or perform some physical act, it is an attempt to be recognized. After some time, they, like the three month olds, will give up. Be careful though. Once I blank faced my ex-girlfriend to the point where she became so agitated that she punched me in the face. Later, she said she hit me because I was not responding to her increasing insults, ignoring her.

The child who received a great deal of attention, whose every need was promptly met, as among the New Guinea Mountain Arapesh, became a gentle, cooperative, unaggressive adult. On the other hand, the child who received perfunctory, intermittent attention, as among the New Guinea Mundugomor, became a selfish, uncooperative, aggressive adult. Margaret Mead.

If attention, touching and love are a necessity for normal development and we have to associate with others to feel whole, how do we satisfy this need and not violate the natural law, the law of doing no harm to others? It seems to be a conundrum in today's society.

We have the taught behavioral phenomena of self-interest, as well as our instinctual need to survive, and our spiritual need for companionship and love.

The reality of the situation is this; we want to satisfy our needs without the risk of being hurt or doing any harm to another. The only solution is to be honest about and aware of our biological, spiritual and psychological needs. We need to be free with the same love and affection that we want returned. I know from personal experience it is a lot easier said than done, but I am still trying.

The Love Drugs

Chemical love is the product of the brain. It is not the love we are so desperately seeking; it is a catalyst. The body wants to feel good and so do the conscious self and the subconscious.

If you sincerely kiss a person, they are yours for life. A kiss is the first tool at the disposal of a lover. It conveys meaning and feelings that seem to be inexpressible in any other manner. A kiss can leave you breathless and yearning for more. I do remember certain kisses and I know why I remember them. "Why did you stop?" is the question that immediately comes to mind when a real kiss ends. Lip to lip or lip to flesh; kiss me whenever you feel like being honest.

Some choose to kiss for money. Others kiss for security. Still others kiss for sex. I kiss to feel the truth. According to the Bible, Judas kissed Christ just before he was arrested.

I kiss to seduce the *Old Brain*. I like to flick the switch to pleasure mode. If the body is distracted enough by pleasurable feelings the real self feels comfortable enough to emerge (bedroom confessions at their best). People will tell a truth more readily in the heat of passion than they will in everyday life unless they are pissed off or on.

I once kissed a woman for hours. Nada was beautiful. Long black hair flowed over her shoulders. Her light brown eyes sparkled when sunlight reflected off them. 127 lbs. inside of a 5' 7" frame made for nice presentation. I had seen her in a bikini and there was not an ounce out of place. She once asked, "Do you think I am fat?" "I would have to see you in a bikini." "Come to the beach on Friday."

We started talking late one night while I was leaning on her car. She said she had to go. I kissed her. She kissed me back. It was a kiss of medium pressure and high passion. We had never had sex nor kissed before. I wanted to and so did she, but (why is there always a "BUT" when you find someone really nice?) … she had had sex with someone I knew and considered a friend and I do not do that. It frequently leads to issues. She felt so special at that moment that I began to question my own rule. The kiss did it. It made me grab her hard and pull her closer. It made me want to be inside of her. Not in the sexual sense, in the sense of actually being one with her. What a kiss (this is another reason I do not kiss).

As she moaned, I thought of the time my friend said she was crazy. I remembered when he said he told her he did not want her during sex. I remembered when I watched her chase a guy, who had gotten what he wanted from her, around a party all night. I remember her telling me that she knew it was destiny that had brought her and my friend together. He told me the same thing, but it scared him. That preceded the "She's crazy" statement. I thought about the male she had a one-night stand with so that she could join his musical group. Her five-year old son came to mind. I remembered her saying, "I am 28-years-old; I have to get married!" I could not do it. Despite the urges coming from below my waist, I knew not to have sex with her. I kissed her more and she slept in the same bed with me. The indicators were there, but I rolled over, placed a pillow between us and went to sleep. I know I will see her again. I wonder what will happen.

Try touching your partner's skin using only your fingertips. Examine the body as if you were a doctor. Watch the physical reactions. Forget about the sex. Go on a journey of discovery. Find out for yourself what the body likes and give it. Do not listen to the distractions. Tell them to be quiet and enjoy it! Close your eyes and smell. Smell past the cosmetics, perfumes, body washes and deodorants. Smell and touch the hair; there is no better indicator of general health. I like to smell a woman after physical exertion, when the sweat pumps have been going for a while. The real them is in that smell (pheromones) and the sense of smell is the only sense that is not routed through the cerebral cortex; it is wired directly to the old brain. If someone does not pass the sniff test, run.

Chemical love is also a product of the body[333]. The chemicals are designed to help humans form pair bonds and encourage dual parent nurturing. It is not the love we are so desperately seeking; it too is a catalyst. Alcohol and other drugs can affect behavior and judgment similarly. They make us feel good. I want everyone to be aware that what they are feeling when holding hands, kissing or having sex is a physical reaction to a chemical stimulant produced in the brain that circulates through the body. If you want to know why males often fall asleep after sex, chemical love is the answer. Most females want to cuddle after coupling. Most males do not; we are done and have achieved our goal, an orgasm. God designed us, males, to go into an almost catatonic state so that females can snuggle up without protest. It is that simply. But, beyond this state of chemical bliss are other levels of pleasure and consciousness that can only be tapped into through other means, none of which require physical contact.

Show Me the Love

I believe that if we showed as much concern for others as we do for ourselves, there would be no war and the world would truly be heaven on earth. If we loved everyone, there would be no famine, violence, envy, greed, fear, hate or the perceived need for revenge because we would all be loved in kind. The need to seek attention, affection and love would be removed. We would come to realize that it is everywhere.

One word frees us of all the weight and pain of life: That word is love. Sophocles[334]

The late Dr. Harold Voth,[335] "It has been shown scientifically that people who are mentally run-down and depressed are far more prone to sickness than those who are not. Hugging can lift depression enabling the body's immune system to repair itself. Hugging breathes fresh life into a tired body and makes you feel younger and more vibrant." The fact that love heals is not a new idea, so why not practice this concept more?

Societies having the highest levels of physical affection have low rates of theft, minimal physical punishment of children and low levels of religious participation. James W. Prescott. PhD

The message of love exists in every culture; it is embedded in music, literature, folklore and religion.

Look at any top ten list of music being played throughout the world. What is the main theme? I guarantee that it is sex, money, love or all three. Look at the headlines of our most popular women's magazines: "How to Please Your Mate", "Ten Ways to Know if Your Man is Cheating", "How to Put the Spice Back into Your Relationship", "Top 10 Sexual Sins", "How to get Him to Pop the Question", etc… Most of the articles in magazines geared toward women are about men. If it has to do with weight, it is about men. If the article is about beauty tips, it is

---

[333]When we are involved in romantic activities, a chemical reaction takes place in the body. The body produces chemicals that are closely related to the amphetamines. They include dopamine, anandamide (also in chocolate), norepinephine and particularly 2-phenylethylamine (PEA).

[334] Sophocles (496-406 B.C.E.): Greek playwright.

[335] Harold Voth MD. (?-2003): Psychiatrist and Psychoanalyst long associated with The Menninger Foundation. (Body-Mind Center: *What Is the Joy Body?*)

about men. If the article has anything to do with exterior modification to enhance attractiveness, it is about men. All of these articles give advice on how to find love. Some even venture into how to keep it. But I have yet to read about appealing to a "Man's" inner self.

Most people seem to think that looking good or having great sex is enough to attract and keep love; it is not. Looks fade, despite modern technology or make-up, and sex is a sport that most like to think they excel. Some seem to think, the best way to keep a male is to have a child or to buy a house. The logic being, "He won't leave his children and he won't want to lose the house. If he does, I'll make him pay for it." My next work is going to be written for righteous women. It is titled: *How to Attract, Engage and Keep a Real Man*, not implying that I am one, but I am going write as if I were. It is not that hard. Just be honest, enjoy sex with your partner, and love yourself and him unconditionally. Love yourself with full knowledge of who you are, what you have done and what you are capable of doing. There is no room for denial in this state of being.

Even our folktales and religions are peppered with the love theme. We are told if we show God love, He or She will return this love in a divine way. Our movies and plays always have a theme of Love. Our lives scream, "Show me the love!" Why? Why is the need to be loved so innate? We swim upstream, spend hours butting heads, laugh at stupid jokes, and put up with things that normally drive us mad, for what?

It is my belief that we need to be loved because we are made of the same material as everything else around us, the dead stars of the Universe[336]. Not just in a physical, but also in a spiritual, and a psychological, sense. If you think about matter and atoms, you will find that we are mostly made up of empty space. If we could enlarge an atom to the size of a racetrack, the nucleus would be the size of a basketball. There is nothing solid between the nucleus and the different shells of the electrons. I believe the same thing that bonds atoms together to form solids to a lesser extent also bonds solids to one another. The bonding is not as strong between objects as it is internally, but it is there.

We interact with everything around us. We share electrons and energy. We are a part of each other and we are driven by unseen, unknown forces to interact, to be popular and to have the praise of others. This force is our oneness with others and the whole Universe. That is why plants and other animals respond to our touch and comforting. That is why people are capable of forming bonds with other animals that may be stronger than their bonds with humans. I will take this a step further and say we have to depend on each other because we are of one entity. In hating another, we hate ourselves; the same is true of love.

I cannot be the first person from whom you have read something like this. Someone older and wiser told me before I was old enough to understand and I am sure you have experienced the same. I have read versions of this philosophy in the Bible, the Qur'an and a number of other

---

[336] We share 50% of our DNA with a flat worm and 99% of our DNA with chimpanzees and we are practically identical to other homo sapiens. I figure that if there are 30,000 (Human Genome Project) different DNA sequences in the homo-sapiens, then we are separated by 9.

religious books. I hear it in song and see it in dramas. Dr. Sally Mendoza[337] also thinks that we are connected. She believes, as I do, that we rarely do anything that does not affect others, and that our connections affect our behavior and decisions. Dr. Mendoza wrote that social interactions change our internal physiology and chemistry. She and I share a common theory: that we are individuals in body only. Our internal chemistry is not individualized. It is designed to interact with the chemistry of others.

Have you ever seen a crowd panic as a group or seen joy spread like wild fire? Have you heard the saying "attitudes are contagious"? You cannot tell me you did not feel the hole left by "The Tsunami" or the Twin Towers. We all know this to be true. We spend most of our time interacting with each other. The concepts of family and community revolve around this concept.

Every culture promotes interaction at work, play and at home, the society dictates in what order. Work is a more pleasant experience when there is gossip, jokes and friendships. We play with each other because it builds relationships. Family life is the basic drive of every animal; it ensures the survival of our genetic line. For many, the best times are those spent with others. If you think of the nature of love as a tree, then our need to belong and interact is in the roots.

Dr. Mendoza does research with several types of primate societies. She noticed that when she removed one squirrel monkey from a colony, there was an instantaneous measurable spike in the remaining animals' stress hormones. The same spike was common throughout the entire colony, even in monkeys that spent little time with the missing animal.

Humans act similarly if not more so. Fear, happiness and stress can spread through a group like a plague. We pick up queues from others and, like it or not, they affect us all. We are connected. That is the main reason I choose to spend the majority of my time with a select group or alone. I do not like to be around people who are constantly vibrating towards the negative. We have all experienced people who constantly complain or always seem to have issues. These feelings are contagious and I would rather not catch the disease that plagues most of humanity, I have had it too long already. Not that I am not affected when I withdraw from society, but I am affected less when I put distance between others and myself.

For one human being to love another; that is perhaps the most difficult of all our tasks, the ultimate, the last test and proof, the work for which all other work is but preparation. Rainer Maria Rilke[338]

The experiences we have, however different, are the same in the end. The lessons and meaning of life push each and every one of us to the same destination, though the road traveled may be different. Some call it Heaven; others call it Enlightenment. While still others call it Nirvana, Paradise, Valhalla, Zion, the Kingdom of God, eternal life or the Elysian Fields. Whatever the name, the concepts are the same, happiness, peace and love forever: a time to rest and enjoy paradise. I think we have lost contact with what makes human beings special, our ability to love without expectation. I had a conversation with someone recently about love. She

---

[337] Sally Mendoza, Ph D.: Psychologist at the University of California Davis. Her principal research interests concern the neuroendocrine mechanisms.
[338] Rainer Maria Rilke (1875-1926): German writer and poet.

said that she did not like being hurt by people who pretended to love her. I told her that she should not feel hurt. She did not see the logic in my statement. I elaborated with, "If you love someone honestly, you should not expect anything in return, not even his or her love." I went further to say, "If someone does not love you or pretends to love you, it is your fault." I really lost her there.

If we do not take the time - and I mean years - to get to know another and his/her motives, we are playing dice with our emotions. Even though there is no wrong in loving, if the expectation is to have that love reciprocated in some form (her form is monetary), one has to be open and honest about the need and be able to recognize early in the relationship when it is not being satisfied and then decide whether to stay or move on (did you notice I did not say try to change the behavior?).

For whatever reason, not everyone will return our love in the form we want. That does not mean that we should not love them or that we should be hurt by their denial. If others hurt us, we have no one to blame but ourselves because we seem to think that suffering is an acceptable part of life.

What We Want

I think on the inside we just want to be loved and will do whatever it takes to find this love. I also think our bodies are programmed to procreate with the best possible mate or mates and will do whatever it takes to accomplish this mission. For many, a compromise between the body and spirit is met. The compromise usually lies somewhere between love, security and physical necessity.

The compulsion for love is directly related to how attractive we think we are. We spend billions each year to make ourselves more appealing to others, when the soul is the essence of beauty. It spurts through the eyes, the open door and a magnifying glass, and it flows from the mouth, an instrument for the soul to play its sweet song. Unfortunately, our culture has de-emphasized inner beauty and concentrates mostly on the shell.

It is natural to have desires and emotions, but they can manipulate our power to reason and our ability to truly know others. I like to think that I could love someone without ever seeing or physically feeling her. That way I could be sure that I am not lusting over a nice body or falling for a pretty face. Emotions and desires have the ability to excite the body to the point of irrational behavior. And, the younger we are, chances are the more excitable we become.

Our minds are seized by desire and, if allowed, the mind will be guided into relationships that we know are not a fit because of the body's wants. Not because of the sex or the feeling of wellness it seeks, but because we often confuse or mislabel desire, emotion and sex as love.

The body is the main cause of the beauty it holds. To enjoy this, we think it is necessary to attain as intimate a union as possible, and sex is the natural way of attaining this union. Sex can be a deceiving way to enjoy another, if you do not know them and love them. It is not a rational choice nor are we moved by the true knowledge of another's soul when we have sex with a stranger and think that the pleasure gained from an orgasm is what we really want, if love is the desired outcome.

I love orgasms, as I am sure you do, but I do not think of a massive orgasm as love for another person. It is the desires of the senses that are being fulfilled. The pleasure that follows is often false and fleeting, if it is thought of as love. When we try to satisfy only the body's desires through sex, two fates await. Either we experience distaste or even hate after achieving what we so desire or once attained, the desire for beauty is not satisfied because we have not found what we are seeking. When trying to satisfy the body with sex there are two usual outcomes: never finding love or worse, attaining true love and finding it distressful because we cannot recognize or return it.

Ideas stimulated by desire sap people's ability to reason. These same desires or emotions are directly proportional to our level of excitability. They persuade the mind to yield. Because of these strong biological influences, we cannot always see truth when trying to fulfill our obligations to the body.

I have witnessed, in others and myself, the repetitive search for beauty and love. This behavior should diminish with age or rather experience. After all, it is easy to forgive the young, but it is most difficult to forgive the older and, supposedly, wiser. Following desire is acting in the same likeness as animals; it is more an instinctive response to a biological trigger than love, reason or inference. It is an attempt to satisfy a need through desire. On the other hand, "*In whose souls the bridle of reason restrains the inequity of the senses benefit from finding true love of beauty and know it to be good and holy.[339]*" With some physical restraint we can find much benefit. The benefit that I refer to is a spiritual and more fulfilling type of love. It is very similar to the kind of love that one experiences with close family or friends. It usually has nothing to do with sex, though in some cases it does.

Some may call it finding a soul mate. I think it has more to do with caring and having affection for someone than with gaining a commodity. It is unselfish and unwanting of anything but love in return. We cannot know spiritual love without knowing the person first and time is the only way to gain true familiarity when it comes to people. And, although familiarity often breeds contempt, it can also breed true love, if both parties are honest about themselves and their expectations from the beginning.

I try not to fall into the trappings of youth, when the body is rebellious and makes thought listen to strong desires. I want to be able to love above the capacity of my desires. I am trying to remedy the impulses, the quickening of the heart, the heat that warms the body and the pleasure gained from contemplation, by alerting reason and recognizing that these are indeed physical reactions to a spiritual need. Quenching the thirst for water with wine will satisfy the thirst for a moment, but the thirst always returns with a vengeance. In fortifying the heart against the attack of desire, I am able to think clearly and choose my course more logically.

---

[339] Baldassare Castiglione (1479-1529): Italian author, diplomat, and soldier. The count of Novilara. Author of the Book of the Courtier.

I have not always been able to do this, nor do I wish to be able to do it all the time. Where would the fun in life be?

Some will never be able to separate physical and emotional feelings from real need. Try to remember that everything we want is not always what is good for us. In the presence of a beautiful woman, I do stare and contemplate, but I also observe and restrain. I want to know if the attraction is real or am I reacting to an innate cue, an animalistic urge to procreate, false advertisement or someone else's desires. Only time and patience can reveal that answer.

Again, I am not arguing that intimacy is wrong. The world would be a better place, if we nurtured more and were not so sexually repressed. Nor am I saying that our instincts, our body's natural desires and defenses, are bad. Our natural reflexes are but one of the many wonderful gifts of nature, when properly used and controlled.

Look at what instincts did for those animals that fled Sri Lanka's national wildlife park at Yala, which houses elephants, buffalo, monkeys and wild cats, very few animal corpses were found. They fled before the Tsunami arrived and so did a group of indigenous people isolated on one of the Nicobar Islands. They recognized the signs because of a folk song passed down by earlier generations.

And, there is nothing wrong with feeling good. After all, a kiss is a wonderful thing, the union of the body and the spirit, the soul wanting to exit the body to be shared with another.

Let him kiss me with a kiss of his mouth - for your love is more delightful than wine.
Solomon's Song of Songs

I am suggesting that when associating with one another, it is a good idea to know what our objectives are and be able to distinguish between affection, attention and love. Mistaking one for the other often leads to conflict and avoidable behavior. It is also a good idea to know what our partners really want. Unfortunately, this is more difficult because very few tell the truth, even to ourselves and fewer still actually know what we want.

We cannot truly enjoy love merely through a physical union. That is just sex and affection. Engaging the eyes (watch), mouth (communicate) and ears (listen) are a must. Examine your partner. Know every part of his or her body. Enjoy the smiles, mannerisms, movements, gestures and grace. Enjoy the sweetness of voice, laughter and modulated sound. Kiss someone and try not to think about sex. Try to feel the something else that lies beneath the biological urges. You would be surprised what joy can be derived from other channels. I have known women who have achieved sexual climax from a verbal exchange over the phone, using only a vivid imagination. I have known some who achieved the same level of satisfaction from visual stimulus alone. I think satisfaction is not about the act of sex for many women. It is about the hope that this union is the one that will fulfill their needs.

We are not surrendering some small token of love when we share ourselves and give our beauty to another; it is a powerful exchange. The subconscious is engaged when we join with someone else. It is a sharing. It may be one sided as hell, but it is sharing nonetheless, and both partners are gaining something or they would not willing be doing it. Try to concentrate on someone's face. It is a fact that we are more intrigued by facial expressions than by a "nice ass". Even infants concentrate on our faces when we hold them. They receive all the information they need just by looking at your face.

Communication without words is having a conversation with the eyes and facial expressions. Try the same technique with people. Look in their faces when they speak, try to listen to what they are really trying to say and ask questions with your facial expressions. Share yourself with someone who truly interests you, not just someone for whom you have a physical attraction, want something, or have a desire. You are sharing a union with a person that does not end with copulation.

Life is divided into two halves, one frozen and the other a flame, the burning half is love.
Kahlil Gibran

We, Ourselves and Us

One of my personal missions is to understand my own motives (biological, mental and spiritual) for wanting love. I am trying to unlearn what I have been taught about beauty and relationships, resist the biological and instinctual responses to stimuli and control the spiritual need to intermingle in order to understand the love equation and myself.

I know it is possible to love without sex. I love some of my family and I love a few close friends. I also know that I can have sex without love. The sex chapter offers testimony to this fact. I want to see if it is possible to interact with another without the prospect of gain, judgment or the advent of competition.

It is my goal to be able to receive and give graciously and without guilt. I want to be able to love everyone, especially those who hate me. I believe that achieving this goal is the path to true freedom, the road to happiness and the fulfillment of my real purpose. With this freedom comes power. The conundrum is figuring out how to achieve this goal and still be able to function somewhat normally in a society that does not promote such behavior. I am not trying to be cynical.

We do not love each other. As our concentric rings of virtue venture further from the center (ourselves) our amount of trust, obligation and love decreases exponentially. The recent breakdown in New Orleans is an example of what happens when resources dry up. Some of us do not love our own family members. This being the case how is it possible to love anyone who is not genetically connected? I say we do not love each other because the United States is one of the most violent countries in the world. It is also the richest nation on Earth, but we have people who are poor, homeless and forgotten.

If our children are raised in affectionate environments, they will not become violent adults. If we loved each other, we would see more 50-year marriages, the level of infidelity would decrease and starter marriages would not be the status quo. Fathers would actually help support and rear their children. The incidence of violence would all but disappear even in the most desperate of situations. And, our economic and security interests would always be our children.

Love is the *only* thing in the Universe that is infinite. You can give away as much as you like and still have an infinite reservoir. We can receive as much as we like without gaining weight or any health risks, though you may have some issues from those who do not wish to see you loved. You can love all day and all night and not be tired. Love will open eyes and free spirits. And, I believe that when you love on such a level, you never have to want or fear anything. I think that prosperity, health and happiness are frequent guests in the home of a person who loves and is loved. I know because every day I see and hear who is happy and who is not, and so do you. And, I am not referring to the drug-induced contentment that many have.

Let me tell you a story to demonstrate the power of love. I flew to Napa, California for a job interview. Before I left I got an idea. I promised myself that I would have a good day no matter what, and that I would try to enrich the life of anyone with whom I came in contact. In short, I planned to act as human as possible.

When I disembarked, I noticed a woman walking in front of me. Here is some insight into the mind of a male. I looked at her butt first. She had wide hips for her 5" 3' frame. I am guessing she weighed about 150 lbs. She had a short Halle Barry type haircut. She was between 30 and 35 years old. I cannot really tell you her exact age because I did not look that hard. I had no interest in her body so I did not have a motive to interact with her further. I did notice that she was struggling with her bag. It was painfully obvious that she was tired; her body language said so. And her feet were hurting; the way she walked told me that.

At first I was more concerned about getting pass the slow moving wide load in front of me. For whatever reason, once I stopped looking at her as a potential mate, I could see her as a person, another person in need of some assistance. I had a rolling bag, so I inquired if she would like to put her bag on top mine for as long as we traveled together. She looked confused and a little weary, but fatigue won the day. We walked and talked a little. She told me her name and I returned the courtesy. When we reached the point where our paths parted I said my goodbyes and headed off toward the rental car agencies. It was not until later that I realized she was the woman who had looked at my shoes when I passed her boarding the plane. I am sure she was confused because I made no attempt to flirt with her and did not even ask for her phone number.

When I entered the Rental Car terminal, I noticed that there were not any other customers in the building. It was around 10:00 PM. The sole woman behind the counter was bored and pissed. It showed all over her face. She really did not look happy. I put on my biggest smile and asked her if they had stayed open just for me. She forced a smile onto her face in response. We went through the reservation process. Through small talk, she told me that she was not happy in her job - "No shit."

I told her she should sit still in a quiet place and ask herself, "What do I want to do?" "When you get an answer, you should do it," I noticed she did not look at my license. She touched it and gave it back (I found out five months later on a return flight from Las Vegas that my license had expired on my previous birthday. Airport security finally caught it after numerous trips.). I told her to have a blessed night.

I found my car, but it had someone else's name on it. I questioned one of the attendants about the mix-up and she radioed the office. I recognized the voice on the radio as the woman who had just helped me. She said, "It's ok. We'll give Mr. Connors another car when he arrives." I thought the car I had was rather nice for a job interview. They usually put me in a compact. I did not realize that the attendant had upgraded me until I reached my destination.

On the return trip the next day as I attempted to check the car in, they were having issues with the handheld units used to give instant receipts. The attendant apologized for my having to go inside for a receipt. I told him I had plenty of time. I did. My ticket was for 8:15 PM; it was 3:30 PM. I was hoping to smile my way into an earlier flight. He said, "Most people are not so understanding." I told him, "I realize that it is not your fault." He said it again. "Well, I guess I am not most people." I said as we parted ways. "Have a beautiful day."

At the counter was a chipper male who was about 23. I explained that I needed a receipt and why. He went about preparing the receipt and we did some small talk. We talked about the upcoming Super Bowl. I told him, "My heart is with Philly, but I think the Patriots will win."

He laughed and said, "Later, Brah." I used to be taken aback when someone assumed I spoke Ebonics and even if I did, when I am wearing a suit and tie, it usually is not a socially acceptable time to do it. I looked at him and smiled. What tickled me is the fact that he actually got it right. If my eyes were closed I would have sworn that an African-American had said it.

On the flight back a male in front of me needed help removing his bag, but would not ask for it. He had placed his bag in the same overhead bin as mine, but it was positioned directly over my seat. He was attempting to reach over his seat and retrieve a bag that was directly in front of me. It was not a small bag. He was going to have to do some work to get it. I asked, "You want me to get that for you?" He thanked me and said, "Not many people would do that." I said, "If more people did, we would have less war." "We would definitely have different leadership." is the last thing he said to me as we disembarked.

As I sat waiting for my ride, I noticed a strange looking kid. He was dressed like a nerd and toting a box of books on a pull along. He passed me by and asked the 21-year-old beside me if he wanted to buy a book. The potential customer yelled at him. "No! Go away!" I could see by now that the vendor had a license to sell and that he was handicapped. He lowered his head and walked away, looking crushed and humiliated. I wanted to buy a book just to make him feel better, but I only had $25 left from my overnight trip and I was unemployed. That is the excuse I told myself in order to justify not reaching out to uplift an obviously hurt person. I wish I had bought a book.

Instead I asked the kid beside me, "I wonder why he went to you?" I was being funny. There were three of us on the bench. One had on hip-hop gear, one was in Jeffery Bean casual and the other was in a suit. Two of the males were African-American. To whom do you try to sell your book? He said, "I know. Can't he see that I am in a bad mood?" I said, "What is her name?" He gave me a puzzled look.

If a guy that age, with his obvious upper class upbringing was that upset, it had to be a woman; he does not have any other real worries. He told me that he had broken up with his girlfriend of four years because he wanted to experience other women. He had gone to France for eight months and sown some wild oats. Now he was back and ready to start anew, but she had a new beau. I asked why he was upset. He said he loved her. I told him, "You will love many people, if you live long enough." That puzzled look returned. I asked him if he and his father were close. He said, "Yes!" I suggested that he ask his father how many loves he has had. He said, "My Mom and Dad have been together like forever." "What does that have to do with it?" He paused for a few seconds and then he said, "I do not know if we are that close…" were his last words. His father's car pulled up to the curb. I wonder if he asked…

I have one last experiment. First, I ask that you define love? After you map out your definition, ask yourself how many people you have said you love really fit into it?

I am not sure I have ever loved. If I apply the definition that I have of love today to all of my relationships, I have not been in love, and at the same time realize that I have those precious and fleeting moments. I have used others to get what I want. I have formed strong bonds with those who have provided something I have desired, but I am not sure it was love or fulfilling one of the more self-centered needs. I do not think I know what love is because I still have hateful and angry thoughts.

My understanding of love has changed over the years. It has moved from individuals to the human group as a whole. It has grown to include all living things. I wish I could maintain and restore my body with only water and sunlight. I am pro-life remember? So, I love what I eat and thank it for its sacrifice. I eat as little as possible as a sign of respect and thanks and as a reminder that there are others who have little or nothing, even though there is enough to go around.

Love is the hurt one endures. Love knows who you are and what your purpose in life is. Do you know? Love is the unconditional sacrifice of self to some cause or purpose. Love is the peace that comes from knowing there are no accidents. Love is coming to terms with our past choices and being proud of future promises, if we have the fortitude to make and keep them. Love is the bond between us all. Love is our connection to the one. Everything we experience, in one form or another is love.

Our personal barriers have to be talked and thought through. Some of us are fortunate enough to be able to pay a professional to listen and give us pills, some of us resort to other forms of self-medication, and some have good friends. We all seem to need a sounding board, a release and someone to hear us out. I try to communicate with everyone as honestly as I can. I talk to God and myself as only I can. I find a quiet place within where I can be still and then I question and ask. It is free and answers come eventually to those who are patient enough to listen and brutally to those who are not.

There is nothing wrong with us, if we have love in our heart - One world, One race, One God. I have drawn my battle lines. Love is my shield and Truth is my weapon.

Only one true emotion exists and that emotion is love. Everything else is a misrepresentation, misinterpretation or misunderstanding of that one emotion. Fear is love. Lies, jealousy, envy, judgment, right and wrong are fear's children and love's grandchildren. Furthermore, relationships and sex are just a search for love. I believe that love is the most powerful motivator there is, the end of everyone's journey, and the cure for "What's Wrong with Us."

You may ask how I came to this conclusion after such a life. In a moment of desperation I screamed, hollered and cried. I demanded proof, and then I saw God's face.

Imagination is more important than knowledge. The important thing is to not stop questioning... Imagination is everything. It is a preview of life's coming attractions. Albert Einstein[340]

---

[340] Albert Einstein (1879-1955): Physicist, Philosopher and Mathematician.

If

If I knew us, I would know that the steep road holds more wealth and righteousness than the more traveled path. I could have unimaginable knowledge and peace. Hate would dissolve in a solution of brilliant love and we would call everyone friend and brethren.

If I am knowing me through others; their actions and thoughts are my own. The trespasses are identical, the desires parallel: different paths, yet the same destination.

If I had a dollar for every lie I have heard, I would be rich, yet without trust.

If I had a dollar for every lie I have told, I would be equally well off, yet without friends.

If there were a book that contained all I know, it would have a finite amount of pages.

If there were a book containing all that I do not know, it would be infinitely larger. Knowledge is a quest that will never end.

If I aged a year for every time I have been afraid, I could have been a waiter at the last supper. Fear is made and sustained in the hearts of people.

If I steal, things will be stolen. No need to question why in any particular occurrence. Actions past always come to visit, whether invited or not.

If I weighed my worth on a balance of humanity versus the animalistic urges, knowing the loves I have had and lost, having my heart broken and breaking in kind, would I pass the test?

If I dared to live as naturally as we were meant to, I would be scorned, labeled and ridiculed, but happy returning to the whole and embracing its laws as my own.

If I knew what true beauty was, time would not have been spent in search of what is all around me. All things made are perfect. It is my sight that is flawed.

If I choose to worship a gracious and forgiving Creator, one who I need not fear because of pure love, clarity of life is my reward.

If I could see life as if looking down, I could see into the spirits and hearts of myself and know what we could, should be.

If I could experience life as a child again, I would see things as they really are, not good or bad, but as lessons, a part of a curriculum designed long before awareness.

If I could find contentment in my own possessions and still have growth, I would know that what is mine cannot be taken or given away. It must be used up in its entirety for the purpose planned.

If I weighed my deeds on a balance beam of humanity, would I fall left or right or remain centered?

If I knew myself, I could know others.

If I choose to worship a benevolent God, I need not fear anything. A Citadel of Love protects me, the gift of life is my reward and then I will be able to extend my hand to every person without fear.

If I choose to master desire and bridle emotion, I could love all beings.

If I knew happiness, I could share with those who are not.

If I could kiss the hand of God and not cry for shame nor squint from guilt, then I would know that I have lived up to the charge issued long before my birth: the charge to evolve, to become a human being.

I have stopped searching for love. I have found it years ago and I will not let it go again.

Mikaku Oyasin![341].

---

[341] Lakota language: We are all related. The Lakotas (or Sioux) are any of seven groups of Aboriginal-Americans from what are now Minnesota, North Dakota, South Dakota, Nebraska, and Wyoming.

Bibliography

Abraham, Mental. "Mommy's Little Secret" The Globe and Mail, [Toronto] December 14, 2002 Print Edition.

American Academy of Child and Adolescent Psychiatry (AACAP). "Children and Lying No. 44." 2005. http://www.aacap.org/publications/factsfam/lying.htm. (05 Jan 2004).

Barash, David Ph D. "Deflating The Myth of Monogamy." http://www.trinity.edu/rnadeau/FYS/Barash%20on%20monogamy.htm. (05 Oct. 2006).

Baker, R. R. and Bellis, M. A. "Number of Sperm in Human Ejaculates Varies in Accordance with Sperm Competition Theory." Animal Behavior. 1988. Volume 36. P 936-939.

Baker, R. R. and Bellis, M. A. (1995). Human sperm competition: Copulation, Masturbation and Infidelity. Chapman and Hall, London.

Barna Research Group. "How America's Faith Has Changed Since 9 – 11." Truth Views Radically Altered. http://www.barna.org/FlexPage.aspx?Page=BarnaUpdate&BarnaUpdateID=102 . (23 Dec. 2003).

Basler, Roy. The Collected Works of Abraham Lincoln Volume III: Fourth Debate with Stephen A. Douglas at Charleston, Illinois. September 18, 1858. 1990. New Jersey: Rutgers University; Reissue edition.

Blüher, Matthias, Kahn, Barbara and Kahn C. Ronald. "Extended Longevity in Mice Lacking the Insulin Receptor in Adipose Tissue." Science. January 24 2003. Vol. 299.

Burch Rebecca L. and Gallup Gordon G., Jr. "Semen Displacement as a Sperm Competition Strategy in Humans." The Human Nature Review, Evolutionary Psychology. 8 February 2004. 2:12-23.

Blum, Deborah. Love at Goon Park. 2002. Boulder, Co: Perseus Publishing.

Boeree, George C. Ph D. "Personality Theories" Abraham Maslow 1908 – 1970. 1998. http://www.ship.edu/~cgboeree/maslow.html. (4 Jan. 2004).

Brosnan, Sarah, B. M de Waal, Frans and Schiff, Hillary C. "Tolerance for inequity may increase with social closeness in chimpanzees." Proceedings of the Royal Society. 2005. Volume 272, Number 1560.

Bureau of Justice Statistics. Crime and Victims Statistics. 2006. http://www.ojp.usdoj.gov/bjs/cvict.htm. (23 Mar. 2004).

Bureau of Justice Statistics. <u>Prisoners on Death Row by Race</u>. 2006. http://www.ojp.usdoj.gov/bjs/glance/tables/drracetab.htm. (25 June 2004).

Buss, David M. <u>The Evolution of Desire: Strategies of human mating</u>. 1995. New York: Basic Books.

Castiglione, Baldassere. Edited by Walter Raleigh. <u>The Book of the Courtier</u>. 1900. London: David Nutt.

Davis, Jefferson. "Slavery in the Bible." <u>Quotations by learned men from the 19th century</u>" 1995. http://www.religioustolerance.org/sla_bibl.htm. (15 Mar. 2004).

Diamond, Jared. <u>Guns, Germs and Steel: The Fates of Human Society</u>. 1999. New York: Norton and company.

Dostoyevsky, Fyodor. <u>The Idiot</u>. 1955. London: Penguin Books.

Etcoff, Nancy. <u>Survival of the Prettiest.</u> 2000. New York: 1st Anchor Book Edition.

Gray, John PhD. <u>Men are From Mars, Women are From Venus</u>. <u>A Practical Guide for improving Communication and Getting What You Want in Your Relationships</u>. 1992. New York. Harper Collins.

The First Family Institute of Kansas. "Family University." <u>Infidelity Facts.</u> http://www.family-university.org/tips/infidelity_facts.html. (05 Jan. 2004).

Fisher, Allen and Gittinger, Ted (2004). "LBJ Champions the Civil Rights Act of 1964." <u>Summer 2004</u> National Archives Vol. 36, No. 2. http://www.archives.gov/publications/prologue/2004/summer/civil-rights-sidebar.html. (14 June 2006).

Fisher, Mary. <u>Living Religions</u>. 3rd Ed. 1997. London. Prentice Hall.

Flaherty, Lorraine and Wehner, Jeanne. "Gene That Influences Fearfulness in Mice Detected." <u>Nature Genetics</u>. National Institute of Mental Health. November 1997.

Giles, Lionel. "Sun Tzu: The Art of War." <u>The Oldest Military Treatise in the World</u>. http://www.kimsoft.com/polwar.htm. (25 Feb. 2004).

Giller, Ester. "About Trauma. What Is Psychological Trauma?" <u>Passages to Prevention: Prevention across Life's Spectrum</u>." 1995. http://www.sidran.org/whatistrauma.html. (27 Mar. 2004).

Gopnik, Blake. "Science, Trying to Pick Our Brains About Art." <u>The Washington Post</u>. January 25, 2004; N01.

Gordon, Randy. "Causes of the Civil War." 1995. http://ngeorgia.com/history/why.html. (20 Mar. 2004).

GPO Access. "Overview of the President's 2005 Budget." 2005. http://a255.g.akamaitech.net/7/255/2422/02feb20041242/www.gpoaccess.gov/usbudget/fy05/pdf /budget/overview.pdf (21 June 2005).

Harris, Marvin. Cultural Materialism: The Struggle for a Science of Culture. 1979. New York: Random House.

Hencke, David. "Child Support Agency Forced to Pay Back Wrongly Accused Men." The Guardian. November 28, 2005.

Hite, Shere. The Hite Report on Male Sexuality. 1981. New York: Alfred Knopf; New York: Bertelsmann.

Hite, Shere. "The Hite Report: A Nationwide Study of Female Sexuality." 1987. New York: Macmillan; New York Bertelsmann.

Holmes, B.W. "Reasoned Spirituality" Exploring spirituality, the meaning of life and the concept of God. Parts 8 and 19." 1998. http://www.reasoned.org/index.html. (09 Feb. 2004).

International Bible Society. Holy Bible: International Version. 1981. Grand Rapids, Mi: Zondervan Publishing.

Kant, Immanuel. "1790 The Critique of Judgment Part One." 2000. http://www.4literature.net/Immanuel_Kant/Critique_of_Aesthetic_Judgment/. (Feb 2004).

Kemerling, Garth. "The Discipline of Logic." http://www.philosophypages.com/lg/e01.htm. (23 June 2004).

Kinsey, Alfred C. Sexual Behavior in the Human Female. 1953. Philadelphia: W.B. Saunders; Bloomington, IN: Indiana U. Press.

Kinsey, Alfred C. Sexual Behavior in the Human Male. 1948. Philadelphia: W.B. Saunders; Bloomington, IN: Indiana U. Press.

Lovejoy, Paul E. "Transformations in Slavery-A History of Slavery in Africa. No 36." The African Studies Series. 2000. Cambridge: Cambridge University Press.

Matschullat, Beth M. "Government Strategy Concerning the Protection of the Child in Difficulty Romania's New Child Welfare Reform Effort" Will It Make A Difference? 2000. http://www.factbook.net/countryreports/ro/Child_protection.htm. (13 Jan. 2004).

McDowell, Josh. "Right and Wrong" A Case For Moral Absolutes. 2005. http://rbc.gospelcom.net/ds/q1107/q1107.html. (12 Feb. 2004).

Mead, Margaret. <u>Cooperation and Competition among Primitive Peoples</u>. 1961. Boston: Beacon Press.

Mendoza, Sally P. and Barchas, Patricia R. <u>The Evolution of Cooperation</u>. 1985. New York: Basic Books.

<u>Merriam-Webster's Collegiate Dictionary</u>. 1993. 10th ed. Merriam-Webster's, Inc.

Morris, Charles G. <u>Psychology: An introduction 9th edition</u>. 1996. Springfield: Prentice Hall.

National Archives and Records Administration. <u>Emancipation Proclamation</u>. http://www.archives.gov/exhibits/featured_documents/emancipation_proclamation/index.html.

National Institutes of Mental Health. "Suicide Fact Sheet" <u>Suicide Deaths. U.S., 2001</u>. http://www.nimh.nih.gov/research/suifact.cfm. (17 Mar. 2004).

<u>The New Book of Knowledge</u>. 2001. Grolier Incorporated, Danbury, Conn.

<u>The New Webster's Dictionary of the English language</u>. International Edition. 1989. Lexicon International, New York.

Pope Gregory XVI. 1839. "In Supremo Apostolatus: Condemning the Slave Trade." http://www.catholic-forum.com/saints/pope0254j.htm. (13 Apr 2004).

Prescott, James W. "Alienation of Affection." <u>Psychology Today</u>. December 1979. http://www.violence.de/prescott/pt/article.html. (15 Nov. 2003).

Prescott, James W. "Body Pleasure and the origins of Violence." <u>Bulletin of the Atomic Scientists</u>. November 1975. p. 10-20.

Reagan, David F. "Early Corruptions: Bible Preservation." 2006. http://www.learnthebible.org/preservation_corruptions.htm. (28 Feb. 2004).

Rowatt, Wade C. "Deception to get a Date." <u>Personality and Social Psychology Bulletin</u>. 1998. 24, 1228-1242.

ST. Augustine. "Church Fathers: On Lying." <u>DE MENDACIO</u>. 2005. http://www.newadvent.org/fathers/1312.htm. (10 Mar. 2004).

Waal, Frans B. M. de. "Primates Bonobo Sex and Society: The behavior of a close relative challenges assumptions about male supremacy in human evolution." <u>Scientific America</u>. March 1995. 82-88.

Walsch Neale Donald. <u>Conversations with God: An Uncommon Dialogue, Book 1</u>. 1995. Charlottesville, Va.: Hampton Roads Publishing; New York: G.P. Putnam's Sons.

Walsch Neale Donald. <u>Conversations with God: An Uncommon Dialogue, Book 2</u>. 1997. Charlottesville, Va.: Hampton Roads Publishing.

Wikipedia, "Diebold Election Systems" http://en.wikipedia.org/wiki/Diebold_Election_Systems#Diebold_and_Kenneth_Blackwell (Oct. 10, 2006).

Williamson, Marianne. <u>A Return to Love: Reflections on the Principles of "A Course in Miracles."</u> 1994. Harper Collins Publishers.

Wong, Paul T. P. "The Positive Psychology of Love" <u>Fear has driven away love!</u> http://www.meaning.ca/articles/presidents_column/print_copy/psychology_love_june03.htm. (19 Mar. 2004).

Zeki, Semir. <u>A Vision of the Brain</u>. 1993. Oxford: Oxford University Press.

LaVergne, TN USA
27 October 2010
202246LV00003B/1/P